"Just Dummies"

"Just Dummies":
Cruise Missile Testing in Canada

John Murray Clearwater

UNIVERSITY OF
CALGARY
PRESS

© 2006 John Clearwater

Published by the University of Calgary Press

2500 University Drive NW

Calgary, Alberta, Canada T2N 1N4

www.uofcpress.com

Library and Archives Canada Cataloguing in Publication

Clearwater, John

   "Just dummies" : cruise missile testing in Canada / John Murray Clearwater.

Includes bibliographical references and index.

ISBN-13: 978-1-55238-211-0

ISBN-10: 1-55238-211-7

   1. Cruise missiles—Canada—Testing—History—20th century.   2. Canada—Military relations—
United States.   3. United States—Military relations—Canada.   I. Title.

UG1312.C7C54 2006   355'.03109710973   C2006-904569-0

We acknowledge the financial support of
the Government of Canada, through the Book Publishing Industry Development Program (BPIDP),
and the Alberta Foundation for the Arts for our publishing activities. We acknowledge the support of
the Canada Council for the Arts for our publishing program.

Printed and bound in Canada by AGMV Marquis

♾ This book is printed on 60 lb. Rolland Enviro 100 natural text

Cover design, page design and typesetting by Mieka West

to Mom

Contents

ix   List of Photographs

xi   List of Figures

xiii   Acknowledgements

xv   List of Acronyms

1   Introduction

3   Chapter 1: The Race to Test the Cruise

63   Chapter 2: Testing, Testing, 1–2–3 ...

99   Chapter 3: Litton, Direct Action, and the CMCP

111   Chapter 4: Stealth Cruise Over Ottawa

141   Photographs

151   Chapter 5: Liberals Create, Tories Renew

177   Chapter 6: All Things Must End

199   Conclusion

211   Notes on Sources

217   Annex A: Chronology of Test Flights

223   Annex B: Agreements and Arrangements

231   Notes

265   Index

List of Photographs

1. AGM-86B test ALCM in flight over United States.
2. B-52 bomber with twelve test AGM-86B test cruise missiles.
3. W80-1 nuclear warhead.
4. Greenpeace protestors and RCMP officials near CFB Cold Lake.
5. W80-1 nuclear warhead about to be lifted into ALCM.
6. Greenpeace protestors in a blizzard outside CFB Cold Lake.
7. B-52 launches test ALCM from bomb bay.
8. Landing at Primrose Lake after a full flight test in early 1985.
9. ALCM on Primrose Lake with parachute still attached, early 1985.
10. AGM-86B airlifted by Huey helicopter after a test in early 1985.
11. Canadian Forces crew with recovered missile at Primrose Lake in early 1985.
12. ALCM lifted being lowered on to a trailer for shipment back to the United States after being recovered on Primrose Lake weapons range, 24 February or 1 March 1987.
13. CF-18 fighter aircraft escorts an ALCM over Canada, 27 January 1989.
14. Two CF-18 fighter aircraft escort an AGM-86B cruise missile over Canada, 19 January 1988.
15. AGM-129 stealth Advanced Cruise Missile in flight over desert.
16. B-52H of 410 Bomb Wing, K.I. Sawyer AFB, in flight with twelve AGM-129 stealth Advanced Cruise Missiles mounted on under-wing pylons.
17. A CF-18 flies with an AGM-129 Advanced Cruise Missile.
18. The author with a W-80 nuclear warhead from an ALCM.

List of Figures

Figure 1	Test # 84-1,6 March 1984
Figure 2	AGM-86B Air-Launched Cruise Missile
Figure 3	W-80-1 Nuclear Warhead
Figure 4	Test # 85-x, 15 January 1985
Figure 5	Test # 85-y, 19 February 1985
Figure 6	Test # 85-z, 25 February 1985
Figure 7	Typical AGM-86B ALCM flight in Canada
Figure 8	Test # 86-1, 22 January 1986
Figure 9	Test # 86-2, 25 February 1986
Figure 10	Test # 87-1, 24 February 1987
Figure 11	Test # 87-2, 1 March 1987
Figure 12	Test #87-3, 27 October 1987
Figure 13	Test #88-1, 19 January 1988
Figure 14	Test # 88-2, 26 January 1988
Figure 15	AGM-129 Advanced Cruise Missile
Figure 16	Test # 89-(ACM-1), 2 March 1989
Figure 17	Test # A91-01C, 7 November 1990
Figure 18	Test # 92-1, 29 October 1991
Figure 19	Test # A93-04S, 29 March 1993
Figure 20	Test # 89-4, 27 January 1989
Figure 21	Test #90-4, 23 January 1990
Figure 22	Test #90-4A, 29 January 1990
Figure 23	Test # 91-4, 31 January 1991
Figure 24	Test # 91-5, 9 February 1991
Figure 25	Test # 92-4, 10 February 1992
Figure 26	Test # 93-4, 29 January 1993
Figure 27	Test # A94-06 (A193), 6 March 1994
Figure 28	Briefing Note for the Minister of National Defence "Canadian Forces Maritime Experimental and Test Ranges (CFMETR)"

Acknowledgments

This book could not have been possible were it not for those anonymous individuals who made access to information requests to the Department of National Defence and the Department of Foreign Affairs for information about cruise missile testing. The material all became available to the general public after being released to the applicants, and forms the basis of this book.

I am therefore indirectly indebted to the access to information staff of the Department of National Defence and the Department of Foreign Affairs, as well as to the Privy Council Office. I am also directly indebted to National Defence for processing all of my access requests. Their work was crucial to demonstrating the veracity of the information presented in this book. I give thanks to Bonnie Petzinger, Sue Lajoie, and Judith Mooney, the three access coordinators at National Defence, and all their staff, especially John O'Connell and Tara Rapley. The staff at Privy Council Office were as forthcoming as possible, given the constraints of the twenty-year rule for cabinet material. On the negative side, the access division at Foreign Affairs stalled every step of the way during the research for this book, with many documents remaining hidden behind its refusal to engage in proper work, and its wholesale deletions of legally releasable documents. Although many of the documents used in this work are from Foreign Affairs, many more remain hidden by this maverick department.

My thanks also go out to Project Ploughshares and their past and present staff for sharing with me their extensive files on these subjects.

Since almost none of the technical information flowed to Canada, I had to make use of sources in the United States. The United States Air Force (USAF) has been extremely forthcoming with records and photographs. Many *Freedom of Information Act* (FOIA) requests were made to various USAF agencies and bases. I am grateful to the FOIA officers at Minot, Barksdale, Tinker, Eglin, Nellis, and Langley Air Force Bases. I also appreciate the work of the FOIA staff at Air Combat Command Headquarters, Strategic Command Headquarters, United States Air Force Headquarters, and various other agencies and bases.

Los Alamos National Laboratory has provided declassified photographs through the FOIA process. I give thanks to the National Atomic Museum for allowing me access to their document collection and library. I am also grateful to the museum for providing me direct access to their cruise missile W-80 nuclear warhead.

Lastly, I thank Sharpsword for insightful and helpful comments on the military and nuclear aspects of this book.

Acronyms

ABM	anti-ballistic missile
ACC	Air Combat Command (USAF)
ACM	advanced cruise missile (stealth)
ADI	Air Defence Initiative
ADM	Assistant Deputy Minister
AETE	Air Experimental Test Establishment
AFB	air force base (USAF)
AIA	Access to Information Act
ALCM	air-launched cruise missile
ARIA	advanced range instrumentation aircraft
ASL	above sea level
ATIP	Access to Information and Privacy
AWACS	Airborne warning and control system
B-	bomber
BMD	ballistic missile defence
BoMARC	Boeing and Michigan Aeronautical Research Center
BUIC	Back-Up Interceptor Control
CAF	Canadian Armed Forces
CANUS	Canada-USA
CC	Cabinet Confidence
CDC	Cabinet Defence Committee
CDLS(W)	Canadian Defence Liaison Staff (Washington)
CDS	Chief of Defence Staff
CEO	Canadian eyes only
CEP	circular error probable
CF	Canadian Forces
CFB	Canadian Forces Base
CFMETR	Canadian Forces Maritime Experimental Test Range
CINC	Commander-in-Chief
CMCP	Cruise Missile Conversion Project
CMDI	Cruise Missile Defence Initiative
CSRL	Common Strategic Rotary Launcher
DEFCON	Defence Condition
DEW	Distant Early Warning
DND	Department of National Defence
DM	Deputy Minister
FOIA	Freedom of Information Act (USA)

FOL	Forward Operating Location
FOT&E	follow-on test and evaluation
GLCM	ground launched cruise missile
HQ	headquarters
INF	intermediate nuclear forces (see TNF)
JAG	Judge Advocate General
JSP	Joint Space Program
KAL	Korean Airlines
KGB	Committee for State Security
kt	kiloton
LANL	Los Alamos Nuclear Laboratory
LRNA	long range nuclear attack
MC	Memorandum to Cabinet
MIRV	multiple independently targetable re-entry vehicles
Mk	Mark
MND	Minister of National Defence
MOU	Memorandum of Understanding
MP	Member of Parliament
MX	Missile Experimental
NATO	North Atlantic Treaty Organization
NDHQ	National Defence Headquarters
NDP	New Democratic Party
NMD	national missile defense
NORAD	North American Air/Aerospace Defence Command
OSD	Office of the Secretary of Defense
PCO	Privy Council Office
PJBD	Permanent Joint Board on Defence
PM	Prime Minister
PMO	Prime Minister's Office
RCMP	Royal Canadian Mounted Police
SAC	Strategic Air Command (USAF)
SALT	Strategic Arms Limitation Treaty
SCC	Standing Consultative Committee
SCEAND	Standing Committee on External Affairs and National Defence
SDI	Strategic Defense Initiative ('star wars')
SIOP	Single Integrated Operational Plan (for nuclear warfare by USA)
SLBM	sea launched ballistic missile
SLCM	sea launched cruise missile
SNDV	strategic nuclear delivery vehicles
SoD	Secretary of Defense (USA)
SRAM	short range attack missile

SSEA   Secretary of State for External Affairs
START   Strategic Arms Reduction Treaty
STRATCOM Strategic Command (USA)
SWOAC   Southwest Ontario Area Commander
T&E   test and evaluation
TEP   test and evaluation programme
TERCOM   terrain contour matching
TNF   theatre nuclear forces (see INF)
UNSSOD   United Nations Special Session on Disarmament
USAF   United States Air Force
USN   United States Navy
W-   warhead (nuclear)
WTO   Warsaw Treaty Organization
z   zulu (Greenwich Mean Time)

Introduction

It is incredible that in a democracy Canadians are
given so little information about such a matter.
Pauline Jewett, MP, 11 March 1982

This is the third volume in the nuclear weapons in Canada trilogy that began with the 1998 book *Canadian Nuclear Weapons*, and was followed in 2000 by *U.S. Nuclear Weapons in Canada*. This volume brings the project up to date by telling the definitive story of cruise missile testing in Canada between 1978 and 1995, and demonstrates how the structure of politics and the military in Canada is set up to serve the military requirements of the United States.

This book is about the process by which the Canadian government came to view the cruise missile program as essential to maintaining good relations with the United States. It is about how Prime Minister Pierre Elliott Trudeau and his cabinet made decisions based on little information. It reviews the ongoing negotiations between Canada and the United States concerning how weapons would come to be tested. It reveals the secrecy with which the entire program was treated in order to prevent the public from being able to mount an effective opposition. Lastly, the book is a blueprint for how the Canadian government makes unpopular decisions, hides them from the public, makes justifications when secrets leak, and in the end does what needs to be done to keep the United States happy.

I titled the book "Just Dummies" as this was a phrase uttered by the defence minister, Gilles Lamontagne, after a cabinet meeting on Thursday, 11 March 1982, describing the warheads in the cruise missiles to be tested over Canada. The wonderful irony of this statement, seeming to refer to both the confused cabinet members worried about testing and the test warhead units, made for the perfect title.

Arranged chronologically, the book covers the negotiations to begin cruise missile testing; the testing itself; protests; the advanced cruise missile; renewal of the agreement; and, finally, the termination of cruise testing.

For those who wish to investigate the veracity of the claims made in this work or to see the documents, I invite them to examine the copies of the originals which have been deposited at the archive of the Directorate of History and Heritage (DHH) at National Defence Headquarters in Ottawa, and are available for viewing by any persons, be they academics, reporters, or interested citizens. These files are part of the Clearwater Nuclear Weapons Fond (Acc. 98/15). The material in this book is from official government sources, albeit sources never meant to be seen by the public. All of the documents used are actual declassified Canadian and U.S. government military and political records.

John Clearwater
Ottawa, 2006

The Race to Test the Cruise

We all know that the cruise is at the end of the road.
Prime Minister Pierre Elliott Trudeau

THE NEGOTIATIONS AND THE SECRETS

The modern air-launched cruise missile came into the arsenal of the United States Air Force (USAF) when President Jimmy Carter, on 7 July 1977, cancelled the B-1A bomber in favour of the small, unmanned nuclear delivery system. Carter had killed, at least temporarily, the expensive B-1 bomber and had substituted the cruise missile. Although not originally well received by the military services, the cruise missile became indispensable to the U.S. military. They required thousands of them, and would deploy them around the world and in all three armed services before one was ever tested in Canada.

For Canada, the birth of the issue dated back to 26 May 1978, when Prime Minister Pierre Elliott Trudeau offered his "suffocation" proposal to the United Nations. He stated that the arms race should be cut off by ending testing of advanced weapons systems. This would come back to haunt the man who had little time for foreign affairs and defence policy.

1980

The first firm indication of cruise missile testing in Canada came to the attention of the military high command through the office of Colonel Lorne Broughton, the director of Continental Policy at National Defence Headquarters (NDHQ) in Ottawa. The United States Air Force's Strategic Air Command (SAC) had suggested in late 1979 that the new cruise missile be tested over the Soviet Union-like geography of Canada.[1] Colonel Broughton wrote a memo on 29 August 1980 which stated that beginning in 1981 or 1982, the U.S. military wanted to use Canadian air weapons ranges for testing its new cruise missile due to the terrain's similarity to Eurasia at high latitudes. The colonel, recognizing the political sensitivity of such a request, suggested that any negotiations be handled in a compartmentalized manner, separate from anything else. But, fearing that the situation might become difficult, he warned that the benefits to Canada "are not so clear."[2]

Cruise missile testing was first raised informally with officials of the Department of National Defence (DND) and the Department of External Affairs (DEA) at a meeting in Ottawa in early September 1980.[3] The initial suggestion was followed by a full United States Air Force team giving detailed briefings on the proposal to External Affairs and National Defence senior staff at National Defence Headquarters on 9–10 September.[4] This first informal suggestion was followed in October 1980 when Dr. William J. Perry, the Pentagon's chief science advisor who would later become the secretary of defense, wrote to National Defence to request on behalf of the U.S. Air Force, use of Canadian airspace for cruise missile testing and for various other testing schemes.[5] Although the whole issue had yet to be recognized for what it was, Commodore G. L. Edwards noted the "potential political sensitivity" of such negotiations.[6] The government would manage to keep everything secret for just under two years.

On 30 December, Perry wrote to Assistant Deputy Minister of Defence for Material (ADM Mat) L. D. Crutchlow to recapitulate what he thought was the state of the discussions on two issues: the United States' use of Canadian weapons testing sites, and the use of Canadian airspace for air-launched cruise missile (ALCM) testing. No reply to this letter would be forthcoming for several months, and it would be answered only the day before the new secretary of defense, Caspar Weinberger, met with the minister in April 1981. Crutchlow's reply was dated 14 April 1982, and by this time, Perry was no longer at the Pentagon as control of the White House had changed from the Carter Democrats to the Reagan Republicans. His successor was told that the Canadian reply would become known only once the minister of national defence (MND) had conveyed it to Weinberger.[7]

1981

The first known reference to formal military talks on cruise missile testing in Canada comes from the 158th meeting of the Permanent Joint Board on Defence (PJBD or Board), which met at the United States naval base in

Charleston, South Carolina, 17–20 February 1981.[8] Although a wide range of items were discussed, Canadian chairman George Hees drew Prime Minister Trudeau's attention to the second item, which was the beginning of a U.S. request to test cruise missiles in Canada.[9] It was at this meeting that Richard Ledesma provided the Canadian delegation with a sample, four-year working plan for the tests.[10]

Prime Minister Mackenzie King and President Roosevelt's Ogdensburg Declaration in August 1940 created the Permanent Joint Board on Defence as an advisory body to the two leaders on mutual defence matters. Through informal discussion, the Board is to reconcile the requirements of North American defence with the social-political-economic situations in each country. In the early years, decisions of the Board became recommendations to the prime minister, which became executive documents, and which were then formalized into cabinet documents for decision and action. This format would subsequently be taken over by other channels of direct communication, but the PJBD continued to provide the single most important forum for discussion of mutual military matters due to the presence of officers, parliamentarians, and diplomats from both countries. With the end of World War II, the Board slipped in importance, only to be resurrected in 1950 as an instrument of Cold War cooperation and control. Agreements for the radar sites known as the Pine Tree Line, the Mid-Canada Line, and the DEW Line were negotiated through the PJBD. In addition, the NORAD agreement and the agreements for nuclear weapons in Canada were formulated and presented and negotiated at the Board.

The Permanent Joint Board on Defence, made up of senior military and diplomatic personnel, and chaired by a Member of Parliament appointed by the prime minister and by a White House appointee, reports directly to the prime minister and to the president of the United States. Formal meetings take place three times each year at various military bases: October in the United States, June in Canada, and February alternately in each.

The Military Cooperation Committee (MCC or Committee) was set up pursuant to a recommendation by the PJBD in January 1946 that called for a secondary forum for the free and comprehensive exchange of military information on the security of North America. The MCC was immediately responsible for the Basic Security Plan for Canada-United States defence; a responsibility it still holds almost sixty years later. The basic job of the Committee is joint military planning for the defence of North America. Formal proposals or initiatives are presented in working groups as either a Canadian or a U.S. document, negotiated, and finally can become an agreement or service-to-service note. The Committee is also responsible for the annual updates of the Basic Security Plan series and supporting plans. Lastly, the MCC administers the catalogue of the several hundred military agreements between Canada and the United States. The Military Cooperation Committee meets twice annually: in the spring in Ottawa and in autumn in Washington.

Canadians did not see any of the secret workings of the PJBD or MCC, but in the spring they did notice that with little fanfare and with no real debate, the North American Air Defence Command agreement (NORAD) was renewed on 31 March 1981, and came into force again on 12 May. The previous renewal had taken place on 12 May 1980, only one year previous. The document was signed by Minister of Defence Gilles Lamontagne, Secretary of State for External Affairs Allan MacEachen, and United States Secretary of State Alexander Haig. The new version of the agreement contained substantive changes from the previous version of the agreement. The United States had insisted that NORAD be updated to take account of space as well as air, and NORAD became the North American Aerospace Defence Command. Space was the new primary interest of the United States, and Canada would have to go along with it.

During March the wheels were secretly turning at the Department of National Defence in preparation for the joint ministerial meeting. Politically, the race to test the cruise missile in Canada got its start at the closed meeting at National Defence Headquarters conference room A, between Caspar Weinberger, the new United States secretary of defense, and Gilles Lamontagne, the minister of national defence,[11] on 15 April 1981.[12]

The Honourable Gilles Lamontagne was born in Montreal in 1919 and joined the RCAF in 1941. He qualified as a pilot and served with the "Les Alouettes" bomber squadron until he was shot down over the Netherlands and imprisoned until the end of World War II. He was first sent to the House of Commons for the Langelier constituency in a 1977 by-election, and was then named the parliamentary secretary to the energy minister. After the 1980 election which returned the Liberals to power after the Clark interregnum, he was appointed minister of national defence until his replacement on 12 August 1983. He left federal politics to become the Lieutenant-Governor of Quebec, and recently retired as chairman of the board of the Royal Military College (Kingston, Ontario). Caspar W. Weinberger was born in San Francisco in 1917, and graduated from Harvard Law School in 1941 before enlisting in the U.S. Army to serve in the Pacific theatre as an intelligence officer. After the war, he held a variety of private and governmental positions, the most important being the vice-president and general counsel of the military contract company, Bechtel Group. He was chosen by the Reagan staff to serve as the secretary of defence from 21 January 1981 to 23 November 1987. He is remembered as the man who spearheaded the nuclear weapons program to acquire and deploy the B-1B bomber, the F-117 stealth fighter and B-2 stealth bomber, the LGM-118A 'MX/Peacekeeper' ICBM (inter-continental ballistic missile), the Trident D-2 MIRVed SLBM (submarine-launched ballistic missile), and several tactical nuclear weapons.

The Weinberger-Lamontagne meeting was the setting for the first, formal political request by the United States for testing rights. Weinberger told Lamontagne that Washington regarded testing in Canada as very important. Although it opened up the distinct possibility of protest, it was deemed a manageable risk as the cruise missile was basically only a particular kind of aircraft. Fred Ikle, Weinberger's assistant, suggested that the tests be done "under cover" of an existing agreement, and noted that a careful choice of words, instead of ALCM or cruise missile, would be helpful in obscuring the real purpose of the tests from the public.

Lamontagne thought that the general attitude of the public would be favourable, but told Weinberger that the U.S. *Freedom of Information Act* (FOIA) and the upcoming Canadian *Access to Information Act* would ensure "ample access to what was involved." Lamontagne pointed out that to many people in Canada and abroad, cruise missile meant nuclear weapon. Commiserating, Weinberger told the minister that freedom of information could "present problems" for testing in Canada, and that in the United States, FOIA resulted in a situation of "freedom and candour run wild." Lamontagne understood this, as recent revelations from Washington about the testing of Agent Orange at Canadian Forces Base (CFB) Gagetown had created difficulties for the minister and the government. In fact, officially, swift and punishing action was demanded. On orders from the secretary of state for external affairs, the Canadian embassy in Washington had demanded that the U.S. State Department investigate and plug the leak about chemical weapons testing conducted over Winnipeg in 1953. However, it turned out that under a *Freedom of Information Act* request the Pentagon had released the documents to the Church of Scientology, and that the U.S. State Department had no input. In any case, the State Department declared that since no Canadian documents were involved, it had no requirement to consult Ottawa. The minister's office demanded that anything pertaining to activity in or over Canada must be cleared through the Canadian embassy.[13]

The meeting ended with the conclusion that more informal talks would be necessary, and that an entirely new agreement would have to be drafted. Both parties also agreed that a massive information campaign would be needed to convince an increasingly anti-nuclear public of the wisdom of such testing. Finally, Lamontagne and Weinberger agreed to keep the talks at the military-to-military level, and to not involve cabinet for the time being. The only public reference to the meeting, written in advance, announced that the two men spoke about the CF-18 fighter jet program.[14]

With the Canadian decision to proceed now communicated to both Weinberger and the Canadian military, it was time for increased activity at the formal discussion level. At the next meeting of the Permanent Joint Board on Defence at CFB Greenwood in Nova Scotia on 16–19 June 1981, the two delegations slightly advanced the talks and began formulating an agreed framework as suggested the previous year by the Pentagon.[15]

In the Soviet Union the fear that the West was about to unleash a 'hot' war was growing. The installation of the Reagan regime and its inflammatory rhetoric had so concerned the Soviets that at a session of the KGB high command and senior staff, General Secretary Leonid Brezhnev and KGB chief Yuri Andropov stated that the United States was actively preparing for a nuclear attack on the USSR. It was announced internally that the KGB and Soviet military intelligence would mount a new intelligence collection operation aimed at monitoring nuclear preparedness and to warn of U.S. nuclear war preparations. The intelligence alert sought information on key U.S./NATO political and strategic decisions about the USSR and the Warsaw Treaty Organization; early warning of U.S./NATO preparations for launching a surprise nuclear attack; and new U.S./NATO weapons systems intended for use in a surprise nuclear attack. Code-named Operation *RYaN* for *raketno-yadernoye napadenie*, or nuclear-rocket attack, agents spread across Europe and the rest of the world in search of the signs of an impending U.S. attack on the Soviet Union.[16] *RYaN* remained a significant operation for the next two years.

The question that has been raised is why something as unusual as Operation *RYaN* was undertaken at all. Reagan's rhetoric was certainly frightening but nothing new in an election campaign.[17] The Soviets probably concluded that once diplomacy got underway with the new regime calmer heads would prevail. However, the Reaganites promptly launched or enhanced previous anti-Soviet campaigns and military provocations, such as the repeated secret naval incursions in Soviet waters in early 1981, or mock attacks by bombers over the North Pole. Such a massive increase in military testing, incursions, and practice attacks on the Soviet homeland had the effect of convincing Andropov that the United States was preparing for all-out nuclear war, just as Reagan had said in his presidential campaign.

Cabinet first dealt with the cruise missile issue during the 17 July meeting of the Cabinet Committee on Foreign and Defence Policy. At this time, only the United States proposal and the recent Weinberger-Lamontagne talks were discussed with no formal decision being reached. Informally, they decided that the secretary of state for external affairs and the minister of national defence would negotiate a five-year arrangement, and that Canada would proceed cautiously. At this time, the first memorandum to cabinet was jointly prepared by National Defence and External Affairs. As it was common practice for discussion papers attached to cabinet submissions to be made public if requested, New Democratic Party (NDP) Member of Parliament Pauline Jewett was told that no attachments or discussion papers were included with this submission. This was a falsehood. The United States had already provided, and both ministers shared with cabinet that day, the early notional list of tests they wished to perform over the next four years.[18] As a result of the cabinet decision, the Canadian government solicited a formal request from President Reagan, asking Prime Minister Trudeau to agree to weapons testing. The letter would come and Trudeau "signed a positive reply."[19]

The most interesting part of the submission featured the commercial considerations facing Canada. Cabinet read that the Department of Industry, Trade and Commerce was an "enthusiastic backer" of the proposal, and that a Canadian firm with government financial backing was manufacturing guidance units for cruise missiles. The draft of the submission revealed that Litton Systems of Canada in Toronto had received the contract as part of the industrial benefits package resulting from National Defence's purchase of the CF-18 fighter, and that the Canadian taxpayer had given Litton Systems of Canada nearly $40 million in grants through the Defence Industry Productivity Program (DIPP). This was viewed as an indication of existing Canadian government support for the new ALCM program. Cabinet was asked to believe that "a positive Canadian reaction could increase opportunities for new contracts."[20]

With the initial, though not formal cabinet-level decision having been made, and with joint discussions proceeding to the stage at which a framework would have to be agreed upon, the Trudeau Cabinet office found itself in a bit of trouble. Prime Minister Trudeau had already begun making noises about the need for peace and arms control, and for a reduction in Cold War tensions. For this reason the Prime Minister's Office (PMO) now had to deal with the contradictions inherent in the real policy versus the declared policy. Philippe Clement, Perry Anglin, Stan Carlson, and Susan Carter in the PMO wrestled with the problem of how to reconcile the Trudeau statements on suffocation of the arms race with "our allowing the U.S. to make use of Canadian territory to test their cruise missiles."[21]

The 160th meeting of the Permanent Joint Board on Defence during 20–23 October included a short discussion of the issue, but nothing was resolved.[22] Trudeau was kept informed but did nothing at this point, although he was considering replacing the chairman, George Hees.[23] Trudeau did order his staff in the Prime Minister's Office (Fowler, Pitcairn, and Wightman), to draft the strategy for the Canadian approach to the U.S. ALCM testing request.[24] But more action was needed, and it would have to provide a clear direction. This point was understood both in Ottawa and in Washington.

The Cabinet Committee on Priorities and Planning met several times during October and November, and it was at these meetings that further informal progress was discussed. It was also at the 27 October meeting that the cabinet committee made the formal decision to approve the original cabinet memorandum[25] and to proceed to negotiate a full agreement on weapons testing with the United States.[26] Minister of External Affairs Mark MacGuigan would later comment that the late 1981 cabinet approval-in-principle of the proposal cleared the way for formal negotiations, and that the talks then proceeded without trouble.[27] MacGuigan said that "there had to be Cabinet approval in order for the ... talks to proceed." The strange aspect is that this decision was not communicated to Washington, and the Pentagon and White House had become convinced that the previous nine months of seeming inactivity demonstrated that Trudeau was unwilling to move on the issue.

MacGuigan's confirmation of the cabinet approval drove Trudeau to extremes of pique, but he would say nothing for almost a year. Although the External Affairs minister had said that cabinet had given approval to negotiating an agreement on weapons testing, it was reported as an agreement on cruise missile testing. By March 1983, both Prime Minister Trudeau and the new External Affairs minister, Allan MacEachen, were denying that MacGuigan had ever said that cabinet approved of cruise missile tests.[28] The government was increasingly desperate as protests mounted and divisions appeared in its own ranks.

At this point the Reagan regime intervened. At first it was thought that the Reagan letter was the result of White House impatience with their little brother to the north, and that Weinberger had prevailed upon Reagan to write to Trudeau. However, it is now known that the Canadian government actually "solicited a formal request from President Reagan."[29] What the Trudeau government had hoped to do, and partially succeeded in doing, was to use the letter to show that Canada was just helping out a close ally which, on its own, had requested assistance. In reality, Trudeau's people had asked the White House to send the letter, thereby giving themselves a propaganda item in the war for public opinion they knew would come.

The 18 December letter asked that Canada move forward with the proposed joint agreement on weapons system testing. It did not mention the cruise missile, and this may be due to the Canadian government's interest in the words not appearing in any official document.

Again the PMO trio, Fowler, Pitcairn, and Wightman, drafted the reply which was ready and on Trudeau's desk on 23 December.[30] Trudeau waited a week before signing his response to the new U.S. president. The short note thanked Reagan for his letter and closed with wishing him a happy new year and expressed the hope for "real progress in the search for world peace and stability." But the crux of the matter was covered by Trudeau telling Reagan that his cabinet agreed to the testing, and that the secretary of state for external affairs had been authorized to negotiate and conclude and sign an agreement on this issue. Trudeau assured Reagan that the Department of External Affairs would very soon be in touch to finalize the agreement.[31] As with the Reagan letter, this one never mentioned the cruise missile.

The year ended with the first Boeing production-model AGM-86B air-launched cruise missile being rolled out of the factory at Kent, Washington, before a large crowd of invited guests and reporters. The reception was warm, and the new weapon was soon embraced by the U.S. Air Force.

1982

The outcome of the letter and Trudeau's directive was that External Affairs immediately sent a draft of a proposed agreement to the State Department in Washington as the basis for consultations. By the end of

February, the U.S. government had decided that it liked the draft, but was uncomfortable with certain provisions related to legal wording. Due to the wording of the data exchange provision, the U.S. team worried that what they considered proprietary data from the weapons and/or the tests could end up in Canadian hands. Lastly, there was still the question of what role the Canadian Forces would have during any tests, and how the entire program would be funded. On or about 25 February 1982, the U.S. counter-proposal was sent back to Ottawa, and Canadian officials began consideration of the new points.[32] By this time the United States had already agreed to total U.S. funding, and to not use live warheads of any type. The United States also agreed that Canada did have the right to block any tests, and that all Canadian environmental laws which applied to the Canadian Forces would also apply to the U.S. military.

The world-wide nuclear weapons situation, and the cruise missile situation specifically, was ominous as 1982 began. The arms control negotiating team from Washington had already communicated to the Soviet Foreign Ministry that cruise missiles would not be included in any arms reduction proposal. In Washington, the annual Department of Defense report from secretary Weinberger called for increasing spending on the acquisition of strategic nuclear forces, including cruise missiles, from the then current $16.2 billion to a new high of $23.1 billion. By the end of February, the Pentagon had announced that the first forty LGM-118A 'MX/Peacekeeper' ICBMs would be deployed in silos at Warren Air Force Base in Wyoming, Colorado, and Nebraska. The new ten-warhead MX missile was partly responsible for the plan to add seventeen thousand new nuclear warheads to the U.S. arsenal of some twenty-five thousand existing warheads over the next fifteen years. The massive build-up required Reagan to ask for an extra $1.1 billion to speed warhead production for the following five years. By this time, the belief was that the Soviets had deployed some three hundred RSD-10 'Pioneer' (NATO designation, SS-20) INF missiles.

By the end of August 1982 the U.S. team had provided a list of weapons systems they wished to test in Canada over the following three years. The tentative list included the ALCM, artillery equipment, helicopters, surveillance and identification systems, and aircraft navigation systems. Initially, a rumour persisted in Ottawa that the United States would ask to test the ground-launched cruise missile (GLCM) – the weapon bound for European Intermediate Nuclear Force (INF) deployment.[33] However, this seems to be wishful thinking by officials who desperately needed to justify the cruise missile decision with a NATO cloak. When the list was provided on 26–27 August 1982, it was then confirmed that the GLCM was one of the proposed items, but that the air-launched cruise missile was the one to be immediately tested. Since the list was considered secret, the Canadian government could not even use it to justify their tenuous argument.

At the next Permanent Joint Board on Defence meeting on 16–19 February 1982, the Canadian and U.S. delegations discussed the formal proposals as directed by Trudeau and Reagan. Hees reported little progress to Trudeau.[34] In reply, Trudeau told Hees that he was glad that his decision to allow "certain defence system" tests in Canada helped to establish a positive atmosphere in the talks, but that "the decision was taken only after a certain amount of soul-searching." Trudeau continued by telling Hees that "in the end, we recognized that, like it or not, we have a vested interest in the improvement of the United States deterrent capability." Trudeau ended his letter by telling Hees that he hoped that the positive decision on cruise missile tests would have a positive impact on the direction and outcome of other upcoming defence-related issues.[35] From this we can conclude that Trudeau was trying to manage Canada-U.S. military relations, which had been difficult since Diefenbaker's term, by at least giving the United States something important, something which they seemed to want so dearly.

The importance of the meeting was that the U.S. team was proposing to remove the restriction on arming weapons to be tested. The Canadian team had included the phrase, "cruise missiles shall be unarmed," in the very first draft considered by both ministers in early 1981, and then given to the U.S. team. The legal division of External Affairs determined that by removing such language from the agreement and placing it in the attached arrangement, it would cease to be legally binding and would have to be repeated with each arrangement; they preferred to have it settled once and for all by its inclusion in the formal agreement.[36]

Cabinet had to start laying the groundwork for what would become one of the most unpopular decisions of the Liberal government. The following months saw increased, but low-key, propagandizing efforts by cabinet. In committee, Minister of External Affairs Mark MacGuigan told Pauline Jewett that the Liberal government had no problem with nuclear weapons system components being created and manufactured in Canada, nor with Canadian taxpayers' money going for industrial support to do so. He said, "it would not offend any of our principles that we are doing so."[37] MacGuigan already knew that cabinet had decided to proceed with cruise missile testing, and that various components on nuclear weapons systems were made in Canada by Canadian and US subsidiary companies in Canada.

Then it happened – what they all feared and knew might happen – the cover was removed and the story leaked to the press. The leak arose from a question relating to a totally different issue. The purchase of the CF-18 aircraft from McDonnell-Douglas Aircraft Corporation in the United States seemed to come with a price tag a bit on the low side. One U.S. Air Force officer commented that the United States should be lenient on CF-18 price issues as, after all, Canada was going to test the cruise missile for the United States Air Force. This inadvertent comment led to an article which let Canadians know what their government was secretly up to.

On 9 March the U.S. Air Force told the story to two reporters in Washington.[38] Canadians awoke on Wednesday, 10 March 1982, to find out that their government had again been saying one thing and doing another. The news was broken to an astonished public by Don Sellar and John R. Walker of Southam News. "U.S. wants missile tests over Canada," boomed headlines in the *Ottawa Citizen* and every other Southam newspaper. A U.S. Air Force spokesman confirmed that the negotiations were underway, but because it was known to be a very sensitive subject, "did not want to pre-empt anything the Canadian government might say about it." It was already too late for that sentiment. The Trudeau Liberals cabinet had been hoping that the entire affair could be signed and sealed, and testing begun, before the Canadian public heard anything about it; they had made no plans to ever make public any details.

The Sellar/Walker article was full of information the Canadian government never wanted the public to know or to discuss. The state of the negotiations, and the fact that the agreement would be an umbrella document allowing for various weapons system tests, was revealed. Sellar and Walker found out that the United States and Canada were officially considering both air and ground-launched cruise missile tests, and that there were many other, still secret, weapons being considered. The USAF told them that the tests should take place in northern Canada as the winter months provided "more realistic flight profiles." They further told the public that the B-52 bomber would release the ALCM at a target over twenty-five hundred kilometres away. One other detail that successive Canadian governments did not want the public knowing about or talking about was the depth of Canadian government, industry, and tax-supported involvement in the nuclear weapons business. Sellar and Walker told their readers that when McDonnell-Douglas Aircraft Corporation won the contract from the Liberals for providing the CF-18 fighter aircraft to the Canadian

Forces, it also received a grant of at least $545 million in industrial benefit credits to make guidance systems for the ground-launched cruise missile at their sub-contractor facility run by Litton Systems (Canada) Ltd. of Toronto. The Canadian public was now thrust into the centre of a highly divisive issue that would drag on for another twelve years.

Minister of National Defence Gilles Lamontagne was briefed by PMO staff before entering the House of Commons that morning. General D. P. Wightman gave him several talking points which would prove useful in deflecting discussion. Wightman's talking points boiled down to the following assertions: the agreement would cover any weapons testing but specified none; the United States was expected to ask to test the ALCM; "Canada would have an absolute veto over any and all tests"; no live weapons will be tested and all delivery systems will be unarmed; testing information will flow to the benefit of Canadian industry; and this was done to enhance the NATO posture and to improve the deterrent force.[39]

Upon leaving the House of Commons, Lamontagne was immediately besieged by reporters. In a scrum outside the Commons, Lamontagne had a number of points to make, and the desperation was already evident. Aside from saying that the negotiations were only a few weeks old, and that the cruise missile was just one of the items that the United States might want to test, his answers to reporters were limited to the party line.[40]

When asked about the difference between weapons and delivery systems that may or may not have nuclear warheads, Lamontagne launched into his rhetoric, exclaiming that "there is a big difference, because if it is live it might explode, might hurt and might do some damage, but this is just dummies, like we have sometimes with shells that are made of wood or just lead or something like that. There is no explosive whatsoever in these weapons, they are strictly a question of testing, as I say, if we agree on this cruise missile delivery system, it will be strictly the delivery system that will be tested, there will be no weapons tested." He added that "there is no question of testing weapons, it's a delivery system which they are asking us to be able to test in Canada." The next day the headline exclaimed, "They'd be just dummies."[41]

Lamontagne then tried to play the NATO card. This would become a standard ploy of the public relations personnel in Ottawa as the testing program proceeded. When asked if the testing contradicted Canada's general stance on disarmament, Lamontagne stated that it did not, and that the NATO dual-track decision of 1979 called on all members to improve the NATO deterrent capability by modernizing weaponry. When asked if such a contradiction weakened Canadian credibility, Lamontagne again responded that strengthening NATO's nuclear weapons would improve our position, "and may give the Russians a better argument for discussing disarmament." External Affairs Minister MacGuigan told reporters days later that "because we belong to a military alliance, NATO, which is a nuclear alliance... we need these weapons in order to advance towards peace."[42] This argument would be used even after the Cold War ended and the USSR collapsed.

The NATO argument was favoured by Canadian politicians because they knew Canadians generally favoured NATO. It was a relatively safe debating trick under normal circumstances, but these were not normal circumstances, and many Canadians understood that air-launched cruise missile (ALCM) testing in northern Canada had nothing whatsoever to do with any NATO commitment or the dual-track decision of 1979. Pierre Trudeau stated that "If NATO in Europe did not need these missiles, I would guess we would not consider testing them."[43] At the behest of British Prime Minister Margaret Thatcher, the United Kingdom's high commissioner to Canada, John Moran, weighed in saying that NATO had collectively decided to counter the Soviet SS-20 missiles, and that Canada was merely fulfilling its commitment to NATO.[44] So strongly attached were Trudeau and his cabinet to the NATO argument that he even used it as a straw man against the idea of an election. Trudeau stated that not to test the cruise missile would mean Canada was leaving NATO, and that could only be done as a consequence of a national election in which that was the main question.[45] In the end it was probably put best by former United States Secretary of Defense Robert McNamara, who told the parliamentary Joint Committee on External Affairs and National Defence that "there may be no military requirement for the missiles, but there is a political requirement." Trudeau and those who followed would use the NATO fig leaf to cover their political deeds.[46]

Lamontagne was amazing in his capacity to evade the real issue and to cast it against the naysayers. Despite nuclear weapons still stationed in Canada for immediate use, he responded, "there is no question of nuclear weapons in Canada, that's very very decisive. I don't think that the prime minister or myself, we agree both of us on that, that there should be no nuclear weaponry, even nuclear weaponry tested in Canada, not at all." At the time fifty-two W-25 nuclear warheads for Genie rockets were still stored at Canadian Forces Bases Bagotville and Comox.

One reporter brought up the very problem the Prime Minister's Office had feared and already discussed – how this worked in light of Trudeau's suffocation speech at the United Nations in 1978. Spokesmen for the prime minister denied that there was a contradiction, saying that Trudeau had merely 'floated' the idea. Lamontagne continued by noting that testing was okay if it increased the chances of the suffocation for which Trudeau had called. There was no good answer to this question, and the very real contradiction, denied in public but acknowledged by Trudeau and the PMO, would remain a sore point for Trudeau and a striking point for activists.

Around the world, the spring was full of protests against nuclear weapons. On 4 April as many as one hundred thousand people rallied at Comiso Air Base in Italy against the proposed cruise missile deployments expected there. On 18 April another fifty thousand marched in Munich against the Intermediate Nuclear Force deployments. Rome was besieged on 5 June by one-quarter million protesters angry at the Italian government for allowing the deployments. By the end of June the Italian campaign would gather one million signatures against the cruise missile.

Canadian protests were also growing. Ordinary Canadians such as Perry Padgham, the president of Edmontonians for a Non-Nuclear Future, and Nancy Burger of the Lakeland Area Non-Nuclear Coalition, helped organize the first mass protest near CFB Cold Lake. More than six hundred Canadians gathered at the high school in Grand Centre, Alberta. They came in buses from across the province, carrying signs such as "cruise now pay later," "peace is everybody's business," and "remember Hiroshima." The general mood was that if this was such a good idea, and if it was so safe, then the missiles should be tested in Ottawa, or better yet, in Washington. The Reverend Glen Eagle, another organizer, was thankful for the support from around the province and around the country. Normally conservative Alberta was sprouting protesters and protests faster than imagined by politicians in Ottawa.

External Affairs swung into action, prompted by reading about the secret negotiations and testing in the newspapers, and by the fact that the negative calls were already coming into the minister's office.[47] No response had yet been prepared. The next day all major embassies were cabled informing them of the new party line. In case of any questions, embassy officials were to state that test flights of unarmed ALCMs were consistent with Canadian arms control policy because Canada only supported mutual restraint based on signed agreements; the government disavowed any use of unilateral restraint on testing and development of nuclear weapons; the ALCM was in place to prevent war and to ensure peace for North America; and NATO required these weapons to demonstrate solidarity and to force the Soviets to the negotiating table.[48] The one interesting item they were allowed to say was that other systems to be tested might include "artillery weapons, helicopters, surveillance and identification systems and aircraft navigation systems." But such minor actions directed to embassies would be of little use if the Canadian public came out in force against the issue. The Department of External Affairs would eventually send a large information package on the prospective agreement and cruise missile testing to all of its consulates around the United States. Embassy and consulate staff were supposed to read the material "and consider ways in which the agreement might be publicized in their territory so as to redound to Canada's credit."[49]

The public affairs machine was in full swing at the Department of National Defence. Cruise missile testing was wildly unpopular, and National Defence had identified four major problems that it and the government would encounter. First, in addition to cruise missile testing, it had become known to the public that the U.S. Air Force wanted to set up another B-52 low-level training route in Alberta. Second, multiple missile crashes had raised fears of possible life-threatening situations in Alberta. Third, the public was not buying the artificial distinction between captive-carry and free-flight tests; to the public a test was a test, and all tests were protested. Captive-carry tests had the missile attached to the bomber for the entire route. Free-flight tests had the missile fly by itself to the target. Finally, the White House also caused problems. The Department of National Defence lamented that the White House had announced that it was about to exceed the treaty limits on bombers in the SALT II agreement, and that the B-52 was the ALCM carrier. The public affairs staff noted that it would be a cruise missile carrier which would break the treaty, and that the anti-cruise missile movement would use this as ammunition.

In the end, National Defence chose to maintain a low-key, but detailed, information approach. Questions would be answered with as much detail as possible, but National Defence would not go looking to tell its story.[50] But one military figure was not agreeing with the party line. Retired General E.L.M. Burns, the first peacekeeping force commander and later the government's advisor on arms control, announced that he was against any action which increased the proliferation of nuclear weapons. He opposed testing the cruise missile and said that this was something the Canadian government should stand against.[51]

Terry Sargeant, an anti-nuclear New Democratic Party member, was the first Member of Parliament to take action. He immediately wrote to the prime minister and challenged the decision. The Trudeau reply was at once a masterwork of subterfuge, and a confused response on an issue no one in government could publicly deal with by telling the direct truth. The prime minister started honestly enough by telling Sargeant that at this stage the agreement was only an umbrella agreement under which it would be possible to test various weapons systems, but that none had yet been agreed to. He also admitted that "we have no doubt" that the United States would soon ask to use Canadian ranges and airspace for the testing of unarmed cruise missiles.[52]

Trudeau then sprung into a disjointed and rambling defence of the decision based on unrelated NATO events. He told Sargeant that there were many considerations, among them Canadian membership in NORAD and NATO, and the joint Defence Production Sharing Agreement. Trudeau continued by telling Sargeant that Canada and his government fully supported the 1979 NATO "dual-track" decision on INF weapons, and that for Canada now to not test U.S. systems and to follow only one track "would clearly jeopardize whatever chances there may be of reaching disarmament agreements with the USSR." The prime minister's letter then further digressed by confusing NATO forces with the U.S. strategic arsenal, and stating that the Soviets would have no incentive to negotiate if Canada did not allow for the modernization of the strategic deterrent. He concluded by trying to assure Sargeant that his commitment to disarmament "will continue undiminished."

A week later Sargeant asked the minister of national defence if there was a connection between the testing and the CF-18 deal previously signed by the Liberal Cabinet. His question in the House of Commons on 17 March went unanswered in public. No reply was given, and it would remain a point of debate and conjecture.

But National Defence and External Affairs were not the only offices under attack. An army of Canadians was besieging the Prime Minister's Office. Telephone calls and telegrams and letters were pouring in. In typical Canadian fashion, there was no screaming, and protesters were described as "very polite" by Trudeau's office staff.

At the NATO foreign ministers' meeting held 17–18 May, U.S. Secretary of State Alexander Haig told his colleagues that the United States would offer to discuss cruise missiles and bombers with the Soviets, but that Washington feared Moscow would demand cuts. MacGuigan later told reporters that although the ministers expressed solidarity with the concept of the talk, there was no endorsement of the U.S. position articulated by Haig.

The Liberals could wait no longer; they had to go on the offensive or risk losing even more public opinion. On 19 March, in one of his increasingly rare and brief appearances in western Canada, Pierre Trudeau chose the Saskatoon Centennial Auditorium as the venue for his first public appearance on the cruise missile issue. In this hastily produced news conference, the prime minister had to dodge some tough questions, but tried to keep the proceedings light and to his advantage. He began by saying that he was flattered that so many Liberals had shown up for his interview, and that he was ready to talk politics because, "well, that's my gig and I'm ready to start." Although the glow of the late-1960s Trudeaumania had long since faded, the prime minister still acted in a flamboyant, though increasingly desperate, manner. He would be gone from politics in two years.

In a pre-speech briefing, Robert Fowler told the prime minister that the proposed testing might have direct economic benefits for Canada, and would surely have indirect benefits such as encouraging more defence production north of the 49th parallel.[53] This line would continue and become even stronger as time went by. In fact, with the renegotiation of the agreement to add Canada's right to test in the United States, the government was able to put forward this argument.

After the speech the scrum did not go well for Trudeau. One reporter asked Trudeau why he had chosen to proceed with an order-in-council rather than with parliamentary debate and a resolution to approve the testing agreement. The prime minister responded with no real answer by saying, "well, there is nothing new or astonishing about that."

Another asked if the entire weapons testing policy was in direct conflict with the prime minister's earlier policy of strategic weapons suffocation that was to ban flight tests. Trudeau used the opportunity to once again tout his vision of disarmament in which the nuclear arms race was suffocated by ending work "in the laboratories, or in the testing areas." At the same time he finally did admit, in a roundabout way, that "there might be a contradiction with our policy of suffocation." Various reporters, and Trudeau himself, pointed out that in 1978 Trudeau had told the United Nations Special Session on Disarmament that one answer to the arms race was to cut off testing of new items. In response, Trudeau said that he still thought that the idea was a significant one, but that "it wasn't accepted by many people, particularly by the Soviets." Trudeau did not have to explain that it was not the Soviets testing weapons in Canada. Reporters never followed up on his curious assertion.

Reporters in Saskatchewan brought up the notion of western alienation from eastern Canada, and some wondered if the two affected provinces, Alberta and Saskatchewan, had been consulted. Saskatchewan Attorney-General Roy Romanow told the press that his government had not been consulted or even informally told of the proposed tests, and that this was "a source of mild irritation to Alberta and to Saskatchewan." The reality was that the Prime Minister's Office had chosen to consult the provinces only when the agreement was within weeks of signature. Original criticism by the NDP in Saskatchewan was muted when the federal team showed up in Saskatoon on 27 April, the day after the NDP had been defeated in the provincial election. The federal Liberals now had to deal with the accommodating provincial Conservatives. The PMO feared that to consult earlier would increase the risk of a leak to the Canadian public.[54]

In one of the oddest points of the discussion, and one seeming to have been calculated to play on the fears of Canadians and the lack of information available to them, Trudeau stated that the Soviets had tripled their number of "cruise missiles known as the SS-20."[55] The SS-20, formally known as the RSD-10, is a ballistic missile that has nothing in common with any form of cruise missile. However, Trudeau hoped to make an equation in the minds of Canadians and thereby prop up his case for the testing as a bulwark against the Soviet Union. Even odder was Trudeau's assertion that Canada and NATO must match the Soviets 'gun for gun' in the arms race, as this had never been a policy adopted by NATO, which instead had chosen to rely on nuclear weapons as an alternative to massive conventional forces.

In the days prior to this news conference, Soviet General Secretary Brezhnev had announced that he was willing to halt deployments of the RSD-10 missile. At the same time, massive public rallies against the GLCM and Pershing missiles were taking place across Western Europe. Trudeau therefore had to dance around the issue of new tests even as an accommodation on the INF missile issue in Europe seemed possible. He told reporters that even though Soviet deployments would probably stop now, it was up to NATO to match the deployments, and that "the cruise missiles which are being tested now would have that [matching] effect." No reporter asked whether the ALCM to be tested in Canada had any connection to the GLCM being fielded in Western Europe and NATO, and Trudeau chose not to bring up the discrepancy that he and his cabinet members had introduced. The perpetually vague and tenuous link between the NATO cruise missile and the U.S. Air Force cruise missile was maintained by successive Canadian governments as just about the only palatable way they had of justifying the testing in Canada. Polls showed that Canadians would probably support NATO, but that there was little support for simply helping the United States increase its strategic offensive forces. Perhaps Trudeau's oddest statement of the day was the simple argument against weapons testing. In closing the discussion he boldly claimed, "We must reduce our cruise missiles."

The Canadian press may have bought the idea of the NATO link, but the public was disbelieving, and certain Members of Parliament took the government to task. Pauline Jewett, the NDP Member of Parliament and member of the Standing Committee on External Affairs and National Defence (SCEAND), called Mark MacGuigan on the carpet for his evasive and sometimes contradictory statements. When MacGuigan tried to use the NATO argument, Jewett immediately cut him off simply saying, "Red herrings," and later noting that the Canadian testing had nothing to do with NATO policy and the 1979 dual-track decision. She rightly pointed out that these missiles "are not for deployment in Europe under the theatre nuclear forces modernization NATO decision.... They have nothing to do with that, and therefore the minister simply draws a red herring."[56]

Only when questioned by a sympathetic committee member did MacGuigan get to state, "we want to promote the idea that there should be general agreement not to test new weapon systems." He also decided that it would be a good time to cast a new light on the reason for the government's embarrassment over the issue. MacGuigan therefore told the committee that the only reason the Liberals were shy about the whole thing was that the leak had come before they could consult Alberta. The meeting then recessed.

The reality was that despite all the propaganda about the agreement dealing with various weapons systems and not about the cruise missile, it was always about testing the ALCM. Documents released by the Prime Minister's Office years after the fact revealed a memo stating, "the testing of cruise missiles has been the aim of the exercise from the outset."[57] Everything else was window dressing.

During the meeting of the Standing Committee on External Affairs and National Defence (SCEAND), Douglas Roche, the red Tory (Conservative Party) from Alberta, suggested that perhaps the minister and cabinet could stall the agreement at least until after the next United Nations Special Session on Disarmament (UNSSOD II). In fact, given that there was so much attention on the issue, and given that the PMO already recognized the inconsistency of the policy positions, it was decided that this was the best route to follow – somewhat. MacGuigan and Lamontagne agreed that the governments would proceed normally towards the agreement, but that any subsidiary arrangements which would allow, say, cruise missile testing, would not be concluded until later in 1982, and "in any event not until after UNSSOD II."[58]

By this time the U.S. State Department had already replied to the Canadian drafts with proposals of their own. Its April response prompted further work at both National Defence and External Affairs, and both ministers always knew the status of the negotiations, even if they chose to hide them from committee. To push the Canadians, U.S. Secretary of Defense Weinberger called Lamontagne to the U.S. delegation office at NATO for instruction. Lamontagne received in no uncertain terms the official position on air defence, Goose Bay, NATO commitments, armoured vehicles, and U.S. tests in Canada. All that Lamontagne could tell Weinberger was that work would proceed, but the arrangements would not be in place until after UNSSOD II.[59]

Minister of National Defence Gilles Lamontagne was the next cabinet member to appear before committee. The same session of SCEAND was to hear his testimony on the military budget estimates, but everyone knew that the cruise missile would be the primary topic of discussion. Lamontagne was briefed extensively by his staff at National Defence as he prepared for the mighty conflict.[60] He was advised of the prime minister's experience in Saskatoon, and of the grilling MacGuigan had experienced in committee. He was given their answers as well as new answers compiled by National Defence. As expected, he spent a great deal of his statement time misdirecting debate by telling everyone how the entire decision was based on the need to support the NATO dual track decision.[61] The government had decided on the propaganda line, and nothing would budge it from this course.[62]

The next day, formal consultations with the provinces began as the Department of External Affairs, the Department of National Defence, and the Federal-Provincial Relations Office at PMO, met with British Columbian officials in Victoria. The 28 April meeting was the first opportunity any provincial official had to discuss the issue with federal officials. However, the talks were limited to briefing British Columbia on the environmental and flight safety aspects of the proposed flights. The provinces would be ignored.

The slow Canadian reply to the State Department came on 12 June 1982. After having been through drafting at External Affairs, National Defence, and the PMO, the Canadian team transmitted its draft of the agreement and accompanying arrangement back to Washington through the Canadian embassy.

Internationally, protests were mounting against nuclear weapons and against the Intermediate Nuclear Force deployments. Two thousand people blocked the entrance of the Lawrence Livermore National Lab in California where nuclear weapons were designed, and some nine hundred people were arrested. Strategic nuclear weapons were high on the agenda of many around the world, and the Reagan administration was forced by public opinion to engage in arms control talks. Having campaigned against the SALT II Treaty, Reagan and his team made a new proposal on 9 May 1982 for new talks under a new name, Strategic Arms Reduction Talks (START). The Soviets did not accept the name immediately, preferring their own Strategic Arms Limitation and Reduction Talks, which they announced on 31 May. The initial U.S. position was that bombers would be limited to four hundred aircraft carrying no more than twenty ALCMs each.[63] This was more than the entire U.S. bomber inventory, and the extreme upper end of the cruise missile war load of the B-52, so there was no reduction or even limitation. The lesson was that the ALCM was too important to the United States Air Force to be bargained away in reducing nuclear weapons.

Many Canadians were angry with government lies and with what they perceived as the extension of the arms race to Canadian territory. National Defence Headquarters acknowledged answering some six hundred letters between mid-March and June 1982, while External Affairs had to answer at least one thousand letters.[64] The number of letters addressed to the prime minister remains unknown. Upset with the secretary of state for external affairs, several Canadians in Vancouver spit on Allan MacEachen, who had been caught in another massive demonstration held in Robson Square by the local chapter of the Canadian United Nations Association. His assistant, Jim MacDonald, incredulously called out, "you can't spit on the minister!" Canadian politicians needed intestinal fortitude now more than ever.[65]

Sister Mary Jo Leddy, one of Canada's most active social consciences and activist for the poor and powerless, stated that Canadians were being tested as human beings. She told Canadians that in this time of trouble you were either standing by and aiding the destruction of the human race, or you were pulling people from the flames. She called on Canadians to take up the challenge and confront the evil that was happening in Canada, whether it be the production of cruise missile navigation systems by Litton in Rexdale, Ontario, or the testing of the cruise missile itself.[66]

In Moscow the Soviets were now proposing to forego their European missile deployments in exchange for stringent cruise missile restrictions. On 16 July 1982, U.S. negotiator Paul Nitze and Soviet negotiator Yuli Kvitsinsky went for the now famous and fabled 'walk in the woods.' They agreed on an INF compromise to severely limit INF systems on both sides. This comprehensive framework for reductions and limitations was forwarded to Moscow and Washington the next day. It was immediately rejected in both capitals. The war machine was stepping up, and on 21 July Washington revealed that the U.S. Army was seeking pre-clearance to use tactical nuclear weapons without waiting for a further presidential decision in times of war. While approval of this remains uncertain, it is known that the U.S. Congress authorized funding for one thousand of the 155 millimetre neutron bomb artillery shells for use by the army.

The teams from the U.S. State Department, the Pentagon, National Defence, and External Affairs met again in Ottawa 26–27 August 1982. This resulted in a revised draft agreement as well as a supporting memorandum of understanding (MOU). It was at this meeting that the Canadians believed that all outstanding issues of substance were resolved.[67] However, no French text had yet been prepared, and the Canadian government would not agree without a French text. For their part, and because French wording often differed considerably from the original intent, the U.S. would not give approval to the Canadian package pending the receipt of the draft French translation from Ottawa.

While the French translation problem stood in the way of completion, the meeting revealed to the Canadians why the United States had for so long insisted on removing references to cruise missiles being unarmed when tested in Canada. At the same meeting the U.S. team told National Defence and External Affairs staff that they wanted to propose "the testing of conventionally armed short range cruise or ballistic missiles possibly launched from ships to overfly exposed portions of the coast of New Brunswick with a view to determining their accuracy in shore bombardment when they impacted on the Gagetown range."[68] The CFB Gagetown range, south of Fredericton, is a massive artillery range used by armoured groups and the Royal Canadian Regiment.

United States naval vessels would have to steam into the Bay of Fundy and fire the missiles some one hundred kilometres inland through the coastal area west of Saint John, New Brunswick. This was at a time when the United States was still experimenting with early generation precision-guided munitions, and live warhead tests were common. Upon hearing of this plan, Canadian officials expressed relief that they had been insistent earlier, and resolved that they would continue to hold the line on including the reference to unarmed weapons. However, years later, the government would allow the use of St. John's harbour as a staging area for sea-launched cruise missile (SLCM) tests by the U.S. Navy.

But it was not just naval cruise missiles and ballistic missiles that posed a problem. An even greater, unseen problem was coming over the horizon. In early August 1982, William Perry wrote that the stealth ALCM could become operational within the year, and that it had a radar cross-section only one-one thousandth that of a B-52 bomber. By the end of the month the chief Soviet military negotiator on arms control, General Viktor Starodubov, said that any arms control agreement would be meaningless and of no value if the United States started a cruise missile race while seeking a reduction in heavy missiles. The Soviet team then proposed an unspecified limit of strategic warheads, under which would be counted all thirty-eight hundred planned United States Air Force ALCMs. The Soviets, now resigned to new MX heavy missiles, were hoping to at least limit cruise missiles.

Just over two weeks later, Secretary of State for External Affairs Allan MacEachen was advised by his deputy minister, de Montigny Marchand, and his assistant deputy minister, W. T. Delworth, that the agreement, pending U.S. acceptance of the French text, was ready to be signed. Delworth and Marchand wrote that the latest negotiating sessions had satisfied virtually every Canadian concern, and that now only an order-in-council was needed to enable the secretary of state for external affairs to conclude the agreement. On 16 September 1982, both recommended that MacEachen sign the Submission to Council that would ultimately give him that authority.[69] The only problem was that the agreement was not ready for signature. First, the United States had still not agreed to the French text. Second, the U.S. team had, at the last moment, introduced new language on financing that Canada could not accept. The agreement would not be signed anytime soon.

The government was already seeking a way to soften the impact of signing the final agreement. Delworth and de Montigny recommended to Allan MacEachen that the agreement be signed by the Canadian ambassador in Washington, D.C. Having Alan Gotlieb sign the document in Washington would "give the exchange a lower profile in Canada than it would have if the Exchange of Notes were signed in Ottawa" by the secretary of state for external affairs and the U.S. ambassador. In addition, the previous minister, Mark MacGuigan, had planned for the agreement to be signed before Parliament reconvened, as this would obviate the normal practice of tabling the document in the House of Commons the day it was signed.[70]

The 163rd meeting of the Permanent Joint Board on Defence was held 19–22 October at CFB Petawawa, Ontario, and a brief discussion of the finalized agreement took place. There was no need for any informal talks as the decision had already been translated into an agreed text.

An eleven-day event was just beginning in Vancouver. Coinciding with United Nations Disarmament Week, Target Vancouver was a massive teach-in and series of anti-war activities including movies, marches, speeches, discussions, and plays. Organizer Peter Prongos told supporters that their actions were important because Canadian support for the U.S. military machine was considered important south of the border. If they could hold back the cruise missile, they would be making an important contribution to peace. To drive home the message, at least nineteen municipalities in British Columbia had already signed on to conduct a referendum on nuclear disarmament. Montreal's events included a talk by Nobel laureate Linus Pauling on the arms race, and numerous activities revolving around missile testing.

The new United States secretary of state, George Shultz, visited Ottawa to chat with MacGuigan and to lobby for cruise missile testing. The 24 October 1982 meeting, on the heels of the Litton bombing (see chapter 3) focused on pushing forward the agreement to a near-term signing.

On Saturday, 30 October 1982, over fifteen thousand Canadians converged on Parliament Hill. It was one of the largest protests ever held on the Hill. The moderator of the United Church, the Reverend Dr. Clarke MacDonald, begged Trudeau not to back down now in the fight against nuclear weapons. Despite the cold, another six thousand people gathered in Winnipeg. In Bagotville, Quebec a group of some one hundred protesters demonstrated at the gates of CFB Bagotville. Although the protests across Canada were about the cruise missile, the question in Bagotville was one of nuclear weapons at the base. National Defence officials denied that the base contained any nuclear weapons; an assertion now proven to have been completely false as declassified documents show Bagotville was home to the second last VooDoo squadron armed with Genie nuclear rockets until 1984.[71]

Allan MacEachen told reporters that even the thousands of protesters had no effect on the government's policy, as Trudeau's attitude had not changed and cabinet remained committed to the testing.[72] However, as 'Refuse the Cruise' protests mounted all across the country, the Liberal

Cabinet pushed away the signing date again and again. The autumn gave way to winter.

The Liberal Party convention took place in the winter. Pierre Trudeau tried to rally the Liberal faithful, many of whom were losing faith in their great leader and self-professed peacemaker. Trudeau told the Liberal multitudes, "this, once again, is the situation we are in. I don't like it. I am not happy with testing cruises in Canada. And as I said in my speech at the United Nations, I hope to hell that we don't do it."[73] On 6 November 1982, Trudeau persuaded the party policy committee to approve a motion saying that the Liberal government should allow the testing. To this day the party remains split on this issue and on the issues that followed, such as missile defence. In the long term, the current Trudeau hagiography may well give way to serious scholarship about the split he produced between the party leadership and the grassroots members over this major issue.

Back in Ottawa Gilles Lamontagne received another extensive briefing on the issues surrounding the production, deployment, and use of cruise missiles.[74] Immediately after this, both Lamontagne and MacEachen received their initial copy of the draft communication plan on 3 November. R. P. Cameron, the chief of international security policy and arms control affairs for MacEachen, told him that "it might have been desirable to limit public discussion on the cruise missile testing issue at least until the agreement with the U.S. had been signed." Cameron bemoaned the fact that with the signing still weeks if not months away, public debate was being stimulated "by a variety of groups opposed to the conclusion of an agreement."[75] He also warned that demonstrations were being organized on a regular basis, and that with Parliament ready to return to session, the issue could be raised at any time.

On the other side of the world, an era was coming to an end. After an iron rule which had lasted eighteen years, Leonid Brezhnev, the general secretary of the Communist Party of the Soviet Union, died at 8:30 A.M. on 10 November 1982. The greatest build-up of Soviet nuclear power had occurred during his rule, but his country lacked the capability to compete with the west on a long-term financial and technological basis.

Lamontagne met one more time with U.S. Secretary of Defense Weinberger, and both men discussed NORAD and the test and evaluation negotiations. Within a week of this meeting, negotiations finally came to an end on 30 November 1982 when the two sides finalized the wording in Ottawa.[76] Both sides finally overcame problems injected by the U.S. team that had added vague wording on financial arrangements. The Canadian team insisted on language ensuring U.S. financial responsibility for all costs. A spokesman for External Affairs said that "both sides went away happy" and that "we are very optimistic."[77] The minister of national defence was told that the agreement would be ready for signature within two weeks or by late November.[78] U.S. Secretary of State George Shultz would later commend Allan MacEachen for moving the agreement to completion, as the White House "attach[ed] considerable importance" to concluding the Canada-United States Test and Evaluation Agreement [CANUS T&E]. Shultz thanked MacEachen and Trudeau "for the strong stand you have taken in defending this agreement against domestic criticism in Canada."[79]

One week later Ottawa provided its approved French text to the State Department, and thereby began what seemed like the endgame for the signing of the agreement.[80] Coincidentally, Liberal Party headquarters in Toronto was besieged by noisy protesters carrying banners, placards, and megaphones. They played protest songs, chanted, and blocked traffic. The crowd was buoyed by the news that Toronto City Council had unanimously voted to condemn the testing.[81] Mayor Art Eggleton, who would later become the minister of national defence in a Chrétien Liberal government, was on record as opposing cruise missile production at Litton. Eggleton even supported a national referendum to determine the level of support for and against cruise missile testing, with the results being binding on the government.[82]

In Ottawa, several women held a vigil outside National Defence Headquarters in solidarity with the women of Greenham Common in Britain. With their 'Refuse the Cruise' banner, Deb Ellis, Deb Powell, and ten others said they were weaving a web of life to remind the politicians and the military of Canadian opposition to the cruise missile. On the other side of the Atlantic, some ten thousand women, some with ling in their hair, had encircled Greenham Common Air Base in Britain in opposition to the upcoming deployments of ground-launched cruise missiles. Their action would have little effect on the cabinet meeting three days later.

The Cabinet Committee on Foreign and Defence Policy met on 13 December 1982 and received an update on the status of the negotiations from Secretary of State for External Affairs Allan MacEachen. There was little to report other than that the Canadian team was now satisfied with the new wording, and that "virtually all of the principal Canadian concerns" had been met. Prior to the meeting, MacEachen's chief advisors told him that the United States and Canada had not yet engaged in formal discussions dealing with the arrangements for testing the ALCM.[83] In the

House of Commons Trudeau announced that he was willing to entertain a debate on the issue, but that all Liberals must vote the party line without exception. At the same time he reportedly told close friends, "show me a consensus against testing and I will cancel it."

The ALCM world changed dramatically at this point. On 16 December 1982, the first USAF B-52 bomber squadron, stationed at Griffiss Air Force Base in New York, became fully operational with twelve ALCMs on each aircraft. The sixteen bombers would stand ground alert twenty-four hours each day. The weapons, without ever being tested in Canada, were already operationally deployed. These B-52G bombers already had externally observable differences as required by SALT II. As it had to be clear as to which bombers carried the cruise missiles, the U.S. Air Force spent $89 million adding features to the wing root visible from space. In addition, the Reagan administration decided to forego violating SALT II by limiting ALCM deployments to twenty missiles per bomber instead of the recommended twenty-two missiles.

One week after the cabinet meeting, Deputy Minister Marchand told MacEachen that the United States secretary of state was prepared to sign the agreement as early as the following day, Wednesday, 22 December 1982.[84] Confirmation came on 22 December when the following formal United States Diplomatic Note arrived in Ottawa:[85]

EMBASSY OF THE UNITED STATES OF AMERICA NO. 397

The Embassy has the honor to inform the Department of External Affairs that the appropriate United States authorities have approved the English and French texts, the latter as provided to the Department of State by the Canadian Embassy in Washington on December 9, of the Agreement on the Test and Evaluation of US Defense Systems in Canada on which negotiations were concluded November 30, 1982 on an ad referendum basis in Ottawa.

Ottawa, December 22, 1982

Robert Fowler and General Wightman from the PMO sent Trudeau a large study from National Defence's Operational Research Division on considerations affecting and arising from the testing of cruise missiles in Canada. Both men pointed out to Trudeau that for his purposes the best part of the report explained why cruise missiles would stabilize the deterrent.[86] The ground-launched cruise missile, planned for a European deployment, failed its first of seven tests on 17 December when the engine did not start and the missile crashed back to earth after a few seconds of ballistic flight. Even more important for Canada, the 19 December flight test of the air-launched cruise missile in the United States ended in total failure after controllers lost contact with the in-flight missile and it crashed.

The beginning of the most significant protest in history took place in Europe. On 13 December 1982 some thirty thousand women gathered at Greenham Common Air Base in Britain to protest the cruise missile deployment plans. They would stay in place until the last missile was removed. With the base now closed, a monument to their tenacity and vision has been raised using the remains of the cruise missile complex.

1983

Winter soon passed into the new year. Little was being done on the agreement as it was already complete. However, much effort was being expended putting together propaganda to accompany the release of the text. Work began immediately after the new year and the first drafts were ready on 7 January 1983.[87] The most significant meeting on this issue occurred on Tuesday, 11 January, when officials from both External Affairs and National Defence gathered at the Pearson Building (External Affairs Headquarters) to discuss the proposed information packages. Their task was to finalize the propaganda packages that would be passed to both ministers and to prepare a possible submission to cabinet of the same material. The committee was also to finalize a briefing package for government members and another for opposition members.[88] The day before the meeting, J. R. Francis of the Defence Relations division at External Affairs submitted its draft of the press release and accompanying information package to the ad hoc committee. The initial draft was twenty-three pages in length, and included the two-page press release; eight pages on Soviet missiles and a short paragraph on Canadian arms control policies; a four-page description of the ALCM; one page on safety considerations; one page on the Trudeau suffocation policy of 18 June 1982; and seven pages of anticipated questions and ministerial answers.[89]

However, the battle taking place in cabinet could not be hidden by the work of the two major departments and the PMO. Trudeau had been unable to manage his cabinet members and news of a major conflict had leaked out from behind normally impenetrable cabinet secrecy. Those opposing the agreement pointed to the massive opposition within the

Liberal Party itself, and to the majority of Canadians who took a dim view of such activities. Proponents dragged out the tired NATO argument, already largely discredited by the facts. The 17 January 1983 cabinet defence committee meeting was apparently one of the toughest ever, with members actually sweating. Nothing was resolved, but Trudeau and his chief security members had a difficult time putting down what was becoming an open revolt.

The nuclear world looked just as dangerous in 1983 as it had in 1982. The year began with Reagan asking Congress for an extra $8 billion for strategic nuclear offensive forces. Part of the money would go to doubling the funds for converting B-52 bombers into air-launched cruise missile carriers. In addition, $6.6 billion would be for the MX 'Peacekeeper' ICBM, $6.9 billion for the B-1 heavy bomber which was a planned cruise missile carrier, $2.5 billion for another Trident ballistic missile submarine, and nearly $1 billion for an ABM system (later known as 'Star Wars'). Total strategic offensive force spending would rise by 30 percent to $30 billion.

Toronto was the place to be for anti-nuclear activists in Canada. Mayor Art Eggleton, presented a motion to Toronto City Council banning nuclear weapons from the city. On 14 January the city council passed the motion banning the "production, testing, storage, transportation, processing, disposal or use of nuclear weapons and their components" within the city boundaries. Eggleton said he was aware that his nuclear-free city had no legal standing as far as the federal government was concerned, but that it was an indication of his and the city's support for disarmament. Such feelings would quickly slip away from Eggleton once he became a Liberal federal cabinet minister. Of course, his actions as mayor quickly came to the attention of the secret police office responsible for collecting material on anti-cruise missile activities, and his participation in this supposed communist plot was noted in the Cruise Missile Conversion Project file kept by the RCMP.

T. James Stark, already famous for having successfully fought for municipal disarmament referendums across Canada with Operation Dismantle, announced on 19 January 1983 that a coalition of peace and disarmament groups would challenge the cruise missile testing in court. The coalition and its lawyer, Lawrence Greenspon, planned to argue that the testing, and by extension the entire nuclear arms situation, was contrary to Article 7 of the new Charter of Rights and Freedoms, which guaranteed the right to "life, liberty and security." Federal Court case T-1679-83 was registered in Ottawa and sent for scheduling, but with no apparent activity on the government front, the case simply waited for a mid-year or autumn hearing date.

Time was passing, and the *New York Times* concluded that the Canadian government was faltering under pressure from the increasingly vocal, militant, and massive anti-cruise missile movement. Michael Kaufman revealed that the Canadian government had asked Washington to be patient while Ottawa tried to sway public opinion. It was not working, and on 20 January 1983 MacEachen decided to put the signing off for two weeks.[90] MacEachen was to be in Geneva at the Conference on Disarmament talks, and Lamontagne would be visiting several military establishments in western Canada. On 24 January 1983 cabinet deferred the signing by ten days.[91] The Liberals had finally realized they were on the cusp of the Progressive Conservative political convention the following weekend, and wished to avoid giving ammunition to the opposition Tories. So on Tuesday, 25 January, the Canadian embassy in Washington told reporters that there would be no signing ceremony until at least February. The formal reason for the delay, as given to the press, was that MacEachen was away in Europe and wished to be back for the event. Again the secretary of state for external affairs denied that the protests had any effect on the government.[92]

Protesters recognized that the agreement was still coming even if delayed slightly. Washington was only slightly more pleased. Having worked so hard to gain Canadian acceptance of the agreement, and unwilling to push too hard, U.S. Secretary of State George Shultz wrote to Secretary of State for External Affairs Allan MacEachen that he was pleased at the progress. Prodding Ottawa, Shultz said that the United States attached considerable importance to this agreement, and "we have very much appreciated the strong stand which Prime Minister Trudeau [has] taken in defending this agreement against domestic criticism in Canada."[93]

Protests were growing across the country and had even invaded formerly sacred places. On the same day that embassy staff told the press to wait until February, several people held a demonstration against the cruise missile in the public gallery of the House of Commons. All were immediately arrested. The Canadian press chose not to give coverage to the event, but the British Broadcasting Corporation in London did and tied the protest to the expected signing.

Already a majority of the public opposed testing. The *Toronto Star* revealed its own polling which showed that at least 71 percent of people had heard of the proposed testing – a significantly high number. A full 50 percent opposed testing, while only 40 percent supported it.[94] These numbers would gradually shift as more and more people grew aware of the situation and voiced their disapproval. And while Canadians were ready to have their voices heard, politicians were cowering from the issue. Two out of three Members of Parliament would not even state their position on cruise missile testing. The *Toronto Star* found that of the 281 Members of Parliament, only 56 would say that they supported the tests, while 42 declared their opposition, and a full 183 refused to say anything. The opposition, which constituted only 15 percent of the House of Commons, would never reflect the majority of opposition by Canadians.[95]

Southam News, always a supporter of the Canadian establishment, tried to minimize the public opposition by conducting their own polls. Southam polling revealed that 41 percent of those polled supported testing; hardly a massive groundswell of support over earlier polls.[96] What made this polling especially suspect was that at the same time other polling in generally right-wing Alberta and the prairie provinces revealed that 59 percent opposed the tests while only 35 percent supported them. The Southam pollsters pointed out that 40 percent of Albertans supported the tests, but that a clear majority were opposed.[97] These numbers hardly deviated from the national norm.

The U.S. Air Force now had 192 ALCMs with nuclear warheads deployed at Griffiss AFB in New York. Five bombers were on alert with 12 ALCMs each, and the remaining 132 were stored on base for use as more bombers became available. Deliveries had also begun to bomber bases at Wurtsmith in Michigan and Grand Forks in North Dakota, just south of Winnipeg. The Air Force was planning to have at least 105 B-52G bombers equipped with the missiles. And even though the deployments had begun in earnest, the test program continued. Boeing declared that sixteen of the twenty flights had been a success, as were thirteen of the last fourteen flights.[98] It was unclear to Canadians why the flights now had to be flown in Canada.

It seemed more than a little ironic that Trudeau sent Secretary of State for External Affairs MacEachen to Geneva to speak for Canada at the United Nations Conference on Disarmament. On 1 February 1983, the minister addressed the conference and told them of Canada's intention to sign the umbrella agreement that would allow the testing of ALCMs and other weapons in Canada. Staff at External Affairs believed that with MacEachen just having been to the United Nations in Europe, he would be in a good position to deal with opposition and press questions on the link between cruise missile testing and disarmament.[99]

Immediately after his speech, MacEachen had R. P. Cameron, his chief of international security policy, telephone Ottawa and tell External Affairs staff that he would not be setting a date for the signing until after his return the following day. Staff were preparing for a disastrous decision, as they expected MacEachen would try to rush to have it signed the day after on 4 February 1983. All were against this as they knew it would be virtually impossible to gain agreement on the information packages, to translate the texts, and to prepare two thousand copies for distribution.[100] In addition, the perception was that it was unfair to give the U.S. State Department less than twenty-four hours' notice.

The standard nuclear-armed air-launched cruise missile became less newsworthy when it was revealed on 1 February that the Pentagon had cancelled further acquisition of the missile in favour of a new cruise missile. The ALCM-B program had called for 4,348 of the missiles to be built, but it was announced that only 1,499 would be built. The money, which had already been appropriated, was to be spent on development of the new stealth cruise missile. Pentagon briefers had secretly told select congressmen that the ALCM line item in the budget had been submitted in order to fool the Soviets into thinking that there was no second type of missile, and that the funds were only for the ALCM.[101] However, by the middle of the month, U.S. Air Force officials were already telling Congress that lack of adequate funding meant that it might not be possible to buy as many stealth cruise missiles as desired. The stealth cruise missile would eventually come to play a minor but important role in Canadian politics.

Back in Canada, MacEachen told the public on 3 February that the agreement would be signed the following week. This was contrary to the Department of National Defence's position that there should be no mention of the timing or authorization for the agreement until after it had been signed. National Defence argued that to let people know what government was doing would remove the initiative from ministers and that it would make it difficult to reverse course.

Now the Liberal government first denied knowing about a U.S. request to test the advanced cruise missile, better known as the stealth cruise missile. It is most likely true that the secretary of state for external affairs had not heard of any request as the timing of the initial U.S. proposal on the ACM would be somewhat later. Even at this late date, no formal or informal request had been made for any project arrangement covering the test of any U.S. weapons systems.

The next day MacEachen announced to his staff that the agreement would be signed by Ambassador Gotlieb at 2:00 P.M. on 8 February

1983.[102] Once again this date would not be kept. However, MacEachen and Trudeau already had more to worry about. Reports of a new cruise missile – an advanced or 'stealth' cruise missile – were now circulating. A day earlier, CTV's morning news program "Canada AM" broadcast a short item on it; the Canadian Press wire reports carried the news; the authoritative journal *Aviation Week and Space Technology* had written about it; and worst of all, Secretary of State Weinberger's annual report to Congress mentioned it. The issue was coming to Canada well ahead of the missile itself, of which Canadian officials knew almost nothing. There had been no talk of it from the U.S. team. However, MacEachen had been briefed to respond that this potential new Strategic Air Command weapon would, if deployed, enhance "NATO" forces.[103]

It was not only the public that worried the Trudeau government; the provinces were not particularly cooperative. In the days before the signing, MacEachen followed up on the direct briefings his staff had provided to the affected provinces with telephone calls to various premiers. The western premiers and their staffs were not told anything which would not be revealed to the public through press releases, briefings, and the tabling of the actual agreement. However, the personal telephone calls served to dampen opposition within official circles.

DAY OF THE SIGNING

Thursday, 10 February 1983 is a day remembered by many an anti-cruise missile protester. The secrecy plans were only somewhat effective, as reporters knew the agreement would be signed even though they were not invited to the signing. Canadian embassy spokesmen told reporters that under orders from Secretary of State for External Affairs MacEachen, all press was banned from the event. External Affairs believed that if the date could be kept secret, then it might be possible to avoid provoking disarmament groups into seeking a temporary injunction to prevent the signing.[104]

On that Thursday afternoon, Canadian Ambassador Allan Gotlieb drove the short distance from the old embassy on Massachusetts Avenue to the State Department. He was escorted to the diplomatic reception rooms on the top floor, which were closed for the event. There, at 3:15 P.M., he and the United States Acting Secretary of State Kenneth W. Dam signed the Canada-United States Testing and Evaluation (CANUS T&E) Agreement

At the ceremony, Kenneth Dam gave a short speech to the assembled guests, of whom there were almost none save a few officials and the State Department photographer.

It gives me great personal satisfaction to participate in the exchange of notes which brings into effect the agreement covering the test and evaluation of U.S. defense systems in Canada. Close defense cooperation between Canada and the United States is essential to our own security and to that of our NATO allies. Canada and the United States threaten no one. Our governments and our people remain committed to the peaceful resolution of international differences. This agreement bears witness to our shared belief that peace can be preserved only through preparedness and that meaningful reductions can be negotiated only if we demonstrate our determination to remain strong and free. I would like to thank the government of Canada for its willingness to work with us through this important agreement to strengthen peace and stability.

Formally called Note #64, Exchange of Notes constituting an agreement between the Government of Canada and the Government of the United States of America concerning the Test and Evaluation of the U.S. defence systems in Canada, the document was a mere five pages long and represented the Trudeau Liberals' final break with their anti-nuclear policies of the past fifteen years.[105] Canada signed the agreement itself, and the United States signed a reply accepting the Canadian text. Copies were exchanged and quickly sent off to Ottawa by diplomatic bag.

By the time Gotlieb returned to the chancery, the press was waiting. Spokesmen distributed copies of the short speeches made at the ceremony and handed out film taken by a U.S. government photographer. Gotlieb is said to have come into the room and dropped his pen on the table in front of the reporters saying, "that's the pen, a ballpoint," in reference to the usual practice in the United States for the pens used to sign important legislation and treaties.[106] He explained that the secrecy was in place to allow the minister to be the first to table the agreement and bring it before Parliament.

Back in Ottawa, Allan MacEachen stood in the House of Commons and tabled the agreement. The totality of the announcement was confined to this short statement in English: "Madam Speaker, in accordance with the provisions of the Standing Order, I would like to table in both official languages an exchange of notes between Canada and the United States constituting an agreement between our two governments on the use of Canadian facilities and airspace for the testing and evaluation of U.S. defence systems. The notes are being signed today in Washington by the Acting Secretary of State, Mr. Kenneth W. Dam, for the United States, and by Ambassador Gotlieb for Canada."[107] Strangely, it seems that MacEachen jumped the gun and tabled the agreement minutes before Gotlieb and Dam signed it.

Both the opposition Progressive Conservative Party (which supported the U.S. nuclear build-up) and the New Democratic Party (which did not) were clamouring for a full debate and the presentation of the agreement to Parliament or at least to the House of Commons Standing Committee on External Affairs and National Defence. Tory defence critic Allan MacKinnon stated that while he did not object to the testing of the cruise missile, he was worried about the two defence departments concluding agreements on their own "without Parliament looking at them."[108] This was something the Liberals had feared, and they had sought to keep Parliament from having any say in Trudeau's affairs. Prior to the signing, MacEachen had asked his staff to find out how other defence agreements and arrangements had been handled, and if it was possible to keep them out of Parliament's hands.

The Defence Relations division at External Affairs responded that the only precedent they knew of was the NORAD agreement of 1957 in which the text was examined first by cabinet committee, then by cabinet, and was then tabled in the House of Commons. At that time Prime Minister John Diefenbaker made a short statement and allowed a very brief debate. The Liberals followed the same pattern when NORAD came up for renewal in 1968, 1975, and again on 11 March 1981.[109] This was just what MacEachen needed; the history to show that Canadian governments never have submitted defence agreements and arrangements to the will of Parliament. Despite having a majority, the Liberals already knew that an open debate and vote would reflect badly upon Trudeau's judgment. Trudeau's decision had to be protected against the unruly masses in the House of Commons, as it was already known that at least twenty Liberal backbench Members of Parliament were ready to vote against his policy.

For the next several days, minister MacEachen had to repeatedly deny that a secret agreement on the cruise missile had been reached between Trudeau and Reagan. Questions and statements by the leader of the NDP, Edward Broadbent, and defence critic Pauline Jewett had to be denied several times. A statement by the Member of Parliament for Thunder Bay, Paul McRae, also pointed to the fact that things did not seem quite right. Even Trudeau was pulled into the fray when on 15 February 1983 he had to stand in the Commons and state that "there has been no agreement to test the cruise."[110] While this was technically true in that there was no written arrangement, it was false in that the entire CANUS T&E Agreement was a charade to cover for the initial U.S. request to test the cruise missile. MacEachen went on the offensive to defend the agreement, saying that refusal now would allow the Soviets to exploit the West and NATO's weakness.[111] He did not explain how this would be done or what the probable outcome would be.

Although a clear majority of Canadians opposed the cruise, the Tory members of the opposition generally favoured such military cooperation. Trudeau even went so far as to suggest that there was absolutely no need for a debate as all the Progressive Conservative leadership candidates, including the eventual winner Brian Mulroney, agreed on testing cruise missiles in Canada. Trudeau glossed over the fact that it is the job of Her Majesty's Official Opposition to ask the hard questions, even if they agree with the overall policy, especially when massive numbers of Canadians are opposed.

The issue was always a problem for Trudeau and he clearly had contrary ideas about it. After the signature he stood in the House of Commons and explained that he would concede "from the outset that the Government had been contemplating the possibility of testing the cruise. We knew that this was at the back of the mind of the American administration when it was asking for a weapons-testing system." He then admitted that "we all know that the cruise is at the end of the road."[112] It was therefore odd that the prime minister would deny once again in the House of Commons that there had been a decision to test cruise missiles, yet on 15 February he again stood in the Commons and issued a direct denial. He later said that if asked about the issue he would tell a caller to "drop dead."

Project Ploughshares printed their own open letter to the prime minister in the *Globe and Mail* on 24 February. Signed by many prominent Canadians such as Margaret Atwood and David Suzuki, the letter said that given the large number of Canadians opposed to testing, "there is no public mandate for such testing." The letter ended with the signatories urging Trudeau "to refuse to allow testing of cruise missiles in Canada, and to press for productive negotiations towards disarmament." Readers were encouraged to clip the form, fill it out, and mail it free of charge to the prime minister's office.

For weeks after the signing, members of the federal cabinet had their time filled with denying that there was already an agreement to test the cruise missile. Although technically this was still true, matters were not helped when the U.S. ambassador to Canada, Paul Robinson, said that it would be a breach of the commitment and a diplomatic row would ensue if Canada refused cruise missile testing.[113] Once again MacEachen had to deny that any such thing was true. However, by this time, Canadians were having a hard time believing anything the government said on the subject.

At the same time as the agreement was being drafted, the two teams were also negotiating the memorandum of understanding (MOU) which would accompany the primary document. It was intended that the memorandum would be concluded between designated representatives of both defence departments, and in late February the Pentagon informed National Defence that they wanted the memorandum to be signed by Secretary of Defense Weinberger. Deputy Minister of National Defence D. B. Dewar immediately counselled Lamontagne not to agree to this plan. Officials warned that since MacEachen and U.S. Secretary of State George Shultz had not signed the agreement, it would call undue attention to the memorandum of understanding if Lamontagne and Weinberger made an effort to sign it.[114] Lamontagne then decided the issue and verbally informed his colleagues at the 9 March 1983 cabinet meeting.

War preparations by the United States and NATO now truly alarmed the Soviet leadership. Cruise and Pershing missiles in Europe; nuclear artillery and neutron weapons in Europe, and cruise missile testing in Canada all conspired to present a dreadful picture to the USSR. Yuri Andropov ordered that Operation *RYaN* be stepped up to full national importance. Orders were issued on 17 February 1983 to "uncover any plans in preparation by the main adversary for nuclear-rocket attack and to organize a continual watch to be kept for indications of a decision being taken to use nuclear weapons against the USSR or immediate preparations being made for a nuclear rocket attack."[115]

More Canadians were willing to take direct action to bring the dangers of the time into view for others. John Willis and Karen Pierce chained themselves to the front door of Parliament on Friday, 11 February as a direct protest to the signing of the agreement. However, Parliament Hill guards had cut their chains only minutes after the pair of Greenpeace members had chained themselves in place. Martin Zeilig, then with Operation Dismantle, warned that this was only a small sample of the number of Canadians who were taking to the streets to confront their government.

The scene shifted to Washington where George Shultz was asked about the consequences of Canada not signing the operative arrangement to test cruise missiles. Shultz replied that "the Canadian government has made an agreement with us and we expect that will carry forward."[116] Pressure would now have to mount from Washington as the situation became more difficult for the Liberals. United States Ambassador Paul Robinson weighed in on Saturday, 12 March, warning (some said threatening) that Canada would risk the United States' wrath by holding back the tests. Robinson, like many Canadian government officials, also warned that failure to test the USAF air-launched cruise missile "would be contrary to Canada's NATO commitments."[117] Whether he knew there was really no connection between the ALCM and the NATO deployments, or whether he was incredibly ill-informed, remains unclear. Only days before, Robinson had attacked anti-cruise protestors saying they were "misguided" to oppose the testing. Of course, many people recognized that Robinson was a political appointee of the Reagan administration with little tact and even less professional diplomatic skill.

The first ALCMs were deployed to Griffiss AFB near Rome, New York, and early in March the Soviets asked the Cubans to overfly the base in the hope of discovering what was going on. One regularly scheduled flight between Havana and Montreal deviated substantially from its authorized route and flew over the Griffiss AFB area. Although this is a serious violation of procedures and would have been subject to Federal Aviation Authority action, the U.S. State Department immediately reacted by imposing a two-week suspension from 24 March to 7 April on Cubana Airlines. When questioned, the State Department refused to comment on the security implications of the case. By early May, the bombers were already practising simulated launches as they flew over Canada. A group of B-52s was heading to the joint Maple Flag exercises at Cold Lake and executed a simulated launch of cruise missiles as they passed from the Grand Forks region into Manitoba. Although the Canadian Forces denied any nuclear weapons training or activity, military officials at Griffiss acknowledged what for them was a common training routine.[118]

In Ottawa a freelance filmmaker named Karen Harrison began a hunger strike in the public gallery of the House of Commons on 7 March 1983 in her effort to force a free debate on the cruise missile tests. With passes from her Member of Parliament, Liberal Party member Aideen Nicholson, Harrison spent each day in the gallery wearing her "fast for peace" tee shirt. Security surrounding Trudeau had become oppressive, and one reporter who tried to question the prime minister was attacked by a bodyguard and was being dragged to the basement of the Parliament buildings for questioning when the two were surrounded by other reporters.[119] Reporters had promised not to scrum Trudeau if he held weekly news conferences, but Trudeau had long since tired of having to speak to Canadians, so he was once again fair game for questioning outside the House of Commons.

United States Vice President George Bush visited Trudeau in Ottawa to discuss a wide variety of the Reagan administration's initiatives and concerns. During his meeting with the entire cabinet, two ministers who were not identified told Bush that there was significant opposition to the tests. Bush responded that this did not surprise him because he had already encountered it in seven NATO countries as well.[120] Trudeau made it plain that he would literally rubber-stamp any U.S. request to test the cruise missile by saying that Canada would have to withdraw from NATO if it refused the cruise missile test.[121] When Bush spoke to Parliament, Karen Harrison was there to heckle him, despite being weakened after more than two weeks of living on water and lemon juice.

At the state dinner held by Trudeau for Bush on 23 March 1983, the prime minister said several very interesting things. First, he was heard to confidentially say to Bush, "Don't worry George, we'll test the cruise for you,"[122] and publicly that Canada was allowing the testing "because the Europeans have asked us to do this for them."[123] Another source said that Trudeau actually stated, "If we test the cruise missile it will not be because the United States asked us, but because the Europeans asked us."[124] There has never been any evidence of such a request, nor is there a single record supporting the assertion. It is most likely that Trudeau said it because he needed the NATO rationale; he was sure to be attacked for praising cruise missile testing in the presence of the U.S. vice president, and it was better to look as though it was not subtle U.S. pressure which brought the testing upon his cabinet and the country.

The prime minister's public affairs spin on the NATO connection was laid bare when Chief of Defence Staff General Ramsey M. Withers told the Standing Committee on External Affairs and National Defence that the question of testing in Canada referred to the air-launched cruise missiles for the U.S. Air Force, and not to the ground-launched systems being deployed to NATO Europe.[125] Trudeau never again claimed there was a formal NATO request.

Internationally, the month will be remembered as the time when President Reagan announced his Strategic Defence Initiative (SDI), better known as 'Star Wars.' This was the final straw for the Kremlin leadership, and Andropov now publicly accused Reagan of preparing plans and weapons for a nuclear war against the USSR.[126] Andropov talked about

U.S. weapons and deployments, as well as the secret and never discussed Soviet arsenal he said was there to deter Washington's aggression. Even if the Soviets had a ballistic missile defence, cruise missiles would still penetrate into the USSR to attack vital targets; they might even set off a doomsday device by accident.

The day after the Bush visit, on 25 March, the United States government, represented by Secretary of Defense Caspar Weinberger, signed the Memorandum of Understanding (MOU). The document was passed to the Canadian embassy and shipped to Ottawa by diplomatic bag. It must have been a slow trip, as the memorandum would not be signed in Ottawa for nearly another month. Although Lamontagne had decided to sign it himself but did not intend to table it in the House of Commons, he was at least willing to make it public "if there is a demand for it."[127]

During his meeting with the NATO Nuclear Planning Group in Portugal, Lamontagne met with Weinberger and his staff and agreed on how the memorandum would be signed. At this point, the U.S. embassy told External Affairs that the first request for a real test would come shortly after the memorandum had been signed by Lamontagne at the completion of his world tour.[128] The United States ambassador, Paul Robinson, told the CTV that testing would likely start within a year, and that he anticipated cabinet's approval of the request that he would deliver.[129] During the same talk, Robinson also echoed the Reagan line that acid rain was not caused by sulphur dioxide emissions, as Reagan himself had advanced the idea that acid rain came from both bird droppings and cow flatulence. More pressure was being applied by Washington. During his 10–11 April visit to Washington, D.C., Secretary of State for External Affairs Allan MacEachen was lobbied by Secretary of State George Shultz for several hours. MacEachen told reporters that he refused to tell Shultz in advance what the Canadian response would be to the first request.[130]

Two things would happen on 19 April 1983 and only one would be of lasting significance. Allan MacEachen wrote a form letter to all of his House of Commons and Senate colleagues on both sides of the Commons trying to explain the decision in terms of NATO solidarity and the dual-track decision.[131] More importantly, the Parliament Hill peace camp was erected, and would remain in place for several years. Originally set up to protest the completion of the agreement, the upcoming memorandum, and the actual cruise missile testing, the peace camp would take on a wide variety of social causes surrounding nuclear disarmament and peace. The peace camp, which was started by Abraham Weizfeld of Montreal with only four participants including Dave Savage and Stephanie Coe of

Calgary, was expected to last only three days. Weizfeld, later arrested on Parliament Hill and fined five hundred dollars for trying to put up a pup tent, had set up the original peace camp with only an information table, a mock missile, and a tarp.

Finally, on Thursday, 21 April 1983, the Canadian government, represented by Minister of National Defence Gilles Lamontagne, signed the memorandum of understanding and returned a copy to the Pentagon. It was now done, and they simply had to wait for the formal specific request for testing to arrive. The memorandum was a general implementation arrangement between the Department of National Defence and the Department of Defense for the use by the Department of Defense of Canadian Forces test sites, training areas, and ranges, and Canadian airspace for the test and evaluation of U.S. weapons pursuant to the 10 February agreement. It stipulated that the process would be overseen by a joint committee chaired by the assistant deputy minister of defence for material in Canada, and by the U.S. under-secretary of defense for research and development. It was the United States' responsibility to provide Ottawa with the probable tests list for the next four years, as well as an estimate of the financial requirements, need for airspace, and services to be provided by Canada.

The oversight of the process was accomplished at the Department of National Defence by a two-tiered structure made up of a steering group and a co-ordinating group. The steering group has authority over the entire CANUS T&E program and recommends projects it views as acceptable to Canada. The definition of 'acceptable' is very broad. The co-ordinating group reviews individual projects and provides overall administration of the CANUS T&E program. When the annual thirty-month forecast from the Pentagon is received, the steering group examines it and recommends it to the minister of national defence who may take it to cabinet, or who may approve it without further reference. Once the United States is informed of the approval, individual U.S. services can request specific tests, which are then examined by the co-ordinating group and a project arrangement is jointly agreed to. Then testing can begin.[132]

Protests were sweeping the nation. The largest set of anti-cruise missile demonstrations in Canada took place on 23 April 1983, when the mayor of Vancouver, Michael Harcourt, led at least seventy-five thousand people through the streets to Sunset Beach, where more than eighty thousand people attended a rally. In Toronto a small demonstration of some fifteen thousand took place at Queen's Park, the site of the Ontario provincial government. Led by Toronto aldermen John Sewell and Jack Layton, the crowd moved down Bay Street, the heart of the financial district. Others gathered all over the country, from the northern city of Whitehorse to the southern towns past Toronto. Saskatoon, not the largest of Canadian cities, managed to bring together at least three thousand marchers who followed a replica cruise missile through the streets in protest. In Cold Lake thirteen people were arrested for trying to block the entrance to the base. There were over one hundred thousand people in the streets that day. These protests would continue to grow as the danger of the times and the implications for peace and security grew clearer to Canadians.

In the spring Prime Minister Trudeau visited Washington and had extensive meetings with U.S. officials, including a 27 April 1983 meeting with George Bush. The next day he met for two hours with President Ronald Reagan, although the Prime Minister's Office denied that either man discussed cruise missiles.[133] Before leaving for this trip, Trudeau was warned that the U.S. presentation of a list of proposed tests was now only a couple of weeks away. The United States was keenly aware of the problems the cruise missile proposal had caused for the Liberals, and had decided to make their initial request for an unrelated test. However, it would be "closely followed by the cruise request."[134] During the visit it is likely that Trudeau told Reagan that he intended to distribute a letter to all the newspapers in the nation explaining the cruise missile and weapons testing decision and agreement.

Trudeau's open letter to Canadians entitled, "Canada's position on testing cruise missiles and on disarmament," was sent by Nicole Senecal, the PMO press secretary, to all editors-in-chief across the country. Although the first drafts came from PMO staff members, Trudeau himself worked on the final version. One reporter discovered that the PMO had already counted at least 6,570 personal letters to the prime minister from Canadians, and this figure did not include the piles of form letters, postcards, and petitions which had been pouring in at many times the letter rate. Only 1.8 percent of writers supported his decision.[135] Cruise missile letters far outnumbered those for any other topic in 1982. Senecal explained that the massive number of letters and petitions which had poured in could not all be answered individually, so the prime minister wished to address the nation collectively. She wrote that publishing the letter would be a public service, and indeed, many newspapers chose to print the five-page explanation and request for understanding. Trudeau rarely ever addressed the public as a whole, and this was the only open letter to English Canadians he would ever issue. His general unconcern for western Canadians, over whose land the missiles would fly, was well known.

The crux of the 9 May letter was an attack on Canadians who protested his decision. Trudeau desperately lashed out against the hundreds of thousands of Canadians who were becoming politically and socially active, and who were opposing his authority to allow the testing. He tried to drive a wedge between Canadians, condemning the "hypocrisy" of some citizens. He called on right-thinking Canadians to support the United States on testing "when the going gets tough," and attacked those who he said would take refuge under the American nuclear umbrella, but do not want to hold it. No mention was even made of what his own office acknowledged as the contradiction and hypocrisy of the testing with the suffocation of strategic arms policy – only the public were hypocrites, never the philosopher prince himself.

The prime minister spilled a great deal of ink trying to equate the ALCM with the NATO dual-track decision, and with Pershings and SS-20s. Again and again Trudeau referred to the relationship to NATO programs and to Canadian support for NATO. He never addressed the clear and irrefutable fact that the ALCM was never a NATO weapon and was never intended to be a NATO weapon.

The letter ended as it began, in teary-eyed sentimentalism. Trudeau recalled the great outpouring of Canadian concerns and how they weighed heavily upon him. He then said that he still had faith in his notion of suffocation, and that although the great powers refused to accept it, he hoped that the eventual recognition of the idea "frees us all from moral anguish and fear." Despite this beginning and ending, the most striking feature of the letter was the bulk of attacks against people who disagreed with Trudeau, and who were making their disagreement known in the streets and in the newspapers. As *Ottawa Citizen* reporter Richard Gwyn said, the letter told Canadians nothing new about the subject, but it did tell them a lot about Trudeau: "mostly that he's tired, stale, and peevish."[136]

Two weeks after the open letter was published, an anti-cruise missile group under the umbrella of Project Ploughshares delivered another thirty-five hundred objection letters to the Prime Minister's Office. A fluid and ad hoc organization of church groups and development agencies had coordinated the write-in campaign in response to the prime ministerial letter to Canadians.[137] Mother's Day on Parliament Hill was the setting for a touching and heartfelt demonstration by at least two thousand mothers and children against cruise missile testing. Although the RCMP denied them permission to protest, hundreds of women held hands and encircled the centre block of Parliament, hugging and kissing the police and the RCMP. In Chicago Dr. Benjamin Spock told a massive Mother's Day rally that, like them, he was willing to do what was necessary "to demonstrate against the arms race." The Ploughshares effort, and the efforts of many other grassroots organizations, came right on top of the first request.

On 13 May 1983 the request from Washington was received by Deputy Minister of National Defence Bev Dewar at National Defence Headquarters. Dewar then visited General Wightman at the Prime Minister's Office to tell him of the request and to start the process of consultation with the Privy Council Office (PCO). As Dewar had surmised, the first request was not for the cruise missile but for LANTIRN, the Low-Altitude Navigation Targeting Infra-Red for Night system. The tests were conducted between October and December 1984 over CFB Gagetown and portions of New Brunswick by F-16s operating from Loring AFB in Maine.[138]

At the time, the American embassy suggested to Dewar that the cruise missile request would follow in one week.[139] The timing is curious in that only the day before, the minister of national defence, Lamontagne, told the Standing Committee on External Affairs and National Defence that the United States had not yet made any request to test any weapon system.[140] During his mid-May visit to Canada, Mikhail Gorbachev, the young and influential Politburo member who would soon become the Soviet leader, asked the Canadian government to not allow cruise missile tests. He told the Joint House and Senate Standing Committee on Foreign Affairs that the tests greatly concerned his country, as the only reason the U.S. Air Force sought to test in Canada was that it had "conditions similar to those of our country."

It was at this time that Trudeau was trying to get his message across to an incredulous public. In his first English interview in many years he spoke first and at length about the cruise missile decision in the hopes of reaching the majority of Canadians who were already alienated on this issue. Trudeau assured people that he was concerned about nuclear weapons, and that he was proud to have de-nuclearized Canada's forces in NATO. Then almost immediately the prime minister struck out at those with anti-cruise missile sentiments by saying they were anti-American and hypocritical; no real arguments would be entertained by the philosopher king. Then he repeated the tired arguments that the cruise missile was only a delivery system, that no nuclear warhead would be tested, and that this was all to support the NATO dual-track decision calling for Pershing and GLCM deployments. Again Trudeau brought up the SS-20 missile without ever showing how the testing of the ALCM in

Canada was somehow a response to the deployment of the SS-20 by the Soviet Union in Europe. He closed with an interesting recognition that many Canadians had come to their beliefs about the warlike nature of the Reagan administration because Reagan and his people "have given some justification for those fears."[141]

Former U.S. Secretary of State Henry Kissinger, in Canada for a meeting of the secretive Bilderberg Group, said that Ottawa would naturally authorize the tests. He informed the press that various cabinet members had told him this was a done deal, and the meeting with Trudeau on 1 June did nothing to change this impression.[142]

Canada was already deeply involved in the cruise missile program, but from a different angle than most thought. Since the Low-Angle Measurement (LAM) agreement had been signed on 29 November 1979, a joint Canada-United States program was underway at thirty-five sites in Alberta and at more than sixty-five other sites to ostensibly improve the ability of military and civilian radar systems to distinguish low-flying objects from ground clutter. This testing by a team from the experts from the Massachusetts Institute of Technology Cruise Missile Technology Group was clearly to improve the survivability of cruise missiles in the face of ground-based air defence systems. The Liberal government initially vehemently denied this was the case.[143] However, under continuous pressure from NDP defence critic Terence Sargeant, Lamontagne finally admitted on 7 June that the radar testing had cruise missile applications.[144]

Now Gilles Lamontagne was told that the U.S. Air Force would want to test the air-launched cruise missile "in Canadian airspace during the first quarter of calendar year 1984, to evaluate the missiles' navigation system performance over snow covered terrain." Deputy Minister of Defence Bev Dewar informed Lamontagne that the recent cruise missile flight test failures would not have a negative impact on the Canadian test. Dewar and his staff laid out the timeline necessary for such testing: testing in January 1984 would require forty-five to sixty days of preparation after a project arrangement had been concluded in mid-November 1983; and the project arrangement in turn would require three months after Canadian approval was received. This meant that Lamontagne would have to inform cabinet in early August and then approve the individual test no later than mid-August 1983. In 1983 the problem was that cabinet would be shut down from mid-July until late August, so any decision would have to be considered by cabinet on or about Canada Day 1983. The Department of National Defence sought to avoid having the minister make the kind of announcement that would set a precedent. Dewar told Lamontagne that the minister should not allow people to expect that each new test would be announced. Dewar preferred to plant a question in the House of Commons and to then let the minister of national defence answer that a request had been received.[145]

Although it would have been possible to keep all of this reasonably secret up until the time of the actual test, flight safety was a consideration that was not strictly military in nature. The Department of Transport needed to determine the air routes and the altitudes to be used, and to print notices to airmen (NOTAM). This could take as long as six months, and the distribution of thousands of NOTAMs would surely bring the upcoming test to the attention of many people.

Paul McRae, the former NDP member then with the Liberal party, wrote a twenty-page letter to Trudeau meticulously outlining the anti-cruise missile positions of Liberals and the Canadian public. He hoped to persuade the prime minister against the tests that were soon to be requested. However, instead of having the desired effect, the letter galvanized the pro-testing segment and a full lobbying effort was launched by the prime minister's allies. The letter was dissected and shredded in a frantic effort to discredit anti-cruise missile forces. The speed and ferociousness of the attack, and the swiftness of the move to accept the tests, surprised McRae and his allies. Washington would have to be appeased and the voice of the Liberal Party members would be ignored to that end.

Meanwhile, Trudeau was being kept informed and was still the driving force behind the decision and the process. With the aid of General David Wightman and Robert Fowler, Trudeau decided on the process for cruise missile decisions on 9 June.[146] This was immediately communicated to Minister of National Defence Lamontagne who would have to take the lead as National Defence received the actual testing proposals from the United States. The next day National Defence swung into action, and the organization and staff procedures for dealing with the expected request were being promulgated.[147] The Department of National Defence was put on alert to expect both the request on 13 June and to have it ready for cabinet within four days. The new co-ordinator of the CANUS Test & Evaluation program at National Defence Headquarters, Brigadier General A. C. Brown, told his staff that U.S. requests would have to be staffed in the shortest possible time from now on.

The first written request for a specific cruise missile test was delivered to National Defence Headquarters by the U.S. embassy's defence attaché on Monday morning, 13 June 1983. The U.S. Air Force wrote that it wanted to test between four and six cruise missiles between January and March 1984 over the realistic flat, featureless, snow-covered terrain in the extreme cold weather of the far north.[148] The United States also wrote that the ALCM would be unaccompanied for part of the trip. Prime Minister Trudeau was immediately informed of the request by Robert Fowler and a full briefing was provided the next day.[149]

Although the request had been expected since the end of March, it was a momentous event. What made it very odd was the fact that the USAF had only two weeks before it suspended all ALCM testing after two failures on 19 December 1982 and 24 May 1983. In the late May incident, the ALCM crashed in the desert between Utah and Nevada. This now meant that two of the last three tests had been failures. In other nuclear news that gave Canadians reason to worry, the first test of the MX 'Peacekeeper' ICBM on 17 June was a total success. The missile and its six unarmed warheads flew from Vandenberg AFB in California to the target area near Kwajalein Atoll. The USAF said it wanted to begin deployment as soon as possible. The Soviets responded immediately by announcing on 20 June that they would test two ICBMs each day for four days (29 June–2 July).

The Prime Minister's Office had been preparing for this event for months. Everything was worked out to the minute. The PMO had scheduled the entire event, writing that it began with the receipt by National Defence of the USAF cruise missile request at 10:00 A.M. on 13 June, followed two hours later by the publication of a press release announcing the receipt of the document. One hour later Minister of National Defence Lamontagne was to release a statement – already approved by Trudeau – on the request. At the same time, National Defence would inform the affected provinces and territories about the proposed tests. Cabinet would then give formal permission. It is interesting to note that in the documents it is clearly assumed that there will be a positive response to any cruise missile testing request. The PMO planned to have Secretary of State for External Affairs MacEachen issue a press release at 5:30 P.M. on 22 June informing Canadians of the government's decision to allow cruise missile tests.[150] Everything was scripted to the last minute, and everything assumed that a 'yes' decision was inevitable.

The initial request from the U.S. Air Force had a test route which included the communities of Norman Wells, Fort Good Hope, Fort Simpson, and Fort Liard in the Northwest Territories; Fort Nelson, Fort Saint John, and Dawson Creek in British Columbia; and Grande Prairie, Alberta, at the southern boundary of the corridor.[151] The Canadian concern was that although the missile was almost impossible to see, it should not fly over or near or endanger any community. What they wanted to do was to ask that the final route take the missile away from even the smallest community so that no reproach could be made by those opposed. The Canadian Forces also recognized that not nearly enough explosive ordnance demolition soldiers were available at CFB Cold Lake, the main site for test support. The view of the director general of ammunition was that additional ordnance demolition staff could be moved in from Edmonton, Wainwright, Dundurn, and Winnipeg for the tests.[152]

One interesting aspect of the initial U.S. proposal was that the duration of the project was to be for the normal "life cycle of the weapon system." Major Hunt, the Director of Law (International) for National Defence Headquarters, warned that this was far too vague and that it should be a more finite time in keeping with the original agreement and arrangement.[153] This would eventually be changed to reflect a more reasonable state.

In direct response to the news of the cruise missile test request, two Greenpeace members, John Willis and Dave Harris, scaled the Peace Tower on Parliament Hill with their anti-cruise missile banner. At just past eight o'clock in the morning on Thursday, 23 June, the two men climbed above the main entrance to the centre block of Parliament and unfurled their banner reading, "No cruise, Greenpeace." Several hours later the RCMP, with the help of an Ottawa Fire Department ladder truck, removed the two men, who spent the time getting a better suntan. The commander of the Royal Canadian Regiment, Colonel Thomas Lawson, told a counter-demonstration in Halifax that protestors should be sent to Moscow to see "the alternative to our way of life."[154] Quaint an idea as it was, Lawson was unable to describe any real connection between testing cruise missiles and preventing Canadians from becoming dull, drudging Muscovites.

Downtown Toronto was also the site of direct activism. Thirteen anti-cruise missile protesters staged a sit-in at the downtown Canadian Forces recruiting centre on 8 June. They were forcibly removed and later convicted by Justice Gordon Rennie. Their lawyer, Aaron Rynd, argued afterwards that the conviction set a dangerous precedent for freedom of speech, as this was apparently the first time that peaceful demonstrators had been convicted of a criminal offence in a case where there was no property damage. The penalty was a fine of two hundred dollars or thirty days in jail.[155] The government was now making it clear that freedom of speech would have to be exercised very discreetly in Canada.

Defence Minister Lamontagne announced the receipt of the request in the House of Commons, indicated that cabinet would decide, and then rushed out to avoid reporters. Trudeau refused comment. The advice of the Privy Council Office, which had formerly sought to keep everything a secret, was now that the news should be made public "immediately if not sooner" in the hope of avoiding charges that the Liberals were trying to hide events.[156] Former Tory defence minister Allan MacKinnon told reporters that he expected the Liberals to wait until after Parliament adjourned on 30 June to make and announce their decision as this would have left no room for debate.[157]

The day after the announcement was made by Lamontagne, NDP leader Edward Broadbent proposed in the House of Commons that cruise missile testing be opposed. His motion, which read "The House should express its opposition to the escalation of the nuclear arms race by any nation and, in particular, its opposition to Canada's participation by testing in Canada any nuclear weapon or nuclear weapon delivery vehicle such as, and including, the cruise missile," was defeated 213 to 34. Although Trudeau had absolutely refused to allow a free vote in the House of Commons, many Liberals declined to vote for the government (David Weatherhead, Doug Firth, Peter Ittinaur, Paul McRae, Ron Irwin, and George Baker all abstained), while one, Warren Allmand, voted against Trudeau. Four Tories (John Fraser, Doug Roche, Jack Murta, and Walter McLean) also voted against testing. Gilles Lamontagne led the debate for Trudeau's government, noting that, amongst the public, "the upsurge of anti-nuclear sentiment is one of the most important problems" faced by the government.

Concern was spreading to other aspects of the testing. It was already known that the cruise missile would be carried by the venerable workhorse of the Strategic Air Command (SAC) bomber fleet, the eight-engined B-52 Stratofortress. However, a series of crashes the previous December had raised concerns, and several members of the House of Commons wanted to know about the flights over Canada. Minister of Defence Lamontagne and Vice Chief of the Defence Staff Lieutenant General Theriault assured Members of Parliament that all of the crashes were during low-level flights, and they led the members to believe that in Canada B-52s, such as those requiring the use of oxygen at all times, flew only at very high altitudes.[158] This was a total falsehood as SAC flights in Canada in the early 1980s were often at very low altitudes. This was clearly shown by the flight profiles in Transport Canada charts provided to Canadian civil and commercial pilots so that civilian aircraft did not collide with low-flying USAF bombers on various flights paths across Canada.

Cabinet was originally expected to deal with the request at its 20 June meeting.[159] Lamontagne had to tell his colleagues that the navigation equipment and radars on the ALCM had the potential of disrupting civil microwave and other communications transmissions. He was coached to explain this to cabinet in non-technical terms and to assure them that this would not violate the International Telecommunications Union. Later analysis revealed that it was more likely that civil communications would have a greater chance of interfering with the cruise missile flights than vice versa.[160]

More bad news for Ottawa came the day after the cabinet meeting. After the USAF's statement to the Southam reporters who broke the original story in March 1982, Trudeau's staff ordered that a diplomatic complaint be lodged with the U.S. State Department. The State Department conferred with the White House and the Federal Bureau of Investigation (F.B.I.) was ordered to investigate the matter. On 12 June, with the authority of the U.S. Attorney General William French Smith, the F.B.I. called Don Sellar, the Southam Washington correspondent, in for an interview. The meeting took place at the Washington field office of the F.B.I., after Sellar rejected going to an annex of the White House, and the F.B.I. rejected conducting the interview at the National Press Building. It looked to many like Trudeau had asked Reagan to plug a leak that had severely embarrassed Ottawa. The reality is probably closer to the Reagan administration itself ordering a massive leak investigation aimed at other departments. This was quite ironic as the Reagan White House is reputed to have leaked more than any other in history.

In Ottawa another group announced that they were going on an anti-cruise missile fast. On 12 July the five participants, Robert Light, Dave Morrison, Sue Power, Wilfrid Raby, and Stephanie Coe, told the press that they would fast until cabinet made a final decision on cruise missile testing. The five participants were part of the anti-cruise missile peace camp set up on Parliament Hill three months earlier in mid-April. They camped out below the Peace Tower during their fast, and indicated that they expected a bad decision to be forthcoming.

Friday, 15 July 1983 was a busy and significant day in cruise missile history. The Cabinet Policy and Planning (P&P) Committee met to discuss the cruise missile in the morning, and a full meeting of the entire cabinet took place in the afternoon. At this second meeting the entire cabinet authorized the testing of USAF air-launched cruise missiles in Canada the following winter. The decision was brief: "The Cabinet agreed that the United States Air Force be permitted to test unarmed cruise missiles in Canada"; and that "the U.S. immediately be informed of Canada's agreement to permit unarmed cruise testing."[161]

The letter that Secretary of State for External Affairs Allan MacEachen would send to U.S. Secretary of State George Shultz had already been written when cabinet gave its approval. MacEachen went from the cabinet meeting back to his office and signed the letter to Shultz which informed the United States that Ottawa "has decided to approve the request" for live cruise missile testing over Canada.[162] Trudeau had ducked the responsibility of making the announcement, instead leaving the unenviable task to MacEachen and defence minister Gilles Lamontagne. When the press conference at the National Press Building just off Parliament Hill began ninety minutes behind schedule, the public was given much information about the Canadian commitment to arms control and to NATO membership, and how Canada had renounced nuclear weapons. Authors of the announcement even managed to include references to the planned tests, telling Canadians about the route a B-52 would fly over northern Canada.[163] Roy McFarlane, an Operation Dismantle member, stepped in front of Lamontagne's car just as the minister was trying to get away from the press conference. McFarlane blocked the car for about fifteen seconds in silent protest. Although it was not as memorable or as significant as the student who would stand in front of the tank in Tiananmen Square in China in 1989, it was a powerful reminder to the government that Canadians were not as complacent as the Liberals hoped.

Trudeau left his office at 7:00 P.M., refusing to answer any questions from reporters. He and his three sons promptly left Ottawa for a six-day trip across the Arctic region, starting in Yellowknife where he was greeted by an anti-cruise missile protest.

Even Allan McKinnon, the defence critic of the right-wing Progressive Conservative Party, attacked the Liberals for being premature with the decision, saying that it would have been far better to await the outcome of the Geneva talks. He doubted that Canada's cruise missile testing would have any effect at all on the Soviets, much less push the USSR towards arms control concessions.[164] The New Democratic Party (NDP) immediately raked Trudeau and MacEachen over the coals for dragging Canada further into the new Cold War emanating from Washington. Its external affairs critic, Pauline Jewett, commented that the decision was hardly a surprise, and that she thought it had in reality been made at least one year earlier. She went on to characterize the 6:30 P.M. announcement on a Friday afternoon at the height of the summer as "a typical sleazy Liberal tactic" to avoid criticism and press coverage.

Moscow was not forced to the negotiating table. The only Soviet comment was that a "massive tide of angry protest" had been unleashed by the United States-authored Trudeau decision.[165]

Although some conservative members would attack Trudeau's Liberals over the cruise missile, one party activist put it another way. The local Conservative campaign media officer in Nova Scotia told the press that Canadians do not care about cruise missile testing and "all that commie shit."[166] He refused to comment on the number of apparent commie Canadians who were now turning out in record numbers to protest the testing.

Protest was swift and vociferous. The Canadian Union of Postal Workers, the Canadian Union of Public Employees, and the United Auto Workers all vowed to fight the decision. Across Canada the chapters and headquarters of Physicians for Social Responsibility condemned the decision. James Stark of Operation Dismantle told the press that his group would seek a court injunction to prohibit testing under the Constitution. When Trudeau visited Yellowknife, Northwest Territories just after the decision was announced, he was greeted by a determined group of cruise missile opponents wearing black arm bands.

The Cruise Missile Conversion Project (CMCP) in Ottawa planned a march to Griffiss AFB in Rome, N.Y., to protest the testing. According to Brian Burch and Pete Dundas of CMCP, the group would start in Kingston and cross the Peace Bridge near Ganonoque, Ontario if allowed by U.S. authorities. The U.S. Immigration office at the border said that each person would be treated individually, because the United States "afford[ed] everyone the right of free speech." Only one man was turned back at the border, while 135 Canadians, 89 U.S. citizens, 3 Britons and 1 citizen of France were admitted. Once they arrived at Griffiss AFB, 35 Canadians would be arrested for exercising the right of free speech on land considered part of a high-security facility. Chaos reined on the nuclear cruise missile base during the protest.

On 22 July, in the most despised act of protest of the decade, Toronto art student Peter Grayson splashed red ink on Canada's Constitution at the National Archives in Ottawa. He was immediately charged with damaging public property, and eventually sentenced to eighty-nine days in jail, two years of probation, and one hundred hours of community service with the John Howard Society. The ink has resisted all attempts to remove it from the second copy of the Constitution signed in April 1982. Archivist K. F. Foster has advised that about thirty different solvents have been unable to remove the stain, but have succeeded in dimming the red colour. A conflict has arisen between those who believe the marked document is a valuable record of the time, and those who wish to erase any trace of the event that makes this copy unique. In the long term this copy of the Constitution will be a valuable record of a different part of Canadian history, where protest took many forms and cruise missiles had taken centre stage in the daily political life of the nation.

Groups began week-long vigils outside Liberal offices in Toronto, Halifax, Vancouver, Regina, Saskatoon, and Calgary. Liberal Party headquarters at Yonge and King Streets in Toronto was the prime target of many protests. One organizer, Angela Brown, said that the demonstrations and vigils would continue at the party headquarters and at Queen's Park for a week and then culminate in a massive set of nation-wide protest marches. The Toronto protest march drew some four thousand to eight thousand people, all of whom were immediately branded as criminals by Toronto police who cited a 1964 law banning marches on Yonge Street. In a dramatic move, protesters later set fire to a giant model of an ALCM outside the U.S. consulate on University Avenue. Matthew Clark of the Toronto Disarmament Network said that the thousands who had protested so far would grow to tens of thousands then hundreds of thousands now that the Liberals had announced their final decision to test. Canadians were mobilizing, even in foreign countries. Several members of Mobilization for Survival were arrested in Boston when they unfurled a banner on the Canadian consulate; other events took place at consulates throughout the United States.

The new minister of national defence, Jean-Jacques Blais, now had to deal with protesters on a regular basis. Scheduled to speak on the state of the Canadian Forces at the Garrison Officer's Club in Alberta, the minister instead spent his time attacking Canadians who disagreed with Trudeau's policy. He slammed citizens for weakening the free world and impairing the quest for peace. Trying to shift public opinion, but instead preaching only to the converted, Blais told his military audience that he never saw people protesting Soviet missile testing.[167] He declined to mention that the Soviets had tested their missiles in the USSR, and that the ALCM was being tested in Canada by a foreign power then bent on prevailing in a nuclear war. Keeping vigil at the site was Richard Gomberg dressed in his cruise missile costume. The notion that free speech would weaken NATO was greeted by many with disbelief.

The announcement of the decision to allow specific testing motivated the federal court action on the part of the anti-cruise missile coalition. The ad hoc group, largely led by James Stark, called on their lawyer Lawrence Greenspon to immediately file for a temporary injunction against the tests. Stark told the media that Operation Dismantle, along with other members of the coalition, was filing for an injunction in federal court to temporarily stop implementation of the cabinet decision. Greenspon said that he would file court papers on 19 July and sought a hearing within seven to ten days.

"Even if cruise is tested, the larger issue isn't over. All along the cruise has been a symbol of Canada's involvement in the arms race and will remain so," said Jamie Scott of the United Church. The government opposed the case reaching a federal court hearing by arguing that cabinet decisions were not subject to constitutional restrictions, and were certainly not subject to review by the courts. But Canadians and coalition members were elated when, on Thursday, 15 September, Federal Court Justice Alex Cattanach ruled that the hearing could proceed, and ordered that lawyers for the government had to present a defence statement within thirty days. Cattanach called on the federal Justice Department to respond with a statement showing why the testing was justifiable in a free and democratic society. Greenspon joyously told the press that this was the first time that a cabinet decision would come before the courts. Trudeau responded to the ruling by telling the House of Commons that "as far as the Government is concerned, it has taken a decision and announced a policy and it will stand until the court strikes it down."

However, Trudeau did more than just make a statement. He immediately ordered that a full appeal be set in motion in order to test the limits of both the courts and cabinet authority. Justice Minister Mark MacGuigan argued that in Canada "there are certain kinds of decisions which are not reviewed by the courts." The Federal Court disagreed. Justice Cattanach wrote that all decisions of Parliament and cabinet could be challenged in court if they appeared to violate the Canadian Charter of Rights and Freedoms. Cattanach's nine-page decision noted that individuals have the right to challenge an act of Parliament, and that executive decisions of the government are subject to the Charter. The Justice Department filed a thirty-three page brief calling for the case to be struck down on appeal, saying that the decision eroded the three-hundred-year-old doctrine of parliamentary supremacy. Each side's position would be heard on 11 October by a three-member panel of federal court justices.

During the Federal Court appeal, case A-1331-83, the lawyer for the government, Associate Deputy Minister of Justice Ian Binnie, insulted the justices by saying that appointed judges did not have the aptitude to deal with complicated political questions. At the 11 October hearing, Binnie sought to have the anti-cruise missile case thrown out and the supremacy of cabinet decisions reserved away from court oversight. Greenspon and Irwin Cotler argued that the Charter applied to all actions of government and that the case should proceed on its own merits according to the Cattanach decision. Justices William Ryan, Gerald Le Dain, Louis Marceau, Louis Pratte, and James Hugessen did not agree with the anti-cruise missile case. Greenspon argued that unless there was clearly no case at all, the justices should not interfere with the original ruling. The ruling would come in late November.

The world of 1983 was increasingly dangerous as the Cold War seemed to get far colder in terms of superpower relations, and far hotter in terms of actual small wars and conflicts. In autumn, two events would galvanize hostilities. On 1 September a Soviet Air Defence Force (*PVO Strany*) Sukhoi-15 jet, using two missiles, had shot down Korean Airlines (KAL) flight 007, a civilian passenger flight, over Sakhalin Island, killing all 269 people onboard. The Reagan regime used the shoot-down as a rationale for a request to Congress for a massive increase in the nuclear weapons budget, including funding for the MX first-strike ICBM. Then, on 24 October 1983, the United States Navy, Marines, Army and Air Force invaded the tiny island of Grenada. They were cheered on by Reagan's White House, which claimed that the ex-British colony had fallen under the military occupation of Cuban forces who were engaged (with British government assistance) in building a commercial runway which would be big enough to handle tourist flights from Europe.

Pro-cruise-missile activists used the KAL incident as a justification for testing. Paraded before a group of supporters, the father of KAL flight 007 passenger Mary Jane Hendrie asked the group, "how many examples do they [anti-cruise protesters] need" of Soviet evil before they approve of testing. The government was never able to use the tiny and infrequent actions by pro-cruise missile demonstrators to their advantage, as large numbers of Canadians did not identify with the groups promoting militarism during the height of concern over nuclear destruction.

At the end of the year people finally got a glimpse of what the United States and NATO had planned for the Pershing and cruise missiles. NATO selectively released parts of a target planning document which said that NATO had "more than 2,500 high-priority targets, about two-thirds are located in the non-Soviet Warsaw Pact and the remaining one-third in the Soviet Union." It also noted that the twenty-five-hundred-kilometre-range ground-launched cruise missile based in the United Kingdom could strike "approximately 87% of the high-priority targets, including Moscow itself."[168]

The war scare in the Soviet Union was now of greater intensity than at any time in history. The public was genuinely worried and often alarmed at what they saw of U.S. and NATO nuclear activities. Starting with the secret decision to begin operation *RYaN*, and then making the concern public, the Soviet regime seems to have been extremely fearful that the Reaganites were bent on launching a nuclear-rocket attack. Of this, the cruise missile testing in Canada was just one aspect.

At a meeting in Halifax, U.S. Secretary of State George Shultz praised the Trudeau government for allowing the ALCM tests. Shultz, a staunch Cold Warrior, toasted MacEachen and the Trudeau Cabinet as having contributed to international peace by testing offensive nuclear weapons systems.[169] The irony was not lost on the Canadian public who were increasingly taking to the streets in opposition to Pierre Trudeau's policies. However, behind the scenes, the meeting was not all smiles. The U.S. team announced that the USAF would only be doing "captive-carry" tests over Canada. The Canadian government, having put up with a year of attacks often centred on safety issues surrounding testing, shot back that if they had known about this in the first place a great deal of public concern and controversy could have been averted.[170]

All the planning done in Canada up to this point had been based on the assumption, which the U.S. side showed no interest in changing, that the cruise missile would fly on its own down the entire test corridor. However, the USAF began an extensive modification program on their Advanced Range Instrumentation Aircraft (ARIA) meant to control the missile and monitor the flight test. The modifications were to include the installation of a second remote control and communication unit for enhanced safety, but this upgrade would not be completed before the February–March 1984 testing period. The government now actually had the added bonus of announcing that free flights would be put off for a year while additional safety measures were put in place.

An international day of protest against Pershing and GLCM deployments had been planned for 22 October, and Canadians were joining in with their anti-ALCM protests. Two million people took part in the demonstrations around the world. Massive protests took over the streets in Toronto, Hamilton, London, Windsor, Thunder Bay, Ottawa, and Kingston in Ontario; Halifax, Saint John, Charlottetown, and St. John's in the Maritimes; Winnipeg, Regina, Saskatoon, Prince Albert, Calgary, and Edmonton on the prairies; and Vancouver, Victoria, and Vernon on the west coast. It was estimated that some five hundred anti-cruise missile and pro-peace groups had sprung up across the country, joined only by the Canadian Disarmament Information Service (CANDIS) of Toronto. CANDIS, housed in the Peace Chapel of the Holy Trinity Church in downtown Toronto, was originally funded by the city and the Department of External Affairs. Washington retaliated against the swelling peace movement by speeding up the deliveries of cruise and Pershing missiles to Europe.

Harvie Andre, who would later become the second-in-command at National Defence as the secretary of state for defence under the minister of national defence, said that the entire Canadian peace and anti-nuclear movement was financed by communists and Moscow. He admitted having no evidence, but was sure that "they [the USSR] are supplying funds and being helpful."[171] Andre was unable to explain, even with information supplied to him by National Defence, how cruise missile testing served some strategic defence need for Canada, but he was certainly getting into stride for his upcoming job attacking protestors and defending testing.

Canadian communists, or at least the Canadian Communist Party (CPC), admitted to being involved in the anti-cruise missile movement. Party leader William Kashton told reporters, "we are very much a vigorous part of this whole movement,"[172] and pointed out that this was not hidden. Given that the CPC regularly attended protest marches carrying large banners identifying themselves as communists, it was hardly an intelligence coup to discover that there was communist interest in anti-cruise missile activities. After the fall of the Soviet Union, files in Moscow did show that some little money had moved to anti-nuclear groups and communist organizations in the West. However, the bulk of protest was indigenous and self-funded, with no Soviet connection whatsoever. In fact, one of the largest sectors of public protest at the time was the church-based anti-war and pro-peace movements which crossed all sectarian boundaries.

In Washington, the U.S. Congress moved against arms control. Ultra-right wing members of the Senate stated that due to the outcome of a vote on U.S. compliance with SALT II, the treaty was rejected. Led by Jesse Helms and Stephen Symms, they said that observance of and compliance with a non-ratified treaty is illegal under U.S. law, and thus U.S. compliance had ended. This 4 November non-decision came about as a result of a failed vote (fifty to twenty-nine) for an amendment from Helms and Symms which ordered that no U.S. military programs be impeded in any way in order to comply with SALT II, and that all compliance should cease. Their later theory was that since only one-third voted for an amendment, the treaty would not get the necessary two-thirds required for ratification and, therefore, the treaty was dead. This was not accepted by all involved, but was a clear indication of the pro-nuclear mania engulfing Washington. Within days, several other congressmen pointed out that within a few months the United States would be in direct violation of SALT II when the seventh Trident ballistic missile submarine was deployed.

Senator Dale Bumpers told Reagan that "If we go over the 1,200 missile limit, it would be an open invitation to the Soviets to follow suit and break out of the SALT II limits which they are currently observing." This could not be allowed to stand, and an unidentified senior Pentagon official told the editors of *Arms Control Reporter* that the Soviets had told the Standing Consultative Commission (SCC) that they had indeed violated SALT II by deploying more bombers equipped with air-launched cruise missiles than permitted under the 1,320 limit for MIRVed ICBM/SLBM and cruise-equipped bombers. While many observers said this report was nonsense, the Pentagon stood by their strategic leak.[173]

The outcome of the long awaited Federal Court of Appeal case was illuminating; each side won something. Trudeau was told that by a unanimous decision the court had overturned the Cattanach decision and thus ended the challenge to cruise missile testing. One justice, Louis Marceau, called the original case "manifestly frivolous and vexatious," and militantly sided with autocratic government rule. The government's loss came when the majority decided that cabinet decisions were subject to Charter restrictions and that such decisions could be reviewed by the courts. Only Marceau slavishly defended the absolute right of cabinet to be free of any and all constitutional restrictions. The case seemed to be at an end.

On 11 December, the fourth anniversary of the NATO dual-track decision, thirty thousand demonstrators surrounded Greenham Common Air Base in Britain, the site of the ground-launched cruise missile facilities. The anniversary also attracted protestors at the cruise missile site in Sicily and in the Netherlands. The first parts for the GLCMs had just arrived in Sicily, and would be stored at Signolla until construction of the facility at Comiso was completed. The first GLCM components arrived in Britain on Monday, 14 November. In Canada, John Cashore handcuffed himself to the front door of Parliament, and Toronto police and the RCMP arrested 114 men and women in front of Litton. Deputy Crown Attorney Norm Matusiak, the chief prosecutor of the Litton protesters, said that those he took to court were primarily motivated by anti-Americanism, not by a commitment to a more peaceful world. It was in this atmosphere that Minister of National Defence Jean-Jacques Blais announced on 16 November that the first flight test in western Canada would happen in March 1984.

Trudeau ended the year by meeting with Reagan in Washington. During their 15 December 1983 get-together, Reagan apparently told Trudeau that he supported the prime minister's peace mission. The domestic intelligence staff of the security office at CFB Cold Lake ended the year worrying that protesters would initiate Christmas violence; it never happened. 'Peace Mom' Pauline Davis ended the year in her tent in the Don River Valley in Toronto in her continued attempt to get better lines of communication opened between citizens and the prime minister.

The coalition of anti-cruise missile groups ended the year by winning the right to be heard by the Supreme Court of Canada. On 20 December, Chief Justice Bora Laskin, Justice William McIntyre, and Justice Julien Chouinard took only five minutes to decide to grant a hearing for an appeal of the November Federal Court of Appeal decision. The short hearing became very tense when Laskin said Greenspon "was pretty close to contempt" for his comments, and then cut off federal lawyer Ian Binnie by telling him that the court already knew that the case was politically charged. Laskin stated that unless the government had an immediate reason why the case could not proceed, the justices were inclined to grant leave to hear the appeal. Laskin, McIntyre, and Chouinard decided to hear the appeal of the cruise missile decision, and to examine whether courts could examine cabinet decisions. As the year ended no date had been set for the appeal.

2

Testing, Testing, 1–2–3 ...

It is not a test of technology, it is a test of
Canada's obedience to Washington.
Dan Heap, Member of Parliament

Worldwide preparations for war continued in 1984. For the first time in a decade, the United States Navy deployed nuclear-powered and armed submarines to the North Pole, and the Soviets began deployments of their new, massive *Typhoon*-class submarines in polar waters. Once again the nuclear competition moved through and north of Canada.

1984: TESTING BEGINS

The now annual U.S. Department of Defense forecast of test projects in Canada was received in Ottawa on 9 January 1984. The air-launched cruise missile (ALCM) featured prominently, as did lesser systems such as LANTIRN.[1]

Prime Minister Trudeau continued to lecture the world about nuclear restraint and peace. On 9 February he told the House of Commons that he would soon tell both President Reagan of the United States and General Secretary Andropov of the USSR about the ten principles of common ground between the two nations. Ironically, Andropov was already dead. He would be replaced by Constantin Chernyenko four days later. At the funeral in Moscow, Trudeau would meet with the new General Secretary and pass on the principles. Trudeau's ten principles were:

1. Both sides agree that nuclear war cannot be won;
2. Both sides agree that nuclear war must never be fought;
3. Both sides wish to be free from the risk of accidental war or surprise attack;
4. Both sides recognize the dangers inherent in destabilizing weapons;

5. Both sides understand the need for improved techniques of crisis management;

6. Both sides are conscious of the awesome consequences of being the first to use force against the other;

7. Both sides have an interest in increasing security while reducing the cost of defence;

8. Both sides have an interest in avoiding the spread of nuclear weapons to other countries;

9. Both sides have come to a guarded recognition of each other's legitimate security interests; and

10. Both sides realize that their security strategies cannot be based on the assumed political or economic collapse of the other side.

The leap year seemed fortunate for Canadians who opposed the cruise missile, when on 29 February Pierre Trudeau announced that he would finally retire. However, just days later, Minister of National Defence Blais was briefed on the test series for 1985; the tests seemed unstoppable. The minister of national defence was told that the United States Air Force (USAF) would conduct three tests: one captive-carry and two free flights. The Pentagon had notified the Canadians that up to six flights per year could be expected in the near future.[2]

The first cruise missile would not fly by itself. The ALCM made the entire first trip, called mission profile 20, on 6 March attached inside the bomb bay of a B-52G. The B-52G was from the 319th Bomb Wing at Grand Forks AFB, North Dakota, just south of Winnipeg, Manitoba. The government had initially thought that the first test would be accomplished by a B-52 from the 436th Bomb Wing at Griffiss AFB in Rome, New York.

TEST # 84-1

Date: 6 March 1984
captive carry
Mission profile: 20
Unit: 319 Bomb Wing from Grand Forks AFB, North Dakota
Bomber: B-52G
Note: No information has ever been released about this test. It is the position of the Deputy Director of the U.S. Air Force Aircraft Directorate, as the only repository for such information, that the documentation does not exist.

Although the missile never left the bomber, the first test was perhaps the most controversial political and military event in Canada that year. Hundreds of reporters and protesters showed up at CFB Cold Lake to stand witness. Reporters were unable to cover the event as they were relegated to the town of Cold Lake, as the base had been sealed by extra-well-armed security troops, and as only telephone calls were allowed into the public affairs centre. The military had refused to arrange a press conference to discuss the test or the outcome, but eventually, besieged by reporters and telephone calls, the Canadian and U.S. military public affairs officers hosted a joint news conference. Although no press was welcomed at Cold Lake, the U.S. Air Force greeted their press with open arms at Grand Forks. The U.S. media were allowed to witness the giant bomber being prepared for the test flight. The Department of National Defence later said that it did not make allowances for the media because they feared that protesters would use the occasion to try to score political points.[3]

It was at this time that the commander of CFB Cold Lake and his security staff made an interesting observation: Cold Lake, being one of the world's largest air bases in terms of surrounding area, had no fence. Since death threats had been reported against the base commander, Ottawa quickly replied to a request for funding the building of a fence, and a standard airport chain link fence was erected within months.

TESTING THE CRUISE MISSILE

The annual tests were designed to evaluate the operational suitability and effectiveness of new and operational cruise missile systems, and to help maintain the system safety and security. The overall test objective in Canada was to evaluate missile performance over terrain representative. of operational areas.

By U.S. standards, Canada offered the best and most realistic test routes outside of Siberia in the Soviet Union. The combination of terrain, weather, and northern latitudes would push the cruise missile's Terrain Contour Matching navigation equipment to its limits under operationally realistic conditions. Free-flight tests, where the missile would fly on its own to the target at Primrose Lake, would take place only during the winter months when snow was on the ground. This limited free flights to the January–March period each year. The U.S. Air Force estimated that some 153 personnel would be directly involved in each test. About fifty would be deployed to Canada in support of the test, while the remaining 103 would be with USAF aircraft or at mission sites in the United States.

Testing weapons is an expensive activity. By 1990 the cost of flight testing the AGM-86B cruise missile was up to an estimated $250,000 per captive-carry flight, and up to $400,000 per free flight.[4]

THE CRUISE MISSILE

Cruise missiles are a class of weapons which work by flying exactly like a conventional aircraft, with the exception of not having a pilot. The small, winged AGM-86B is powered by a turbofan jet engine that propels it at sustained subsonic speeds. After launch from the host B-52 bomber aircraft, the folded wings and tail surfaces, and engine air intake unfold or deploy. Newer systems as well as updated old cruise missile variants around the world are being upgraded with the addition of Global Positioning System (GPS) hardware into the guidance system. The AGM-86B has a radar return only one-one-thousandth that of the host B-52 bomber. Small radar signature and a low-level flight capability greatly enhanced both the survivability and the effectiveness of the ALCM, and gave the U.S. Air Force a good chance of catching the Soviet air defence forces with their pants down.

AGM-86B Air-Launched Cruise Missile

Strategic nuclear cruise missile

Primary contractor: Boeing Missile & Space Division
Wingspan: 3.64 metres
Wing sweep: 25 degrees
Length: 6.3 metres
Diameter: 0.622 metres
Weight: 1,450 kilograms
Engine: Williams Research Corp./Teledyne CAE F-107-WR-101 turbofan
Engine weight: 66 kilograms
Thrust: 600 U.S. pounds
Fuel: JP-9
Guidance: inertial with TERCOM (Litton Systems Canada)
Targeting: up to 10 pre-selected targets in computer
Accuracy: 10–30 metres in 1984
Range: 2,500 kilometres
Speed: Mach 0.73 (880km/h)
Warhead: W-80-1 (5, 150-170kt variable yield)
Total built: 1,715 (1980–86)
Place built: Boeing Aerospace, Seattle and Kent, Washington.
Cost (missile only): $1,247,000 each
Deployed: up to 20 on each B-52H bombers; up to 12 on each B-52G.

The missile is comprised of a body with four major sections: the guidance system in the nose, the warhead compartment, the fuel tanks, which take up most of the space, and a small engine section in the extreme rear of the fuselage. The fuel tanks are actually the load-bearing structure of the body. A tiny three-piece tail section provides control surfaces, and small thin wings swept back at a twenty-five degree angle provide the aerodynamic lift needed to sustain flight.

Guidance was provided by the Litton System of Canada TERCOM terrain contour-matching guidance system. The ALCM can fly complicated routes to a target through the use of the TERCOM system. During flight, this system compares observed surface characteristics with maps of the planned flight path, which have been stored in the computer, to determine the exact location of the missile.[5] This system is updated with location information every sixty seconds while still attached to the host bomber. After launch, the TERCOM system will regularly match the received and stored images, but will increase the resolution and pairing of the images in the terminal phase of the flight as the weapon nears the target. Matching seems to take place every sixty to ninety minutes, and a normal long distance flight will see a matching at landfall, several (two to five) matchings along the route, and a final more detailed matching in the terminal phase of the flight.

When Secretary of Defense Bill Clements ordered the re-orientation of the cruise missile from decoy to weapon on 30 June 1973, the cruise missile concept changed from an armed or unarmed decoy carried by the bombers as a defensive measure, to a decoy that was now the actual weapon. Later, in February 1974, the Nixon administration allowed the U.S. Air Force to ask Boeing to develop the AGM-86A ALCM. This test system was never produced as a weapon, but served as the basis for the AGM-86B authorized by the Carter administration in January 1977. President Carter had opted for the AGM-86B, which was two metres longer and weighed an additional 550 kilograms. But it was not quite that easy, and the Carter administration ordered a fly-off competition to determine the better weapons for the U.S. Air Force – the AGM-86B or the Tomahawk. The AGM-86B ALCM was confirmed the winner on 25 March 1980.

The new weapon was to be used to extend the operational life of the B-52 fleet, to replace the costly B-1 bomber, and to complicate Soviet air defence. Production began in March 1980, and a total of 1,715 ALCMs had been built by October 1986. In early 1983 the Pentagon cancelled the

AGM-86B in favour of the advanced cruise missile (ACM). Production would continue for another three years to meet operational requirements.

On 11 January 1981, two ALCMs were delivered to the weapons maintenance unit at Griffiss AFB in New York, and were used for environmental and maintenance testing and training. The first operational training flight by the U.S. Air Force with the ALCM occurred on 15 September 1981, followed shortly by the first operational test launch on 21 September. The first squadron of sixteen B-52G bombers at the 416th Bombardment Wing at Griffiss AFB, New York, armed with twelve ALCMs each, became fully operational in mid-December 1982. Success with arming the G-model bomber had prompted the U.S. Air Force decision in September 1981 to arm B-52H with ALCMs.

One small problem that arose was that because the warhead compartment is unheated, the W-80 warhead had to be able to withstand extreme cold for several hours. But the warhead had not been designed for such extremes inside the ALCM, and had to be fixed after initial deployment. The missile itself was tested under such conditions on 27 January 1982 when an ALCM thickly coated with ice was successfully launched in Utah.

The AGM-86C, a conventional variant of the AGM-86B, was first used in combat when seven B-52s from Barksdale AFB flew to the Arab Gulf region and launched thirty-five missiles at targets in Iraq at the beginning of the January 1991 war. The bombers flew thirty-five hours continuously to return to their home base without landing during Operation Secret Squirrel.

Four to six tests would be planned per year, but only two or three free flights would be flown. Many of the ALCMs could be reused, as they were recovered intact. The ACM crashed after passing the target and was thus unrecoverable for further flight. Each flight would be supported by twenty-two USAF aircraft: the B-52 bomber, the ARIA instrument aircraft, one AWACS, up to ten tankers, and eight to ten fighters to act as chase planes. Testing of the AGM-86B is called 'Global Cruise' by the USAF, and comprises four to six launches per year during the operational life of the weapon system.

STRATOFORTRESS

The B-52 *Stratofortress* eight-engine intercontinental nuclear bomber was the icon of Cold War arsenals. The bomber had entered the popular culture as the deliverer of death in the movie *Dr. Strangelove*, and was seen nightly on television news dropping thousands of tonnes of high explosives on South East Asians during the U.S. war against the Vietnamese and Cambodians. The B-52 has been the primary manned strategic bomber in the United States' arsenal for half a century, and is expected to continue in service until perhaps the year 2020.

Design began at the end of World War II and was settled during the weekend of 26 October 1948 at Wright-Patterson AFB in Dayton, Ohio. The first aircraft, XB-52, rolled out of the Boeing factory in Seattle, Washington on 29 November 1951, but did not fly first due to a massive systems failure which destroyed the wings. The second airframe, YB-52, made the first flight on 15 April 1952. The first production line aircraft flew on 5 August 1954, and the first B-52B, #52-8711, was delivered to the United States Air Force at Castle AFB on 29 June 1955. The era of the B-52 had begun, and a grand total of 744 of the massive bombers would be built.

The 193 airframes of the B-52G model were built at the Boeing plant in Wichita, Kansas between May 1958 and August 1960. The definitive version, the B-52H, with 102 units produced, was built between September 1960 and June 1962. Technically, the aircraft can be described as a cantilever semi-monocoque structure with anhedral (drooping) wings with a thirty-five degree sweep and a variable incidence tailplane, sitting on two tandem landing gear sets, and powered by eight turbofan jet engines. The bomber has a six-person crew and can carry up to 31.5 tonnes of ordnance under the wings and in the 29.5 cubic metre bomb bay. The H-model will cruise some 10,000 kilometres at 820 kilometres per hour without refuelling. The refuelled range is limited only by the endurance of the crew.

Starting in 1978 the U.S. Air Force and Boeing began the modifications necessary to make ninety-eight B-52G and ninety-five B-52H models cruise-missile-capable by installing the computers and the pylon system which would be fitted under each wing. The first B-52 unit to receive the entire ALCM and B-52 weapons system was the 416th Bomb Wing at Griffiss AFB in New York in early December 1982. Work continued on the modifications until the final aircraft was given back to the U.S. Air Force in late 1989. As part of this program, the Common Strategic Rotary Launcher (CSRL) was placed on eighty-two B-52H aircraft during 1988. This gave the H-model the ability to carry eight ALCMs in the bomb bay and twelve under the wings, for a total of twenty deliverable weapons. Earlier bomb bay carriage had been accomplished using a modified SRAM launcher refitted for the larger missile.

The B-52 could carry up to 31.5 tonnes of bombs, and in the fifty years that it has been in service, the bomber has operated with the B28, B43, B53, B57, B61, and B83 nuclear bombs, and the AGM-69A SRAM, AGM-28 Hound Dog, AGM-86B ALCM, and ACM-129 ACM missiles. It has a maximum cruise missile load of twenty ALCMs, or twelve ACMs.

The B-52G was the first ALCM carrier. Of the 193 built, 98 were converted to carry the missile, and by 1987 the AGM-86B was operational with the 2nd, 97th, 379th, and 416th Bomb Wings until the aircraft itself was retired in 1994. The B-52H, still in service, saw 96 of the original 102 aircraft converted to the ALCM role, and later to carry the ACM. By the late 1980s, the aircraft and missile combination was flown by the 7th, 92nd, 410th, and 416th Bomb Wings.

With the 1979 signing of SALT II, the B-52G would have to be modified slightly to meet the requirements of the arms control treaty. Bombers carrying cruise missiles had to have external observable differences from non-ALCM bombers. These structural differences also had to be observable from space. Boeing and the U.S. Air Force decided to add strakelets to the area where the leading edge of the wing meets the main body of the airframe. The B-52H model did not need any modification, as the engines were sufficiently different and clearly observable to satellite-based inspection. By decision of the Reagan administration, the USAF was directed to violate the un-ratified SALT II agreement by deploying over 130 ALCM-equipped heavy bombers. The 131st aircraft, B-52H #60-0055, was delivered to United States Air Force at Carswell AFB on 28 November 1986. With more than a little sense of irony and bad taste, the air force had nicknamed that aircraft *Salt Shaker*. In the early 1980s, with nuclear dangers at the highest level, Canadian commentators noted that the B-52 was something most young people would not live to be, and added that the definition of 'radioactive half-life' was B-26.[6]

THE WARHEAD

With the decision to pursue work on both sea- and air-launched cruise missiles, it became necessary to acquire a suitable warhead for the planned confined space aboard such a missile. The W80 warhead, a Los Alamos product, is a re-engineered version of the successful Mk-61 bomb used by the U.S. Air Force, and was actually intended to be the replacement warhead for the Short Range Attack Missile (SRAM). It has two nuclear yields in the 5 to 170 kiloton range.

Developmental engineering for the warhead began at Los Alamos National Laboratory (LANL) in June 1976, testing took place in 1978, and production engineering started in January 1979. Initial production warheads were delivered two years later in January 1981. It was only then that a problem with the insensitive high explosive component became obvious.

The original design was not robust enough to withstand the extreme cold temperatures experienced for many hours at maximum altitude. Soon after the first units were manufactured, LANL discovered that the system did not work in the cold. During a test detonation of the primary (fission) section of the warhead in shot *Baseball* of Operation *Guardian* on 15 January 1981, after production had begun, LANL was alarmed to note that the warhead gave only a fraction of the rated yield at below minus forty degrees Celsius. In fact, the primary section did not have enough power to ignite the secondary (thermonuclear) stage of the weapon. Both Los Alamos National Labs and Lawrence Livermore National Labs worked to rectify the problem, and a new design for the primary was soon released. This new warhead design was successfully tested below minus fifty degrees Celsius in shot *Jornada* in Operation *Praetorian* of 28 January 1982.

W-80-1 Nuclear Warhead

Lightweight, two-stage, variable yield nuclear warhead.

Designed: Los Alamos National Laboratory (LANL)
Built by: Mason & Hanger-Silas Mason, Pantex Plant, Texas.
Yield: two selectable, 5 to 150–170 kiloton (variable)
Length: 0.798 metres
Diameter: 0.29 metres
Weight: 132 kilograms
Weight of arming/fusing system: 4.5 kilograms
Shape: Cylindrical body with hemispherical nose for primary
Permissive Action Link (PAL): Category D PAL (six dig-
    it lock with limited try and lockout)
Number deployed to USAF: 1,000 for ALCM; 400 for ACM
Development begins: 6/1976
Production Engineering: 1/1979
Initial production begins: 1/1981
Deployment on ALCM begins: 9/1981
Quantity production begins: 2/1982
Production ends: 9/1990
Deployment on ACM begins: 1991

Rectification of the freezing problem meant that the full production units did not come out of the assembly bays at the Amarillo, Texas, Pantex Plant for delivery to the U.S. Air Force until mass production began in February 1982. At least 1,650 units were hand-built by the time production ceased in September 1990. The warheads are divided roughly two-thirds for the ALCM and one-third for the ACM. The plutonium pits and various sub-systems are being updated, and responsibility for the Los Alamos designed warhead has been transferred to Lawrence Livermore National Laboratory. The W-80 warhead was not carried on any of the free-flight tests over Canada due to both the ban in the agreement and the risk of both a loss and an accident.

The year 1984 was significant for nuclear weapons in Canada for reasons other than the cruise missile. This was the year that nuclear warheads would finally leave the Canadian Forces forever. The nuclear warheads for the BoMARC anti-bomber missile, the Honest John battlefield rocket, and the free-fall weapons on the Starfighter bomber had been acquired under a 1963 agreement signed by Trudeau's predecessor, Prime Minister Lester (Mike) Pearson, in order to keep a campaign promise. Pearson originally thought that he could simply turn the weapons around and send them right back to the United States, but it was not to be. The deployment of several hundred warheads in Canada and West Germany with the Royal Canadian Air Force and army lasted until 1972 when the bulk were returned to the United States for use by their forces. However, more than fifty W-25 warheads remained in Canada for use with the Genie anti-bomber rockets carried by the CF-101 VooDoo. The bases at Bagotville, Quebec, and Comox, British Columbia hosted fifty-two nuclear warheads until their final withdrawal in April and June 1984 when the weapons went to their immediate destruction in Amarillo, Texas.[7]

In Europe, opponents of Intermediate Nuclear Force (INF) cruise and Pershing missiles mobilized thousands of people. On the Easter weekend, a traditional time of peace marches in Europe, at least 100,000 people demonstrated at six German INF sites. The new Canadian government of Brian Mulroney received a peace petition signed by 420,000 Canadians. Mulroney, quite subservient to U.S. interests, rejected the petition out of hand saying, "there is no change in our thinking."[8] The entire petition was tabled in the House of Commons on Tuesday, 13 November. Although one-third of the signatures were symbolically tabled by each major party, the Tories quickly distanced themselves from Canadian feelings by declaring that they had no intention of heeding the call from the masses; they answered only to the White House. In fact, so great was Mulroney's reliance on Washington for cues that the White House had come to expect total obedience. This caused a problem when U.S. Secretary of Defense Weinberger told the press during the Mulroney-Reagan summit that anti-cruise missile missiles would soon be stationed in Canada to strike Soviet missiles. The Mulroney team spent several days trying to deny that any such thing would happen, and trying to reassure Canadians that Ottawa was really in charge.

The United States Navy (USN) was also entering the cruise missile world after several years away from the field. Although they had early experience with primitive cruise missiles in the 1940s and 1950s, the modern Tomahawk sea-launched cruise missiles were just coming on line. In late June, the first nuclear-armed SLCMs became operational with the United States Navy aboard four nuclear-powered attack submarines.

The intensive U.S. cruise missile activities had stimulated Soviet interest in longer-range systems. Previously, cruise missile work inside the USSR had been limited to short and medium-range attack cruise missiles, mainly for anti-ship missions. However, once the United States proved small long-range missiles were feasible, and once the Soviet design bureaus could produce a small and efficient engine, the interest in building such a system rose. The Soviet programs came to fruition in the spring of 1984 with flight-testing of the early models.

In a break from a secretive tradition, the Soviet Ministry of Defence announced in *Pravda* that it was flight-testing long-range cruise missiles. *Pravda* went on to state that such weapons were bad for arms control and international security.[9] Later in the summer, the Soviet United Nations Mission released a statement saying that the country was testing a system that would help restore the balance between the USSR and the United States, and between the Warsaw Treaty Organization and NATO.[10] What this all meant was that the system was quite far along in development, and indeed, deployment began in early October on a tiny number of strategic bombers. At this time only about six Tu-95 bombers were equipped to carry the AS-15 ALCM, but there were probably plans to convert up to 69 of the 101 bombers to carry the new missile. Although initial production units were being sent to a couple of bomber bases, they remained in a pre-operational mode pending further flight-testing with regular bomber units. At the time, Soviet cruise missile stocks were made up of only the AS-15 and the BL-10. The only real Soviet cruise missile shock in North America remained a secret from the public. On 30 November, the first Soviet long-range Tu-95H bomber armed with cruise missiles flew a mock attack against North America. NORAD intercepted the aircraft and noted that the USSR now had the initial capability to attack with cruise missiles.

In the United States Ronald Reagan was re-elected as president for a second term on 4 November. Although called wildly popular, and his victories described as stunning electoral landslides, Reagan was returned to the White House with 59 percent of the popular vote in an election with less than 53 percent voter turnout. Even amongst those who chose to vote that day, polls revealed that most voters held views contrary to Reagan's on the deployment of nuclear weapons.[11]

Without Ottawa's prior knowledge, and certainly without much public affairs preparation being done for the scared Canadian government, a spokesman for the U.S. Air Force announced on 6 December that Canada had agreed to allow free-flight cruise missile flights during the January–March 1985 testing season. Captain Jim Berg said that there would be two captive-carry and two free-flight tests, including the very first free flight. Canadians learned of their government's earlier decision from United States' sources in their morning paper on 7 December. Caught by surprise, National Defence directed Captain Luigi Rosetto to brief the media now clamouring for details.

By the end of the year the United States Air Force had conducted twenty-four free-flight tests of the AGM-86B ALCM, mostly over the Utah test route.

1985

The weapons testing season of 1985 opened with a new prime minister in the Langevin Building on Parliament Hill. Brian Mulroney was informed on 9 January that the winter tests would take place on 15 January, and on 12 February and 15 February. The first would be a captive-carry test in which the missile rode the entire route attached to the bomber. The next two tests would be free-flight runs in which the ALCM navigated the course under its own power.[12]

TEST # 85-x

15 January 1985
Global Cruise ALCM test (code means follow-on test
    and evaluation (FOT&E) of ALCM)
west route, captive-carry (last before free-flight tests)
Missile profile: 14 (second flight, also called 85-4/14-NS/MO214)
Unit: 319 Bomb Wing from Grand Forks AFB, North Dakota

Bomber: B-52G/57-6480 (may be B-52G/58-0223)
Crew: E-31
Primary missile: 81-0512 (may have been 81-0355)
Payload: NTIK-17
Position: RP-2 (pylon #90)
Secondary missile: 81-0449
Payload: NTIK-18
Position: LP-2 (pylon #86)
Additional stores: 81-0474 on RP-5, and 81-0451 on LP-5.
Launch mode: manual
Launch altitude planned: 10,000 metres above sea level (ASL)
Initial flight altitude: 1,830 metres ASL
Launch time (simulated): 16:46:30.13
Time on target: 21:10
Flight time to target: 4 hours, 24 minutes, 57 seconds
Note: The simulated launch of the primary missile was delayed over two hours
    due to support aircraft, weather, and maintenance problems, but was ac-
    complished on the first hot pass of launch point. This test marked the
    completion of the second phase of the three-phased testing in Canada.

The second season of winter tests attracted much opposition. In Winnipeg, protesters braved extreme cold to be on the streets day after day for each test. Numerous members of the Winnipeg Coordinating Committee for Disarmament even went to the Canada-U.S. border town of Emerson at the end of February for a quiet vigil on the 49th parallel. Cole Summer, the spokesman for the group, said that they had gathered for a solidarity meeting in the face of tests scheduled so close together.[13] Prince George, B.C. was the site of a cruise missile burning. Over one hundred people gathered in Carrie Jane Gray Park to witness Susan Stevenson ignite the fuel-soaked full-scale model of the ALCM.

The anti-cruise missile coalition took its case back to the Supreme Court, asking for a temporary injunction to stop the first free-flight test. After hearing ninety minutes of arguments, a five-judge panel ruled against the group and denied the injunction. Led by the new Chief Justice Brian Dickson, who was joined by justices Julien Chouinard, Willard Estey, William McIntyre, and Bertha Wilson, the group took ten minutes to decide that the case was without merit. James Stark, head of Operation Dismantle, was resigned to the decision, hoping only that no one was injured or killed during the test.

While attention was focused on cruise missiles, the Canadian government was authorizing other nuclear delivery system tests outside the Test and Evaluation Agreement. The U.S. Air Force had approached the Department of National Defence in January with an urgent request for flights along the western ALCM corridor by a B-52 outfitted with a new offensive avionics package. The tests were unrelated to the ALCM flights, and were characterized by the United States as an unforeseen requirement.[14] The offensive avionics package was designed to aid the aging aircraft in delivering nuclear weapons to hard targets inside the Soviet Union.

AIR COMMAND PARTICIPATION

Air Command was tasked with providing air forces for the protection of Canadian and NORAD regions against air attack from the USSR along northern attack routes. It was also tasked with training forces for air defence, and assisting other forces in weapons training and testing. This is where the ALCM tests enter the Air Command area of interest. The headquarters in Winnipeg noted that military personnel would benefit from direct participation with the ALCM tests, and that pilots would benefit from flying both with and against the missile.

There were two methods of testing the ALCM over Canada: 'captive-carry' tests in which the ALCM remained attached to the bomber, and 'free-flight' tests where the missile was launched from the bomber. In each case telemetry was gathered and contour mapping accomplished. In each case the CF-18 fighter and Aurora maritime patrol aircraft could be used.

Air Command's CFB Cold Lake provided the physical support for the very first ALCM test on 6 March 1984. As there was no free flight there was no need for a CF-18 escort aircraft with each missile. However, even the early flights sometimes had CF-18s accompanying the bomber. When a missile flew on its own it was always accompanied by escort aircraft, and early tests had CF-18 fighters flying with the missile at the Primrose Lake end of the flight. CFB Cold Lake's job was to provide forces for escort of the ALCM; helicopters for recovery of the missile; and ground support to USAF range aircraft that stopped in Canada. The B-52 bombers were never to stop in Canada. Later, in 1986, CF-18 fighters would be provided for the mock interception of the ALCM during NORAD training and exercises.

It was during the early Mulroney years that many of the old nuclear weapons agreements and arrangements were terminated.[15] Canada had rid itself of the last of the old U.S. nuclear weapons systems back in 1984 when the final Genie W25 warheads for the Genie rockets carried by CF-101 VooDoo interceptors were returned to the United States for dismantling. Other systems, such as the BoMARC, the Honest John, and the gravity bombs for the Starfighter, had been returned between 1967 and 1972. Likewise, the United States had stored nuclear weapons in Canada at Goose Bay, Ernest Harmon AFB, and Argentia naval station — all in Newfoundland and Labrador — until they too were returned to the United States between 1966 and 1971.

But the arrangements persisted. The Mulroney staff, on the advice of National Defence and External Affairs, asked the joint Military Cooperation Committee (MCC) to review the old arrangements.[16] The MCC then turned their recommendation over to the full Permanent Joint Board on Defence which concurred in June 1986. The outstanding matter of five arrangements was referred to a sub-group of the Board which met on 26 August 1986.[17] The sub-committee members all agreed that it would be prudent to immediately cancel most of the old nuclear weapons agreements and arrangements.[18]

The problem was that after all these years of writing and signing arrangements and agreements allowing the U.S. military to do everything in Canada, no one knew how to cancel such legal texts. It had certainly never occurred to the Pentagon that a client state would try to cancel an agreement, and few if any of the documents came with termination clauses. The office of the secretary of defence had begun in late 1984 to examine agreements which seemed to cover nuclear deployments in Canada.[19] Pentagon lawyers began working on the theory of termination in the spring of 1985 and were still at it in the late summer of 1986. The June 1986 PJBD meeting was a disappointment to the Mulroney government as the U.S. side was both unprepared and unwilling to address Canadian proposals for cancellation.

The office of the secretary of defense was most adamant that nothing be done to the agreements that allowed the U.S. Air Force virtually complete freedom over Canada with nuclear weapons, and they were similarly unhappy with the new Canadian wording for the non-nuclear consultation and authorization agreement.[20] The United States viewed this house-cleaning exercise as symptomatic of Canadian nuclear "allergy." Ottawa had to assure Washington that the sole objective was to review and update joint military agreements bearing on nuclear deployments to ensure they addressed current circumstances, plans, and capabilities.[21]

In the end, Ottawa decided to simply send a letter proposing cancellation of the listed agreements, and to let the office of the secretary of defense sort out who within the Pentagon could agree to accept the letter or any part applying to their projects.[22] Thus seemed to end the life of the nuclear agreements Canada had signed. Eventually, the United States felt more comfortable with the outcome, especially once they realized that many of the nuclear weapons and nuclear weapons carriers in question were no longer in use or even in existence.

This did not mean that nuclear agreements no longer existed between the United States and Canada. A classified "CANUS Index of Agreements" in 1990 had four pages listing nuclear agreements and arrangements.[23] At least twelve were nuclear-related.[24] While none of these agreements directly call for Canada to host nuclear weapons operations, they did entangle the country in a web of activities involving the physical, technical, military, and political support for nuclear weapons and nuclear warfare operations. It is not just the few nuclear agreements which are important in this context; it is all the supporting agreements and arrangements for flights and shipping and exercises which further embroiled Canada in the web of the U.S. nuclear infrastructure.

Of greater significance are the number of agreements Canada had signed in the field of 'Air Defence.' The nine pages list thirty-six separate documents, not all of which are limited to air defence. There were ten items on military nuclear cooperation.[25]

The CANUS index included several other sections listing nuclear-related agreements and arrangements. From operations in Canadian airspace, to refuelling, to nuclear-powered ships in Canadian ports, there was a document to cover everything.[26]

The important question here is why National Defence lists the 1963 agreement for provision of nuclear weapons to the Canadian forces as a current agreement still in force in 1990. NORAD had been denuded of nuclear weapons when the last of the W25 warheads for the Genie rocket were disassembled in December 1984. This seems to be a simple case of the administration not having caught up with reality. Most of the other air defence documents refer to BUIC, the DEW Line, CADIN, PINETREE, and various other radar stations.

Scattered throughout the mammoth index are various agreements that call on Canada to support a wide variety of U.S. nuclear activities. Almost without exception, these agreements were made on a military-to-military basis with little, if any, political input from bureaucrats and politicians who had neither the time, the training, nor the inclination for strategic thought.

By 1997 the CANUS index seemed to have been pared down substantially. Only six documents now referred to nuclear weapons activity, but other items had not actually been declared dead.[27]

THE SECRET AGREEMENTS

Although we now know much about the agreements that exist, this was not always the case. As recently as 1985 the government was still desperately covering its tracks by hiding information even from Parliament itself. In 1985, William Arkin, one of the world's finest nuclear weapons policy experts, told the Standing Committee on External Affairs and National Defence (SCEAND) that the list of military agreements given by the Mulroney government to the committee was missing some crucial items. The original list had been given to SCEAND by the minister of national defence, Erik Nielsen. Nielsen told the press that the censored titles "are classified documents that go to the heart of the nation's security...that traditions prevent from being disclosed."[28]

The eight agreements that the government thought were too emotionally charged to even mention, according to Arkin, were:

1. Exchange of Letters giving formal effect to the "Security Agreement Between Canada and the United States of America." September 1950.
2. Exchange of Notes on an Agreement between Canada and the USA to govern the establishment of a Distant Early Warning System in Canadian territory. 5 May 1955.
3. Exchange of Notes and Statement of Conditions governing the maintenance and operation of Upper Atmosphere research and cold weather testing facilities at Fort Churchill. 14 June 1960.
4. Exchange of Notes on consultation prior to the release of nuclear weapons. 16 August 1962. Note: There is no such agreement of this date, but there is the "Exchange of Notes on Consultation and Procedures related to NORAD alert status and the use of nuclear air defence weapons by CINCNORAD." Canadian Note #352 of 17 September 1965. The actual prior "authorization letter" to CINCNORAD released in February 2004 by DND. The EoN on consultation was exempted from the list.

5. Canada-USA Agreement concerning nuclear weapons for United States Air Defense Forces at Goose Bay and Harmon Air Force Base. 28/30 September 1963.

6. Exchange of Notes on storage of airborne nuclear anti-submarine weapons in Canada for U.S. forces. 27 July 1967.

7. Exchange of Notes on the Operation of United States nuclear-powered warships in foreign ports. 20 February 1967

8. Agreement between 24 NORAD Region and CFB Moose Jaw for IFR Flush Procedures at CFB Moose Jaw. 6 March 1973.

Prime Minister Mulroney himself weighed into the fray and directed his staff to find out exactly what was going on. They reported that the eight agreements "were inadvertently left off the released list," but also that National Defence and External Affairs had "sanitized the eight classified agreements from the list" the previous July. Staff were chastised and told that there would have been no tempest had they displayed better judgment when the list was first released in 1980 and then sanitized for the Standing Committee in July "without explanation."[29] Mulroney was satisfied with his staff's actions and let the matter drop.

Mulroney was told that they now planned to declassify agreements 2 and 8; retain the classification on agreements 1, 4, and 7; and cancel agreements 3, 5, and 6. He was then informed that once the cancellation took effect, "there will be <u>no agreement which calls for either the stationing in or deployment of USA nuclear weapons to Canada.</u>"[30] However, the new problem, aside from cruise missiles, was that the United States now wanted the right to transit the Strait of Juan de Fuca while submerged. Worse still for Ottawa, the United States felt no particular obligation to consult Canada on any of these operational deployment matters.

Within a year, three agreements would be cancelled and a few others would become redundant. Yet so great was the fear of the reaction posed by the public that the minister chose to obscure reality rather than admit the truth of the extent of the Canadian military complicity with the U.S. nuclear infrastructure.

The Mulroney government directed that a review of the state of Canada-U.S. defence arrangements be conducted and that those found without use would be cancelled. The problem was that no one really knew anymore which agreements were of use and even which were in effect. The Department of National Defence review took place during most of 1986 and even then turned up few of the older agreements. A message from David Karsgaard of the Defence Relations Division at the Department of

Foreign Affairs and International Trade (DFAIT) showed that National Defence held no records at all for at least thirty-one Canada-U.S. defence agreements.[31] External Affairs had to deal with the tricky relationship between the U.S. military and the Canadian government. Ottawa had to assure Washington that the review was "not a symptom of nuclear allergy," and that it was only for the purpose of updating joint defence arrangements. External Affairs instructed the Canadian embassy in Washington to tell the United States that the "door is also open to consideration of new proposals."[32]

One other secret alluded to by Arkin was that the United States planned to deploy about thirty-seven Mk-57 nuclear depth bombs on U.S. Navy P-3 patrol aircraft to CFB Comox in British Columbia and to CFB Greenwood in Nova Scotia during heightened tensions or emergencies. The Canadian government absolutely denied that this was the case, and said it had no knowledge of any such plans. External Affairs was charged with making discrete inquiries in Washington.

Since Ottawa was unsure of what plans really existed, External Affairs directed Ambassador Gotlieb to make enquiries. On 15 January External Affairs explained to Gotlieb in Washington that the whole affair had surfaced because of news items in Iceland and Bermuda. Ottawa faxed what little material it had to the United States and said that the next step "would appear to be for us to ask [the] USA to confirm or deny [the] accuracy" of the assertion. Ottawa warned that this "be done initially in a low key manner."[33] National Defence was also brought in and directed to make "discreet service to service enquiries to ascertain the validity of [the] allegations."[34]

The U.S. side was circumspect in dealing with Ottawa, fearing that anti-nuclearism had hardened even in the otherwise compliant Mulroney government. The assistant secretary of state told Gotlieb that as a result of their research, the United States had identified "certain agreements that might be seen to cover deployment of USA nuclear weapons to Canada." However, the secretary refused to comment on the content of the plans. The embassy had a bit more luck with the deputy director of the Office of Canadian Affairs, who gave embassy staff a list of "relevant agreements" which were immediately faxed to Ottawa.[35] Strangely, Deputy Secretary of Defense Fred Ikle later told Gotlieb that there were no such plans.[36] This was probably an attempt by the Reagan administration, which treated its partners in a less-than-forthright manner, to avoid telling the truth to a close ally about a very sensitive subject.

Now worried, U.S. officials asked if Ottawa was proposing a veto over such planning. The embassy wisely replied that the United States officially recognized that Ottawa already had a veto over actual deployments to and over Canada, and while the government had no intention of stopping theoretical exercises, there was a point at which such became plans. The view at External Affairs was that plans had to be passed to Ottawa "somewhere before the president signed [them]."[37] It soon became clear, when External Affairs told the ambassador it was true, that the Canadian government acknowledged that the agreements could be interpreted as the basis for nuclear deployments to Canada.[38]

What all this meant was that although the Mulroney government worked long and hard to clear the nuclear agreements from the books, at least one and possibly more agreements and or arrangements were still in place to allow the United States to deploy nuclear weapons to Canada for their own forces. This remains hidden from the Canadian and the U.S. public.

Having weathered his first captive-carry test, the prime minister was told a week in advance that during the next two tests the ALCM "will be *released* from the B-52," and will fly to the target area under its own power and guidance. Mulroney was warned that since this test involved an operational test profile, it was expected to "engender more objections [and] criticisms" than did the earlier captive carry tests.[39]

THE FIRST FLIGHT TEST

The first, live free-flight test of a cruise missile over Canada was considered most newsworthy in the United States. Journalists were briefed by officers at Grand Forks AFB in North Dakota before and after the test. Called 'Global Cruise,' test 85-5/14-NS/MO314 took place Tuesday, 19 February 1985, when missile #81-0512 was launched from the right wing pylon at 2:32 P.M. (7:32 P.M. local time). The B-52 captain, Major William Fitzpatrick, speaking about the launch said, "There was a thump and then it was gone." It took the missile nearly four hours to reach its target twenty-five hundred kilometres away, and it still managed to arrive two minutes early. Two CF-18 fighters were on hand for the final minutes of the flight over Primrose Lake. Greenpeace launched a 'cruise catcher' fishnet strung between several balloons near Wandering River, Alberta. The group had improved the catcher after a failed catcher-test the previous month. The ALCM passed within seventy-five metres of the airborne net and was also observed in flight by people in the North West Territories.

TEST # 85-5

19 February 1985 (Tuesday)
Global Cruise ALCM test
first live launch over Canada / first free flight over Canada
west route, free-flight
Missile profile: 14 (third flight, also called 85-5/14-NS/M0314)
319 Bomb Wing from Grand Forks AFB, North Dakota
46th Bomb Squadron
B-52G/58-0227
Crew: E-31
Captain: Maj. William Fitzpatrick
Co-pilot: Michael Walker
Electronic warfare officer: Mark Ashton
Navigator: Lt. Steve McKay
Radar navigator: Roger Gustafson
Gunner: William Pangborn
Primary missile: 81-0512 (launched)
Payload: NTIK-21
Position: RP-5
Secondary missile: 81-0525
Payload: NTIK-22
Position: LP-5
Launch mode: automatic
Launch altitude planned: 1,830 metres ASL
Launch time: 14:32:50.060 (07:32 local)
Engine ignition: 14:32:50.155
Warhead arming manoeuvre: 17:33:21
Fuze over target: 18:16:16.157
Time of arrival error: 147 seconds early
Flight time to target: 3 hours, 44 minutes, 26 seconds
Flight path distance: approx. 2,500 km
Notes: This mission was to have been flown in B-52/59-2594, but this
    aircraft was found to be unserviceable, so crew E-31 switched
    to 58-0227. Other aircraft involved in the test included two ARIAs
    from Fairchild AFB, and one AWACS from Tinker AFB. After the
    launch the B-52 returned to Grand Forks AFB and was loaded with
    ALCM 81-0449 to act as back-up bomber for 25 February test.

Once the missile passed over the target and performed a mock-detonation it was to fly until it ran out of fuel, at which point a parachute was deployed from the warhead compartment under the nose. The missile then flipped over and floated down to the snow-covered ground. As it fell it was tracked by Canadian Forces personnel in helicopters from CFB Cold Lake who would be the primary recovery team. A helicopter would airlift the missile, upside down, and deposit it on a snow pile near the recovery trailer. A fitting was attached for crane handling, and the missile then moved to its trailer for the trip back to Cold Lake and on to a base in the United States. Several missiles were re-used; one missile on display in the United States Air Force Museum flew more than five flight tests.

By the time the first cruise missile flew over northern Canada, the U.S. Air Force had already received over 850 ALCMs with the same guidance system used in the test version. Canadians realistically asked the question of why the tests of the guidance system were necessary if it was already approved for production and operational use. Was this the biggest gamble in acquisition history, or was the testing merely political in nature? Most Canadians seemed to conclude that the testing was nothing but a political action to please Washington.

TEST # 85-5A

25 February 1985
Global Cruise ALCM test
second free flight over Canada
west route, free-flight
Mission profile: 14 (fourth flight, also called 85-5A/14-NS/M0414)
319 Bomb Wing from Grand Forks AFB, North Dakota
B-52G/58-2594 code-named "Magma 1"
Crew: E-27
Primary missile: 81-0474 (launched)
Payload: NTIK-17
Position: RP-5
Secondary Missile: 81-0430
Payload: NTIK-18
Position: LP-5
Launch mode: Automatic
Launch altitude planned: 1,830 metres ASL
Time error: 63 seconds early to launch point
Launch time: 14:31:12
Fuze time: 18:16:58
Time to target: 3 hours, 45 minutes, 46 seconds
Note: "The missions were extremely successful for both weapon analysis and US/Canadian relations." (31 March 1985, "History 4201st Test Squadron January–March 1985," DCoS Ops, SAC/USAF, SECRET/NOFORN/RD)

It was still early in their ten years of being in office, and the Tories did not expect the anti-nuclear or the anti-cruise missile protests to continue. In fact, Brian Mulroney was told that future protests would be poorly attended, and that any opposition would be merely pro forma. While protests were dropping off in numbers and attendance, Canadians were still firmly opposed to the tests. The year would experience the height of support for the tests, but opposition would never be lower than a fully committed 50 percent. The anti-cruise missile groups were moving into a period of transition to other forms of protest. Canadians were out in the streets protesting the tests, while inside, government officials assured each other that the anticipated demonstrations "should not have any undue impact."[40]

With two free-flight tests now complete, the United States finally came to thank the Canadian government. The official military record of the second test notes "the missions were extremely successful for both weapon analysis and US/Canadian relations."[41] There was little in the way of acknowledgement for the Canadian effort to please Washington. At the 171st meeting of the Permanent Joint Board on Defence the U.S. team finally expressed their "appreciation for the co-operation and excellent support provided during the testing of the air-launched cruise missile in Canada."[42]

Typical AGM-86B ALCM flight in Canada

(mission 22 January 1986)

15:37:30.843	Launch
15:37:30.932	Separation verification
15:37:33	Engine ignition
15:37:49	Engine 100% revolutions per minute
15:42:01	Level at initial flight altitude
16:35:38	First map update
17:02:50	Second map update
17:28:38	Third map update
17:53:51	Fourth map update
18:10:25	Fifth map update
18:27:15	Sixth map update
18:32:07	Warhead arming manoeuvre #1
18:44:01	Seventh map update
18:49:06	Warhead arming manoeuvre #2
18:58:52	Eighth map update
19:10:16	Ninth map update
19:14:xx	Environmental Sensing Devise set
19:15:01	Arming system enabled
19:15:32.264	Fuze (simulated warhead detonation over target)
19:29:05	Tenth map update
19:41:37	Drop in engine power
19:41:45	Missile impact at range recovery zone

Flight to target time: 3 hours, 38 minutes, 2 seconds
Total flight time: 4 hours, 4 minutes, 15 seconds

The final legal chapter of the anti-cruise missile case was now being written. On 9 May 1985 the Supreme Court of Canada handed down its written decision on the cruise missile case, the appeals, and the question of court oversight of cabinet which had been heard over two days in February 1984. The Supreme Court of Canada ruled that there was no legal basis for any action against the testing of cruise missiles. The peace and disarmament movement was dismayed.

The court also ruled that decisions of cabinet could most certainly be reviewed by the courts. Cabinet was livid. The court had unanimously ruled that "the executive branch is duty bound to act in accordance with the dictates of the Charter." Chief Justice Brian Dickson added that the court had the authority to review any government decision. The legal struggle was over. Cruise missile testing would remain a fixture of the Canadian political and military landscape for another nine years.

In the summer of 1985, the Canadian military proposed becoming more involved in cruise missile tests. Up to this point they had been merely observers, but had concluded that fighter pilots could train against the small, hard-to-spot, pilotless aircraft in the high Arctic. The air defence staff considered the proposal, and it was then forwarded to the U.S. Air Force, with the expectation that actual interception flights would take place early in 1988. The reason for the significant planned delay remains unknown.

1986

The possibility of bad news for the Permanent Joint Board on Defence arose at the beginning of 1986. Brian Mulroney and Ronald Reagan had agreed at the Quebec Summit to make greater use of the PJBD on issues of international security. However, as the prime minister learned in January, the United States was now proposing to use the Board as a way of getting the Canadians to discuss Arctic sovereignty and joint Arctic defence strategies; they had in fact already brought up the subjects at the 25–27 November 1985 meeting. Mulroney was advised that both Minister of National Defence Neilsen and Secretary of State for External Affairs Clark believed that this was a dangerous road and that nothing should be allowed to happen through this channel.[43] Mulroney was willing to listen to the advice of two of his closest cabinet ministers.

The introduction of the second test corridor, known as the east corridor, was truly badly timed. The new route overflew less-populated areas, and had been planned for some time. However, it was announced immediately after the failed tests and the crashes of two ALCMs in early 1986. The public was led to the almost inescapable conclusion that the Canadian government no longer considered the system to be safe, but was still determined to continue testing. The new route would not be flown until an ALCM was captive-carry tested on 27 October 1987. The four-hour flight validated the new test route as suitable for ALCM use.

The Wednesday, 22 January test included something new – fighter attacks on the cruise missile. NORAD had seen the value of providing realistic training against a system that resembled a Soviet cruise missile in the real environment. The Commander-in-Chief, NORAD, ordered that both Canadian and U.S. air defence forces would fly mock defensive attacks against the USAF cruise missile as it flew from the far north to the Primrose Lake weapons range. Before the age of drug interdiction and the fear of aircraft being used as missiles, NORAD was mainly concerned with the Soviet long-range air force bomber threat to North America.

The media carried stories about penetrating Soviet forces and cruise missiles at this time, and it helped to justify ALCM testing in Canada. The fact that the USSR did not field an operational ALCM until at least 1990 was of little concern. The big scare was the emerging threat of the Tu-160, the world's largest and heaviest bomber, and its ALCM-carrying capabilities. In the end, the USSR acquired eleven bombers and then Russia obtained two new bombers from the factory in 2000-2001.

The result was the Cruise Missile Defence Initiative (CMDI). NORAD conceived of a program where pilots would train against the ALCMs being tested by Boeing and the USAF/SAC. Although Air Command was involved in every cruise missile test, only spotty records have been maintained of the participation of Canadian CF-18 fighters and Aurora maritime patrol aircraft. The Auroras were used to train crew in ALCM detection and tracking.

Although cruise missiles tend to fly slowly and in relatively straight lines, interception is strangely difficult. The first time that Canadian fighter aircraft participated in CMDI was in 1986. The event would grow with increasing participation of aircraft from both Canada and the United States. By 1990, the size and scope of the exercise had grown to a point where it concerned National Defence. Worries were expressed that there were too many fighters in Canada; that the size and scope of the exercise was too large; and that there were environmental and political concerns to be addressed. An internal debate was settled when it was decided that there would be no real problem, "assuming the exercise does not grow beyond reasonable levels."[44] This remained NORAD's only direct role in the tests.

Not all CMDI was done in Canada. There are several instances of Air Command sending pilots and aircraft to the United States for further ALCM interception practice. Much of this was done near Hill AFB in Utah which was a prime ALCM testing area.

TEST # 86-1

Date: 22 January 1986 (Wednesday)
Global Cruise ALCM flight test
Route: West route, free-flight
Mission profile: 20 (first flight, also called 0120/20-NS)
Unit: 379 Bomb Wing from Wurtsmith AFB.
Bomber: B-52G/58-0175
Crew: S-30
Primary missile: 81-0115
Position: LP-4
Secondary Missile: 80-1054 (launched)
Position: RP-6
Additional missiles: 10 on external pylons with train-
    ing ferry payloads or no missile at all
Launch mode: Automatic
Launch altitude planned: 1,830 metres ASL
Time of arrival error: 13.324 seconds early
First attempted launch: 14:36:54 (failed)
Launch time: 15:37:30
On target time: 19:15:32
Flight time to target: 3 hours, 38 minutes, 2 seconds
Premature missile termination: 19:41:45
Total flight time: 4 hours, 4 minutes, 13 seconds
Notes: The 21 January test was cancelled due to a fuel pump problem on
    the instrument aircraft. The back-up missile launched after the primary
    missile experienced a flight control system fault, but experienced high
    headwinds. Two CF-18 aircraft intercepted the ALCM en route. The mis-
    sile crashed five minutes before the scheduled end of the mission when
    it failed to perform S-curve manoeuvres to burn off fuel before landing.
    A search took several hours to find the ALCM twelve kilometres from the
    designated landing zone. As the fail-safe system and emergency para-
    chute system failed to function, the missile crashed and was found in
    three pieces. Four Greenpeace protesters were arrested during this test
    after forming a human chain to block the road into CFB Cold Lake.

Now Canadian protesters were being joined by high profile foreigners. In the past, Canadians had travelled to other countries to engage in protest; now others were helping Canadians. Mike Farrell, star of the popular M.A.S.H. television show, lent his support to anti-cruise missile forces while making a movie in Banff, Alberta. In Peace River, Alberta, the safety superintendent of the Canadian Aviation Safety Board, as well as the local RCMP, paid an unexpected visit to the home of an inventor. The man had designed a hot air balloon out of a dry-cleaning bag which was draped with thin metal strips designed to send back radar signals. He and a local group were planning on using the device as an anti-cruise missile protest when the 25 February flight passed overhead. After his idea was given to the Peace River *Record Gazette* but not published, the RCMP and the aviation safety inspector showed up at his home and informed him of the danger to low-flying aircraft. He declined to fly the balloon, but the cruise missile test flight failed anyway.

One of the more novel anti-cruise missile groups had no such trouble with the authorities. The Edmonton-based *People in Sport for Peace* started a petition for a nuclear-free Alberta and its staff jogged to the legislature to present their views.

The 1986 testing season was particularly embarrassing for the United States Air Force. Their 25 February free flight was a conspicuous failure when the cruise missile plummeted to the ice-covered surface of the Beaufort Sea. When the missile was loaded onto the carrying pylon under the wing of the giant B-52 bomber it already had an engine intake cover installed. The cover was to protect the small and delicate engine during the flight to the launch point. At launch a cord attached to both the cover and to the pylon would jerk the cover free as the missile fell away from the bomber. The lanyard was never hooked to the pylon. When the missile was released from the bomber the cover remained in place, depriving the engine of oxygen. So after only two and a half minutes of free flight, the unpowered missile smashed into the ice.

TEST # 86-2

25 February 1986
Global Cruise ALCM flight test
west route, free-flight
Failure
Profile 21 (first flight, also called 0120)
92 Bomb Wing from Fairchild AFB, Washington
B-52H/57-6495
Crew: S-01

Primary missile: 81-0238 (launched)
Payload: NTIK-6
Position: LP-5
Secondary Missile: 81-0239
Payload: NTIK-9
Position: RP-5
Additional missiles: 10 on external pylons with training ferry payloads
Launch mode: Automatic
Launch altitude planned: 1,830 metres ASL

14:29:48.721	Launched from B-52
14:29:48.811	Separation verification received by crew
14:32:10	ALCM level at pre-planned initial altitude (gliding)
14:32:28	ALCM impact on Beaufort Sea ice

Notes: This test failed when the missile impacted on the Beaufort Sea ice after two minutes, thirty-seven seconds of free-flight. An error in rigging the intake cover, which was not removed at the time of launch, caused the engine to fail to ignite. The B-52 was impounded at Wurtsmith AFB upon return. All other information on this flight remains a secret. A full investigation was held, and no problems found with the ALCM or with the bomber.

With the closing of the cruise missile testing season, attention was once again turned to other military matters. The North American Aerospace Defence Command agreement (NORAD) was renewed on 19 March, and came into force again on 12 May. There was no substantive change from the previous version of the agreement. This time the renewal documents were signed by Prime Minister Mulroney and President Reagan, while previous renewals had taken place at the foreign ministerial level.

Failed flights produced bad publicity and were used by opponents to rally thousands more against the tests. The Canadian government therefore proposed to use the 26 August cruise missile meeting at CFB Cold Lake as a venue to suggest that more captive-carry tests be carried out prior to resuming free flights in Canada. What they discovered was that more free flights had already been flown after the incidents in Canada. In fact, the planning teams had already tentatively agreed to one captive-carry test in Canada for 20 October 1986 and four free flights in the new year.[45]

Although the government put a hold on more tests after the accidents, it would not last long. When the decision was made late in the summer to resume testing, National Defence drafted a new public relations plan and statement, and then met with the privy council office and the prime minister's office to gain concurrence. The public statement, still classified as secret, did not mention the accidents but stressed that Canada was aiding in the quality assurance of its own deterrent, and that a second routing would soon be flown.[46]

Public relations continued to be a big problem for National Defence.[47] Although not responsible for the testing, National Defence bore the brunt of the opposition attacks. Two recent crashes of test ALCMs and the news of a newly proposed low-level flight training route in Alberta had stirred opposition. In addition, there was no difference in the minds of Canadians between captive-carry and free-flight tests: a test was a test, and all tests were unpopular. Another reason National Defence was experiencing problems was that the Reagan administration had publicly stated that it would violate SALT II limits with an ALCM-equipped B-52 bomber. In the minds of Canadians, these things were all reasonably connected, and they did not like what they were seeing and hearing. Brian Mulroney met with his security cabinet in mid-November to discuss the proper Canadian response to the U.S. break-out. The only outcome was that the Canadian government signalled its displeasure with the SALT II situation by asking that the ACM test request be withdrawn while allowing the continuation of the ALCM flights.[48]

The year ended with a bad omen for arms control and a harbinger of nuclear weapons to come. On 28 November the U.S. Air Force deployed the 131st ALCM-equipped B-52, thus violating the SALT II limits. When NATO foreign ministers met in Halifax, several denounced the U.S. policy as harming security by destabilizing the nuclear arms balance. NATO ministers were of course ignored by the very unilateral White House.

The U.S. violation of the SALT II limits strained Canadian credibility on the cruise missile. Instead of dealing with the facts and the real problems, the Mulroney government again lashed out at Canadians, thereby shifting the blame. Joe Clark, former prime minister and now minister of external affairs, said that protestors were playing into the hands of the Soviets and were serving to derail arms negotiations.[49] Clark said Mulroney had written to Reagan saying that it was an error not to respect SALT, but Clark continued his attack by spewing vague notions of freedom without showing any direct connection to the testing.

The Liberal Party, now free of Pierre Trudeau and not having to govern, fully endorsed a nuclear-free policy and the end of cruise missile tests. At the national party convention at the end of November, delegates overwhelmingly supported an end to the cruise missile tests. Lloyd Axworthy, one of the closest Trudeau associates, said that this was an about-face by the party, when in fact it was simply the grass roots of the party now being able to assert itself with positions it had always held on the cruise missile issue.

The new year looked bad for future testing, as it began with Prime Minister Mulroney sending a letter to President Reagan informing him that due to the U.S. stance on SALT II, "I'm afraid that on this particular issue we must agree to disagree." Mulroney wrote that Canadians would not understand why the West was seeking deep arms cuts while simultaneously exceeding the high ceilings on arms already in place. That said, Reagan was assured that "we in Canada remain ready to do our part to support the U.S. deterrent, and will, as I stated to you before, continue to test the air-launched cruise missile over Canada."[50]

The original CANUS T&E document stated that the agreement would run for five years, and be renewed automatically for a further five years unless there was an objection. Given that a twelve-month notice was required for withdrawal, the Canadian government would have to inform Washington of its intention not to renew by 28 February 1987. This never happened.

TEST # 87-1

Date: 24 February 1987 (Tuesday)
Global Cruise ALCM flight test
Route: west route, free-flight
Profile 21 (second flight, also called 0221)
Unit: 97 Bomb Wing from Blytheville AFB, Arkansas
Bomber: B-52G/57-6485
Crew: S-01
Primary missile: 82-0412
Payload: NTIK-18
Position: LP-5
Secondary Missile: 82-0407
Payload: NTIK-26
Position: RP-5
Additional missiles: 10 training ferry payloads
Launch mode: Automatic
Launch altitude planned: 1,830 metres ASL
Launch: 14:32:09.121
Fuze: 18:11:14.775
Flight time to target: 3 hours 39 minutes, 5 seconds
Total flight time: 3 hours, 52 minutes

Distance to target: 2,200 km
Time error: 47 seconds early over target
Notes: This was the first successful ALCM test after several failures in
the United States, and the crash on the Beaufort Sea in 1986.

Test personnel carefully monitored the use of engine cover lanyards to
prevent a recurrence of the previous loss of a missile. Despite the adverse
headwinds during the first third of the flight, the missile arrived early over
the target. Along the flight path the ALCM was intercepted by CF-18, CP-140
(Aurora) and USAF F-4 and F-16 aircraft as part of the initial Cruise Missile
Defence Initiative (CMDI) tactics flight tests. This was the last of the tests
conducted under the original CANUS T&E Agreement. The agreement was
renewed for a further five years immediately after this successful test.

The U.S. Air Force secretly flew the SR-71 spy aircraft over Canada
during this test mission. Results of this part of the test remain secret.
Three Greenpeace members were dug in at the edge of the Primrose
Lake, prepared to be under the target site in an attempt to foil the
test. The missile missed the impact zone and crashed into a wooded
area where it was later found in the proper upside-down position.

TEST # 87-2

Date: 1 March 1987
Global Cruise ALCM flight test
Route: west route, free-flight
Mission profile 21 (third flight, also called 0321)
Unit: 97 Bomb Wing from Blytheville AFB, Arkansas
Bomber: B-52G/57-6517
Crew: E-42
Primary missile: 83-0201
Payload: NTIK-26
Position: RP-5
Secondary Missile: 83-0202 (launched)
Payload: NTIK-21
Position: LP-5
Additional missiles: 10 training ferry payloads
Launch mode: Automatic
Launch altitude planned: 1,830 metres ASL
Launch time: 15:33:24.125
Fuze time: 19:12:32.353
Time error: 44 seconds early over target
Time to target: 3 hours 39 minutes, 8 seconds
Notes: Numerous weather problems, mostly in Alaska, caused the mis-
sion to be held back. The back-up missile was launched due to lack
of "identification friend or foe" (IFF) response from the primary mis-
sile. Moderate headwinds were encountered, and the missile was in-
tercepted by CF-18 and CP140 (Aurora), USAF F-4, F-16, and AWACS
engaged in Cruise Missile Defence Initiative (CMDI) flights. The U.S.
Air Force again secretly flew the SR-71 spy aircraft over Canada during this test mission. Results of this part of the test remain secret.

Cruise missiles came up again in the House of Commons when the New Democratic Party advanced a motion to end the tests. Mostly as a reaction to the U.S. violation of the SALT II limits, Pauline Jewett, the NDP foreign affairs critic, proposed "That this House, alarmed by the role of air-launched cruise missile deployment in violation of SALT limits and alarmed by threats to the integrity of the Anti-Ballistic Missile Treaty, aware also of the possibility of a negotiated elimination of all medium-range nuclear missiles in Europe, calls for strong initiatives by the government to strengthen arms control and disarmament measures including the termination of cruise missile testing in Canada."[51]

The vote was taken on 9 March, and under strict Canadian parliamentary party discipline, the Liberals, not even the ruling party by this time, once again flew in the face of public and party opinion. The motion was defeated: 27 votes in favour, 122 against.[52] Four Liberals voted with the NDP, showing cracks in the Liberal facade that would break open by the autumn.

Summers usually tended to bring a lull in cruise missile interest, and in 1987 Canadians pondered the dramatic Meech Lake Accord. But the agreement would never become law, as it failed to gain the approval of all the provincial legislatures. Manitoba led the fight against more power for Quebec by voting against the Accord, thus causing its death in June 1990.

It was now that Canadians learned that the Canadian government had finally raised concerns over the safety and environmental aspects of the cruise missile test corridor. Over 60 percent of the route was redrawn with the aid of Canadian Forces Northern Region. Colonel George Landry told Canadians that there was concern over areas of potential impact and that some portions of the route had been altered by more than one hundred kilometres.[53] This seemed odd as the environmental aspect had always loomed large in the cruise missile debate. Activists warned of environmental consequences that never materialized, and apologists said there was never any danger of anything at all. Of course, this was difficult to prove as the Initial Environmental Evaluation (IEE) had been done despite the exclusion of a crucial federal department; Environment Canada had not been invited to participate. In fact, the initial evaluation was so secret that National Defence told the press it would probably never be released. This eventually resulted in a raft of *Access to Information Act* requests for the document, all of which were denied by National Defence, and the denials upheld by the Information Commissioner. The report only came to public light when a reporter borrowed it from the National

Defence Headquarters library in Ottawa, promising to return it the very next day.

The Liberals, now in opposition, moved against the tests. On 1 October 1987 Liberal Party leader John Turner told the House of Commons, "the time has arrived to move forward in the world search for peace and for Canada to suspend cruise missile testing in Canada."[54] Liberal members rose as one and applauded the statement of their leader, now finally in line with party membership thinking.

The ruling Conservatives did nothing in response. The military planners had already sought and received authorization for flights in the new U.S. fiscal year beginning in October. In fact, one of the few cruise missile tests to take place outside the usual January–March season promptly took place on 27 October to validate the new, eastern flight path with a captive-carry missile. In the new calendar year free flights were scheduled for 19 January and 22 January.[55] The Liberals felt offended at this apparent slap in the face, but the timing of the flight was only a coincidence.

TEST #87-3

Date: 27 October 1987
Global Cruise ALCM flight test
Route: captive carry, eastern route validation
Mission profile: 32 (first attempt/first captive flight, also called 0132/32)
Unit: 92 Bomb Wing from Fairchild AFB, Washington
Bomber: B-52H/61-1031
Crew: S-01
Primary missile: 82-0597
Payload: NTIK-23
Position: RP-5
Secondary Missile: 82-0342
Payload: NTIK-21
Position: LP-5
Launch mode: Automatic
Launch altitude planned: 1,830 metres ASL
Launch time (simulated): 14:31:00
Fuze time: 18:26:00
Time of test flight: 3 hours, 55 minutes
Notes: This was the first flight over the eastern flight path. The missile remained in captive-carry mode, attached to the B-52 for the entire flight, and provided the data necessary to validate the suitability of the new route.

The year ended on a far more hopeful note for arms control and disarmament. United States President Reagan and Soviet General Secretary Gorbachev signed the INF Treaty banning medium-range nuclear missiles. The weapons, including the Soviet RSD-10 (SS-20) and the U.S. Pershing II and ground-launched cruise missiles, were to be totally destroyed.[56] This inevitably led to calls in Canada to end the testing as it had originally been justified as a support to NATO. The reasoning was that if NATO no longer needed or even had the weapons under a treaty with on-site inspection provisions, then Canada no longer needed to test the cruise missiles. A public opinion poll conducted by the Canadian Peace Alliance after the treaty was signed showed that 84 percent of the 8,655 people polled believed that testing should cease, while only 16 percent favoured continued testing. Even the Gallup poll showed that there was a 9 percent increase in opposition to testing. However, testing had to be done to please Washington, and the NATO argument was nothing more than a public relations justification.

1988

Once again cruise missiles came up in the House of Commons as they did during every testing season. Pauline Jewett proposed that the government give notice under the CANUS T&E "for the termination of cruise missile testing in Canada."[57] The motion never made it to the vote stage, as the Conservative majority had ensured that under procedures devised to keep non-majority business off the floor the motion died when the official time for private member's bills expired. What was different now was the level of outright Liberal support for the motion. Andre Ouellet, who would become foreign minister when the Liberals were returned to power in 1993, supported the NDP motion, saying that there was no longer any reason for Canada to continue to act as though nothing had changed in the nuclear weapons world.[58] Ouellet would have to bite his tongue in 1994 when Liberal leader Chrétien allowed the continuation of the tests for several more months. But that was still six years away.

█ TEST #88-1

Date: 19 January 1988
Global Cruise ALCM test
Route: east route, free-flight
Mission profile 32 (second attempt, first free flight, also called 0232/32NS)
Unit: 379 Bomb Wing from Wurtsmith AFB, Michigan
Bomber: B-52G/58-0168
Crew: S-01
Primary missile: 82-0222 (launched)

Payload: NTIK-29
Position: RP-2
Secondary Missile: 82-0545
Payload: NTIK-24
Position: LP-2
Additional missiles: training ferry payloads on LP-5 and RP-5
Launch mode: Manual
Launch altitude planned: 1,830 metres ASL
Time error: 8 seconds early to target
Launch time: 14:40:32
Fuze time: 18:24:04.485
Time to target: 3 hours, 43 minutes, 32 seconds

TEST # 88-2

Date: 26 January 1988
Global Cruise ALCM flight test
Route: east route, free-flight
Mission profile: 32 (fifth attempt, second free-flight, also called 0532/32NS)
Unit: 379 Bomb Wing from Wurtsmith AFB, Michigan
Bomber: B-52H/58-0168
Crew: S-01
Primary missile: 82-0545
Payload: NTIK-24
Position: LP-2
Secondary Missile: 80-0840 (launched)
Payload: NTIK-28
Position: RP-2
Additional missiles: training ferry payloads on LP-5 and RP-5
Launch mode: Manual
Launch altitude planned: 1,830 metres ASL
Launch time: 16:16:49
Fuze time: 20:00:19
Time to target: 3 hours, 43 minutes, 30 seconds
Time error: 12 seconds early over target
Notes: Mission control AWACS aircraft had no IFF contact with the primary mis-
    sile and only intermittent contact with the secondary missile. Canadian unit
    of CF-18 interceptors had constant IFF contact with the secondary missile, so
    permission was obtained from Canadian authorities to launch that missile.

3

Litton, Direct Action, and the CMCP

Bombing is Madness.
Litton Systems President, 15 October 1982

Covert security force surveillance of the anti-war movement in Canada had waned after the end of the U.S. war in Viet Nam. During that war, the RCMP had tracked hundreds of protests and organizations, and thousands of individuals for opposing the policies of another country. The cruise missile tests brought individual and organized opposition to the forefront again, and the Royal Canadian Mounted Police (RCMP), and subsequently the Canadian Security Intelligence Service (CSIS), was there to watch and spy and harass.

Protests against the testing of the cruise missile were closely watched by both the RCMP and by CSIS. Since the early cruise missile events predate the creation of CSIS, most of the covert security forces' involvement centres on the RCMP. Both forces were quite busy keeping track of Canadian citizens. The RCMP dutifully watched as young and old men and women peacefully marched on Parliament Hill.

But the most famous protest act of the cruise missile era was not at all peaceful, and no one in Canada saw it coming.

LITTON AND DIRECT ACTION

In 1979 Litton Systems Canada Ltd. entered the consciousness of a small number of Canadians, mostly in the aerospace and financial sectors, when it was announced that the Rexdale, Ontario company had won a massive contract to build guidance systems for the air-launched cruise missile. The company was pleased to announce fifteen thousand man-years of work, and the federal government was pleased to try to take some credit for those new jobs. The Canadian government had put up a $26.4 million grant of taxpayers' money to support the Litton bid and factory upgrade, and had also provided a $20 million interest-free loan to Litton to begin production.[1]

Litton received the contract, not from the U.S. Air Force, but from McDonnell-Douglas Corporation, the prime contractor on the air-launched cruise missile (ALCM) project. With an estimated worth of more than $1 billion over several years, this was one of the largest foreign military contracts ever awarded in Canada. In 1979 Litton built inertial navigation systems (INS), a computer that understood where it was on the planet at any time and could guide an airplane to any other location with an error of less than two kilometres per hour of flying time. Advances over the past two decades have increased the accuracy to within several metres.

Remembrance Day 1981 was the scene of one of the first mass protests at Litton, well before news of cruise missile testing had reached Canadians. Police arrested twenty-two people for protesting the production of nuclear weapons components in Canada. The Cruise Missile Conversion Project (CMCP) began to protest Litton weapons production, and to press for conversion to more peaceful items. This was completely misunderstood by Litton, whose executives thought that it was an attempt to unionize the workers rather than a plea for peaceful output. Soon Litton would install security to guard more against CMCP than against Soviet spies and saboteurs.

On 9 March 1982, just one month before the first navigation unit was completed, news of U.S. testing in Canada broke. People would quickly make the connection between the work done by Litton and the new weapons that would be tested in the Canadian northland. The first unit of the initial contract order for 102 guidance systems, costing two hundred thousand dollars, was handed over to U.S. Navy Admiral W. M. Locke, then director of the United States joint services cruise missile program, on Friday, 10 April 1982. Present at the ceremony was Minister of Supply and Services Jean-Jacque Blais, as well as a team of admirals, generals, and colonels from both countries. The initial contract for 102 guidance units to be delivered in 1981–82 was followed by another contract for 305 units in 1982–83. At the ceremony Locke commented that it was politically risky for the U.S. government to have allowed such a contract to be granted outside the United States, but that Litton had come through with a quality product ahead of schedule.

A seemingly unrelated event took place on the other side of the country. Four Cheekeye-Dunsmuir power-line power transformers on Vancouver Island were blown up. Two months later, more than a tonne of dynamite was stolen from the British Columbia Highways Ministry explosives storage facility near Squamish. A group calling itself Direct Action claimed responsibility for the 31 May blast that destroyed the four 109-tonne transformers. They would become known as the Squamish Five.

Brent Taylor had driven from Vancouver to Toronto in April 1982, and assuming a disguise, drew and photographed the Litton facility in Etobicoke, Ontario. In late July the group stole thirty-eight cases of DuPont dynamite stored by the British Columbia Highways Department and moved it a short distance into the woods. It would not be seen again until it destroyed part of the Litton plant on the other side of the country.

Commemorating the thirty-sixth anniversary of the atomic bombing of Hiroshima, some one hundred people marched for hours outside the gates at the Litton plant. Sixteen were arrested for trespassing, blocking traffic, and mischief. Police re-arrested organizer Tom Joyce, who had returned to the protest after being arrested the first time.

Of the one tonne of stolen dynamite, some 250 kilograms would be packed off to Toronto. Once the group arrived in Toronto with their explosives and blasting caps, they stole a blue 1980 GMC van from the Gauley-Gage Cartage Company and hid it in a rented garage. Taylor, assisted by Gerry Hannah and Juliet Belmas, set the explosives in the van and wired in the detonators. On the night of 14–15 October 1982, the van was carefully driven by Taylor to the Litton facility on Cityview Drive in Etobicoke, pulled up on the grass, and left partially obscured by shrubbery. He then placed an orange-coloured box in front of the van, and on top of it he placed two sticks of dynamite and a note. The note warned "DANGER EXPLOSIVES" and explained that the van contained more sticks wired to explode within twenty-five minutes.

At 11:18 P.M. the Etobicoke Police Department received a telephone warning from a woman about the bomb. She told them that the van contained an explosive device, and that as proof the police should look at the cardboard box in front of the van. She warned that "the threat was not to be taken lightly." Three police officers were sent to the scene; the first two, looking into the back windows of the van, saw a load of explosives. The third, Sergeant Harry Dungery, who arrived just before the explosion, said he saw an orange box of explosives on the ground in front of the van. He was walking towards the van as the two others were running away from it and towards him.

As the officers were wisely running away, the bomb detonated twelve minutes early at about 11:30 P.M. Constable Guy Courvoisier suffered a concussion that took him off work for two weeks. The Etobicoke Fire Department sent ten trucks and forty firefighters who dealt with the small blaze in only ten minutes. The hotel across the street lost many of their more than 520 windows. The front windows of the print shop five hundred metres down the street were blown in. By the end of the night eight people had been admitted to Etobicoke General Hospital, and another man was sent to Toronto Western Hospital for treatment.

The most seriously injured that night was the Litton security guard, Barry Blundon, who had been no more than ten metres from the van at 11:30 P.M. He suffered a skull fracture, broken leg, and other serious wounds, and he was seen bleeding from the chest. He was immediately admitted to the neuro-intensive care unit. He would remain off work for more than a year, spending most of that time in the hospital. Terry Chikowski, another security guard, was partly disabled with post-crisis depression. James Tayles, a Litton factory worker, broke his foot and suffered minor cuts and bruises. Leo Baily, another Litton worker, was off work for two weeks after inhaling smoke from the fire.

The head of Litton Canada told the press, without a hint of irony, that "bombing is madness." The explosion did not stop cruise missile navigation systems production. In fact, the area in the factory, well insulated from shock and vibration, remained unharmed. The test pedestals on which the delicate instruments were calibrated remained mounted on their steel and concrete columns sunk far into the soil beneath the factory. After the blast, technicians simply rechecked the alignment of the test-beds with the stars and the earth's axis to ensure the perfection of the TERCOM navigation instruments. Production was not halted.

Direct Action claimed responsibility for the bombing. Though they had never been heard of before in eastern Canada, they were now front page news. Their nine-page communiqué had been mailed to several newspapers, organizations, and individuals. In it they apologized to the injured and chided the Litton security officers for not noticing a strange van parked beside their guard hut. Divided into two parts, the first three pages apologized for injuring people. The remaining six pages was a political manifesto on Canada's role in the nuclear arms race. The bombers wrote, "understand and remember, the terrorists are those who have set the world on the brink of nuclear war, not those who are fighting this insanity and inhuman madness." The Litton communiqué and the one issued after the B.C. bombings were very similar in style and content.

Calling themselves Direct Action may have been the group's biggest stumbling point. Police from Toronto and British Columbia promptly began to investigate the similarities between the two letters from Direct Action, and to monitor a post office box used by *Resistance* magazine. *Resistance* had published both Direct Action letters and asked readers to write in about other actions. The box was rented by a friend of Britt Hansen. By following Hansen, the police arrived at the Squamish Five house at 1414 Tenth Avenue, New Westminster, B.C. The group was now under surveillance, even as they planned and executed a series of fire-bombings of 'Red Hot Video' pornography stores. On 22 December the police broke into the house to assist RCMP Corporal Robert Kuse in planting listening devices in the basement and kitchen.

The Canadian peace movement reacted to the bombings with the same horror felt by the general population. Bombing was a revolting act, and various spokesmen decried any such activities. Ken Hancock of the Cruise Missile Conversion Project (CMCP) said that he had no idea such a thing would happen in Canada, and that his group was "always within the frame-work of non-violence." However, he announced that their Remembrance Day vigil would go ahead and be more confrontational than before.

The Toronto police immediately targeted the CMCP for some violence of their own. The Remembrance Day protest saw more than seven hundred people stand against the Litton production. In direct violation of the rights of Canadians to protest in public areas, the local police had sectioned off part of Etobicoke and required identification for all who would pass down certain streets. Protesters were kept more than one kilometre from the Litton factory, and police carted away more than one hundred people. Although he was not there for this protest, Toronto mayor Art Eggleton, later the minister of national defence in two Chrétien governments, said he did not want nuclear weapon components built in Toronto, and that Litton should cancel the contract. He told reporters that the cruise missile "is just not wanted here." Eggleton was fortunate to not have to be minister of national defence during the first two Chrétien years, or he would either have had to approve more testing or resign.

The Remembrance Day vigil was followed almost immediately by a women's demonstration in which fake blood was splashed about and twenty-nine women were arrested for trespassing at Litton. Police vowed to always have enough officers on hand to deal with any demonstration and to protect Litton from Canadians. Four days later, the last in a series of rolling demonstrations struck Litton when protesters said they would try to make a citizen's arrest of Litton executives arriving for work. Police hauled in forty-four men and thirty-seven women in two buses converted into paddy wagons. Most were kept in prison without bail, having refused to accept as a condition of their release that they stay away from Litton and give up their constitutional right to protest. By the end of the protests, 129 people were awaiting trial.

It was not long before the police descended on the offices of various Toronto peace groups. The first to be hit was the World Emergency Project at Trent University, shortly followed by a raid at the CMCP offices in the Metropolitan Community Church. Four detectives searched the office for four hours, going through drawers, filing cabinets, and even the garbage. The warrant stated that the police were searching for material relating to the possession of explosives, and they carted away several boxes of documents. Police refused to give office coordinator Murray MacAdam and the CMCP lawyer a list of the papers they were removing, but it was noted that membership and contact lists were of prime interest to the police. The only police comment was that the raid had been a success and that it had turned up some new leads. Since the official investigation had already identified all of the bombers and had them under constant surveillance, the raid on CMCP and other peace groups was nothing short of direct and purposeful police harassment of citizens engaged in constitutionally protected free speech.

So eager was the government to bury the peace movement that its overzealous minions sometimes produced the opposite effect. When Ivan LeCouvie, an anti-cruise and anti-Litton activist, was arrested so that he could be questioned about the bombing, police gathered his papers and diary. The Deputy Crown Attorney for Etobicoke, Norman Matusiak, was so eager to convince Canadians that the peace movement was nothing but a Soviet-inspired, anti-American coven, that he made public the contents of Mr. LeCouvie's diary – a document unrelated to the case. The courts had little choice but to immediately release the defendant. Matusiak, the chief prosecutor of Litton protesters, was not forced to apologize and did not lose his job. Some Canadians, such as Sonny Jaworsky, urged in the letters to the editor columns that "it's about time for the RCMP to arrest these dummy protesters."

Direct Action, better known to Canadians as the Squamish Five, was captured by the RCMP thirteen kilometres north of Squamish on Highway 99 three months after the bombing. On 20 January the RCMP had disguised themselves as highway repairmen, stopped the truck, threw tear gas, and broke the windscreen. Two days after the first anniversary of the first cruise missile guidance system delivery, five people were formally charged with the bombing. Brent Taylor, Gerald Hannah, Ann Britt

Hansen, Juliet Belmas, and Douglas Stewart now began their years in jail.

Brent Taylor was the intellectual leader of the group, having written about revolution and urban guerrilla warfare tactics. He was sentenced to twenty-two years in prison for conspiracy to rob an armoured bank truck, explosives and weapons offences, auto theft, and breaking and entering. The nine-year prison term for his role in the Litton bombing was to be served concurrently with his twenty-two-year term already underway at Millhaven Penitentiary. He was eventually transferred to a medium security prison in Kingston, and in June 1989 he earned his bachelor of arts degree from nearby Queen's University.

Ann Brit Hansen, the group's philosopher and radical neo-feminist, pleaded guilty to the Litton bombing, and was sentenced to life in prison on 7 June 1984. The sentence of life was for conspiracy to rob a Brink's armoured bank truck. She also received twelve years for the Litton bombing, six years for the B.C. power station bombing, and several more years for the fire bombing of several pornography stores in and around Vancouver. At her sentencing she screamed at the judge and threw shreds of paper and a tomato. The tomato missed Justice S. M. Toy, who had earlier described Hansen as a menace to society. Hansen was eligible for a parole hearing seven years after being arrested, as her crime did not involve murder. She was released in 1990 and now lives north of Kingston. Her 2002 book on the events is entitled, *Direct Action: Memoirs of an Urban Guerrilla*.

Juliet Caroline Belmas, the youngest of the Direct Action five, was sentenced on 18 May 1984 to a total of twenty years in prison for conspiracy to rob an armoured bank truck, theft, fire-bombing, and the Litton bombing. Belmas had also pleaded guilty to the Litton bombing. She and Hannah, her boyfriend, were the soldiers of the group.

Gerry "Gerry Useless" Hannah, who had predicted that they could be sentenced to ninety-nine years if their bombs killed someone, received a total of ten years in sentences for his role in other group activities, but was not involved in the Litton bombing. Justice Toy, speaking about the actions of Hannah and Belmas, said that the crimes were not political but simply the work of common criminals. Doug Stewart, the electronics wizard for the group and a committed environmentalist, was given a six-year sentence for the power station bombing on Vancouver Island. He had planted the four charges of dynamite which did an estimated $3.7 million in damage. He was not convicted of the Litton bombing.

Direct Action failed to ignite a revolutionary wave of similar actions. It failed to garner support for other anti-establishment actions, and it failed to catch the imagination of the masses of Canadians who opposed cruise missile testing. In the end, Direct Action was a failed experiment by an unconnected group seeking to be the spark and vanguard of a new revolutionary movement. They had no effect on cruise missile production or on testing. The Canadian government's real fear was of the thousands of ordinary working Canadians in the streets protesting each test.

THE RCMP AND CMCP

The Toronto-based Cruise Missile Conversion Project (CMCP) grew out of the early 1980 loose grouping known as the 'April 26 Coalition,' which had as its objective the withdrawal of Canada from complicity with nuclear weapons plans and operations. Within the coalition, the Coalition to Stop the Cruise wanted a narrower focus on cruise missile issues. By the end of 1980, CMCP grew out of this activity. Although there were some one hundred similar groups in Ontario, the covert security force did not closely observe them during this period; the CMCP was primarily singled out for special attention.

The RCMP Security Service was most concerned by the seemingly inexhaustible supply of CMCP volunteers willing to involve themselves in civil disobedience. The covert force was also concerned by the advanced level of political activity and acumen, and their ability to gain steady and positive media coverage. The real problem the RCMP had was an admitted total lack of knowledge other than the address and telephone number of CMCP and that there had been many successful demonstrations.[2]

Immediately after the Litton bombing, the southwest Ontario area commander (SWOAC) for the RCMP approved a ninety-day, level 4 operation against CMCP.[3] The level 4 investigation is supposed to determine the input and influence of known subversives within a targeted group. The initial action was endorsed by RCMP headquarters, but the head of the review committee overseeing such operations said that a full Subject Evaluation Report (SER) would have to be submitted for further approval of the operation. The stated rationale for the operation was the past and present involvement of CMCP members in groups already under full level 4 surveillance by the covert security force.

The belief was that the operation against CMCP "might have some spin off benefits regarding the bomb attack."[4] The reality was that the RCMP never really thought CMCP was involved. The head of the RCMP criminal investigation division stated that his division did not view CMCP as a criminal group, and that it was of no interest to them. Despite these reservations by others, the area commander for south west Ontario, Chief Superintendent R. L. Duff, authorized an expanded operation against CMCP for the purpose of uncovering domestic terrorism and hidden subversives. Duff felt that the CMCP's political motivation was suspect and that it was probably infiltrated by communists.

The problem the covert security force now had was that because the RCMP did not really suspect the CMCP of the Litton bombing, the review committee stated that further investigation of the group should be discontinued as of 4 November, less than three weeks after the blast.[5] The Ontario region reacted quickly, and shot back that CMCP was a legitimate target and that the covert security force should know more about the group than passive collection of intelligence allowed.[6] The head of the daily operation against CMCP, Superintendent J. A. Venner, stated that level 2 operations would be allowed and that the Ontario region should use these powers. He was backed up by the officer in charge of operations for south west Ontario, Chief Superintendent I. W. Taylor, who quoted chapter and verse of the security service operations manual to the review committee, and stated that it was his intention to continue operations against CMCP.[7] The head of the review committee, F. J. Bosse, quickly wrote back that he could not agree to the CMCP being a target of the covert security force as it was not a subversive organization.[8] The Ontario region again wrote back to the review committee on 16 December and was 'shot down in flames' at the 19 January 1983 review committee meeting.[9] Only passive collection of intelligence against suspected subversive elements within CMCP would be allowed.

For the anti-nuclear movement the lesson of the first test remained buried in the files until the end of the century. Of primary concern to the government and to the Canadian military was that Canadians and their peace movement, with "the degree of antipathy to ALCM testing that appears to exist," would attempt to directly and physically interfere with the tests. National Defence worried about CFB Cold Lake being invaded by protesters and the tests being disrupted. On 23 June 1983 a number of Greenpeace protesters chained themselves to the fence at Primrose Lake weapons range. CFB Cold Lake updated its base security plan and everything was reviewed by Air Command Headquarters in Winnipeg.[10] Number seven platoon was placed on four-hour standby to counter potential protesters. Lieutenant Colonel Leigh was the security officer co-ordinating the project. The example of the Litton Industries bombings was still fresh in their minds, but the government misunderstood the Canadian anti-nuclear movement. From its earliest days, the violence had been perpetrated by the government through intimidation, burglary, or outright attacks on peace demonstrators – not the other way around.

Nothing had changed. In mid-June 1983 Canadians learned that either the RCMP or the new covert security force, the Canadian Security Intelligence Service, was currently engaged in tapping the telephones of the Cruise Missile Conversion Project. The information came from the attorney general of Ontario, Roy McMurtry who warned Ken Hancock of CMCP that his telephone had been tapped for "some considerable time."

The other incident which had to be dealt with was that the spy planted by the RCMP in the Parliament Hill peace camp had been exposed. Andrew Moxley admitted that he had spied on the anti-cruise missile movement for the RCMP since April 1982 and had been paid for information and to attend demonstrations. Moxley's handler was identified as RCMP Corporal Bruno Boyer who worked in the security service section. Boyer reportedly even accompanied Moxley to Kingston for a demonstration, staying in the motel awaiting word of events. Moxley had been in the Canadian Forces, had retired, and had worked as a prison guard in Kingston before moving to Ottawa. After the news broke, the peace camp announced that they would welcome Moxley back, but would probably trust him a little less.

In Parliament, Solicitor General Robert Kaplan said that any telephone interception in Toronto would have been done under the authority of the Ontario attorney general, but he promised to investigate.[11] On the Moxley problem Kaplan reported to the House of Commons that the covert security forces were "not performing any surveillance on [the peace movement]. They have no resources allocated to it, there is no one being planted... There is no one bringing information to the security services about it." Kaplan's answer could not have been more direct and clear; it was also not even slightly true. Whether he lied in Parliament or was lied to by the security services is unknown. What is known is that the RCMP had already amassed extensive files on the Cruise Missile Conversion Project (CMCP). Although these were totally hidden at the time, significant sections of the CMCP file have been released under the *Access to Information Act*,[12] and they show an extensive interest in the group and in general peace and anti-cruise missile activities during the exact time that Kaplan said there was no such interest. Canadians have had to accept that they have either a government which lies about its own activities against various constitutional freedoms, or a government which is not in control of the covert security force.

Neither the protests nor the bombing did anything to halt or even slow production, nor did they stop the government from supporting Litton. The Cruise Missile Conversion Project finally ended its attempt to influence this one small part of the nuclear weapons arms race. The group closed its office in August 1987. The protests did make the governments of the day very nervous. No other issue had caused the mobilization of Canadians in such massive numbers. Never had Canadians rallied on Parliament Hill in such numbers, other than on Canada Day and for the 11 September 2001 memorial service. No issue had ever produced such a flood of mail and telegrams and telephone calls. Trudeau was afraid of the ground swell, but chose to be aloof. Mulroney was so afraid that he delayed the advanced cruise missile decision by several years. Chrétien was only saved the embarrassment of the situation by the fact that the Pentagon withdrew the program early in his first term. The lesson is that mass protests work, but that the daily effect is invisible. Litton Systems of Canada still makes inertial navigation systems for both civil and military craft.

4

Stealth Cruise over Ottawa

There seems to be something in the Ottawa air
that fogs the brains of politicians.
Gwynne Dyer, 3 April 1987

BRINGING THE ADVANCED CRUISE MISSILE TO CANADA

Secret for years, the testing of the AGM-129, or advanced cruise missile (ACM), would only become known to the public in 1987, and would
only be confirmed by a frightened government in 1989.The earliest known
mention of the 'stealth' cruise missile as part of the test schedule came
in early 1984 when it was raised in an initial testing program proposal.
By early 1985 the proposal had already been dropped, along with the idea
of testing Pershing II TNF missile and ground-launched cruise missiles
(GLCM) at CFB Cold Lake. Deputy Minister Gordon Smith was relieved
to be able to tell the secretary of state for external affairs, "the USA has not
resubmitted initial proposals to test 'Stealth' cruise missiles in Canada."[1]
However, the public first heard of the idea in late 1983 when open discussions in Washington dealt with the need for testing the newer version of
the cruise missile.[2]

The January 1986 thirty-month forecast from the Pentagon listed the
AGM-129 advanced cruise missile for prospective testing in the distant future. In April the Pentagon submitted a full proposal to test the
ACM. After a preliminary staffing of the issue within National Defence
Headquarters (NDHQ), Minister of National Defence Perrin Beatty was
briefed about the initial proposal on 21 April 1986. However this was
kept quiet. Both National Defence and External Affairs asked for more
information. The Pentagon sent a full briefing team to Ottawa on 2 June,
giving sketchy details of the weapon but pushing hard for acceptance of
the new tests.

The first indication that the secretary of state for external affairs was
formally briefed on the subject came when the deputy minister and the

assistant deputy minister for political and international security affairs, Taylor and Sullivan respectively, told the minister about the proposal and the state of the affair in Ottawa. They warned that "the Canadian public is particularly well informed on ALCMs, and this will undoubtedly become a highly sensitive issue."[3] The secretary of state for external affairs was told that only a limited number of officials even knew of the ACM proposal, and that it was to be kept as quiet as possible. Both ministers now awaited the outcome of the review already begun by the Canadian Test and Evaluation Steering Group.

Another early formal indication of the strong U.S. desire to test the new and stealthy missile came during the 174th meeting of the Canada-United States Permanent Joint Board on Defence (PJBD) 10–13 June 1986 at CFB Chilliwack, British Columbia.[4] At that time, the U.S. delegation told the Canadian team, led by Allan Lawrence, that the United States definitely wanted to conduct captive-carry tests of the advanced cruise missile. The U.S. side also brought up the topic of increased joint co-operation in Arctic defence and the new Air Defence Initiative (ADI).[5] National Defence immediately set to work. Interestingly, although the minister of national defence had been briefed in late April, the deputy minister and the chief of defence staff were told that the Department of National Defence (DND) would have to act soon due to the ministers needing early notification on the ACM proposal. Both were also warned of the dangers of premature disclosure of this extremely sensitive topic.[6]

Lawrence wrote to Prime Minister Brian Mulroney and directly told him of the informal proposal by the U.S. side.[7] News of the proposal spread quickly at the highest levels of government, and within two days it was being discussed between the cabinet office and External Affairs.[8] Also, on 18 July, Assistant Secretary to the Cabinet for Foreign and Defence Policy Reid Morden (later to become deputy minister at External Affairs) gave Robert Fowler, the National Defence assistant deputy minister for policy, a set of Privy Council Office (PCO) comments on the ACM proposal.[9]

Prime Minister Mulroney was told that the cabinet office would be providing him with a detailed document on the implications of this new request very shortly.[10] At the end of the month Mulroney invited Allan Lawrence to meet with him and the two cabinet ministers involved in the CANUS T&E process, Secretary of State for External Affairs Joe Clark and Minister of National Defence Perrin Beatty.[11]

Although Perrin Beatty fought for the tests, Brian Mulroney remained unconvinced that this was the time to entertain another round of U.S. weapons testing. Concern had been growing over the U.S. intention to violate SALT II with ALCM-carrying bombers, and for the future of arms control in general. In addition, a total lack of a communication strategy and a dearth of available information made immediate testing appear to be a very poor idea. At the 12–13 August cabinet meetings in Newfoundland, Prime Minister Mulroney and his ministers decided to request that the United States withdraw the initial test proposal for the time being.[12] All were fully aware that the United States would react very negatively to the decision, and it was emphasized that Washington would have to be told that this was a principled stand based largely on the uncertainties in the direction of U.S. arms control and disarmament policy.[13]

Oddly, the message was not immediately communicated to Washington. When Ambassador Derek Burney and his staff at the embassy in Washington met with State Department officials Bader and Brown, the U.S. team asked about the state of the ACM request. Burney's staff matter-of-factly told the two men that advanced cruise missile issues were under active review in Ottawa; the U.S. team left with the view that it was business as usual.[14] Burney had already learned that despite its request, the Pentagon was still in the process of deciding whether it really wanted to begin ACM testing in Canada. Burney went on to suggest that this fact might make it easier to suggest, at a lower level, that the request be withdrawn.[15] Burney was instructed that the government could not agree to any such proposal at that time due to various arms control and public reaction reasons, and that it would definitely not be possible for the United States Air Force to test the ACM during the 1986–87 testing season. He was told that it would be best for all concerned if, for the present, the United States simply withdrew its request. Of course this was a temporary measure and Ottawa made it clear that "we would of course be open to considering a new ACM test proposal at a later date."[16]

The Canadian government had still not figured out how to tell Washington it was saying no. They came up with the idea of not actually saying no, but rather convincing the United States to 'withdraw' the request. External Affairs took the lead and secretly drafted the new approach. The plan was to begin by stating that Ottawa had for many months asked for background information, which the United States had been unwilling or unable to provide, and that without this information the Canadian government would not mount an effective campaign for such testing. Secondly, Ottawa would point out that both it and the public were experiencing considerable uncertainty as to the direction of U.S. arms control efforts, especially concerning President Reagan's intention to "break out" of SALT II launcher limits. Ottawa would bluntly tell

Washington that "we do not endorse the exceeding of SALT limits in the absence of some new limiting agreement."[17]

By this time two failed tests of the ALCM had been conducted in Canada, and Ottawa told Washington that a resumption of the tests with the ALCM, while the United States was violating SALT II, would bring much criticism from the public. It would be difficult enough to restart ALCM testing without complicating the equation with the ACM. The minister of national defence and the secretary of state for external affairs would therefore ask that under these circumstances the U.S. Air Force request to test the ACM be withdrawn. To back up the statement, it was proposed to tell the United States that "should the request to have the ACM test series removed from the test agenda be rejected, the Government would have no alternative in current circumstances but to refuse the request to test the ACM."[18]

Following the development of the plan, United States Ambassador Thomas Niles was handed a demarche from External Affairs on 9 September telling him of the decision. Niles communicated with Washington and was immediately instructed to visit the minister of national defence not the secretary of state for external affairs. The next afternoon Niles met with Perrin Beatty at National Defence Headquarters and made "suggestions that Canada was not a good ally." Beatty responded that there was no question of Canadian alliance under U.S. leadership, and pointed to the prompt permission given to the U.S. Navy the previous month when it wanted to use the harbour at St. John's, Newfoundland as a staging post for sea-launched cruise missile (SLCM) tests. Niles tried to bully Beatty into changing his mind, but the minister responded that the decision carried the imprint of the prime minister and cabinet. The most important message given to the United States that day was that Ottawa would prefer not to have to say no, as such a response now would make it nearly impossible to say yes later on.[19]

On 12 September, Perrin Beatty flew to Washington to receive instructions from United States Secretary of Defense Caspar Weinberger, and to formally deliver the bad news from cabinet. The ninety-minute meeting at the Pentagon did include discussion of the proposal. Beatty told Weinberger that cabinet had decided to ask Washington to withdraw the proposal. Weinberger agreed that the matter could be taken off the table for the moment. Further to the Canadian penchant for secrecy, the minister of national defence pointed out that the original U.S. request had been made in an unclassified letter to National Defence, and that knowledge of the proposal was now widespread within the military and External

Affairs hierarchy. This meant that the chance of a leak had dramatically increased. Although both men agreed to the plan that the proposal would be withdrawn and treated as though it were not current, Weinberger told Beatty that "a request to test the ACM would likely be forthcoming in the not too distant future."[20]

The Pentagon did withdraw the request, but only grudgingly. The Reagan White House regime was livid that Canada, especially Mulroney, had refused to consent to the testing proposal. No one in Washington was prepared to view this as anything less than a refusal.[21] They would wait less than one year before re-submitting their proposal on behalf of a weapon which was already struggling in testing and being attacked by Congress.

In Ottawa, officials at National Defence promptly set to work as they now expected a full formal request to immediately follow the visit. The Department of National Defence sought to prepare a public information strategy that would support a 'yes' decision by the Canadian government.[22] The reason for the continued action was that although a decision had been made, the issue was discussed within Privy Council twice during the weeks of 11 September and 18 September 1986.[23] But the answer remained a polite 'no.'

Ambassador Niles began regular pilgrimages to External Affairs and National Defence Headquarters to lobby for testing. Only two days after receiving the bad news, he met with the deputy minister at External Affairs and even tried to sound conciliatory, stating that Washington understood how sensitive this was for the government. The deputy minister told Niles that Ottawa felt Washington was "over-interpreting the decision and overreacting to it." Niles was informed that the decision by cabinet was not 'never,' but rather 'not now.'[24]

Not letting up, the United States ambassador met the secretary of state for external affairs for breakfast on 7 October, and harassed him about the bad cabinet decision. Niles said that the decision was especially worrying from the U.S. view – a point he had already forcefully made in his 22 September letter to the minister on the same subject.[25] With diplomatic roads blocked, the Pentagon and the State Department moved to the military sphere. The U.S. delegation once again brought up the subject at the 175th meeting of the PJBD; this time in Winnipeg between 14 and 17 October 1986.[26] Cabinet would not be moved on the issue.

The stage for cruise missiles, and arms control in general, was about to change dramatically. At a historic meeting between President Reagan and General Secretary Gorbachev in Reykjavik, Iceland in October 1986, both governments agreed to equal cumulative ceilings of systems capable of carrying one hundred Intermediate Nuclear Force (INF) missile warheads, none of which would be deployed in Europe. The Soviet Union also proposed a freeze on shorter-range missile deployments and agreed in principle to intrusive on-site verification. The final INF Treaty was now only a year away, and the signature of this distinctly European agreement would send Canadian bureaucrats scattering for new justifications for cruise missile testing.

Back on the diplomatic side, United States Secretary of State George Shultz invited the secretary of state for external affairs to Washington to discuss the matter on 21 November. Shultz was under the impression, as were others in Washington, that this was a decision by one cabinet minister, which could be easily reversed.[27] The State Department did not yet understand that a full cabinet decision had been made, and that it would take another full cabinet decision to reverse course. The secretary of state for external affairs told Shultz that the request had come as a surprise to Ottawa, and that the government was very sensitive to the topic and to public reaction. When Shultz asked the secretary of state if he was telling him that the Canadian government would be able to agree to the request, the answer given was in the negative. However, Shultz was told that it was not possible to know then what the outcome would be if the matter were carefully managed.[28]

Having been lobbied by the Pentagon, the State Department, the Permanent Joint Board on Defence, and the White House, members of the Cabinet Committee on Foreign and Defence Policy met on 26 November to take stock of the situation. Aside from discussing the new defence white paper, both the minister of national defence and the secretary of state for external affairs told their cabinet colleagues about the loud overtures from Washington. External Affairs noted that Minister of National Defence Perrin Beatty was overly optimistic about the arms control environment, especially as the United States was going ahead with violating SALT II.[29] Of course, no reversal of the decision was made, and the answer remained a polite 'no.'

The one overriding concern of both the government and the bureaucrats was that the secret would leak. The original request was unclassified and fairly broadly known at the higher levels of the military and diplomatic communities. Both the minister of national defence and the secretary of state for external affairs were fully prepared for questions from the press or from members of Parliament. They were to state, but only if asked, that "there is no request now under consideration for the testing of the ACM in Canada."[30]

THE STEALTH CRUISE MISSILE

Following on the heels of the unstable but successful stealth fighter aircraft, in 1983 the U.S. Air Force awarded General Dynamics a contract to develop the AGM-129 ACM. Initial deployments began in 1991. The USAF wanted one thousand copies of the advanced cruise missile (ACM), but this number was progressively reduced to 640 and then 460 in 1993, the year production wrapped up.

AGM-129 Advanced Cruise Missile

stealth strategic nuclear cruise missile

Prime contractor: Hughes Missile System Company
Wingspan: 3.10 metres
Length: 6.35 metres
Body diameter: 0.64 metres (height) x 0.70 metres (width)
Weight: 1, 250 kilograms
Engine: Williams International F112-WR-100 turbofan
Thrust: 732 U.S. pounds
Guidance: Inertial with terminal laser radar
Range: 3,680 kilometres
Speed: 800 km/h
Warhead: W-80-1 (150-170 kt yield)
Total built: 460 (1987-1993)
Cost (missile only): $6.9 million each
Cost (test payload): $500,000 each
Deployed: up to 12 on each B-52H and 18 in each B-2

Various features contribute to the stealth of the ACM. The shape of the body and nose lowers the radar cross-section signature of the missiles, and the design of the jet exhaust area minimizes the infrared heat signature produced by the engine. The addition of radar absorbent paint, and minimal-vibration wings and tail, produce little to radar track the missile. However, the entire ACM appears clearly to radar from above.

The guidance system uses lasers to map the ground image, thereby reducing the electronic signature of the missile itself and adding to the stealth characteristics. Terrain updates and an inertial mid-course guidance system will take the missile from the host bomber to the target area.

A laser radar terminal phase guidance system will then take the missile on a dive to within a few metres of the target.

The ACM is deployed to half of the remaining B-52H fleet, and is carried on the under-wing pylons. The missile can also be launched from the rotary system in the twin bomb bays of the B-2 stealth bomber. Several missiles have been converted to conventional weapon carriers for use in ongoing wars. Operational flight testing of the AGM-129 ACM was called 'Global Shadow' by the United States Air Force.

1987

During a January meeting in Ottawa, U.S. Deputy Assistant Secretary of Defense for International Security Policy J. Maresca told the assistant deputy minister for policy at NDHQ that they were still very interested in testing the advanced cruise missile in Canada. Robert Fowler responded that he hoped for a minimum delay between the official request, the official response, and the actual flight testing.[31] Maresca left Ottawa quite pleased with the Canadian attitude, thinking that Ottawa would soon be saying yes.

So far, all had been kept secret; then a cabinet minister chose to tell an untruth in the House of Commons, and the Mulroney government was exposed. It all started when the peace group Project Ploughshares asked a researcher to request cruise missile documents from National Defence under the *Access to Information Act* (ATIA). Ken Rubin, renowned as Canada's most prolific ATIA requester, found the 'smoking gun' records. The documents were heavily over-severed, but a staff officer in the policy office had failed to delete a single reference to the minister of national defence being briefed about the AGM-129. The document, entitled briefing note #50, and captioned "Project Proposal for Captive Carry Tests of the AGM-129 Advanced Cruise Missile," showed that Minister of National Defence Perrin Beatty had known about the U.S. request since at least 21 April 1986.[32]

Project Ploughshares researcher Bill Robinson gave the document to Pauline Jewett, an NDP Member of Parliament. On Monday, 2 February 1987, Jewett used it as a weapon when she asked Beatty if the United States had made such a request. Beatty denied it, and Jewett said that a document from his own office proved otherwise. Trying desperately to defend his government Beatty stated, "there is no request before Canada at the present time to test the advanced cruise missile."[33] Although this was technically true, as Mulroney had told the White House not to make any requests on this difficult subject, it was not the whole truth; the matter was simply in abeyance. Beatty was promptly confronted by Ms. Jewett, who said it was clear that either he was keeping the Commons in the dark or he had no idea what was going on in his own department.

Beatty had failed to follow the advice of his office, which had already told him that the proper answer to any question was that there was no such request before the Canadian government. Beatty had simply said that there had never been such a request from the United States, and everyone already knew this was false.[34] He equivocated on the subject, as National Defence had done just days before it received the new 1987–88 forecast of intended U.S. tests from the Pentagon, and cruise missiles were now mentioned only in the generic.

Beatty's first act upon leaving question period that day was to rush back to National Defence Headquarters and order a clamp-down in the Access to Information Directorate (DAIP). From that moment nothing would be allowed to go out without being vetted by staff from the minister's office. This situation would persist until Beatty was replaced by the slightly more flexible Bill McKnight in 1989. The next day Pauline Jewett again attacked Beatty for being evasive. This time she asked for the official response to the original U.S. request to test the advanced cruise missile. Beatty, hoping to avoid yesterday's mistake, answered that there was no current request, but avoided answering the actual question.[35]

Having acquired the title of the briefing note, Project Ploughshares went after the document itself. A request to the Department of National Defence yielded nothing, and a complaint to the Information Commissioner yielded the same. The Information Commissioner had been convinced by the government that the entire briefing note, administrative markings, signatures, and so forth had been received in confidence from a foreign government, and that the release of any part of the document would damage the national defence of the country and harm the conduct of Canada's international relations.[36] Given that the note was from the assistant deputy minister for material at National Defence, this is not a reasonable interpretation.

The Mulroney government wanted desperately for this issue to go away, and they made all possible efforts to ensure that information did not get out, even by legal means. The Department of National Defence was in violation of the bilateral agreement on these matters, which had been negotiated with the United States. By agreement Canada stated that the release of information on any project under CANUS T&E "shall require" prior consultation and coordination with the Pentagon.[37] National Defence had failed to undertake consultations, and the Information Commissioner had failed to enforce the regulation.

The cat was out of the bag, but the Tories would try for the next two years to keep detailed information from leaking out, and to keep this issue at arm's length. In fact, Mulroney and his security cabinet tried to hold off this request for almost three years. They had a deep and abiding fear of the public on this issue, having witnessed several years of massive protests, and knowing that cruise missile testing had never been popular anywhere in Canada. Even normally right-wing Alberta, a Tory stronghold, had a great number of cruise missile protest groups and thousands of citizens openly demonstrated in the streets. Letters, cards, telegrams, and telephone calls continued to pour into the offices of cabinet ministers and the prime minister himself. By the thousands of pinpricks, the anti-cruise missile movement had made an impact and frightened the government into inaction. It was only the eventual massive pressure by Washington which forced the issue in Ottawa. Had Washington not made it clear that the ACM would be tested, it is very probable that the Mulroney government would never have authorized the project.

The Reagan administration continued to press Ottawa for a yes answer. Secretary of Defense Weinberger again wrote to Perrin Beatty on 12 May, telling him that ACM testing was an urgent matter and that preparations were well under way. However, National Defence had learned from contacts inside the Pentagon and from the office of the secretary of defense that the ACM testing program was not that advanced, and that the United States was still not yet ready to fly the stealth weapon in Canada. National Defence believed that an actual request "may not in fact be imminent."[38]

Over the next ten months, Prime Minister Mulroney received advice from various quarters in Ottawa, and pressure from Washington. The pressure came in the form of the renewed request received by National Defence from the Pentagon on 23 July. The U.S. Air Force now requested consent to carry out two captive-carry missions during the first quarter of 1988 on the same route used for the air-launched cruise missile.

On 13 August 1987, Mulroney finally decided on his response,[39] and directed that the U.S. government be told "the Government of Canada wishes to acknowledge receipt of the U.S. request to test the advanced cruise missile (ACM) over Canada. This is an important issue for Canadian government policy, one which touches upon a variety of considerations including progress in East-West relations, Alliance security requirements and bilateral relations. The Government wishes to accord this request the full and deliberate consideration it deserves. A final decision on this issue will therefore take time. I would expect, however, that we may be able to come to a decision by the end of the year."[40] Washington was again on notice to stop asking difficult questions.

Back in Europe, at the June 1987 meeting of the North Atlantic Council, NATO foreign ministers had decided to support global elimination of all U.S. and Soviet intermediate-range and shorter-range missile systems. Canada also supported this resolution. An Intermediate Nuclear Force deal was at hand which would destroy all ground-launched cruise missiles and the government's excuse for testing.

The Tories had to appease the United States or at least not incur its wrath. This meant keeping the door open to the proposal without necessarily letting it in. In a way, Prime Minister Mulroney was saying, "Not necessarily cruise missiles, but advanced cruise missiles if necessary," much as Mackenzie King had said decades before when he speaking of conscription. Lines of communication were kept open on 2 September 1987 with a well-worded letter from Perrin Beatty to Caspar Weinberger.[41] Drafted by the Privy Council[42] and vetted by External Affairs,[43] the Beatty letter would serve to satisfy the Pentagon by promising to consider its request at a future date, and by tacitly stating that a yes answer was very possible if the request was held back for some months.

One important factor that made the entire process more difficult for the Tories was that their opposition to the cruise missile was tied directly to an arms control agreement. In the autumn of 1987 it became obvious to Ottawa that the United States and the USSR would be signing the INF Elimination Treaty, and that the only requirement the Tories had laid down for ending the tests would be fulfilled. The fact that they were now being pressured by Washington into accepting ACM tests made the whole situation worse in Ottawa.[44] While in opposition, the Tory defence critic had told the House of Commons that the Conservatives had undergone a rigorous debate on the topic, and decided that they would end their support for testing if an INF elimination treaty was signed. When Jeff Sallot of the *Globe and Mail* telephoned Colonel Fraser, the chief of continental policy for assistant deputy minister (policy), he specifically asked about the Tory commitment to ending testing. Fraser told Sallot, "nowhere has the government committed itself to cessation of cruise missile testing in the event of an INF agreement."[45] The nuclear world was changing quickly.

On 8 December 1987, Mikhail Gorbachev and Ronald Reagan signed the historic Intermediate Nuclear Forces Elimination Treaty, which would result in the destruction of hundreds of missiles in the European theatre over a four-year period. In late April and early May 1991, the United States eliminated its last BGM-109G cruise missiles and Pershing II ballistic missile systems covered by the INF Treaty. The last Soviet SS-20 was destroyed on 11 May 1991. A grand total of 2,692 missiles were completely obliterated under the sweeping treaty provisions. The Mulroney government went out of its way to ignore this entire event and to ensure that it never had to live up to a commitment made in the House of Commons while it sat on the Opposition benches. Given that at one point the United States had proposed testing the ground-launched cruise missile in Canada, the Mulroney government just wanted it all to quietly go away.

The public, witnessing the signing of the INF Treaty, the diminishing of the Cold War, and the United States moving to test the advanced cruise missile (ACM), was once again in a mood to protest. In Winnipeg, Canadian Forces reservist Private Doug Harney of the 17th Service Battalion was seen participating in a march on Portage Avenue protesting that day's cruise missile test over northern Canada. Harney was disciplined in a court martial, pleading guilty on 27 January 1988 to a charge of committing an act to the prejudice of good order and discipline under the *National Defence Act*. He was fined an undisclosed sum. His crime was that he wore his uniform in the march. The Department of National Defence stated that as a private citizen he had every right to protest, but that he could not wear the uniform or winter dress while doing so.

Another year had gone by, and continued pressure forced the prime minister to directly address President Reagan.[46] Joe Clark, once the prime minister himself, and now the secretary of state for external affairs, sent a memo to Mulroney urging action on the request.[47] Clark was feeling the heat as well, and was asked a written question (Question 242) that had been tabled in the House of Commons by Dan Heap. Heap asked whether Canada had ever agreed, formally or informally, to permit ACM testing, and on or for what date. Clark responded in the negative.[48] In fact all Clark would say was "no." While successive governments in Ottawa had the habit of being less than direct with the public, this issue was straining even the Mulroney cabinet.

1988

The new year began with Secretary of State for External Affairs Joe Clark being lobbied by United States Secretary of State Shultz at a meeting in

Paris on 6 January. Shultz said that the U.S. Air Force wanted to fly two captive-carry tests of the ACM in March, and needed an answer by the end of January. Clark told Shultz that he and Beatty had already submitted a recommendation for testing to Mulroney, and that he expected cabinet to deal with the issue before the end of the month.[49] In Washington, Derek Burney had become convinced that Shultz would approach Joe Clark on the issue again in five days and warned that the request was now being seen as a litmus test of Canadian solidarity.[50] Just before the 11 January meeting with Shultz, Mulroney instructed Clark to obtain an overall reading of the importance of the ACM to the White House, and on the state of the general bilateral relationship.

Shultz did not like what Clark had to tell him, and on 3 February a follow-up letter arrived in Ottawa.[51] Shultz indicated that the United States was prepared to wait until 12 February for a positive response, but that the question was growing more and more urgent. The big push for a response came from United States Ambassador Thomas Niles who wrote directly to Minister of National Defence Beatty for an answer. Niles reiterated what Bob Fowler had already told his minister about the advanced cruise missile proposal.[52]

On 4 February a U.S. briefing team appeared in Ottawa to press the technical case for testing. Bev Dewar and David Karsgaard from External Affairs would be briefed by Brigadier General Glenn from the office of the secretary of defense, George Bader from the NATO office in the Pentagon, and Lt. Colonel McCreary from the Pentagon. Ambassador Niles also sat in on the briefing at the Fort Pearson (External Affairs headquarters) A-2 operations centre conference room. Karsgaard assured the team that the room had been swept for bugs. Although the U.S. team put a bright face on the testing and the program as a whole, the Canadian government already knew from government sources in California that the ACM was already some eighteen months behind schedule. Ottawa was finally starting to get some good information.

Despite the good information and the knowledge that the majority of Canadians were against even the ALCM (air-launched cruise missile) tests, Joe Clark was advised to recommend the tests to Mulroney and cabinet. On 9 February Joe Clark was told that a decision to refuse or further delay ACM tests would be criticized by many in Washington "and could cause serious damage to our security relationship." In addition, refusal could "undermine acquisition of technology central to the success of our new defence policy."[53] The only real warning given was that too prompt an acceptance might be portrayed as an attempt to buy the North American Free Trade Agreement then being finalized.

The security cabinet met on 11 February 1988 and decided once again, despite all the pressure being applied by the U.S. administration and Ottawa bureaucrats, to say no to the new tests. Joe Clark immediately telephoned George Shultz and explained the decision. Clark then followed up with a letter stating that "the Canadian Government is not in a position to respond positively to the United States' request," and that the government concluded "it is not in our best interests to proceed at this time."[54]

The White House swung into action, immediately firing off a letter from the president to the prime minister. Written as though from a parent speaking to a child who refuses to behave in the understood manner, the letter began with Reagan telling Mulroney, "I am deeply disappointed to learn of your government's decision not to approve" advanced cruise missile testing. Reagan then blamed Mulroney for increasing the costs of the ACM program and for setting back the testing program, and ultimately for stalling the modernization of U.S. strategic nuclear forces. In closing, Reagan refused to accept no for an answer, telling "Brian" that he hoped "that you will reconsider this matter on an urgent basis."[55] The letter was all the more meaningful because the relationship between Mulroney and Reagan was one of the few which was both personal as well as official, and was considered to be of a very special character by the White House.[56]

Mulroney knew that the Reagan letter, coming from his closest political ally, would require a direct and apologetic response. He personally wrote to Reagan on 16 February, telling him that although the U.S. request could not be considered "at this time," he and his cabinet would "consider seriously a formal request to test the ACM at a later date."[57]

It was at this point that the government decided to change their public information tactics from evasion and half-truths to direct responses based on reality. The Prime Minister's Office, External Affairs, and National Defence agreed on 29 February that questioners would be told 'yes' if they asked whether a request had been made, and that the Canadian government's reply had been that it was not then prepared to approve such tests for the testing season ending 31 March 1988.

Again the U.S. delegation put the issue on the agenda for the Permanent Joint Board on Defence talks at the 1–4 March 1988 meeting at Fort Ord, California,[58] and again the Canadians said no. Under such continued pressure, Mulroney directed Joe Clark to speak with Secretary of State George Shultz about the matter during the NATO meeting on 9 June.

Mulroney hoped that this might allow the NATO summit to be a basis for the ultimate decision.[59] Clark was instructed to tell Shultz that the February decision was not a rejection of strategic modernization; rather, it reflected the government's judgement that it was not in Canada's best interest to proceed at that time.[60] It also appears that Clark led the U.S. team to believe that a final decision could be expected from cabinet by the end of January 1989.[61] This would provide the four weeks of preparation time required to set up the two ACM captive-carry tests scheduled for March.

Government offices were deluged with public enquiries about the new tests. National Defence was the recipient of most of the letters and calls, but had no power to make a decision and was not responsible for any part of the program. The Department of National Defence appealed to External Affairs and the Prime Minister's Office to come up with a public line which would be of some use in dealing with questions. The PMO agreed that the External Affairs line was the best and directed that it be shared with DND.[62] Many were amazed that the secret remained a real secret. The External Affairs deputy minister wrote that the knowledge has "by a miracle not leaked yet," especially as the U.S. military "go on talking openly about it to all sorts of people, Canadian and American, who have no need to know about it."[63] Apparently the head of the U.S. Strategic Air Command was telling various people about plans to test in Canada, and these words had made it back to diplomatic ears in Ottawa.

Chief of the General Staff General Manson and Deputy Minister Dewar provided the minister of national defence with a quick briefing and recommendation on the release of information on ACM testing.[64] The minister was told not to answer questions and to continue to say that any such negotiation was a secret. This reiterated the advanced cruise missile testing public disclosure policy set on 13 April and 31 May 1988,[65] but was contrary to that agreed to by PCO, External Affairs, and the Pentagon.

During the late summer of 1988, Mulroney was bombarded with more information on the ACM proposal.[66] He put off making any final decision, hoping that circumstances would change, and that his government would not have to be the ones to allow this new series of tests which were so unpopular with Canadians. It was a faint hope strangely based on intelligence coming from Washington on the state of the ACM program. The Canadian government had learned that the missile program was under intense attack by Congress, and that funding was being held up pending a better testing record. This meant that the probability of the U.S. Air Force seeking tests in Canada to maintain the program and to continue to receive massive infusions of tax dollars had increased. Clark asked Shultz that further requests be put on hold until after the U.S. presidential election that upcoming November. Shultz agreed, but stated that a new request would be submitted before the end of December 1988.

With the election of George Bush as the president to succeed Ronald Reagan, Canada was once again faced with the immediate prospect of more ACM requests. Immediately after the U.S. election, the Prime Minister's Office, National Defence, and External Affairs consulted with each other with a view to once again forestalling any re-submitted request. They agreed to a plan and on 23 November informed the U.S. embassy in Ottawa that "no formal request should be submitted prior to passage of the FTA [free trade agreement] legislation."[67] Clark was briefed and agreed to the plan on 12 December.[68] Clark was to make the case that since free trade and acid rain were of much greater concern to both countries, and since both would generate much heated debate, it would be prudent to remain focused. Conversely, once free trade passed Congress and Parliament, ACM testing could not jeopardize the agreement's prospects. If necessary, Clark would again mention the Canadian stand on waiting for the completion of START, the strategic arms reduction treaty.

A multi-pronged strike against the request began with External Affairs asking the U.S. embassy chargé d'affaires Montgomery to delay the re-submission of the request until the new year. At National Defence, General Huddleston briefed the U.S. military attaché on the need for a delay. In Washington, the Canadian embassy made direct representations to the State Department telling them that "we do not want to receive [the] request before FTA" (the free trade agreement) passes on New Year's Day 1989.[69]

1989

The new year and the final days of the Reagan regime brought new arm twisting to the prime minister's office. On 17 January, only days before finally leaving office, Reagan asked Brian Mulroney to ensure that the advanced cruise missile would be tested in Canada.[70] Of course Reagan was operating on the assumption provided by Canada to George Shultz in Paris that a positive decision could be expected by the end of January, and he now expected it to be done.

Derek Burney immediately visited the State Department, both as an introductory accreditation call, and to discuss various pressing matters with Deputy Secretary of State Whitehead. Whitehead told Burney that on some issues the Reagan team was "not rational," but that the United States still waited for a positive response. Burney limited his reply to stating he was aware the request had been delivered.[71]

As a result of the letter given to Perrin Beatty by U.S. ambassador Niles, and due to the pressure from the Republicans in Washington, a cabinet planning and priorities meeting on the issue was scheduled for 31 January. Both the minister of national defence and the secretary of state for external affairs signed a joint Memorandum to Cabinet on the issue recommending they all agree to testing of the advanced cruise missile.[72]

Minister of National Defence Beatty sought to provide ministers with a detailed package of documentation on the issue, and other members of Parliament with a less detailed package. The package was to be provided to members immediately after the decision would be announced, and the decision was expected to be made the same day as the cabinet meeting. Interestingly, the deputy minister was directed to have samples of packages for both possible outcomes ready by 27 January, three days before the cabinet meeting.[73] Back at Privy Council, staff advised Mulroney on the aspects of the timing of any such announcement,[74] and they seem to have concluded that it was best left to National Defence and the minister of national defence. Ominously, it was discussed as though testing was already a foregone conclusion (a fairly reasonable interpretation), and the final draft of the minister's letter to the United States secretary of defense was done by 23 January.[75] At the Tuesday, 31 January 1989 meeting of the Cabinet Committee on Priorities and Planning the ministers agreed with Beatty to allow ACM tests.[76]

While the Conservatives were trying to figure out how to survive a renewed cruise missile debate, the Liberal Party was holding another convention. Herb Gray, a very senior party member and deputy leader of the opposition Liberals stated that "the Liberal Party called for the Conservative Government to finally shake off its cold war mentality and cancel further cruise missile testing in Canada as a tangible and positive gesture to improving the climate of East-West relations and ongoing disarmament negotiations."[77] Gray noted that "Canada was in grave danger of missing the boat" in regard to changes in the international situation. Such a move was characterized as indicating a "bold willingness on the part of the Canadian government," and it was clearly too bold for Mulroney or Chrétien. In power four years later, Jean Chrétien and his cabinet would ignore the will of the party despite being deeply divided by the same question.

Finally the new minister of national defence, William (Bill) McKnight, informed the United States Department of Defense by direct and informal means that the government had agreed to testing of the AGM-129.[78] The formal note was signed by the minister of national defence and given to United States Ambassador Thomas Niles for transmission to United States Acting Secretary of Defense William H. Taft IV the following day.[79] Ambassador Niles was told by the under-secretary of state for external affairs, J. H. Taylor, that "the Canadian Government is pleased to approve the request"[80]

In order to allow for the captive-carry testing of the advanced cruise missile, the ALCM Project Arrangement would have to be modified. The 1 December 1985 arrangement stipulated only the testing of the AGM-86B ALCM; anything else would need a new arrangement or an amendment.[81] However, this was not the original arrangement. Almost two years earlier, on 4 January 1984, the United States signed the original arrangement with no such restrictive reference in it.[82] The reason for the additional restriction remains unknown. With the approval of cabinet already given, National Defence and the Pentagon moved to finalize "Change 3 to ALCM Project Arrangement" (Change 3 Arrangement), which would allow the captive-carry tests. The assistant deputy minister (materiel) signed for Canada on 28 February, with Robert Duncan from the Pentagon signing the day before in Washington.[83] The Change 3 Arrangement really only added references to the AGM-129 in the opening general paragraphs, and stipulated that wherever the document referred to the ALCM, it was also understood to be referring to the ACM. "The term Air Launched Cruise Missile (ALCM) shall be used throughout this document to refer to both the AGM-86B and the AGM-129."

The Change 3 Arrangement declared that testing of any other missiles or follow-on missiles must be the subject of a separate project proposal. This was misunderstood by many people in the peace movement as the government sneaking testing in under cover of false documents. In fact, only a new proposal was necessary, but the old arrangement could be used again and again with modifications enacted through the Change 3 Arrangement.

Much political blood had been spilled, and External Affairs thought nothing would come to Canada for it. John Noble from External Affairs lamented, "we are not certain that we will get any credit inside Pentagon for agreeing to test ACM and are even less certain how that might play in context of other bilateral issues."[84]

A public announcement was finally made by Minister of National Defence William (Bill) McKnight on 1 February.[85] This time the references to the need for NATO solidarity and INF system imbalances were gone, replaced with a new requirement to match Warsaw Pact cruise missile capability and to support the START arms control process. The Tories had made the switch. Knowing that there would be both an uproar and many calls to fellow Conservative Party members in the House of Commons, McKnight had DND prepare, along with External Affairs, a package for all Tory members. McKnight told his colleagues in a letter that in the coming days and weeks they should expect to face many questions from constituents, especially from people who disagreed with the decision.[86] This was not what Tory members wanted to hear.

In Washington the Pentagon released a memorandum to correspondents that same day around noon. All it said was that the two governments had reached agreement to allow the testing of advanced cruise missiles over Canada; that the ACM was an improved ALCM; and that the agreement represented another example of the close cooperation between the two countries.[87] Soviet Ambassador Rodionov commented that Canada was supporting a deadly nuclear weapons arms race, and he was attacked for his "unwarranted and unwelcome intrusion into Canada's security debate."[88] Only positive comments were acceptable, and comments from Washington were always welcome. A few weeks later, on 26 February, Bill McKnight announced that the first captive-carry test of the ACM would take place two days later; it turned out to be four days later. The U.S. Air Force has never acknowledged this planned test, nor has documentation been found.

TEST # 89-(ACM-1)

Date: 2 March 1989
Global Shadow ACM captive carry test (Global Shadow means ACM)
first ACM captive carry (first ACM in Canada)
Route: east route, captive carry
Unit: 410 Bomb Wing from K. I. Sawyer AFB, Michigan
Bomber: B-52H
Note: No information has ever been released about this test. It is the position of the U.S. Air Force Aircraft Directorate, as the only repository for such information, that documentation does not exist. Minister of National Defence Bill McKnight announced the test and the flight was recorded in the annual report of CFB Cold Lake. It was a notable event as there was no snow on the target range as required by the project arrangement.

The second ACM captive-carry test was scheduled for a 15–19 November 1989 test window. The test never happened because the U.S. Air Force had a more urgent need for the testing units and aircraft. A new test window was scheduled for 24–30 March 1990, and this test was successfully completed on 24 March. Thus, only two test of the ACM were conducted in 1989–90.

Even with a reduced testing schedule, Canadians were still unhappy with the tests. Another in the multi-year series of Gallup Polls revealed the testing was now opposed by 57 percent of Canadians. Support had dropped to its lowest since the question was first asked in 1982, bottoming out at 35 percent.[89] The Gallup organization usually asked the same question year after year: "The United States is using a northern Canadian area to test cruise missiles because the guidance system must be tested in an Arctic-like climate. In these tests the cruise missiles have neither conventional nor nuclear warheads. Do you think Canada should continue to permit the United States to test these missiles in its territory?"[90]

A far more important event was happening on the other side of the world, and it would change the way many more people looked at cruise missile testing. The East German government had decided to let East Berliners freely visit West Berlin, and this curious decision had quickly resulted in the dismantling of the Berlin Wall and the eventual dissolution of the entire country. The rest of Eastern Europe soon followed, and the Soviet empire literally disappeared. NATO no longer faced the Warsaw Treaty Organization, only the Soviet Union. Two years later the Soviet Union itself disintegrated into its warring constituent republics. The Cold War was over. In Ottawa the prime minister was told that if asked about the dramatic changes in the world situation, then he was to say, "we rely on nuclear weapons to deter aggression or intimidation and as long as we do, Canada will continue to uphold our obligations and responsibilities to assist in the maintenance of a credible nuclear deterrence."[91]

Still troubled by the public response to new testing, Secretary of State for External Affairs Joe Clark referred the matter to the Consultative Group Meeting on cruise missiles. The brief they produced on 3 December 1989 was full of the usual tired arguments for testing: there was no harm to the environment; it was not a first strike weapon; it posed no verification problems; it was necessary to counter Soviet development of the AS-19 cruise missile; and it allowed Canadian pilots a superb training opportunity.[92]

During this time, the reach of the cruise missile grew appreciably. The first use of the cruise missile in combat since World War II occurred in the U.S. war against Iraq, with hundreds of ALCMs (air-launched cruise missiles) and SLCMs (submarine-launched cruise missiles) fired against a plethora of targets. Most interestingly, and unknown at the time, was that the initial strikes involved the AGM-129 advanced cruise missiles. Testing was now being done on an entirely different scale.

In Canada, two free-flight tests of the ALCM and one captive-carry test of the ACM were conducted in the 1990–91 testing season. The United States then informed National Defence that they wanted to do another captive-carry test of the ACM between 22 October and 9 November 1991.[93] The U.S. annual forecast was received at National Defence on 26 February, and National Defence promptly set about preparing for a review under ministerial authority.[94] The authorization was promptly provided and soon followed by permission for the specific test. All of the proposed projects had been previously approved or reviewed as part of the 1989 or the 1990 annual forecast,[95] so the only issue was whether the specific test could take place on a certain date and in a certain place.

TEST # A91-01C

Date: 7 November 1990
Global Shadow ACM test flight
Route: east route, captive carry
partial success
Unit: 410 Bomb Wing from K. I. Sawyer AFB, Michigan
Bomber: B-52H/60-0048
Crew: S-01 with 31 TES IRN
Primary missile: 86-0574
Position: LP-2
Pylon: 029
Launch mode: manual
Launch altitude planned: 7,600 metres
Launch time (simulated): 17:32:08z
ACM systems failure: 20:16:06z
Fuze time: unknown, unmet
Flight time (captive test): 2 hours, 44 minutes
Note: The test was designed to test the ability of the ACM systems and software to accurately navigate to the target. The primary missile, 86-0577, was beyond immediate repair and was replaced with the back-up missile for the test flight. The first attempt was terminated when the tanker could not meet the B-52 for refuelling on 31 October. Three in-flight refuelings were done before missile launch. The missile did two TERCOM updates: the first at landfall, 93 minutes into the flight, and the second over land

two and a half hours into the flight. The TERCOM system voted all three maps comparisons good in the first update. Despite the early termination, most mission objectives were met. The pilot and mission director decided to end the test after the ACM began to shut down various internal navigation systems. It was later discovered that this was probably due to a power surge in the #3 generator onboard the B-52 caused the two inertial navigation system (INS) gyroscopes to become unbalanced.

Cruise missile tests were coming under renewed attack by a newly energized peace movement. The fall of the Berlin Wall and the collapse of Stalinism in Eastern Europe brought the inevitable question: why did testing need to continue? The Soviet Union was less than a year from complete disintegration. When opponents asked National Defence why the missile was still being tested, Major Jan Martinsen, without a hint of irony, said that cruise missiles "are still part of the inventories of both sides. They are still considered destabilizing weapons." It passed without comment that the weapon which had been sold to the Canadian public as a stabilizing force, was now considered destabilizing.

The Strategic Arms Reduction Treaty (START I), signed on 29 July 1991 by President Bush and General Secretary Gorbachev, called for sweeping reductions in the nuclear arsenals of the two superpowers. The levels of ICBMs (inter-continental ballistic missiles) and SLBMs (submarine-launched ballistic missiles) in the United States would drop by 29 percent and by at least 36 percent in the USSR. Soviet throw weight would be reduced by some 46 percent, while warhead numbers would be expected to drop by 40 percent in the United States and 48 percent in the USSR. The central limits included: 1,600 Strategic Nuclear Delivery Vehicles (SNDVs); 6,000 accountable warheads; 4,900 ballistic missile warheads; 1,540 warheads on 154 heavy ICBMs for the Soviet side, plus an agreed elimination of 22 SS-18 launchers every year for seven years to achieve this level; 1,100 warheads on deployed mobile ICBMs; and a 3,600-tonne throw-weight ceiling.

This was also the beginning of air-launched cruise missile restrictions. Nuclear-armed ALCMs with a range in excess of six hundred kilometres (long range nuclear armed or LRNA) were affected. New long-range conventionally armed ALCMs that are distinguishable from nuclear-armed ALCMs were excluded, not limited, in START and could be deployed on any aircraft. For the purpose of counting against the six thousand warhead limit, accountable warheads would be attributed to heavy bombers equipped for LRNA as follows: each current and future U.S. heavy bomber equipped for LRNA would count as ten warheads (except as noted below) but could actually be equipped for up to twenty LRNA. Each current and future Soviet heavy bomber equipped for LRNA would count as eight warheads (except as noted below) but could actually be equipped for up to sixteen LRNA. The United States could apply the above counting rule to 150 heavy bombers equipped for LRNA; the Soviet Union could apply the above counting rule to 180 heavy bombers equipped for LRNA. For any heavy bombers equipped for LRNA in excess of these levels, the number of attributable warheads would be the number of LRNA for which the bombers were actually equipped. Multiple-warhead long-range nuclear ALCMs were banned.

Bush followed up the success of START with a new proposal for further nuclear weapons reductions on 27 September. The proposal so worried the Canadian foreign ministry that the secretary of state for external affairs was informed about the consequences, especially as they applied to cruise missiles. The minister was told that neither the Bush nor the Gorbachev proposal included ALCMs, so Ottawa was safe in its pro-test propaganda for the moment.[96]

The nuclear weapons world again changed dramatically in late 1991. United States President George Bush and Secretary of Defense Dick Cheney ordered the stand down of most of the United States' tactical nuclear arsenal and much of the strategic arsenal.[97] The Joint Chiefs of Staff were told to eliminate the remaining stocks of ground-launched theatre nuclear weapons; to remove tactical nuclear weapons from the navy; to stand down the bomber alert; to stand down the ICBM force scheduled for eventual deactivation under START; to terminate the Peacekeeper ICBM railroad project and small ICBM project; and to terminate the short range attack missile (SRAM) program. In a single move, Bush and Cheney had dramatically altered the nuclear world. The Cold War was over.

TEST # 92-1

Date: 29 October 1991
Global Shadow ACM flight test
Route: east route, captive carry
Mission profile A911 (0191/91NS and A91NSA)
Unit: 410 Bomb Wing from K. I. Sawyer AFB, Michigan
Bomber: B-52H/ 61-0025
Crew: E-60
Primary missile: 86-0585 (telemetry failed)
Payload: NTIK–21
Position: LP-2
Secondary Missile: 87-0818 (simulated launch)
Payload: NTIK–18

Position: LP-5
Launch mode: manual
Launch time (simulated): 14:18:58
Missile over target: 19:45:34
Time error: 7 minutes late over target
Flight test time: 5 hours, 26 minutes
Note: This was the first FOT&E Phase II mission, flown in support of initial
    Headquarters Strategic Air Command (HQ SAC) certification of Operational
    Flight Software version 7.0. The TERCOM system made three updates
    based on maps, but did not update at landfall due to testing constraints.
    The back-up missile was simulated launched due to test related data
    problems in the primary missile. The fuzing errors were considered
    too great for Single Integrated Operational Plan (SIOP) operation with
    nuclear weapons, and this test result would not be included in the cumu-
    lative Circular Error Probable (CEP) database. Circular Error Probable
    (CEP) figures for U.S. nuclear weapons are therefore highly selective.

1992

Despite the end of the Cold War, two ACM captive-carry tests were scheduled at the beginning of 1992 on 28 January and 31 January. The public was
now calling into question the rationale that the tests had to be conducted
in Canada because it resembled the territory of the now defunct Soviet
Union. To make matters worse, the tests would come on the eve of the
official state visit of Russian President Boris Yeltsin to Canada.[98] During
the visit, the Prime Minister was bombarded with questions about the
wisdom of continued testing, and CFB Cold Lake was deluged with media
requests. The military suspected that the switch to ACM free flying would
resurrect protests.[99]

Four months after the ACM tests, the first indication of what the U.S.
Air Force planned to do next arrived in Ottawa. The testing agency, 49
TESTS at Barksdale AFB, wrote that they had planned two live launches
of the ACM on 19 January and 22 January 1993. These were called the
'Global Shadow' missions, and would be flown by the 410 Bomb Wing
from K. I. Sawyer AFB in Michigan. The testing unit knew of the problems
Ottawa was experiencing with the public, and said that they were willing
to use the launch dates to fly regular ALCMs. However, they would insist
on at least a captive-carry test of the ACM in the backup launch window
of 2–13 March 1993 if there had been no free flight.[100]

Later that year Yeltsin would meet with United States President George
Bush and agree to negotiate further limits on strategic nuclear systems.
The two leaders agreed to a "Joint Understanding on the Elimination of
MIRVed ICBMs and Further Reductions in Strategic Offensive Arms" on

17 June 1992. The Joint Understanding called for both sides to promptly finish START II which would further reduce strategic offensive arms by eliminating all MIRVed and heavy ICBMs, limit the number of SLBM warheads to no more than 1,750, and reduce the overall total of warheads for each side to between 3,000 and 3,500.

Therefore, the big problem the government would have to face, as expressed by the policy directorate at NDHQ, was, "with the cold war over, there would no doubt be some tough questions asked about the logic of supporting the development of a new weapons system like the stealth cruise missile."[101] As if the captive-carry tests were not bad enough for the Tories, on 10 September 1992 Richard Ledesma from the Pentagon formally presented the post-Cold War proposal for free-flight testing of the AGM-129.

The free-flight request had been expected to arrive in June,[102] but delays in the testing program within the continental United States had delayed such a request. The plan was first to conduct an ACM captive-carry test in October 1992 if the locator beacon was installed; if not, then the test would be put over to January 1993. Second, the free flight of the ACM was scheduled for 19–30 January 1993, but if that was not approved then further testing of the AGM-86B would happen in the same slot. Last, a back-up window for the testing of either missile would be set for 2–13 March.[103] Ken Calder, the assistant deputy minister (policy and communications), told the Materiel office that the request had come in, and that various offices would have to coordinate to produce an amended project arrangement for the advanced cruise missile free-flight testing.[104]

One new twist was that the AGM-129, in testing configuration, had no room for a parachute package. At the end of the test flight the missile would be put into a thirty-degree dive and crash into the ground, thus shattering into a few large chunks and several small bits. Once the missile had passed over the target, it would fly for a few minutes to burn off remaining fuel before diving to destruction. The impact would dig a hole about two metres deep. The United States Air Force ACM test team had searched the flight termination range and found an appropriate impact area. Most important to the U.S. Air Force was that all the remains be carefully and completely collected for return to the United States. Given that the accuracy of modern cruise missiles is so very high, it is interesting that in 1992 the belief was that they would be able to crash the missile only within one-half kilometre of the intended crash target.[105] During September, the director of environmental protection at National Defence wrote an updated assessment of environmental aspects of cruise missile testing with specific reference to the advanced cruise missile. Kavanagh concluded that there was "no new significant or adverse environmental effect."[106]

Changing to ACM testing would not require a new agreement, or even a new MOU; it would only require an amendment to the Cruise Missile Project Arrangement. Deputy Minister Robert Fowler and Chief of the Defence Staff General John de Chastelain presented a brief to the minister, Marcel Masse, on the proposed amendment. It recommended that the minister of national defence "approve amending the existing cruise missile project arrangement to allow free-flight testing of the Advanced Cruise Missile" and then inform the secretary of state for external affairs and other cabinet colleagues.[107] Well armed with communications strategies and public affairs briefings,[108] Fowler pointed out that he had already consulted with the under-secretary of state at External Affairs, the Prime Minister's Office, and PCO on the matter and that tentative approval had been given. Fowler was doing his best to press for a positive response through an appeal to authority argument.[109] The two men did caution Masse that due to lack of public support, free-flight testing of the ACM in January 1993 "will require skilful public communications."[110]

Discussion continued in mid-December between the Department of National Defence and Privy Council Office even as a small delegation from Ottawa traveled to Washington. Admiral Larry Murray and Colonel Keith Coulter were at the Pentagon, meeting with U.S. officials about the new cruise missile.[111] Back in Ottawa, Robert Fowler had made a personal investment in having the free flights approved[112] and he lobbied the minister of national defence extensively. There is good evidence to suggest that Prime Minister Mulroney was not informed of this action until mid-December, when Glen Shortliffe told him that the United States was preparing to request free-flight tests of the ACM.[113] Since this had already happened, it is unclear what Shortliffe was trying to tell Mulroney. It is possible that due to the early confusion in PCO about whether a new project arrangement would be needed for the new cruise missile type,[114] they had not decided to inform Mulroney about the situation.

The explanatory letter to the minister, seeking his guidance on the issue, had been submitted to Minister of National Defence Masse by Robert Fowler and General de Chastelain on 20 November. The men asked Masse to approve an amendment to the Cruise Missile Project Arrangement that would alter the text to include free-flight testing of the advanced cruise missile by removing the third paragraph of the arrangement which referred only to captive-carry.[115] Fowler then told Reid Morden at External

Affairs that the minister had the note and that Fowler would let Morden know "as soon as the Minister has agreed."[116] For Fowler a negative answer was unthinkable.

National Defence recognized that free-flight testing of the ACM was a "bad news announcement" which could not be avoided. The Cold War had ended, and so had their best argument for testing. Public opinion had never been greater than 45 percent in favour, and that was back in 1985. Staff secretly recommended that free-flight tests be announced as soon as possible in order to minimize the criticism. The political astuteness of National Defence was high as they noted that the tests would remain unpopular, and that the best course of action was to acknowledge this fact and simply respond to individual questions. The Department of National Defence did not hope to win the battle, but they sought to at least make their voice heard.[117]

After holding the document for two weeks, Marcel Masse approved the ACM free-flight testing, even though the original cabinet decision in 1989 already allowed such testing. At the bottom of the English and French letters the words "Not Approved" had been struck out, and a signature applied.

Since no new arrangement for the free-flight test was required, the original ALCM Project Arrangement was simply amended to allow for the new activity by deleting the third paragraph, which referred to the fact that no free-flight tests of the ACM were planned. On 29 December, Ray Sturgeon of National Defence signed "Change 4 to ALCM Project Arrangement,"[118] which enabled the new program to proceed. The signature from Washington was kept waiting pending the outcome of the agreement renewal issue, and Dr. Reis did not sign until 3 February 1993. It was now possible to free-flight test.

1993

With the new year came a new minister. Masse was sent away by Brian Mulroney, and in his place was appointed the first female minister of national defence. Kim Campbell, who would later briefly sit as prime minister, took tentative hold of the cruise missile file. Meanwhile, Robert Fowler and his staff were trying to figure out a positive approach to the ACM issue. He was pleased that the advanced cruise missile could be conventionally armed, as this information could be used to sidetrack the anti-nuclear lobbyists. When told that the CF-18 units would have a chance to intercept the ACM, Fowler declared that such a news item "would be a show stopper."[119]

Once all of the administrative actions had been taken, the testing was supposed to continue unabated and unbothered. However, two things conspired to make the spring 1993 testing season an uncertain one. The lack of certainty in the United States over the expected Canadian decision to renew the agreement and the Memorandum of Understanding had caused a delay in planning by the U.S. Air Force. In fact, the testing authority had been denied funding and ordered not to proceed with modification to the test aircraft and missile until a new agreement and project arrangement had been signed. The ACM would require the installation of an ELT, or emergency locator beacon/transmitter, before flying in Canada.[120]

A larger problem was that an ACM had crashed into the desert in Utah the previous December, and the cause was only determined two days after the agreement was signed. This left no time for planning the previously scheduled 26 January and 2 March 1993 ACM tests.[121] However, the U.S. Air Force now proposed to move the first free-flight test to 23 March, with a back-up window of 24–31 March.[122] The 26 January test date was taken by an AGM-86B ALCM not restricted by the Utah accident. This test took place, after two delays, on 29 January. Up to this point, three ALCM captive-carry tests, fifteen ALCM free-flight tests, and four ACM captive-carry tests had been conducted in Canada.[123] The first ACM free-flight test was coming up quickly.

A test advanced cruise missile had crashed twenty-seven seconds after launch at the Utah test range on 16 December 1992. ACM #87-0823, launched by a B-52H from the 410 Bomb Wing, crashed while carrying a test package similar to a W80 nuclear warhead.[124] Testing was put on hold while the USAF investigated the cause of the accident. The following day, Colonel Hincke at National Defence was called by Major Lyter, the USAF test and evaluation officer, and informed that his organization was still pushing towards an 8 January 1993 decision point on ACM tests. However, if the cause and fix was not then determined, the testing window would be used for a regular ALCM flight.[125]

The final report on the mysterious crash revealed that a one-time failure had occurred when a short circuit developed between a junction box and the missile chassis, causing a fluctuation that prevented the electro-mechanical flight controls from properly operating.[126] By this time forty-one free-flight tests of the advanced cruise missile had been successfully accomplished without such an incident. Contents of the report were quickly communicated within NDHQ,[127] allowing the minister of national defence to renew her permission for testing.

In the midst of the testing season, a short exchange on the matter took place in the House of Commons. Lloyd Axworthy, originally associated with the establishment of the agreement, and then with opposition to it, asked Campbell a question that would return to haunt the Liberal government a year later. Axworthy demanded that "the Minister give a commitment today that there be no authorization of any specific cruise missile test without having that proposal submitted to Parliament so that there can be a parliamentary hearing held, where Canadians' voices could be heard, particularly the voices of northern Canadians who oppose this agreement."[128] A year later, with the Liberals back in power, this statement was repeated to them by various public protest groups, concerned citizens, and Member of Parliament Svend Robinson. Kim Campbell would be told one month later that the ACM flight was confirmed for the following week.[129]

The first free-flight test of the AGM-129 advanced cruise missile in Canada did not go as well as the United States Air Force had hoped. After the failure in Utah had put the entire test series on hold, the USAF and the contractors needed a major success to protect the funding. Also, given that in his 1992 State of the Union speech the president had announced an end to procurement of the ACM, success was crucial. To ensure the life of the program, the U.S. Air Force informed the Department of National Defence in the midst of the testing that they wanted to plan for further ALCM tests in 1994. On 22 March 1993, after the B-52 had reached the launch area, the first attempt was aborted due to a landing gear problem on the telemetry aircraft. The second test attempt was also aborted after the bomber had reached the launch area due to the airborne warning and control systems (AWACS) aircraft being caught in bad weather at Elmendorf AFB. The test director aborted the third try on 25 March due to bad weather at Elmendorf. Success finally came on Monday, 29 March when an ACM flew down the east test corridor and crashed, on purpose, at Primrose Lake.

TEST # A93-04S

Date: 29 March 1993
Global Shadow ACM test
first live ACM launch/flight
Route: east route, free-flight
Mission profile: 92
Unit: 410 Bomb Wing from K. I. Sawyer AFB, Michigan

Bomber: B-52H/60-0003
Crew: R-71
Primary missile: 91-13057
Payload: NTIK-7
Position: LP-5
Secondary Missile: 91-0136
Payload: NTIK-14
Position: RP-5
Launch mode: automatic
Trajectory: A92NS Rev A.
Launch time: 14:20:59z
Fuze time: 20:06:50z
Time to target: 5 hours, 45 minutes, 51 seconds
Weapons Delivery Sequence -
B-52 take-off: 05:47z
Missile pre-armed: 14:14z
Missile launched: 14:20:59.01z
Missile engine ignition: 14:21:01z
Landfall and first TERCOM update: 16:41:03z
Second TERCOM update: 18:16:16z
Warhead arming manoeuvre: 18:41:07
Third TERCOM update: 19:30:56z
Fourth (terminal) TERCOM update: 19:51:35z
Initial arm enable A1: 20:06:21
Inertial Fuze fired: 20:06:50.936
Prior attempts to test:
   1. Test aborted 22 March after bomber had reached launch when test direc-
      tor aborted mission due to landing gear problems on telemetry aircraft.
   2. Test aborted 23 March after bomber had reached launch when
      test director aborted mission due to multiple problems with the
      AWACS aircraft and bad weather at Elmendorf AFB, Alaska.
   3. Test aborted 25 March after bomber had reached launch when test direc-
      tor aborted mission due to a failure of a system on the bomber and the
      AWACS aircraft being caught in bad weather at Elmendorf AFB, Alaska.
         The test proceeded perfectly. The ACM terminated its flight
      by crashing into the ground at Primrose Lake. The debris was
      gathered and returned to the United States. The Canadian Forces
      called the activities surrounding the test Operation "Sloscan."

Canadians were even more opposed to testing now than they had been
for several years.[130] Although the high-profile protests had faded, opposition and outright hostility to the tests remained. Most Canadians had
not bought into the idea that it was necessary to test in northern Canada
because it looked like Siberia. They were even more wary now that cruise
missiles were being used with live conventional warheads against Iraq. As
Ottawa Citizen writer Charles Gordon pointed out, "Northern Alberta is
not like Iraq. Not even *southern* Alberta is like Iraq."[131]

AGM-86B test ALCM in flight over United States.
Courtesy of U.S. Air Force. Negative # R-1641.

B-52 bomber with twelve test AGM-86B test cruise
missiles. Note the black and white marking to aid in
photographic analysis of test flights. Courtesy of U.S. Air Force.

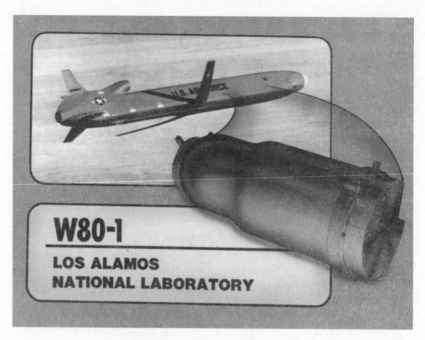

W80-1 nuclear warhead publicity photograph from Los Alamos National Laboratory (LANL). Courtesy of LANL. Negative # CIC-9: CN82-05418.

Greenpeace protestors approaching CFB Cold Lake gate are intercepted by several RCMP officers. Courtesy of CFB Cold Lake.

W80-1 nuclear warhead about to be lifted into ALCM.
Courtesy of U.S. Department of Energy and Los Alamos
National Laboratory. Negative # CIC-9: RN83-045-004.

Greenpeace protestors in a blizzard outside CFB Cold
Lake during a test. Courtesy of CFB Cold Lake.

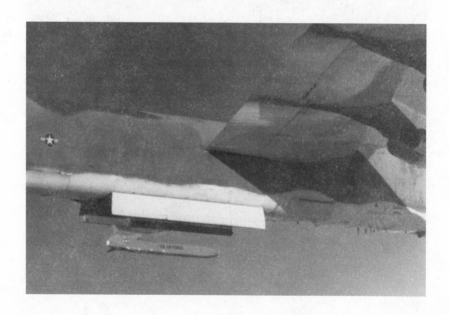

B-52 launches test ALCM from bomb bay. Courtesy
of U.S. Air Force. Negative # B-0782.

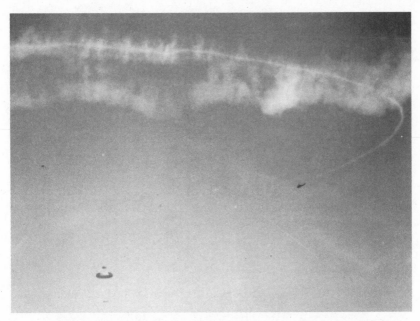

Rare photograph of an ALCM hanging upside down from its parachute, and being circled by a Canadian Forces helicopter prior to landing at Primrose Lake after a full flight test in 1985. Courtesy of National Defence. Negative # CKC85-1101.

ALCM on Primrose Lake with parachute still attached, at the end of an early-1985 flight test. Courtesy of National Defence. Negative # CKC85-1105.

AGM-86B airlifted by Huey helicopter after being
recovered on Primrose Lake weapons range in early 1985.
Courtesy of National Defence. Negative # CKC85-1114.

Canadian Forces crew with recovered missile at Primrose Lake in
early 1985. Courtesy of National Defence. Negative # CKC85-1111.

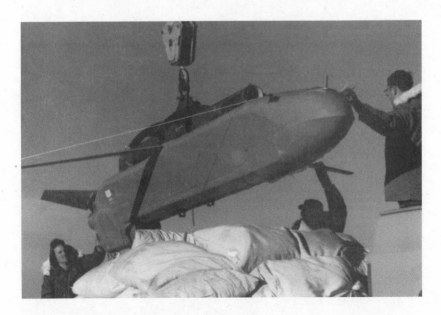

ALCM being lowered on to a trailer for shipment back to the U.S.
after being recovered on Primrose Lake weapons range, 24 February or
1 March 1987. Courtesy of National Defence. Negative # CKC88-497.

CF-18 fighter aircraft escorting an ALCM over Canada, 27 January 1989. Courtesy of National Defence. Negative # AEC89-107-10.

Rare image of two CF-18 aircraft escorting an AGM-86B cruise missile over Canada, 19 January 1988. Courtesy of National Defence. Negative # CKC88-908 W3719.

AGM-129 stealth Advanced Cruise Missile in flight over desert. Unlike the ALCM, the tail on the ACM points downward. Courtesy of U.S. Air Force. USAF Negative # 95-01-158217.

B-52H of 410 Bomb Wing, K. I. Sawyer AFB, in flight with twelve AGM-129 stealth Advanced Cruise Missiles mounted on under-wing pylons. Courtesy of U.S. Air Force and the Tomahawk Business Development office, Raytheon. USAF Negative # CVJ841083.

A CF-18 from Air Experimental Test Establishment (AETE) forms up on an AGM-129 Advanced Cruise Missile over the Primrose Lake Evaluation Range. The shiny material on the cruise missile is radar-reflective tape installed for test purposes to negate the stealth characteristics of the missile. Courtesy of National Defence.

5

Liberals Create, Tories Renew:
The Renewal of Cruise Missile Testing

A decision to end a decade of cruise missile tests would
let Ottawa distance itself from the seemingly relentless
search for new weapons of mass destruction.
Toronto Star, 5 August 1992

Kim Campbell, the first female prime minister in Canadian history, was minister of national defence when the issue of renewing cruise missile testing raised its ugly head. The first renewal crisis had passed relatively quietly, mostly because it turned out not to be real. As the original agreement was automatically renewed after five years, no debate or paperwork was associated with the continuance of the CANUS T&E. This was not to be the case during the 1993 renewal debate, which began in 1992.

THE NON-RENEWAL OF 1988

Back in 1980 the United States proposed an agreement that would be good for ten years and the original Canadian draft stipulated just that. In 1981 either External Affairs or National Defence legal staff changed the wording to "an unknown number." In response, although the U.S. negotiators preferred a ten-year document, they asked for a five-year agreement that automatically renewed for a further five. Paragraph 23 of the final agreement reflected a five plus five life cycle. This feature of the CANUS T&E Agreement led to the false renewal issue of 1987.

The "five + five" format led some in the press to conclude that the agreement would have to be renegotiated and renewed in 1987. However, this was not the case and DND noted that there was no significant difference between the U.S. proposal for a ten-year agreement and the "five + five" formula.

On 24 February 1987 another U.S. Air Force cruise missile made a successful free flight test from the Beaufort Sea that terminated in a parachute landing at the Primrose Lake weapons range in Saskatchewan. Immediately after announcing the successful test, William Chambers, the spokesman for Secretary of State for External Affairs Joe Clark, stated that the CANUS T&E Agreement would be automatically renewed the following year for another five years. The next day the Mulroney government renewed press attention that they certainly did not desire.[1] The strange announcement came as a surprise to the U.S. embassy, and it caused United States Ambassador Thomas Niles to promptly write to Joe Clark thanking him for this action by the Canadian government.[2]

Almost two weeks after the false announcement the government was able to correct the message. Associate Minister of National Defence Paul Dick rose in the House of Commons on 6 March to state, "the agreement was for an initial five-year period with an automatic five-year renewal."[3] Thus ended the non-event, and the issue slipped back to focus on protests and continued flights.

▎ TEST # 89-4

Date: 27 January 1989
Global Cruise ALCM flight test
Route: east route, free-flight, 2nd ANX-Cold
Mission profile 32 (seventh attempt, third free-flight, also called 0732/32NS)
Unite: 416 Bomb Wing from Griffiss AFB, New York
Bomber: B-52G/57-6498
Crew: S-02
Primary missile: 81-0205 (telemetry failed)
Payload: NTIK-114
Position: LP-2
Secondary Missile: 81-0424 (launched)
Payload: NTIK-116
Position: RP-2
Additional missiles: 10 training ferry payloads to obtain cold soak and full load data.
Launch mode: Manual
Launch altitude planned: 1,830 metres ASL
Launch time: 14:35:43z
Fuze time: 18:17:55.815z
Time error: 1 second early over target
Prior attempts to test:
1. Test failed 24 January when, after bomber took off from Griffiss, the airborne refueling aircraft could not take off from Elmendorf AFB in Alaska due to extremely low temperatures and ice fog. The test director aborted the mission at 12:40, approximately two hours before the launch time.
2. Test again rescheduled when 26 January forecast showed severe turbulence in the missile route.

Telemetry was not available from the primary ALCM, so the secondary ALCM was launched. The TERCOM system accomplished seven updates: one at landfall, five en route, and one in the terminal flight to target. Due to strong tail winds, the ALCM used less fuel than planned and flew to optional recovery point. The missile was dragged to shore after landing as the parachute would not collapse in the strong winds, and had to be recovered by hand.

Eight CF-18 and six USAF fighters intercepted the missile during the test flight as part of a NORAD exercise. This was the first time that CF-18s had scrambled from the northern runways at Inuvik and Yellowknife to intercept an ALCM.

Certainly one of the oddest suggestions made by Canada, at least as far as Washington was concerned, was that the Soviets and Warsaw Treaty members would be able to observe cruise missile tests over Canada through the Open Skies Treaty. Canada had helped promote the treaty in Washington, and External Affairs director of arms control, Ralph Lysyshyn, told the press on 9 January 1990 that although the Soviets would not be allowed to closely observe the tests, they could watch the tests from a distance in a jointly-manned observation aircraft.[4] Washington refused comment on the proposal.

TEST #90-4

Date: 23 January 1990
Global Cruise ALCM free-flight test
Route: east route, free-flight
Mission profile 47 (initial attempt, also called 0147/47NS)
Unit: 7 Bomb Wing from Dyess (Carswell) AFB, Texas
Bomber: B-52H/60-0062
Crew: S-01
Primary missile: 83-0451
Payload: NTIK-027
Position: RP-1
Secondary Missile: 83-0418
Payload: NTIK-028
Position: LP-3
Additional missiles: 10 training ferry payload missiles on pylons
Launch mode: Manual
Initial flight altitude: 300 metres
Launch time: 15:02:23
Fuze time: 18:50:22.784
Time to target: 3 hours, 48 minutes
Time error: on time over target
Note: The test flight was normal, and CF-18 and USAF fighters intercepted the missile along the test route. However, due to high winds in the recovery

area, the ALCM drifted into trees on the south side of Primrose Lake. Recovery crew had difficulty reaching the missile due to dense forests.

■ Test #90-4A

Date: 29 January 1990
Global Cruise ALCM test
Route: east route, free-flight
Mission profile 47 (second attempt, also called 0247/47NS)
Unit: 7 Bomb Wing from Dyess (Carswell) AFB, Texas
Bomber: B-52H/61-0021
Crew: E-84
Primary missile: 84-0260
Payload: NTIK-24
Position: RP-1
Secondary Missile: 83-0259
Payload: NTIK-34
Position: LP-3
Additional missiles: 10 training ferry payloads
Launch mode: Manual
Initial flight altitude: 300 metres ASL
Launch time: 15:02:21
Fuze time: 18:50:39
Time to target: 3 hours, 48 minutes, 18 seconds
Time error: 16 seconds late over target
Note: Canadian Forces CF-18 #726 piloted by Richard Corver of Toronto exploded six kilometres from the runway at Inuvik, Northwest Territories on its way to intercept this cruise missile. The waist-deep snow and temperatures ranging from minus thirty-five to minus fifty degrees hampered rescue efforts. Three CF-18 fighter aircraft were involved in the mock intercept (CMDI) of the ALCM.

A CANADIAN DEATH

Operation Sloscan was the joint cruise missile defence initiative exercise conducted in Canada in the late 1980s and in 1990 during which many Canadian and U.S. Air Force pilots gained useful anti-ALCM experience. But the only ALCM-related death occurred during the training. The training demonstrated that it was possible to intercept and down a cruise missile, but it also proved that even with all the experience, operating from the far north was still very difficult and often impossible to accomplish.

During the 29 January 1990 test, 441 Squadron operated out of the Forward Operating Location at Inuvik, North West Territories, and this is where Captain Richard Corver crashed on take-off. It is believed that he mistook the high nose attitude of his aircraft for an impending stall in the darkness and pushed forward on the stick, thus causing his aircraft to dive into the ground six kilometres from the end of the runway. Captain Corver died instantly, but this crash would consume military resources in the far north for almost a half-year. The extreme cold, as low as minus fifty degrees, and the waist-deep snow prevented full recovery until May 1990. With the coming of spring the recovery team returned to the massive crash area and once again began to collect and bag each item of wreckage. Even with the warmer weather, the primary danger was the same — carbon fibres. The composite materials of the aircraft body had dispersed and were a breathing hazard. Richard Corver's death ended Sloscan.

TEST # 91-4

Date: 31 January 1991
Global Cruise ALCM flight test
Route: east route, free flight, low launch
Mission profile 54 (second attempt, first free-flight, also know as 0154/54NS)
Unit: 5 Bomb Wing from Minot AFB, North Dakota
Bomber: B-52H/61-0024
Crew: E-45
Primary missile: 81-0372
Payload: NTIK-34
Position: LP-2
Secondary Missile: 83-0337
Payload: NTIK-46
Position: RP-2
Additional missiles: 2 training ferry payloads on LP-5 and RP-5
Launch mode: Automatic
Launch time: 15:31:31
Fuze time: 19:20:23.945
Flight time: 3 hours, 49 minutes
Time error: 6 seconds late over target
Note: The first test failed on 29 January when, after the B-52 took off from Minot, the test director delayed the mission for forty-eight hours due to bad weather at Elmendorf and Eielson AFBs in Alaska causing several mission support aircraft to abort flight. The missile was launched twenty minutes late due to strong headwinds, made seven TERCOM updates, and arrived over the target three hours and forty-nine minutes after launch.

TEST # 91-5

Date: 9 February 1991
Global Cruise ALCM flight test
Route: east route, free-flight, low launch

Mission profile 54 (forth attempt, second free-flight, also known as 0454/54NS)
Unit: 5 Bomb Wing from Minot AFB, North Dakota
Bomber: B-52H/61-0024
Crew: E-45
Primary missile: 82-0424 (telemetry failure)
Payload: NTIK-47
Position: LP-2
Secondary Missile: 83-0337 (launched)
Payload: NTIK-46
Position: RP-2
Additional missiles: training ferry payloads on LP-5 and RP-5
Launch mode: automatic
Launch time: 15:08:38
Fuze time: 18:57:12.235
Time error: 2 seconds early over target
Note: The 6 February test was aborted because of a support aircraft main-
tenance problem. Due to the primary missile on the primary bomber
leaking oil, a back-up B-52 bomber and missile was used. Most of the
data normally collected was unavailable due to unknown problems. The
missile experienced a large fuze position error that went unexplained.

Attention again turned to other military matters with the closing of
the 1991 cruise missile testing season. The North American Aerospace
Defence Command agreement (NORAD) was renewed on 30 April, and
came into force again on 12 May. The current version was not substan-
tively changed from the previous version of the agreement. The previous
renewal had taken place on 19 March 1986.

1992

As part of his annual State of the Union message in January, United
States President George Bush made a historic announcement on strategic nuclear arms reduction. Ottawa, knowing that the statement was
to be made, but not knowing the exact content, prepared a question and
answer briefing for its diplomats. The Conservatives feared that the Bush
initiative would call into question continued cruise missile testing. The
other problem was that with the announcement coming a day after the
first scheduled test of 1992, Ottawa recognized the possibility of negative
comments from citizens and the media. The embassy staff were to tell
the media and the public that "it remains to be seen how the President's
initiative will affect continued testing."[5]

The Cold War was over, the Soviet Union was gone, and cruise missiles were being used to some effect in Iraq; yet the testing continued in

northern Canada. Gideon Forman of the Toronto Peace Alliance said that official Ottawa was no longer responding to requests to justify the tests. Bill Robinson of Project Ploughshares told the press that testing never made sense, but that it was especially irrelevant now that START had been signed and the Cold War was over. Trying to justify the tests, Alex Morrison of the Canadian Institute for Strategic Studies (CISS) said that although General Motors had built lots of cars, they still tested them.

The testing season of early 1992 did not proceed as well as had been hoped by both militaries. The first attempt to use the common strategic rotary launcher (CSRL) as an operational launch device in Canada was in fact a great success – once all the aircraft made it into the air for the eventual test. The mission was scrubbed on the first attempt due to bad weather in Alaska. Two days later, the second attempt failed when a mission critical support aircraft aborted flight due to an engine fire indication and a landing gear retraction problem. The hat trick of failures came on 4 February when a mission critical support aircraft aborted flight due to another engine fire warning. Success was finally achieved on 10 February when an AGM-86B, #81-0163 was launched from the first position on the CSRL held in the bomb bay of the B-52 from the 92nd Bomb Wing at Fairchild AFB. All previous tests had been conducted using ALCMs attached to pylons under the wings of the massive eight-engine intercontinental bomber. The missile left the bomb bay at 2:58 P.M. and simulated a nuclear detonation over the target just under four hours later at 6:48 P.M. Aside from the usual large number of USAF aircraft which had to participate in the basic test, the Canadian Forces provided a CP-140 Aurora for tracking purposes, two CF-18s as escorts, and a further six CF-18s to conduct mock intercepts of the missile as it cruised towards Primrose Lake. At this disappointing juncture, the U.S. Air Force decided that testing was over for the rest of the season.

TEST # 92-4

Date: 10 February 1992
Global Cruise ALCM test
Route: east route, CSRL launch, low launch, free-flight
Mission profile 54 (seventh attempt, also known as 0654/54NSB)
Unit: 92 Bomb Wing from Fairchild AFB, Washington
Bomber: B-52H/60-0044
Crew: E-12
Primary missile: 81-0163
Payload: NTIK-26
Position: RL-1 (common strategic rotary launcher)
Secondary Missile: 83-0230

Payload: NTIK-34
Position: RL-3
Additional missiles: 12 on pylons, and 6 in all other Common
    Strategic Rotary Launcher (CSRL) positions.
Launch mode: Automatic
Launch time: 14:58:49
Fuze time: 18:48:01.666
Flight time: 3 hours, 50 minutes
Time error: 28 seconds late over target
Prior Attempts to test:
   1. Mission scrubbed on 28 January due to bad weather.
   2. Test failed on 30 January when a mission critical sup-
      port aircraft aborted flight due to an engine fire indica-
      tion and a landing gear retraction problem.
   3. Test failed 4 February when a mission critical support aircraft
      aborted flight due to an engine fire indication warning.
         This was the first attempt to use CSRL mounted in the bomb
      bay as an operational launch device in Canada. The missile ac-
      complished seven TERCOM updates during the flight, but arrived
      late over the target. It was also the only FY92 launch in Canada.

The inevitable request for renewal of the agreement was received in
Ottawa in the spring of 1992. The process began informally enough. In
mid-May the international security division of External Affairs received
a visitor – Mr. Meinheit from the U.S. embassy in Ottawa. He had called
to convey the interest of both the Pentagon and State Department in the
eventual formal renewal of the CANUS T&E Agreement. Meinheit told
J. T. Devlin, the acting director of international security and defence relations, that the U.S. side did not foresee any changes to the agreement, but
merely hoped for a straightforward renewal in February 1993.[6] The move
towards renewal had begun with this visit.

   The Canadian Defence Liaison Staff in Washington had suggested that
there should be more consideration of Canadian interests in the renewed
document. Although Washington wanted a simple renewal, Ottawa was
now interested in adding sections on Canadian research and development, test and evaluation, and acquisition.[7] The concept of reciprocity was
being born, and it would change the face of the CANUS T&E Agreement
to the point where Canada would eventually be conducting more testing
in the United States than the United States was conducting in Canada.

   The word went out within National Defence for suggestions as to what
a new agreement should include, and whether the agreement needed to
be renewed at all. Colonel Leduc, the director of continental policy, asked
the offices of primary interest at NDHQ if there was a need for renewal,

and if so, whether operational staffs of testing agencies required reciprocal access to U.S. facilities under a new umbrella agreement.[8]

Major General P. E. Woods, the deputy chief of Materiel, had complained that the CANUS T&E Agreement did nothing for Canadian Air Force interests. Woods pointed out that while the United States could use Canadian facilities and pay only the incremental costs, as the agreement was one-way in favour of the United States, any use of U.S. facilities by Canadians generated bills for all costs attributable to the testing, not just incremental costs.[9] For the United States, the costing provisions of the agreement meant virtually free testing facilities, while for Canada it meant continued high costs of using any U.S. facility. Woods pointed out that since the increments were so small, Canada could never build up enough to pay for test pilot or flight test engineer training. He warned that without reciprocity the barter system could not be implemented. The suggestion was made that the new agreement be totally reciprocal and have a provision for offsetting the cost of using cross-border facilities without monetary remuneration.[10]

Coincident with the U.S. request, the assistant deputy minister (material) at National Defence, who had the role of Canada's CANUS T&E Coordinator, developed a proposal for a new agreement modeled on the original agreement. The proposal called for all costs directly attributable to testing to be charged to and collected from the United States. Second, it was proposed to make the agreement totally reciprocal by allowing the Canadian Forces the use of U.S. facilities, and to include a provision for an offsetting provision without monetary remuneration (i.e., a facility barter system).[11]

Further along Sussex Drive, staff at External Affairs were involved in a desperate, illegal, and successful attempt to prevent the public from knowing the facts of the situation. An *Access to Information Act* request for records on the topic had been received at National Defence, and DND had found certain records belonging to External Affairs. Upon being consulted regarding the release of the papers, External Affairs responded that everything should be withheld. An internal memo showed the reasoning. The Bureau of International Security warned that "the requester should not be informed of the pertinent facts mentioned in the documents," and that External Affairs should continue to apply section 69 of the Act to prevent release.[12] Aside from the total disdain shown towards the public by civil servants at External Affairs, it is a curious use of a section of the Act referring exclusively to cabinet documents. External Affairs was now using a section of the Act reserved exclusively for cabinet confidences to shield their own records from being seen by citizens.

National Defence was now deciding how to proceed. The deputy minister and the chief of defence staff were told about the new proposal for reciprocity. However, DND still had to determine if renewal was necessary from a Canadian perspective. The fact was that a great deal of public controversy had been generated by the testing, and this was not of much use to the Department of National Defence. However, the question was merely pro forma in that no real decision was required since the agreement would be renewed given the U.S. request in May. National Defence would only have to seek cabinet approval for any changes to the Canadian position on the new agreement.[13] Once cabinet gave approval to renegotiate a newly worded agreement, External Affairs would have to inform the CANUS T&E Steering Group, and National Defence and External Affairs would then begin negotiations with the State Department and the Pentagon.[14]

Cabinet review and approval would be both necessary and crucial. All past decisions had come after cabinet review, and the issue was simply too politically sensitive to be dealt with by a department without reference to the executive. Strangely, the summer had slipped away and little was done by either cabinet or the department.

In the early autumn, Privy Council Office told National Defence that due to the upcoming nation-wide referendum on the Charlottetown Accord on 26 October, no opportunity would be available to brief cabinet before the 18 November meeting of the Cabinet Committee on Foreign and Defence Policy. Any recommendation of that committee would then have to be reviewed by the cabinet Priorities and Planning Committee, and this would not happen before the end of November.[15] The Charlottetown agreement, cobbled together in light of the failure of the Meech Lake Accord, had failed at the hands of Canadian voters who did not want to see more power flowing to Quebec at the expense of the other provinces and the federal government.

Ken Calder, the assistant deputy minister (policy and communications), directed his staff and others in National Defence to promptly prepare a full memorandum to cabinet (MC) by mid-October for the joint signature of the minister of national defence and the secretary of state for external affairs for further staffing and approval. Working with staff at External Affairs, as late as 15 September Calder told the offices involved that in order to impress cabinet the memorandum would have to include the proposed new wording allowing reciprocity, and that this would have to be negotiated before the memorandum to cabinet was written. The Canadian CANUS T&E coordinator, Chief of Staff Military Plans and

Operations (CoS J3), was going to have to promptly contact his counterpart, the American CANUS T&E Coordinator, and work out new wording as Calder had set a deadline of 7 October for an agreement-in-principle on the content of a new agreement.[16] To make matters even more difficult, in a proposal delivered to DND on 10 September, the United States requested that the U.S. Air Force be allowed to free-flight test the advanced cruise missile.[17] Now there were two issues nobody really wanted to handle.

Defence Industrial Relations (DDIR) was the office of primary interest on this topic, and the staff began a rigorous rewriting program by 17 September. LCdr J. J. Priddle from the Judge Advocate General's office (JAG) provided the legal suggestion one week later.[18] Along with the lawyers in Director of Law/Materiel, headquarters staff drafted a new agreement based on the original 1983 agreement.[19] The most important changes would be those reflecting the desired reciprocity. The second paragraph of the preamble was to read: "As a result of further discussions, I have the honour of proposing an expansion of the Agreement to insert an element of reciprocity by permitting test and evaluation of Canadian defence weapons, weapons systems and other defence materiel in the United States."[20]

In order to take full advantage of any testing the United States might undertake in Canada, the lawyers proposed a paragraph which would bestow the right of either side to take part in the testing and evaluation project of the other. This would be a cost-effective means of gathering data and experience, especially for the Canadian Forces. To make the entire process more cost-effective, the proposal stated that each country would value the cost of the test facilities and services provided based on the cost attributed by the other country for such facilities and services.[21] All other proposed changes flowed from the requirement to make the wording reflect Canadian access to U.S. test and operational facilities under the same rules and regulations which governed U.S. access to such places in Canada.

The next day, Colonel Joe Hincke, the Director of Continental Policy, sent the entire new package to Washington through the Ottawa-based United States Defense Attaché Office (USDAO) for review.[22] It now contained the concept of reciprocity, similar cost accounting, and non-monetary trade-offs in exchange for testing services.

Mr. Craig Farr in the Office of the Deputy Director, Strategic Weapons System Assessment/STEP at the Pentagon, had received the memo from USDAO and replied within the week. Farr's immediate comment was that the proposed text appeared acceptable, and that "the concept of a reciprocal, two-way agreement should be beneficial to both countries [and that] charging the same costs for the same services to either side for testing is certainly agreeable."[23] The only problem that Farr saw was that there was no legal way for the Pentagon to establish accounts and reconcile differences in the costs charged. Therefore, he suggested the continuation of the pay-as-you-go method already in use due to the restrictions placed on the Pentagon by certain U.S. regulations.

Work would proceed at an increasing rate of speed in October as it became more pressing to have documents in place and as the decision looked to be on the horizon. LCdr Priddle examined the U.S. counter-proposal within the week, and mostly accepted the minor administrative changes suggested by Craig Farr in Washington.[24] Incorporating both the U.S. counterproposal and the new JAG suggestions and wording, the newest draft text of the renewal note was faxed to Washington. At the same time, Colonel Hincke told Farr that a draft of the proposed memorandum of understanding (MOU) would be coming very soon.[25]

Upon further examination, the team in Washington thought that the costing section should be changed. Farr pointed out to Colonel Hincke that it would be better to specify that only the incremental costs would be reciprocal, as the United States anticipated the volume of testing done by the Pentagon to outstrip that done by Canada.[26] The JAG office again set to work incorporating the U.S. changes into a Canadian document, and had a final version ready by 20 October.[27]

At this point the possibility that the agreement would not be renewed still existed, although this was a slim chance indeed. National Defence was concerned about the issue and directed that a quick note be written by the policy operations staff regarding the consequences for DND programs should the CANUS T&E Agreement not be renewed.[28] This information was immediately circulated within the office of the assistant deputy minister for policy and communications,[29] and would be included in future briefings to the minister of national defence, the deputy minister, and the chief of defence staff as the process progressed. It is suspected that such information was also provided to cabinet in the hope of securing permission to renew the agreement. Colonel Hincke's briefing note on the subject delineated all the main points. He pointed out that if the memorandum to cabinet was approved before December, then all would proceed at a regular pace for an ultimate renewal before the old agreement expired. The U.S. Air Force had told the colonel that a delay in approval of the package would not allow time for mission planning for ACM tests in the January 1993 period, and that the United States Air Force had picked this time in case the agreement was not renewed. However, as the United States still believed that there was no question of eventual renewal and test approval, it was already scheduling advanced cruise missile flights for the spring of 1994.

Cabinet approval and a signed Order-in-Council in mid-January 1993 would still allow for a tight but possible signature of the note and the MOU before the expiry date. Hincke noted that since the House of Commons was normally in recess at that time, he thought that the latest possible time that a decision could be made "that would avoid placing ALCM testing at risk during the next testing season" was mid-December.[30] To drive home the urgency, another U.S. redraft arrived for Colonel Hincke.[31]

As this was going on, National Defence prepared to brief the minister and to work up a memorandum to cabinet on the issue. On 16 October the cabinet liaison staff was briefed and discussed the matter with the deputy minister. Mark Mayhew of the cabinet liaison office talked about the option for renewal and the advanced cruise missile with staff from Ken Calder's office and with Deputy Minister Bob Fowler.[32] The decision to package the renewal proposal and the ACM free-flight test request was made by Assistant Deputy Minister (Policy and Communications) Dr. Ken Calder after a thorough discussion and analysis of the options.[33] Fowler, the powerful and well-connected Ottawa civil service politician, had agreed that this would be the best way to guarantee passage of both proposals. The Department of National Defence gave its view of the situation to a joint meeting of the Privy Council Office and External Affairs the next day on 19 October, and Calder's staff continued work on a memorandum to cabinet (MC) on both issues together. The memorandum was scheduled for completion and approval at the assistant deputy ministerial level by the end of October.[34]

With only four days left in the month, the industrial resources office was still seeking the approval of their assistant deputy minister (materiel), knowing that the final document would be discussed at the upcoming daily executive meeting at National Defence Headquarters.[35] It was at this point that Bob Fowler, the deputy minister, changed the program by directing DND to ask the ministers to approve the renegotiated reciprocal agreement, and at the same time to tell the ministers that Canada was free-flight testing the ACM.[36] Fowler hoped to push the ACM testing through with little attention, as he may have suspected that only the renewal document needed full cabinet approval.

Fowler knew that the January 1989 cabinet decision to allow advanced cruise missile testing had been without restriction – that is, it did not restrict the U.S. Air Force to captive-carry tests and therefore allowed free-flight testing.[37] This did not happen only because the U.S. Air Force was not yet ready to free-fly the AGM-129. External Affairs viewed the ACM issue as a significant one, and insisted that the joint National Defence/External Affairs memorandum to cabinet present it clearly to ministers. The assistant deputy minister's (policy and communications) draft memorandum therefore included the issue of the ACM "so that Ministers will be fully aware of what renewing the T&E Agreement will imply."[38]

The analysis with the memorandum to cabinet provided the ministers with three options: do not renew the agreement and all testing will end; renew the agreement but terminate cruise missile testing; and, renew the agreement and allow continued cruise missile and ACM testing. The bureaucrats recommended in the memorandum to cabinet that the minister of national defence and the secretary of state for external affairs, as well as cabinet, approve the renewal and allow cruise missile testing to continue. As Robert Fowler would present it to the minister of national defence, renewal and cruise missile testing would "serve Canada's foreign policy, security, and defence economic interests."[39]

At the same time, National Defence was trying to work up a plausible communications strategy for use with both the renewal issue, and the even more sensitive ACM free-flight testing proposal.[40] One reviewer of the strategy wrote that the argument was not totally convincing. However, this had to be understood in light of the fact, clearly written in the document, that "public opinion support for cruise missile testing has never been overwhelming," and that the greatest support ever found was 45 percent during the height of the Cold War. Support had fallen by this time to perhaps 35 percent.[41] The analysis revealed there to be "little to no public support for the idea of renewing Canada's involvement in the cruise missile testing program."[42]

The fact was that no public relations strategy was going to capture the hearts and minds of most Canadians on this issue, especially with the Cold War being at an end. The ending of the Cold War had robbed the government of its chief argument in favour of cruise missile testing, a fact recognized by the public affairs staff at National Defence Headquarters. They pointed out that editorial opinion was running against testing, and that various peace and disarmament groups would use the end of the Cold War as a primary argument against renewal. Any announcement would have to "provide a solid post-Cold War rationale acceptable to Canadians," especially in light of Canadians viewing themselves and their government as peacekeepers and peacemakers.

Public Affairs called the renewal and the ACM testing "bad news announcements," and recommended that both be made simultaneously to avoid dragging out the issue and to diminish them as a target for naysayers.[43] Knowing that the issue was not winnable, the strategy called for acknowledging that the issue was unpopular and that any attempt to influence public opinion should be confined to vigorous answers to specific questions. The most National Defence could hope for was, in their words, a balanced public view.

Jim Judd at Privy Council Office, who would later become the deputy minister at National Defence and later still the head of the spy agency, told the cabinet secretary, Glen Shortliffe, that a cabinet decision would have to come soon in order for the U.S. to proceed with the planned ACM tests in the new year. Judd pointed out that no government officials opposed the renewal or the ACM flights.[44] What he did not tell Shortliffe, and it is unknown if Judd even knew, was that further permission was not needed for the advanced cruise missile program. In the words of Dr. Strangelove, the program had passed the fail-safe point; the ACM testing would proceed to its target without further authorization from the national command authority.

Washington was also busy that autumn. The day after Judd briefed Shortliffe at PCO, Craig Farr again provided new comments on the Canadian draft proposal. The good news was that the incremental costs proposal was now progressing. Farr said that U.S. defense department documents for major testing and operations ranges supported such costings. However, the totality of the draft was still being considered in depth by legal counsel.[45] Not only the draft agreement was at issue in Ottawa. The memorandum of understanding (MOU) would also have to be redone as the old one would expire with the original agreement in February 1993. The JAG lawyers were already working on the matter and had drafted a new version based on the original but incorporating reciprocity.[46]

Higher-level decisions were now required. On 5 November Deputy Minister of National Defence Robert Fowler met with Under-Secretary of State for External Affairs Reed Morden to discuss both the renewal and the ACM free-flight testing.[47] Fowler told Morden that renewal was consistent with the Canadian government's commitment to joint operations with the United States and with keeping abreast of emerging technology and the maintenance of combat skills. Fowler also pointed out that it was important that Canada move to "reassure the incoming U.S.

Administration of the value that the government places on Canada-U.S. defence cooperation."[48] Alliance management was at work, and Fowler knew that it was important to continually appease Washington. However, before allowing such reality to slip in to the conversation, Fowler made the usual remarks about the world still being a dangerous place despite the end of the Cold War, and the effective weapons which had been demonstrated in the recent war against Iraq.[49] Fowler also carried with him to the meeting that day a draft of the memorandum to cabinet that both ministers would have to sign. Morden and Fowler agreed that mutually acceptable full drafts of the agreement and the MOU would have to accompany the memo to the two ministers. Fowler and Calder believed it could be done by 4 December, thereby allowing time to complete a full submission to cabinet before the holiday recess.[50]

Another U.S. draft arrived on 13 November. The Pentagon had finally given their firm and legal view on both the agreement and the MOU, and made some significant changes. Various offices replied quickly that they had no problems with the U.S. version. One of the most important respondents was the office of the National Defence Memorandum of Understanding Coordinator (NDMOUC), J. Cabana-Marshall. The NDMOUC office reviewed the proposed MOU and replied with a stack of suggestions on 17 November.[51] Although the suggestions might be characterized as tinkering, they did form an important element of the final document. Speed was important now, especially as Craig Farr had written that it would require some work by both parties to have both documents signed at the same time.[52]

The final push for a draft MOU took place between 13 November and 30 November, in order to meet the deadline set by the deputy minister.[53] Comments from the affected office were solicited for the meeting on 13 November, worked into a new wording by 18 November, and then reviewed by JAG. Between 23 November and 27 November negotiations with the U.S. side on the final wording negotiations would be done by staff in the CoS J3 (formerly the Director of Military Plans and Operations). However, CoS J3 was trying to dump this task and would not continue as the office of primary responsibility for the testing programs. At this point the assistant deputy minister (materiel), the Canada-U.S. Test and Evaluation Program (CANUSTEP) office of primary interest, was prepared to take over the added responsibilities.[54] Possibly the strangest part of this story is that the negotiations were never carried out through the joint Canada-U.S. Steering Committee, which would have been an ideal forum. However, since the Steering Committee had never actually met in the nine years of its existence,[55] there was no real use to it at this point. By the end of the month JAG had reviewed both documents and given approval.[56] The final draft of 1 December was now provided to External Affairs for concurrence. However, External Affairs saw no need to rush despite all the prior meetings and cautions, and gave itself two weeks to review the documents.[57]

One problem for Ottawa was that the advanced cruise missile did not look reliable. During a free-flight test at Hill AFB in Utah, an ACM failed to start its engine and crashed to the ground immediately after release from the B-52. The accident harkened back to the early days of the program in Canada when, on 25 February 1986, an ALCM crashed into the Beaufort Sea ice after two minutes and thirty-seven seconds of free flight. The malfunction of the advanced cruise missile would not be fixed quickly, and the U.S. test director informed National Defence that regular air-launched cruise missiles would be tested in place of the ACM.[58]

Late in the month Prime Minister Brian Mulroney met with the new United States ambassador, Peter Teeley. Teeley had been appointed only six months before and was present for the signing of the NAFTA treaty. When the subject of cruise missiles came up during the 24 November meeting, Mulroney told Teeley only that discussions were well advanced and that cabinet would review the matter "in good time before the renewal date."[59] Teeley reiterated the importance his superiors attached to advanced cruise missiles and to the renewal of the CANUS T&E agreement. To meet at least half those needs, the minister of national defence approved ACM free-flight testing in December, and the Cruise Missile Project Arrangement was amended accordingly on 29 December 1992.[60]

One item which came up repeatedly in official discussions was explained in an editorial from the *Toronto Star* newspaper. Entitled, "End cruise tests as a sign of hope," this 5 August 1992 item had gained a great deal of attention, and was even brought to the attention of the defence minister. The author wrote, "A decision to end a decade of cruise missile tests would let Ottawa distance itself from the seemingly relentless search for new weapons of mass destruction." This would become the primary example of the public and media attitude towards continued testing, which the Mulroney government would continue to ignore.

The text of the renegotiated agreement was readied late in the day on 23 December in both the original language[61] and a French translation. Once reviewed by the Pentagon and the State Department, the translation was to become an issue later. C. A. Kerr from the International Industry Program at National Defence briefed his assistant deputy minister on the final package.[62] Because the assistant deputy minister (materiel) was primarily responsible for the day-to-day administration of the working agreement, all changes had to be routed through that office. Once the office had reviewed and approved the texts, which had already been agreed to by both parties, then Ken Calder would be able to brief Fowler. The review and approval came immediately, and Calder was able to give assistant deputy minister (materiel) a copy of the deputy minister's brief to the minister of national defence and the secretary of state for external affairs the next day. The entire package was then finalized for Bob Fowler to review upon his return from holidays on 4 January 1993,[63] and the whole issue would be examined by the ministers involved in late January.[64] The ministers' brief advised them that the continuance of the program was good for Canadian military industries as the new agreement would raise the profile of those industries in the United States. It was also necessary in that time of strategic uncertainty to keep abreast of cruise missile technology and to continue to train against such missiles on the Cold Lake range. Most interestingly, the ministers were told that free-flight testing of the AGM-129 advanced cruise missile "will begin in January 1993" – the time period during which they would be reading the briefing.[65]

1993

In the new year, the United States' arsenal stood at some 10,500 warheads, with a further 400 in inactive reserve and another 5,850 fully retired but not dismantled. There were still 416 fully armed sea-launched ballistic missiles with some warheads. The intercontinental ballistic missile (ICBM) force was holding steady at 500 missiles with some 2,000 warheads. Strategic bombing could be done with 190 operational aircraft and some 2,900 warheads on cruise missiles and in gravity bombs. The newest nuclear weapon in the arsenal was the advanced cruise missile (ACM), and its production had been cut from 640 to 460 units with the final missile to be delivered later that year. Another promising feature of the U.S. arsenal was the provision of a new SIOP, or Single Integrated Operational Plan. SIOP-94 called for fewer targets than the sixteen thousand in SIOP-85.

The most interesting cruise missile news from the former Soviet Union had to do with the 670 air-launched cruise missiles (ALCMs) remaining in Ukraine after the breakup of the USSR. Ukraine claimed the weapons and the bombers, but the Russians, fearing that the missiles could be directed towards Moscow, had loyal officers remove the guidance packages from the ALCMs and place them under Russian guard in Ukraine. The Ukrainians in turn had placed the Russian facility under guard to prevent the missiles or the components from leaving Ukraine. Canada never tried this, despite having access to the U.S. Air Force ALCM after each test flight.

The big arms control news was that on 3 January 1993, Presidents Yeltsin and Bush met at the Moscow Summit and signed the Treaty Between the United States of America and the Russia Federation on the Further Reduction and Limitation of Strategic Arms (START II). The treaty called for a warhead ceiling of 3,000 to 3,500 warheads, with a sub-ceiling of 1,700 to 1,750 SLBM warheads. Land-based multiple-warhead ICBMs were banned entirely, but no restriction was placed on cruise missiles. It stipulated that there was no limit on the numbers of bombers and weapons, and that the warhead count would be based on the actual number of warheads carried; this was different from past practice. In addition, up to one hundred heavy bombers, carrying ALCMs, that were never counted under START could be converted to a conventional role. In turn, these could be reconverted to a nuclear role and counted under START, but they could never return to a conventional role and then be struck from the START II counting rules. Arms control seemed popular with politicians, while cruise missiles were not.

THE RENEWAL OF CRUISE TESTING

Richard Ledesma, the Pentagon's CANUS T&E Coordinator, initialled the final version of the agreement and the MOU for transmission to Ottawa. Craig Farr then sent the originals along with new copies and a WordPerfect disk by commercial courier to Mike Slack at National Defence.[66] Concurrently, External Affairs had finished their review and provided their comments on the draft to the Department of National Defence.[67] This boded well for the timetable, but a new wrinkle had grown; Kim Campbell, the minister of national defence, wanted to visit Washington as soon as possible. Fowler and Calder cautioned against this as they were aware that the optics of such a visit would make it appear to both the Canadian public and to other ministers that the defence minister was taking advice from the Pentagon and not from cabinet and Canadian advisors.[68] In the end, with the disruption caused by the incoming Clinton administration, no trip was made.

Although everything seemed ready, there was a new problem. Cabinet's timetable was already full and no promising meeting times were left. The Cabinet Committee on Priorities and Planning was scheduled to meet on 27–28 January 1993, which National Defence considered to be too early, and also on 9 February, which was too late as it left no time prior to the expiry for the Order-in-Council and exchange of notes. Originally, the cabinet priorities and planning session at Meech Lake was to deal with the issue on Wednesday, 27 January.[69] Assistant Deputy Minister Ken Calder, in consultation with Deputy Minister Fowler, suggested to Kim Campbell that an ad hoc group of concerned ministers and the prime minister consider the issue in late January[70] or on the margins of the Meech Lake priorities and planning meeting.[71] Calder pointed out that "the timing will be extremely tight if we are to accomplish everything before 10 February," and noted that he had already sent informal copies of the ministerial briefing and memorandum to cabinet to Commodore Dusty Miller (the Arab Gulf War commander) at Privy Council Office, and to Mark Moher at IDD in External Affairs the previous day. Kim Campbell had insisted that Fowler provide her with options.[72] Fowler and Calder were planning on advising the minister of national defence about three possible options: refuse a renewal; renew the agreement but cancel the cruise tests; and renew the agreement and expand cruise missile testing (the DND option).[73]

Once again the final version of the draft went out to various offices for review and concurrence. This was for the last time as the text had already been initialled by Richard Ledesma in Washington, and by Beth Thomas in Defence Industrial Relations, signifying working-level agreement on the wording.[74] Even Revenue Canada was brought into the consultations, as its acceptance was required for the financial and taxation portions of the agreement and the MOU.[75] In fact, no customs duty was payable for military items brought into Canada pursuant to Tariff Item number 9810.00 of the *Customs Act*; DND did not actually pay the goods and services tax (G.S.T.); and Alberta, the location of the Cold Lake range, had no provincial sales tax.[76] Revenue Canada would not be a problem; External Affairs was the new problem.

On 11 January the legal staff at External Affairs put forward twenty-seven suggestions on the new agreement,[77] which National Defence had to immediately work into the text and translate. The translation was important as the Canadian government had decided that an English agreement was not good enough between two English-speaking countries; rather, an English and French text would be authoritative. In addition to the language issue, External Affairs was far behind on the learning curve when it came to process. As late as mid-January, staff in IDR, the regional security and peacekeeping division, were trying to figure out how an exchange of notes came into force in the United States, and whether the United States Senate would have to give approval[78] after the "five-year agreement expired." These and other questions had occurred to the diplomats at their Sussex Drive headquarters only at the last moment. In the end, none of their questions came to be of any importance. Since External Affairs did not even know the duration of the agreement, it was probably best for all concerned that the diplomats were kept at arm's length. Despite their problems, the civil servants believed that they could deliver a positive vote for renewal from their minister.[79] The only real task External Affairs had would be to get the correct name of the Canadian embassy official who would sign the text written into the Order-In-Council. The document required the name of an individual rather than simply a title. In order to keep the Canadian public in the dark about the issue, the normal public release procedure for Orders-in-Council was to be suspended briefly, and the Order-In-Council embargoed until after the agreement and the MOU had been signed.[80]

The plan was to have an ad hoc mini-cabinet meeting of concerned ministers agree to the renewal and ACM flight testing sometime during 27–28 January,[81] possibly at the Meech Lake retreat and cabinet office. In the second week of January, National Defence provided the text of a letter for the secretary of state for external affairs and the minister of national defence to send to Prime Minister Mulroney on 18–22 January requesting such a meeting. Once the letter was sent, the secretary of state for external affairs was to sign the preparatory Order-in-Council.[82] Upon approval of the documents, the exchange of notes would take place in Washington before 10 February. The assistant deputy minister (materiel) would already have a copy of the MOU, and would be prepared to sign it as soon as the exchange of notes had been signed. The signed MOU would then be delivered to Washington for the final signature by the Pentagon's CANUS T&E Coordinator.[83] Since no new person would be in the position due to the change in presidential regimes, someone in an acting position was expected to sign the document. [84] That person turned out to be Dr. Victor H. Reis, the acting under-secretary of defense (acquisition).[85] This was to happen before 10 February in order to avoid a break in the legal framework necessary to keep cruise missile testing alive.

The new problem was that even if everything was signed before the expiry date, the cruise missile testing program would still come to an end.

Only at the last minute did the Pentagon notice that the third level document, the project arrangement for the ALCM/ACM testing, did not refer to any authoritative document other than those which were set to expire. This meant that the project arrangement would also expire on that date and could not be brought back as written. Richard Ledesma suggested that the project arrangement itself be quickly amended to refer to the new memorandum of understanding in the short period between the MOU signature and 10 February when the old memorandum of understanding would expire.[86] Craig Farr also noted the problem, and suggested that a "Change 5" to the project arrangement be signed by both parties right after the MOU. This would serve to keep the project alive.[87] This was acceptable to all parties, and CoS J3 (Chief of Staff Military Plans and Operations) spearheaded this effort for National Defence.

The briefing book on the issue for the minister of national defence went through a couple of quick changes in only three days. Pierre Lagueux, Mark Mayhew, and Ray Sturgeon made comments, as did staff in Defence Industrial Relations and CoS J3. The briefing book was forwarded by Calder to Fowler and the chief of defence staff on 15 January. The deputy minister would brief Minister of National Defence Campbell on the seven-page memo five days later. January was full of briefings for Kim Campbell. She had spent both 5 January and 6 January in introductory briefings on defence matters, and now she was dealing with the most sensitive topic of her entire brief time at the Department of National Defence. On Wednesday, 20 January Robert Fowler gave the minister only two options: "allow the agreement to lapse; or, renew the agreement." Fowler recommended the latter[88] and Campbell agreed to take it to her cabinet colleagues at either the 27 January or 28 January meeting of the priorities and planning committee, or to an ad hoc meeting on the single issue. One of the few questions Campbell asked was about the advanced cruise missile. Colonel Coulter, Director Continental Policy, told her it was a "stealthy" missile with greater range than the ALCM, while the deputy minister passed her a classified photograph of the weapon. The briefing note and briefing for the secretary of state for external affairs was considerably shorter and less intensive. The deputy minister, J. R. Morden, had given it to the secretary of state on 19 January.[89]

▌ TEST # 93-4

Date: 29 January 1993
Global Cruise ALCM flight test
Route: east route, CSRL launch, free-flight

Mission profile: 0157/57NSA, first attempt
Unit: 2 Bomb Wing from Barksdale AFB, Louisiana
Bomber: B-52H/61-013
Crew: R-27
Primary missile: 83-0208
Payload: NTIK-31
Position: CSRL #026 St 2 (inside bomb bay)
Launch mode: manual
Launch altitude planned: 1,500 metres ASL
Launch point: over Beaufort Sea
Launch time: 15:54:22.281
Fuze time: 20:06:11.495
Flight time: 4 hour 12 minutes
Time error: 18 seconds late over target
Note: This was originally conceived as an ACM test, but was changed to an
    ALCM test due to continuing problems with the electronic flight control
    system of the missile. The first scheduled test day was 26 January, but
    the mission was not attempted due to bad weather at a support base. Two
    test missiles had been loaded, but only one was found to be capable due
    to battery availability. The first attempted test failed on 27 January over
    the Beaufort Sea due to forward main bomb door control valve light il-
    luminating when bomb doors were closed. Test Director aborted testing
    for forty-eight hours. The ALCM was launched from the rotary launcher
    inside the bomb bay rather than from the wing pylon. The successful test
    missile made eight TERCOM updates during the four hour flight. During
    the flight, CMDI was accomplished by CF-18 and USAF F-16 fighter air-
    craft. After landing by parachute, and recovery by 417 Helicopter Squadron,
    the missile was refurbished at Hill AFB and sent back to the opera-
    tional inventory. The ARIA aircraft was code-named "Snore Control."

The only public relations problem, aside from the fact that Canadians
hated the testing, was that even though the government was trying to
keep everything low-key up to the signing, they had agreed to a test
scheduled for 26 January. Prime Minister Mulroney was informed that
the minister of national defence and the secretary of state for external
affairs had approved the test, which he had been briefed about before the
Christmas holiday.[90] It was at this point that the new minister of national
defence made an interesting decision. Kim Campbell had chosen to tell
Canadians about the upcoming test even in the midst of the renewal
process. Her decision was based on the idea that the government would
have an advantage in being proactive and presenting their point of view
on the testing and the renewal on their own terms, rather than simply
in response to hostile questions at the discretion of the opposition and
the media.[91] As External Affairs put it for the prime minister as they prepared him to meet the new U.S. president, William Clinton, "this public
concern, however, must be balanced against Canada's broader foreign

and security policy interests."[92] The feelings of the mass of the population would again be ignored.

The minister's personal aide, John Dixon, had pointed to some problems missed by Calder's staff. Aside from the optics of another test during the process, Dixon noted that the economic argument for a renewal was compelling but not necessarily suitable for mass public consumption. He suggested that any such press release be strictly targeted to an industrial audience. His case rested on his belief that Sheila Copps, the Liberal member of Parliament, the media, and the public would certainly ask "given that the international community is now being held to ransom by a monster [Saddam Hussein] who was created by a combination of governmental short-sightedness and entrepreneurial greed among arms merchants, don't you think it is the height of cynicism to suggest that a benefit of this agreement is that we may now get to join in the scramble for cash by spreading some of our home-grown weaponry around?"[93] Dixon had hit the nail on the head; the message was unpalatable to the public and could hardly be advanced in defence of the agreement.

Although a positive decision was virtually assured, it is worth noting that as late as 28 January, less than two weeks from the formal expiry date, the minister of national defence was telling the press that no decision had been made. She was also telling the media that the new agreement would allow for enhanced training by the Canadian Forces against low-level cruise missiles.[94] Minister Campbell announced this as a new benefit despite the fact that Canadian CF-18 pilots had been doing this for several years. It was at this point that Canadians first heard official word of the planned renewal, despite National Defence and External Affairs planning to keep the entire issue buried until the day of the signing.[95] In the House of Commons, Kim Campbell would eventually defend the agreement as one "basically provid[ing] for Canadians the opportunity to develop defensive capacity against low flying missiles." She added that it was financially good for the testing of Canadian-made weapons in a still-dangerous world.[96]

There was no doubt that renewal was imminent. As if to drive home this fact within the military establishment, "Change 5" to the ALCM project arrangement, which would extend the life of the program into the next ten years,[97] arrived from Washington. Strangely, the formal signatures in change 5 required to keep the cruise missile testing program alive were not added until 11 February by Canada and 24 February by the United States.

As the date drew near Prime Minister Mulroney met with President Clinton in Washington.[98] The quick Friday, 5 February meeting at 10:30 A.M., the first meeting of a foreign leader with the new president, made only short mention of the testing issue. It is still unknown what Mulroney told Clinton, but it is prudent to conclude that the Mulroney government held high hopes for quick cabinet approval of the renewal.

The French problem now reared its ugly head. The embassy in Washington was supposed to have had both texts vetted and approved by the State Department during the week of 11–15 January.[99] According to the State Department translators, the Canadian translation of the precise English wording into French had left much to be desired.[100] On the morning of 3 February, the State Department gave the Canadian embassy a long list of problems they had with the French text, and requested immediate clarification and rectification.[101] Embarrassed by their diplomatically inadequate translation, External Affairs replied that afternoon with four pages of corrections.[102]

The expiry and renewal date arrived on Wednesday, 10 February 1993. For unknown reasons, the State Department was now stalling and the note did not get signed until late in the day. Marc Brault, the Canadian charge d'affaires at the embassy in Washington delivered External Affairs Note #24 to the new United States Secretary of State Warren Christopher.[103] Christopher had his assistant, Thomas Niles, sign the three-paragraph reply letter to Brault that same day.[104] The documents were immediately bagged up and returned to Ottawa. One more step was required to keep the testing alive – the ALCM Project Arrangement had to be amended to make it applicable to the new agreement. "Change 5" was signed by Ray Sturgeon the next day.

The late date of the signing had an unintended consequence for testing that season. As the testers could not plan on specific dates while the agreement was being renegotiated, prospective dates were chosen. The original date was 2 March, but the delay led the planners to move the ACM live launch to 23 March. It would not successfully take place until 29 March due to a variety of mission and system failures.

National Defence now had to get the press release, delayed for a day by the minister's staff,[105] out to the media before question period in the House of Commons. In anticipation of a rough ride in the Commons, even the prime minister was briefed on possible answers to questions and heckling about the unpopular renewal.[106] National Defence public affairs told the press that the government had signed a renegotiated weapons testing agreement with the United States, and that the new document gave Canada access to U.S. military and testing facilities for at least ten years. Now that the Cold War was over, continued U.S. testing of weapons in Canada was justified in terms of "increasing instability of the modern world," and supporting actions by the United Nations and for general collective security. The real reason was there as well; the United States was described as a longstanding ally "and trading partner."[107] The Canadian government could not run the risk of displeasing Washington and then have Washington retaliate by either political or economic means. Polling done after the announcement showed that only 35 percent of Canadians approved of the agreement and continued cruise missile testing.[108]

That spring all military units involved in the testing met at Barksdale AFB for the annual "lessons learned" conference.[109] This would be the final, regularly scheduled conference. Cruise missile testing had little more than a year to live, and it would not be the Canadian government that killed the despised tests.

1994

Only one more free flight of the ACM would be conducted under the auspices of the CANUS T&E Agreement, and it would be the final cruise missile flight over Canada. On 6 March 1994, the second and last advanced cruise missile would fly the eastern test route and crash into Primrose Lake weapons range as planned after a five-hour, twenty-four-minute flight.

6

All Things Must End:
The Death of Cruise Missile Testing

CANUSTEP will be an extremely important tool in the
effort to maintain operational effectiveness under
conditions of decreased fiscal resources.
Aide-Memoire for the Minister of National Defence on the value of the
Canada-U.S. Test and Evaluation Program,
7 January 1994

1993

As November 1993 came to an end, staff in the office of Ken Calder, the assistant deputy minister for policy at National Defence, were hard at work on a crucial memorandum to the minister. This document would set out the details of the entire cruise missile test program since 1983, and would request the new Liberal minister to make a decision on allowing the flights previously agreed to by the former Conservative government. As Calder's staff put it, the purpose was to provide background on the test series, to inform about the planned tests in 1994, and to recommend a course of action for the near future.

Calder's memo was to be signed by Deputy Minister Robert R. Fowler and Chief of Defence Staff Admiral J. R. Anderson. Both received copies on 22 November, and both signed the document for forwarding to Minister of National Defence David Collenette immediately.[1] As they saw it, the 1994 tests had been approved by the previous government, and this approval had been communicated to Washington on 26 August. Delay would inconvenience the United States Air Force, and cancellation would impair the Canadian Forces' ability to take advantage of the new reciprocal CANUSTEP.

The first thing that Fowler and Anderson told Collenette was that another test of the advanced cruise missile would take place on 25 January 1994. The minister of national defence then learned that in January 1989 the previous cabinet had agreed to allow testing of the advanced cruise missile. The lesson continued with the minister noting that a list of proposed projects arrived from Washington annually in January, and that the recent list had specifically indicated a desire to continue tests of both types of cruise missiles. On 26 August the previous minister of national defence, Kim Campbell, had agreed to the two 1994 tests scheduled for 25 January and 1 March,[2] and this was immediately communicated by Pierre Lagueux to the U.S. coordinator. Although National Defence Headquarters could rescind permission at any time, the minister of national defence was informed that all approvals were ready and that most were in place for the tests. Only the final safety review needed to be completed two weeks prior on 7–8 December.

The reality was that Washington viewed this as a crucial test. The Clinton administration and especially the Pentagon thought that the new Liberal government would pass or fail based on this test of its resolve. On the same day that Collenette was briefed, the United States embassy staff visited the Department of Foreign Affairs (the Department of External Affairs was now known as the Department of Foreign Affairs and International Trade or DFAIT) to present the official view from Washington. Although the U.S. embassy did not present a démarche, they did indicate that "the government of Canada is aware of the importance the U.S. attaches to these tests and must be aware that the decision will be seen as a litmus test for Canada-U.S. relations in the defence/security sphere."[3]

The Liberals had promised a thorough review of defence policy and commitments during the 1993 election campaign, and the cruise missile would be part of the review. Fowler and Anderson told Collenette that the forthcoming review would examine the Canada-United States defence relationship, and that cruise missile testing and CANUS T&E Agreement were important facets of that relationship. However, the review would not touch on the overall CANUSTEP agreement. The minister of national defence was provided with a two-page, detailed list of projects that the Canadian Forces could now pursue in the United States under the new reciprocal agreement. An aide-memoire for the minister concluded, "CANUSTEP will be an extremely important tool in the effort to maintain operational effectiveness under conditions of decreased fiscal resources."[4]

With this in mind, Fowler and Anderson recommended that the minister of national defence allow "cruise missile testing currently scheduled for 25 January and 1 March 1994 be conducted as planned," and that the public affairs office be directed to develop the ways and means to convey this message to the public in the new year. The most interesting recommendation was that "decisions related to the future of cruise missile testing and of the test and evaluation agreement be held in abeyance pending their examination in the context of the defence policy review."[5] David Collenette read and reread the memo. He discussed it with his closest personal and professional advisors and with the prime minister; on 30 November he wrote "Approved 30/11/93" across the bottom and initialled the document.[6]

While this was taking place at National Defence, the new minister of foreign affairs, André Ouellet, was also being briefed by Gaetan Lavertu, his assistant deputy minister for political and international security affairs. The staff officer on the case, Mark Moher, had drafted an action memorandum on the several issues in joint Canada–United States defence cooperation that now required ministerial decisions. Moher, in consultation with Ken Calder's staff[7] and the associate assistant deputy minister for policy, General John Boyle,[8] was proposing to tell Ouellet about the relevance of NORAD, the new Halifax acoustic submarine tracking facility, the new USAF overflight agreement, and cruise missiles.[9] As the ministry of Foreign Affairs was cognizant that the new Liberal government was wary of allowing further cruise missile tests, and that the question had split party ranks, Foreign Affairs asked the United States government "to confirm the operational necessity for testing in early 1994."[10] The recommendation to the secretary of state for external affairs was much the same as that to the minister of national defence a few days earlier. However, it was known that Ouellet was much less enthusiastic about cruise missile testing than was Collenette. In fact, Moher had told his U.S. counterpart that he could not predict the minister's response on this issue, and that it was possible that Ouellet might turn down the 1994 testing request.[11]

Washington was not inactive in the face of what was perceived as growing Liberal opposition to the tests in Canada. The United States' CANUS T&E annual thirty-month forecast, which was usually received in January, arrived on the desk of Pierre Lagueux, the assistant deputy minister (supply), immediately after being signed on 10 December 1993. Richard Ledesma, the United States CANUS T&E coordinator, was wasting no time and hoped to be heard before the decision which they now felt was sure to come in January. Ledesma pointed out that ALCM tests "have previously been approved in principle by Canada and will be continuing."[12] Lagueux was told that aside from the ALCM, other previously approved tests included the V-22 aircraft, the ribbon bridge transporter, and the B-2 bomber. New test programs now being proposed were limited to a night targeting system and the AN/FPS-117 radar, possibly for the stealth fighter.

Clearly the Pentagon was worried that the new Liberal Chrétien government was going to listen to critics like Lloyd Axworthy and cancel the tests. It had to get the message through to the new minister of national defence and the best way to do so was by pushing forward the date of the forecast letter.

Upon receipt of the secret letter and annexes, Pierre Lagueux quickly forwarded it to Ken Calder. The assistant deputy minister (policy and communications) and his staff then drafted another very detailed and carefully worded memo for the minister of national defence. Although there is no indication that the memo was sent to Collenette, the title and contents are worth noting. Calder's note, to be signed by the deputy minister and the chief of the defence staff and forwarded to the minister of national defence, was titled "Cruise missile testing in Canada - Government Decision."[13] The Department of National Defence command was worried that the Liberals were going to flush away the CANUS T&E Agreement with the cruise missile testing, and it was imperative that Collenette be made to understand that the agreement was still important to DND even without the cruise missile component. Collenette was told that the Department of National Defence was now trying to "avoid jeopardizing our testing activities under the CANUSTEP,"[14] and that for this reason ministerial guidance was needed in this time of transition. The minister of national defence was being called upon to save the agreement so that Canadian weapons and systems could be tested in the United States at the same time as it became obvious that cruise missile testing was coming to an end.

The high command saw a disaster looming if Collenette did not fight for them in cabinet. The renewal of the agreement in February 1993 had added a reciprocity clause which allowed Canadian access to U.S. testing ranges and facilities, and the Department of National Defence was in the last stage of preparing its first testing proposal forecast for transmission to the Pentagon.[15] The document would be ready by the end of January and was to be protected even as the hardest test of the agreement to date was being weathered. The Canadian military conducted a significant amount of equipment testing in the United States, and the new agreement allowed this to be done at reduced costs and increased efficiency. For this reason alone the agreement would have been of value to the military. The second consideration was that a cancellation of the CANUS T&E Agreement might well anger the U.S. government and result in reduced cooperation from Washington. The Canadian military has always had a patron, and the current patron was the United States — so nothing was to be done which would incur the wrath of the political and military leaders south of the border.

In Moscow President Yeltsin of Russia and United States President Clinton formally agreed to change the target sets in their intercontinental ballistic missile (ICBM) forces by 30 May 1994. This was the detargeting agreement, and it stipulated that the missiles would not be targeted at the other country. Each declared that they would not operate their nuclear forces "in a manner that presumes they are adversaries." The United States would remove the codes from 75 percent of their systems and retarget the remainder towards the oceans. The Russians pledged to do the same.

Joined by Ukrainian President Kravchuk, the three leaders signed the "Trilateral Agreement" on the basic terms for the transfer of nuclear weapons from Ukraine to Russia and on compensation to Ukraine for the loss. Under the provisions of START I, Ukraine had agreed to dismantle all of its nuclear weapons infrastructure and transfer all nuclear warheads back to Russia. The Ukrainian government pledged to remove all warheads from their RS-22 ICBM force within ten months, and to deliver at least 200 warheads from the RS-18 and RS-22 ICBMs back to Russia. By the end of the year Ukraine had sent 360 warheads to Russia, including 300 ICBM warheads and 60 cruise missile warheads. A further 700 ICBM warheads had been removed from their missiles and sent to storage near the two ICBM fields in Ukraine. Of the 176 ICBMs in Ukraine, 40 RS-18s from the Pervomaysk missile field were removed from silos and sent to temporary storage. The same was happening in other areas of the former Soviet Union; the arsenal was being drawn down and dismantled.

The U.S. arsenal was still being upgraded. As set out in the Nuclear Posture Review, official plans called on the Pentagon to keep a strategic weapon level of 3,000 to 3,500 warheads, and to keep approximately 450 tactical nuclear weapons deployed in European states that were NATO members. The United States had no intention of lowering the warhead level to below 3,000, and this would remain official policy for the rest of the millennium. The Cold War was over, but news had not filtered down to Ottawa and Washington.

With the coming of the new year Prime Minister Chrétien jetted off to meet President Francois Mitterand of France. When asked by reporters about cruise missile testing on 7 January, Chrétien told reporters in Paris that "we have not discussed that,"[16] and "there is no decision made [and] I will discuss that when back in Ottawa."[17] His answer was not quite true. The decision had been made on or about 30 November of the previous year by Chrétien's own minister of national defence in consultation with the prime minister; yet Chrétien, wanting to avoid more division within the party, chose to lie. That same day, the military operational and safety review took place and concluded that there were no problems.[18]

In Ottawa the media headed for National Defence and cornered Collenette spokesman John Williston, who said that although planning continued for the tests in the January to March period, he could not give the exact dates of the flights more than forty-eight hours before the actual launch.[19] It was a wise thing to say as the Pentagon and NORAD officials had already confirmed that tests would occur in the very near future. Media attention turned to Lloyd Axworthy, who had been a key figure in opposing the tests in recent year. The news division of CTV was now asking Axworthy's staff about the cruise missile testing situation and if the minister thought tests would take place in the very near future.[20] That same day Jim Judd, the Privy Council Office head of defence policy, sent an urgent memo on the cruise missile issue for the prime minister to see "today."[21] The content of the memo is still unknown, but it is thought to contain actual test dates and forward plans.

The high command's offices on the thirteenth floor at National Defence Headquarters was buzzing with activity in light of the statements made by all concerned ministers and their staffs. In light of the problems that had surfaced over this issue the previous week (7–8 January), General John Boyle, the associate assistant deputy minister (policy), demanded a full briefing note from his staff and the deputy minister for the minister of national defence. A draft was ordered by 10 January in the hope that if the problem were solved early enough, DND would be able to stave off a delay in the planned tests.[22]

That day, Robert Fowler and John de Chastelain took the decision "to persuade the U.S. to delay the Jan & Mar CM test by three weeks."[23] Chrétien himself may have suggested the delay in order to give cabinet time to decide the matter. General Boyle immediately informed the Canadian defence staff in Washington and Air Command headquarters in Winnipeg. He told his staff that he would talk with the minister's staff at Foreign Affairs later that day. The Director of Continental Policy was assigned the task to contact the U.S. Air Force in Washington and break the news to them and to the director of aerospace development in Ottawa. Boyle was immediately asked not to tell the U.S. Air Force about the delay, as the Director of Continental Policy (DC Pol-3) seemed to believe that the concurrent effort to resolve the issue might make the delay unnecessary.[24] The advice was not heeded.

Boyle immediately moved to have the United States Air Force told about the change in plans, and requested that the USAF plan for a delay. The message was too late in arriving to halt the request for the final go-ahead for specific tests. That same day, one of the USAF units involved in the test planning, the 939 RQW from Portland, Oregon, requested confirmation of the test date for 25 January.[25] Worse, three days earlier a significant USAF unit, 79 TEG at Eglin AFB in Florida, had also made a similar request for confirmation.[26]

At this time, Prime Minister Chrétien was attending the NATO summit and had the opportunity to speak with the weakened United States secretary of state, Warren Christopher.[27] Chrétien told Christopher that cruise missile testing was becoming increasingly difficult for Canada and the matter would be decided soon. The two men also talked about the situation in Bosnia.

The news was not greeted with great enthusiasm in Washington. The next day, on 12 January, the U.S. State Department told the Canadian embassy that they expected to meet with the charge d'affaires on Tuesday, 18 January at 4:00 P.M. at the State Department.[28] The diplomat, M. Kergin, would have to face Stephen Oxman, the assistant secretary of state for European and Canadian affairs to explain the situation in Ottawa, especially in light of the secret discussion held earlier at the NATO summit between the prime minister and the United States president.[29] Both the prime minister and Foreign Affairs had asked the United States to confirm the operational necessity for testing.[30] Washington was not used to being questioned, even in a benign way.

Kergin was in a delicate situation. He had to appease Ottawa and at the same time not antagonize the senior partner in Washington. Kergin was supposed to tell the U.S. team that the issue would be dealt with soon, but that many new cabinet ministers had well-known anti-cruise missile views.[31] He was also supposed to point out that at various encounters such as the recent Permanent Joint Board on Defence meeting, Canada had stated that with the change in government certain arrangements that had become routine would be reviewed. Foreign Affairs had directed him to say that a decision would be made shortly, but that the time required would necessitate a delay of the 25 January proposed schedule.[32] He was supposed to stall very politely. He never really had a chance.

Kergin met with Stephen Oxman, Assistant Secretary for Canadian Affairs Mary-Ann Peters, Deputy Director of Canadian Affairs Bruce Ehrnman, and Walter Slocum, the deputy under-secretary of defense for policy at the Pentagon.[33] Oxman began the meeting by telling Kergin about the United States' appreciation for the valuable opportunity to use Canadian airspace for testing cruise missiles. He emphasized that the White House was aware of how difficult the testing issue was in Canada, and that they were doubly appreciative for this reason. Then he brought up the reservations that the United States was having. Kergin was told that the 25 January test could be postponed, but at a cost. In fact, the U.S. Air Force had already prepared for the test date being pushed back. Oxman noted that this particular test was covered by an agreed project arrangement, and that if that test were to be cancelled, the United States government would have to reconsider the overall utility of the CANUS T&E Agreement.[34]

Walter Slocum was far less diplomatic and stressed that a cabinet decision to withdraw prior permission for an approved test would pose a serious problem. Kergin noted that Slocum issued a veiled threat by saying that he "hoped it would be possible to discuss such a negative decision, as well as the consequences of such a response, before it was finalized."[35] Although both Oxman and Slocum "left consequences of such a cancellation undefined," the suggestion was made that the CANUS T&E Agreement would have to be reconsidered and that the White House might consider abrogation.[36] Finally, the U.S. team wanted advance notice of a decision so that they could once again state their case in Ottawa. Kergin promised to convey their views to the authorities in Ottawa.

On behalf of the new Canadian government, Kergin told the U.S. delegation that Ottawa had been signalling that since the change of government, "certain arrangements which had become routine with [the] previous government could not be taken for granted when up for renewal." Kergin added that cabinet would deal with the issue of cruise missile testing very soon, and that although no decision had yet been made, the responsible ministers were thoroughly familiar with the U.S. government's view of the situation. Getting to the hard part, Kergin told the assembled group that the lack of decision at this point meant that the Canadian government required "some slippage in the January 25 proposed schedule."

In closing, Kergin cautioned Oxman and Slocum that both public and private discretion and sensitivity was necessary when addressing this issue in the coming weeks.[37] Oxman understood, but Slocum continued to hammer away with his comments.[38]

The meeting in Washington was of little comfort in Ottawa, especially in the material department at National Defence. Pierre Lagueux warned that the U.S. side was now directly linking the entire CANUS T&E Agreement to cruise missile testing, and that any adverse Canadian action could destroy the agreement. Being the "materiel AND Supply" official, Lagueux had a special interest in this matter. He noted that U.S. linkage endangered the close cooperation the two countries now had in the testing field and in the materiel field. Lagueux requested that this aspect of the relationship be taken into account when the assistant deputy minister (policy) drafted the new defence policy review.[39]

Air Command Headquarters in Winnipeg was now in the line of fire, as commanders there had to tell their U.S. Air Force counterparts about the current situation. Those who had made the requests (who had sent messages to Air Command on 7 and 10 January), and others in the U.S. Air Force hierarchy, were told that the Canadian government was currently considering the issue of further testing, but that no decision had been made. Recipients were informed that "until such time as that decision is taken and communicated to NDHQ and AIRCOM staff it is not possible to approve the requests."[40] Air Command then undertook to inform those offices which had the greatest need to know, for the purposes of planning, of any decision immediately by telephone. Late in the evening on 21 January the U.S. Air Force responded by telling everyone involved of the stand-down in testing.[41]

In Ottawa David Collenette was telling the press that the Liberals were committed to a debate the following week, and that only on the Thursday after the debate would a decision be made on allowing the tests. He went on to note that the previous government had approved the upcoming tests, but that the United States had been advised that the Chrétien Cabinet was reviewing the situation. When asked why the debate was occurring at the start of what had been the testing season for the past nine years, Collenette responded by noting that "obviously people on the ground had no reason to believe that tests would not go ahead early this year." Collenette had to duck the question when a reporter, who had been privy to the earlier decision, asked the minister if he had given his permission for the U.S. tests back in November 1993 by writing "Approved 30/11/93" across the bottom of the memo on the tests. The Minister stated that approval had come from the Mulroney Government the previous August, "before we were sworn into office."[42] The Chrétien power structure needed the tests to appease the United States even as the Liberal Party tore itself asunder on the issue.

Prime ministerial staff in the Langevin Block on Parliament Hill were now coordinating a debate on the issue. Herb Gray, the government house leader, and the party leadership had decided that a full debate would be held exclusively on cruise missile testing on Wednesday, 26 January and that a decision would be made after that which would affect the entire testing season for 1994.[43] Gray announced the small initiative, and Prime Minister Chrétien expanded upon it in response to a question by Svend Robinson, the NDP defence critic. Robinson had asked about a full parliamentary debate, as had been demanded of the Conservative government by the Liberals' Lloyd Axworthy when the Liberals were in opposition a year ago. Chrétien stated, "there will be full debate in this House of Commons."[44]

While Chrétien was speaking about the debate in the House of Commons, Mr. Gray's office at Privy Council was preparing the text of a motion to be sponsored by the minister of national defence during the upcoming debate.[45] Of the three proposed wordings, Collenette's office decided that it would be best to say "[That this House,] Recognizing that a bilateral Umbrella Agreement for Weapons Testing exists between the Government of Canada and the Government of the United States, take note of the domestic, international and bilateral aspects of allowing the Government of the United States of America to conduct cruise missile tests within Canadian territorial boundaries, and in particular, two cruise missile tests during the first quarter of 1994."[46]

Staff in the government leader's office also took pains to prepare a series of talking points in favour of testing for any speaker who would support the CANUS T&E Agreement and cruise missile testing in Canada.[47] No talking points opposing cruise missiles were prepared for a Liberal member to use in the Commons. Marcel Masse was instructed to make vague statements if asked about the issue. He was also told that the CANUS T&E Agreement was only "one of about 600 bilateral arrangements between Canada and the Untied States,"[48] but he was not to reveal this due to the storm of protest and debate it would certainly spark.

The Liberal government was now dealing in two realities. With the prime minister's knowledge, the minister of national defence had given his approval to USAF cruise missile tests on 30 November 1993. Concurrently, the Canadian government had asked the Pentagon to delay any testing until after a more formal decision had been made and announced in Parliament. The minister of national defence also asked Washington to put off any testing in February until March. This reality had permeated all levels of government in Ottawa, and was starting to produce cognitive dissonance. The Department of National Defence knew that permission had been granted, but now had to tell its dominant partner that testing would be delayed. This was the reality, and the policy staff at NDHQ began trying to determine who in Washington would receive news of the final political decision. The Pentagon was then going through a period of transition as Secretary of Defence Les Aspin, formerly the senior defence specialist in Congress, was stepping down. The deputy secretary, William Perry, was the Clinton administration's nominee to replace Aspin, but this had yet to be confirmed by the Senate. The Department of National Defence made the decision to formally contact the office of Les Aspin with the news, whether he was there or not.[49]

The USAF Air Combat Command then issued an order to prepare for the final tests of 1994 by stating that the free flights of the ACM were "the best source of information on the operational effectiveness and suitability of cruise missiles," and therefore it was imperative that these test missions occur if at all possible.[50]

In the final stretch leading to the debate, the White House and State Department began to apply more pressure. Late Tuesday, 25 January 1994, the U.S. embassy staff in Ottawa visited their counterparts at Foreign Affairs in the Pearson Building on Sussex Drive and delivered a stern message. While it was not a démarche, the embassy indicated that "The Government of Canada is aware of the importance the U.S. attaches to these tests and must be aware that the decision will be seen as a litmus test for Canada-U.S. relations in the defence/security sphere."[51] The threat was now very real; the prime minister's office, the minister of national defence, and the minister of foreign affairs all knew the consequences of a negative outcome to the debate.

Minister Collenette was instructed to make an opening speech giving broad details of the history of the cruise missile issue. His staff had come up against the same problem that had plagued the Tories before them — how to justify the Cold War missile in the post-Cold War environment. Collenette was to tell the Commons that although the missile had been designed to fight the Soviets and was initially tested in Canada during a particularly low point in the Cold War, it was now needed for counter-proliferation purposes. The minister would tell members of Parliament that with the end of the Cold War many more nations had acquired cruise missile technology, and that testing in Canada aided both western security and the operational training of Canadian Forces pilots.[52] The switch had been made.

The decision had also been made. Collenette was to tell the members of Parliament that despite anything which would be said in the Commons that day that "In the meantime, given the former government had approved in principle the 1994 test series and that extensive planning for these tests is already well advanced, the government has decided to allow the United States to test two unarmed cruise missiles in Canada in 1994. To repeat, the Government will allow two tests of cruise missiles in Canada in 1994."[53]

Debate began at 3:17 P.M. with Collenette speaking for thirteen minutes and proposing the motion given to him by Herb Gray a few days before. The motion was seconded by Minister of Foreign Affairs André Ouellet. The debate would not end until 10:00 P.M., as forty-five Members of Parliament (twenty Liberals, twelve Bloc Québécois, ten Reform, two NDP and one Conservative) spoke to the issue. Twenty-six members made statements and another nineteen asked questions. The only real debate in the House of Commons came from the two NDP members and half the Liberals who chose to speak. Members from the opposition party, the secessionist Bloc Québécois, were totally in favour of the tests. This was more of a surprise than the solid and unequivocal support given to the proposed tests by the ultra-right wing Reform Party.

After Collenette's opening remarks, Lucien Bouchard, a former Mulroney Tory and supporter of the testing, called into question why the government was even holding the debate as they "had made a commitment in principle." Bouchard, who was then trying to lead his province into becoming a sovereign state by participating in the federal Parliament, came out against ending tests as "to stop test[ing] would be detrimental to our interests." Bouchard, having been either ill-advised or out of touch with the realities of the current government, stated that he thought the debate was a cover for the decision to cancel the tests, a decision which had already been made. Most interestingly, Bouchard encouraged Chrétien and the House of Commons to approve a renewal of the CANUS T&E Agreement in 2003 when it expired for the second time.

Reform Party reaction was much more mundane and predictable. Reform led off with Jack Frazer, a former base operations officer at CFB Cold Lake. Frazer spoke about prior commitments and how the old agreement, signed in 1983 during the Cold War, somehow (although he was not specific as to how) guaranteed stability in a volatile world. He pointed out that although the test route ran through his constituency he received no complaints from his Reform Party constituents. The tag team approach next saw Deborah Grey, whose constituency included CFB Cold Lake, talk about the importance of the tests to the local economy. Grey's grasp of economics was clearly not good, as there was no local economic impact to cruise missile testing in the Cold Lake region. However, she continued by noting the benefits derived by the Canadian Forces in terms of operational testing and pilot training, and in terms of increased cooperation with the larger partner south of the border.

The Prime Minister's Office must have been relieved that in response to a question from L. Lavigne, Member of Parliament from Salaberry, another member stated, "the enemy is everywhere!" The debate was going in favour of testing, and the PMO thought that it might not turn out to be the divisive issue first imagined.

The only real challenge to the government came from Svend Robinson, the NDP member for Burnaby-Kingsway, who called on Chrétien to enact the policy the Liberals had developed in opposition, and end the tests. Robinson then drew the knife and asked what had happened to the honesty of the Liberal party. In closing, he asked a real question of the government: will they end cruise missile testing? The government responded that it was a diplomatic question and that "friendly persuasion" was needed when dealing with the United States. Robinson was the only one in the Commons that day dealing with the truth. He stated that the debate was a smokescreen, and that the decision to go ahead had already been communicated to the United States. He also challenged Lloyd Axworthy's absence from the debate. Robinson was correct in stating that a decision had already been communicated, but he did not know that all was on hold now pending a decision by Chrétien after the debate. However, he was correct in that it was a foregone conclusion.

For the ruling Liberals, the opposition parties were not a significant problem. The problem was coming from within the party. The Honourable Charles Caccia (Member of Parliament for Davenport) pointed out that cruise missile testing was a relic of the Cold War, and that real security threats were not strictly military and could not be dealt with by a strictly military means. Caccia stated that the end of stationing of nuclear weapons in Canada should have ended our nuclear commitments. Warren Allmand, who had opposed the testing when it was first proposed, said that he was even more opposed now that the Cold War was over. Allmand opposed the destabilizing effects of the weapon and its contribution to proliferation. This was a good point as the Department of National

Defence had admitted that since the weapon had been developed by the United States and USSR, more than forty countries now had cruise missile capabilities. Roger Gallaway argued that allowing the tests was to accept a reality that existed only in 1983, and that there was no real security benefits to North America derived from testing. Ethel Blondin-Andrew, the Liberal member of Parliament for the western Arctic, refused to speak in debate despite the overwhelming negative feedback from her constituents. Blondin-Andrew had been besieged by the Inuit and others from the region imploring her to take a stand against the testing as many other Liberals had done. She refused and stayed silent. Her silence was later rewarded by Jean Chrétien.

The debate in the House of Commons was a sham. Only later events would turn the tide. The next day, with little to fear other than his own party, Chrétien was briefed by Glen Shortliffe, clerk of the Privy Council, on the outcome of the debate.[54] Reporters for the major newspapers gave a curious view of the long debate. Jeff Sallot from the national *Globe and Mail*, who had covered so many cruise missile stories, centred his report on the views of Bouchard and the Bloc Québécois, while totally missing the actual opening statement of the government endorsing the tests.[55] Allan Thompson of the *Toronto Star* failed to notice that half the Liberals who spoke were not in favour, choosing to mention only Caccia and Parish. He too failed to note the real meaning of Collenette's opening remarks.[56] At least reports from the Canadian Press noted that the debate was marked by the silence of Lloyd Axworthy and Sheila Copps, both vocal critics when they were in opposition.[57]

Chrétien, Collenette, and Ouellet formalized the decision immediately, and this was communicated by telephone to Washington by Ken Calder's staff at NDHQ. However, this fact was hidden for another week. The final planning stages were again set in motion. Within thirty-six hours of the debate ending, the prime testing offices in the United States were gearing up for the first test now only a month away.

The 79 Test and Evaluation Group (TEG) at Eglin AFB in Florida informed all other concerned units that the first test date was 28 February,[58] and that everybody would have to work very hard to accommodate the two ACM tests planned for 28 February and 2 March. The 410 Bomb Wing and all other 410 squadrons at K. I. Sawyer AFB in Michigan were to prepare two B-52 bombers with two AGM-129 ACMs each for the entire thirteen-day period no later than 23 February. The AWACS from 552 OSS at Tinker AFB had to be in place at Elmendorf AFB in Alaska by 26 February. Two ARIA range instrumentation aircraft were required for the entire window, with an early fly-by of the Cold Lake facility before the test. A rescue Hercules from the Air Force reserve in Portland was to be on site for the two weeks, and numerous aerial refuelling tankers would be flown in from the continental United States and Alaska to support all mission aircraft. NORAD would provide a small number of fighter-inter-ceptor aircraft to practice against the ACM.[59]

National Defence Headquarters and the Air Experimental Test Establishment (AETE) were asked to allow a new testing window to start on 28 February,[60] when the first test was now scheduled, through to 12 March, with the exception of Sunday, 6 March.[61] This would be a prob-lem for the government. Cabinet had limited testing to March, and a February date, even if it was the last day of the month, was politically unacceptable.

Ottawa could wait no longer; the announcement would have to be made. Officials in the Prime Minister's Office leaked the upcoming an-nouncement to *Globe and Mail* reporter Jeff Sallot.[62] The issue would be brought up in Parliament, and Collenette was ready. Gilles Duceppe, the future Bloc Québécois Party leader, asked whether the government had made a decision and what that decision was. Minister Collenette said, "the government has decided to proceed with the two tests in 1994 be-ginning with this month."[63] Immediately after the exchange on Thursday afternoon, 4 February, National Defence released a press statement to the media announcing not a cruise missile test, but a review of cruise missile testing. The public affairs writers had come up with a clever means of concealing what had long been decided. The press release was a statement by the minister of national defence without further comment.

The previous Government agreed last summer to allow the United States Air Force to proceed with planning for two tests of the cruise missile in Canada in the first quarter of 1994. In view of the fact that this planning was already well advanced when our Government took office, and that there will be ample opportunity to examine further the matter of cruise testing in the context of the forthcoming reviews of both foreign policy and defence policy, we have decided to allow the tests now planned for next month to proceed. I would like to make very clear that while we have advised the American Government that these tests may go ahead this year, we have stressed the fact that they should make no presumption about the outcome of the defence policy review and foreign policy review which will take place over the course of 1994. Given the depth of feeling within the country and within the Liberal Party on this issue it would be imprudent indeed to presume anything about our Government's willingness to proceed with further cruise missile tests in Canada. That said, we have indicated we will be reviewing these matters with an open mind and we will do so.[64]

The media savaged the Liberals for this clear reversal of party policy. John Ward of Canadian Press put it best when he wrote, "The federal Liberals, who opposed cruise missile testing while they were in Opposition, have approved another set of such tests this spring."[65] The same line appeared in newspapers across the country and on television screens in every home. Sallot quoted David Collenette as saying that the decision had been reached only after much soul-searching, and that "people in our party and many people in Canada have difficulty with the testing of certain kinds of weapon systems ... linked to the cold war."[66]

The last theoretical impediment to testing was gone. Major Chmara, the Air Command Headquarters G3 coordinator, and Colonel R. W. Guidinger, the director of continental policy at NDHQ had told the U.S. Air Force that all signs were go for the test,[67] except that it would have to happen only in March to conform with the direction of the minister of national defence.[68] The 79 Test and Evaluation Group at Eglin AFB put out the word that the testing schedule had been altered to move it out of February, but that the window was now extended all the way to the end of March.[69]

Meanwhile, another issue had come to the fore in Washington. The old U.S. Navy undersea, acoustic, anti-submarine shore-based listening and data processing facility at Argentia, Newfoundland, was being closed and relocated to Halifax. Arrangements were well underway when it became obvious to both the State Department and the Defense Department that the arrangement had certain legal problems. Bad past experiences with the British over sensitive intelligence matters had prompted the United States government to insist on formal agreements and extremely closely associated memorandums of understanding. The new problem was that the proposed document covering the new acoustic facility in Halifax, the so-called *Chapeau* agreement on defence cooperation, was broad enough to cover cruise missile testing. Michael Dawson at the Canadian embassy in Washington was told that for the Pentagon the "experience of cruise missile testing agreement had been something of a shock to the system," and that the new agreement might cause the Canadian government to balk and provoke major debate in Canada on the nature of the entire Canada-United States bilateral defence relationship. The State Department contact told Dawson that "American officials are not entirely sanguine as to [the] outcome of such a debate, based on their reading of [the] cruise missile testing saga."[70]

The Pentagon's thirty-month forecast for CANUS T&E testing arrived the following day. The Department of Defense letter and attachments proposed more follow-on testing of either the AGM-86B ALCM or the AGM-129 ACM.[71] The note followed appropriate channels, and was staffed through junior offices within the international industry program office and the policy directorate.

At this point it was doubtful that the prime minister himself knew when the first test would be. In fact, Glen Shortliffe had to tell Chrétien about the date of the agreed test the day before in a formal memo.[72] However, since the date of the test was a public fact the day before the memo, the prime minister probably read about it in the newspaper just like every Canadian. Transport Canada had issued a notice to airmen on 27 February telling them of the flight path conflict.

The winter of 1993–94 was not an easy one in the far north, and the cold and snow, like anti-nuclear protestors, conspired to halt the tests. At the appointed time the B-52 bomber left K. I. Sawyer AFB and headed for the Beaufort Sea. Only once the bomber was well on its way to the Arctic did the test director abort the mission when it became obvious that none of the aircraft at Elmendorf AFB, Alaska would be able to take off due to zero visibility on the ground. The next day the test was again cancelled when the AWACS aircraft was grounded by weather problems, but at least it was done before the B-52 had taken off and burned several tonnes of fuel. Two days later the B-52 actually reached the launch point far out over the Beaufort Sea when the mission was again scrubbed due to inclement weather in Alaska.

Finally, on the one day that the U.S. Air Force said it did not intend to test, Global Shadow test A94-04 of the AGM-129 started with the ACM being launched the morning of 6 March at 14:15z. The missile passed over the target at 19:39:55z, and then proceeded to dive into the ground and shatter into tiny bits. The final cruise missile had been tested in Canada.

TEST # A94-06 (A193)

Date: 6 March 1994
Global Shadow ACM flight test
Route: east route, free-flight
Second live ACM launch and free-flight
Last official cruise missile test in Canada
Mission profile A93NSA (first attempt)

Unit: 410 Bomb Wing from K. I. Sawyer AFB, Michigan
Bomber: B-52H/60-0011
Crew: E-72
Primary missile: 90-0131
Payload: NTIK-18
Position: RP-2
Secondary Missile: 90-0116
Payload: NTIK-15
Position: LP-2
Launch mode: automatic
Direction of travel at launch: 113 degrees
TERCOM updates: 4
Launch time: 14:15:18.06z
Inertial Fuze time: 19:39:55.02z
Time to target: 5 hours, 24 minutes
Prior attempts to test:
1. Aborted 1 March when, after bomber reached launch area, test director scrubbed mission due to poor visibility at Elmendorf AFB, Alaska.
2. Aborted 2 March when, before bomber took off, AWACS aircraft experienced weather problems at Elmendorf AFB.
3. Aborted 3 March due to bad weather at Elmendorf AFB.
4. Aborted 4 March when, after bomber reached launch point, test director scrubbed mission due to AWACS having weather problems at Elmendorf AFB.
    The missile terminated its flight by crashing into the ground at Primrose Lake. The debris was gathered and returned to the United States. This was the second ACM free-flight, and the last cruise missile test flight authorized in Canada.

The official count noted eighteen ALCM flights, of which three were captive-carries, and five ACM flights, of which four were captive-carries and only one was free-flight.[73] Since there were two ACM free flights, it is unclear why the Department of National Defence listed only one in a secret document.

Testing of weapons must compete with various other operational and training priorities, and the spring of 1994 was a busy one for the U.S. Air Force. Most aircraft had already been tasked for various missions and training schedules, so the support aircraft required for the advanced cruise missile testing were lacking. Lacking the necessary aircraft, the United States Air Force had chosen to conduct only a single test despite having another twenty-four days of test windows available, and the entire test establishment geared up.[74] This news was communicated to the CANUS T&E coordinator and to the assistant deputy minister (policy) by the U.S. coordinator and the U.S. Air Force soon after the success of A94-04.

The 28 TEST Squadron announced to the air force community that the one test concluded cruise missile activity over Canadian airspace for the fiscal year 1994, but that "future plans for FY95 and beyond remain the same. Two air-launched cruise missile (ALCM) tests are still planned for the spring of 1995."[75] Exact dates would be decided at the "lesson-learned" meeting held 1–3 June[76] at Barksdale AFB in Louisiana. Now the air force was certain that cruise missile testing was theoretically to continue, and it was up to the deputy minister and the chief of defence staff to tell the minister of national defence. Ken Calder told the deputy minister and the chief of defence staff that the latest U.S. proposal "includes a request for continued cruise missile testing in the January to March 1995 testing window." Telephone discussions with the testing organizations had shown that more tests were "planned to continue throughout the operational life of the weapons system."[77]

Colonel Guidinger told his officer in charge of the CANUS brief that he was to "ensure that all are aware that no repeat no ALCM testing can be assured for FY95 and beyond. Until Canadian government makes policy declaration all future ALCM testing must be on a contingency basis." The writing was already on the wall, and the colonel closed by writing, "Assuming that there might be [Canadian] government approval is overstating it."[78] The Liberal Party convention was only a month away, and the party faithful had never been keen on cruise missiles.

André Ouellet, now minister of foreign affairs, had been an early opponent of the testing. Now he was in a position of power, and as the convention roared its disapproval of the cruise missile flights in Canada he told reporters that "when we are asked for further testing we will say no. But I suspect the Americans will probably not ask us again."[79] Prime Minister Chrétien tried to duck the issue by saying that he now had to carry out "a commitment of the previous government."[80] On Friday, 13 May, Liberal Party delegates had voted decisively and sent a message to their government to "end all further cruise missile testing on Canadian soil immediately."[81] Ouellet again commented that "testing the cruise missile is not very important and not very necessary."[82] The party had spoken; now the government had to find a middle path between the convention delegates and the United States government.

The real end was soon at hand. On Monday following the convention, new United States Secretary of Defense Dr. William Perry visited Ottawa to meet with David Collenette and André Ouellet. Collenette and his entourage were advised by the assistant deputy minister's (policy and communications) staff that any discussion on the issue should take place not at National Defence Headquarters but at the Pearson Building headquarters of Foreign Affairs. The minister of foreign affairs was to make clear to Perry that this was a "political issue," and that the Canadian government would appreciate the cooperation of the United States government. The note closed by stating that "The best course of action would be for the U.S. *not* to request further testing."[83] (emphasis in original) Another briefing note given to the minister of national defence just before the meeting told Collenette that "A Government decision to refuse requests for further cruise missile tests in Canada is unlikely to alter the close and multi-faceted defence relationship between Canada and the U.S."[84]

Perry met first with Collenette, and as the minister of national defence was advised not to speak of the subject pending talks of all three men at the office of the minister of foreign affairs, the discussion was centred on other more pressing matters. Stepping out of the meeting and into a press scrum at National Defence Headquarters, Perry answered the crucial question: "Back in the late 70s when I was in the Defense Department, and we started the ALCM program, we needed urgently to find an appropriate place to test those. And Canada, because of the natures of its terrain in the far north, turned out to be an ideal location. We were very grateful for the role that Canada played in this testing and we believe that the ALCM played an important and historic role in helping win the Cold War. Today, the requirements are very different and we do not have at this time any requirements for ALCM testing in the near future. So I do not intend at this meeting today to even request additional tests since we do not have any planned."[85]

Even the Pentagon, not known for its sensitivity to the feelings of foreign governments, had noticed that this issue was not a winner for the Canadian government or for themselves. Perry unilaterally declared that the testing was no longer a requirement of his armed forces and by doing so, defused a real irritant in bilateral defence relations. Collenette and Ouellet were most relieved that the difficult conversation would not have to be held, and Chrétien would not have to rein in an unruly caucus. All of these men recognized the potential for other difficulties with the U.S. administration still existed if future test requests were treated in a like manner and testing was denied. In a later interview David Collenette related to reporters that the government was "grateful it appears the U.S. feels it is unnecessary to request further cruise missile testing in Canada."[86]

Despite the public ending of the cruise missile testing issue, it continued to live in official circles. On 1 June 1994, Mr. Kergin of the embassy in Washington was involved in another discussion with the State Department about more cruise missile tests.[87] Alarmed, Pierre Lagueux promptly dashed off a formal letter to Richard Ledesma at the Pentagon telling Ledesma that "we have the benefit of a timely convergence of views on the part of our respective governments" about the termination of cruise missile testing. Lagueux went on to discreetly point out that "While we have agreed on the status of cruise missile testing, I hope that we will continue to reap the benefits offered by the Canada-U.S. Test and Evaluation Program. In closing, I look forward to a continued association in this valuable form of bilateral defence cooperation."[88]

The issue was now dormant pending the final closing activities of both militaries. Air Command Headquarters in Winnipeg hosted the final Cruise Missile Archive Meeting on 3 August and 4 August. The small gathering of people from National Defence Headquarters, Air Command Headquarters, AETE, 49th Test Squadron, 28th Test Squadron, and Transport Canada ended all cruise missile activity by wrapping up the final administrative questions, and directing that all secret files be destroyed and that unclassified files be retained in various locations. John Skynner represented National Defence Headquarters, Captain Heather DeChamplain attended for AETE, and Captain Norman Coull sat in for Air Command Headquarters. The cruise missile building at Primrose Lake was to be turned over to the Canadian Forces, and various offices would have to issue bills and receipts for costs within thirty days.[89]

With the payment of the last bills and the leftover money returned to 28th Test Squadron at Eglin AFB in Florida, the saga of the cruise missile in Canada came to a quiet end. However, testing was not over, and the Liberals made a commitment to keep the CANUS T&E Agreement alive. As National Defence Headquarters wrote in the 1994 White Paper on Defence, "The Government considers the Test and Evaluation Program an integral component of our bilateral defence relationship. The agreement allows us to test in a cost-efficient manner a variety of key Canadian systems in the United States. In turn, we allow the U.S. to test certain systems deemed essential to continental and global security, subject to approval on a case-by-case basis. The agreement is also very flexible, allowing easy adaptation to changing circumstances. Earlier this year, both Governments announced the end of cruise missile testing in Canadian airspace."[90]

It is doubtful that the power structure really accepted that testing was over. On 26 August the Department of National Defence Test and Evaluation coordinator advised his U.S. counterpart that "planning for the cruise missile testing may proceed."[91] By 7 December a joint CANUS group had completed another cruise missile safety review. The ability to test was maintained even after the program had formally been put to rest.

The Department of National Defence was expecting to "maintain Canada's participation in the Canada-U.S. Test and Evaluation Program, the Defence Production and Development Sharing Arrangements, and other existing bilateral arrangements." The new issue, but nobody knew it yet, was that the government was terrified that anyone would find out about the continued U.S. requests to flight test the B-2 stealth bomber at low levels in the cold Canadian air.[92]

Conclusion

In May 2001, the U.S. Air Force flight-tested an upgraded ALCM at the air weapons range near Hill Air Force Base. Boeing received a $59.2 million contract to convert 272 surplus nuclear AGM-86B ALCMs into conventionally armed air-launched cruise missiles (CALCMs) at their facility in St. Charles, Missouri. The three-year development saw old missiles fitted with a new inertial navigation system aided by a global positioning system (GPS). The first avionics sets have already been delivered to the U.S. Air Force for inclusion in various de-nuclearized air-launched cruise missiles.[1]

In October 2001 the first strikes against sites in Afghanistan were made by sea- and air-launched cruise missiles fired from ships, submarines, and bombers. Like the hundreds fired in attacks since 1990, most made their way successfully to their targets. This weapon was never used with nuclear warheads against the Soviet Union, but has been used repeatedly against the developing world.

For the United States there are clear military reasons for deploying the family of cruise missiles, but there is a strong, and possibly predominant, political rationale. Kenneth Werrell, author of the USAF study *The Evolution of the Cruise Missile*, concluded that "cruise missile deployments permit rapid expansion of U.S. nuclear weapons and forcefully demonstrate American will to friend and foe alike. Moreover, missile deployment also seems to involve an element of technological determinism."[2] The Canadian government was willing to take part in the nuclear expansion and was awed by the forcefulness and determination of the U.S. to test their new weapon system in the far north.

The United States military tests weapons in Canada and it has done so for fifty years. To aid in the preservation of the facade of Canadian national sovereignty, the United States makes formal and informal requests for testing rights in Canada. However, no matter how bizarre the weapon, no matter how dangerous the test, no matter how contrary the weapon to stated Canadian foreign policy objectives, Canada has never refused a single testing request from the United States. They have delayed in some cases, but a flat refusal has not been recorded. The plain fact is that the perceived price of refusal is too high for the Canadian government. It has been made clear to the Canadian government, and was demonstrated to

Prime Minister John Diefenbaker, that the government will be destabilized or unseated if it does not accept the U.S. position.

THE CANADIAN 'KIWI DISEASE'

In 1987 the government of New Zealand, in accordance with the wishes of the people of that nation, closed their ports to U.S. Naval vessels that were not certified as free of nuclear weapons. The United States refused to classify its naval vessels and retaliation against New Zealand was swift. To prevent the spread of the dreaded anti-nuclear 'Kiwi disease,' the United States promptly ended the decades-old military relationship with New Zealand.

In June 1997, Dr. Ken Calder, the assistant deputy minister (policy), told the minister of national defence that "denial of access to CFMETR [Canadian Forces Maritime Experimental Test Range] will be viewed by the U.S. as having a direct impact on their national security interests and may lead to a U.S. response out of proportion to the loss of CFMETR itself."[3] Calder pointed out that New Zealand "suffered serious sanctions in response for denying U.S. nuclear ships access to their harbours," and that the United States imposed trade restrictions on that country for failing to support U.S. nuclear deployments. The federal government took the threat and action very seriously, and Ottawa was therefore desperate to ensure that the 'Kiwi disease' did not spread to Canada through action against the U.S. Navy at Nanoose, B.C. Nanoose was not the main issue, and Ottawa realized that access to all of Canada was the real question.

Cabinet knew that the political injury to Canada-U.S. relations and the potential linkage to much larger bilateral issues were far greater than the significance of losing Nanoose. There was no question that Nanoose was a national security matter for the Canadian government. The minister was informed that failure to hold Nanoose open "could damage Canadian international opportunities such as the Government initiative to establish a NATO Flying Training Centre."

As noted for the Minister, the reality is that "the U.S. is by far Canada's most important defence partner. Canada has over 80 treaty-level agreements and over 250 MOUs with the U.S. for a broad range of defence activities. U.S. politicians and officials increasingly claim Canada is not bearing a responsible share of North American and NATO defence burden. Loss of access to the U.S. Navy would be seen as one more reason to question Canada's reliability as a defence partner."[4] For the

Canadian government, Nanoose has always served as a means of showing Washington that Ottawa continues to be compliant and mindful of the desires of the Pentagon.

SECRET (CC) (Cabinet Confidence)

BRIEFING NOTE FOR THE MINISTER OF NATIONAL DEFENCE
"Canadian Forces Maritime Experimental and Test Ranges (CFMETR)"

ADM Policy, National Defence.

12 June 1997
Impact of Termination of Access to CFMETR.

- Denial of access to CFMETR will be viewed by the US as having a direct impact on their national security interests and may lead to a US response out of proportion to the loss of CFMETR itself.

- The experience of New Zealand is an example of this type of US response. It has suffered serious sanctions in response for denying US nuclear ships access to their harbours. In addition to ceasing all defence relations, the US imposed trade restrictions on New Zealand.

- The US is by far Canada's most important defence partner. Canada has over 80 treaty-level agreements and over 250 MOUs with the US for a broad range of defence activities.

- US politicians and officials increasingly claim Canada is not bearing a responsible share of North American and NATO defence burden. Loss of access to the US Navy would be seen as one more reason to question Canada's reliability as a defence partner.

- Termination of US access to CFMETR could bring into question Canada's commitment to continued cooperation with our allies and could damage Canadian international opportunities such as the Government initiative to establish a NATO Flying Training Centre in Saskatchewan and Alberta.

- Canada benefits from a rules-based approach to international relations, including those with the US. Termination of US access to CFMETR would undermine our commitment to this principle. The political injury to Canada-US relations and the potential linkage to much larger bilateral issues is far greater than the significance of the loss of CFMETR.

SECRET (CC)

Canadian politicians and generals have long operated under the assumption that failure to live up to the expectations of the great power south of the border would result in a loss of more sovereignty, perhaps even outright destabilization of the government itself. Ottawa's sobering lesson came from New Zealand, which flatly refused to host nuclear-armed ships after 1987.[5] Washington immediately threatened rapid, punishing, severe, and punitive sanctions; rumours began to circulate of a covert attempt to undermine the government. The lesson was that no Canadian government could afford to catch the dreaded 'Kiwi disease' and deny the United States access to Canadian sites and ranges.

PAST AND FUTURE

With the removal of nuclear weapons based in Canada in June 1984, Canada's role in the U.S. nuclear sphere reverted to providing a battle-ground, early warning, and testing space.

The specific story of cruise missiles in Canada curiously began and ended with the same person, William Perry. In 1980, Perry was the senior scientist for the Department of Defense in Washington. During a visit to Canada he quietly mentioned to defence officials that the United States Air Force would be interested in testing their new cruise missile over the cold and vast Canadian landscape. Fourteen years later, and now the secretary of defense, Perry told reporters in Ottawa during a ministerial visit that cruise missile testing in Canada was no longer necessary and that the flights were over. With a few words this individual both started and ended one of the more important events in Canadian civil-political and military relations.

There is a useful parallel between the events of 1994 and those of 1963. In both cases Liberal government leadership was faced with an unpopular nuclear weapons issue, opposed by both the party membership and by the public, and chose to try to be on both sides of the issue. In 1963, Prime Minister Lester B. Pearson decided that his government would acquire nuclear weapons under a commitment made by a previous government, but would immediately move to divest Canada of the weapons. It took twenty-one years to do so. Between 1993 and 1994, Prime Minister Jean Chrétien faced the dilemma of continuing the testing and alienating the party and the population, or ending the testing and angering the United States, the senior partner in the relationship. Chrétien said that Canada "faced a commitment of the previous government on cruise" and that "we said we will accept for this year, but the policy of our government does not allow us to do this forever."[6] It would be the Mackenzie King bargain — not necessarily cruise testing, but cruise testing if necessary.

When Pearson reversed the Liberal Party policy of opposing nuclear weapons for the Canadian Forces to accepting the deployments, he was not really changing Canadian policy. From the beginning of the nuclear age Canada had been directly complicit in the sphere of nuclear weapons by having mined uranium, helping develop the atomic bomb, providing bases for nuclear attack, and allowing the deployment of nuclear weapons through and over Canada.

Tommy Douglas, leader of the New Democratic Party, characterized the Pearson decision as being "made in the U.S.," and the action so annoyed a young Pierre Trudeau that he quit the party. Trudeau said that Pearson was the "defrocked priest of peace," and later noted that the entire episode was manufactured south of the border, saying "why [should] the U.S. treat Canada any differently from Guatemala when reasons of state requires it and circumstances permit?" This knowledge would lead Trudeau almost twenty years later to the decision to allow cruise missile testing; anything less could be a danger to his rule and place him in a position not unlike that of John Diefenbaker who was displaced in favour of a friendlier Liberal government.

The original public justification for the testing was that northern Alberta looked a lot like Siberia in the Soviet Union, and since testing in Siberia was not possible, Alberta would have to stand in. Strangely, the dissolution of the Soviet Union and the end of the Cold War did not bring about the end of the tests. Even stranger, the USAF was at that same time starting a bombing campaign in Iraq which would eventually see hundreds of cruise missiles seek their targets in the desert country. As editorial writer Charles Gordon wrote, not even southern Alberta looked like Iraq.[7] Further testing seemed redundant if the missiles were already being used successfully in a real war. Foreign Affairs secretly told its minister that ALCM testing in Canada was "not linked to any cold war mind set," yet it was at a loss to fully explain why this was necessary other than to say the two militaries liked it.[8] Any original public justification for the testing was gone, yet the Conservatives and then the Liberals persisted in supporting the policy. All this served to show Canadians that the testing was a farce which had more to do with U.S. control over the Canadian government than with military necessity.

The Canadian military, with few modern weapons and diminishing prestige, became "voyeurs of USAF cloud-shovelling" in an attempt to keep up with those south of the border, to regain some of their former glory, and to remain a player in the world of nuclear weapons. Poor spending decisions, coupled with a hideously bloated and top-heavy hierarchy, had robbed the sharp end of the stick of much of its fighting power. Despite being one of the world's most expensive armed forces, the Canadian Forces had little to show in terms of raw combat ability and equipment for the vast sums of taxpayers' dollars spent. Lacking these attributes, attachment to the massive United States military machine was the best option for maintaining a viable military infrastructure of personnel and training. Cruise missile testing, although not an absolute favourite of the Canadian Forces, at least allowed it a glamorous role, and provided it with live practice opportunities against cruise missiles. It also allowed the Canadian Forces to look as though they were making a contribution to the U.S. military, and would therefore be looked upon favourably in the future.

One of the great lies of this entire episode in Canadian politics was that cruise missiles were just a part of a larger program that came first. Successive governments denied that the cruise missile was the focus of the exercise all along, and tried to propagate the myth that the testing agreement was primary, with cruise missiles being only one possible testing item. This was a total and unequivocal lie by politicians directed towards the public, and there is no evidence to support the ludicrous assertion. The truth is that "originally, the U.S. approached Canada on the testing of cruise missiles only."[9] The umbrella testing agreement was nothing more than a cover invented later to divert attention from the unpalatable reality.

Trudeau decided that cruise missile testing was essential to the well-being of the Canadian government's tattered and battered relationship with the United States. After more than a decade of sour relations, Trudeau knew that a grand gesture would be necessary, and that cruise missile testing offered what seemed like a cost-free opportunity. Mulroney, President Reagan's close friend, could not back away from the testing which his friend in the White House demanded and which the right wing elements tended to support. However, the public pressure had grown so strong that he was forced to keep advanced cruise missile testing at bay for a couple of years. Both men did what they did in the belief that it was necessary for the health of the government-to-government relationship with the United States, and because they believed that there was an almost unstoppable momentum to the process. The United States would not be denied this field of play, and in the end testing was only ended when the Pentagon decreed it was over.

PROTESTS

Cruise missile testing and the Canadian public's response highlighted the blatant hypocrisy in which official Ottawa is mired. Massive waves of protests, especially those by the Cruise Missile Conversion Project and

Operation Dismantle, brought out the worst in the government. Police and RCMP harassment of opposition activities and legitimate protest continued as long as cruise missile testing itself. Many protesters would be arrested without charges ever being laid, even though arrest for questioning is illegal in Canada. Continued infiltration of the peace movement showed the fear of the anti-cruise missile groups felt by the government and secret police. The lesson for protest groups is that the government does pay attention, but that the attention is usually unwelcome and will often involve illegal activities and mild repression. Opposition groups should also learn that a massive outpouring of emotion and activity impairs the actions of governments.

CANADA AS A NUCLEAR OPPOSITION

Canada was caught in the middle of another Cold War arms build-up, which outlived the death of the Soviet Union. But perhaps the most important factor that led to the Canadian government allowing such tests was the belief that to not do so would lead to conclusions too frightening for Ottawa to contemplate. The political outcome of a lack of perceived freedom by the government is an unwillingness to undertake any initiatives or to follow any leads which may seem unwelcome in Washington.

In a larger sense, the Canadian government is not without real choices but seems incapable of exercising real options. The New Agenda Coalition, formed to seek an unequivocal commitment from the nuclear weapon states to commence negotiations leading to a program for the elimination of nuclear weapons, has never had Canada's support. When the issue was first raised in the United Nations First Committee (Disarmament) in 1998, Canada abstained saying that the parliamentary committee had not yet finished its review of Canadian nuclear weapons and arms control policies. In 1999 Canada once again abstained, even though Foreign Affairs was willing to move to a 'yes' vote, as National Defence took the matter to the prime minister, who backed Washington's pro-nuclear stand. Prime Minister Chrétien said that Canada could not lead the NATO countries into voting yes.[10]

To this absurd stand Senator Doug Roche commented:

To drive home the point that the Canadian government considers itself not free to vote principled positions on nuclear disarmament, Canada also abstained on a new resolution introduced by China and Russia on the

Anti-Ballistic Missile (ABM) Treaty. The ABM Treaty was established by the U.S. and the former Soviet Union in 1972 to limit defences against nuclear weapons in an effort to slow down the development of new nuclear weapons. The ABM Treaty has long been considered as a cornerstone for maintaining global peace and security and strategic stability.

Canada has always been an ardent upholder of the ABM Treaty. But now the U.S. wants to either weaken or abrogate the Treaty in order to deploy a new national missile defence system. Billions of dollars are being spent on the development of this system. The Russian-Chinese resolution called for continued efforts to strengthen the ABM Treaty and "to preserve its integrity and validity so that it remains a cornerstone in maintaining global strategic stability and world peace and in promoting further strategic nuclear arms reductions." The resolution went on to urge countries to refrain from the deployment of such systems and "not to provide a base for such a defence..." If Canada seriously intended to uphold the ABM Treaty, it would have voted yes. Even France voted yes. The U.S. voted no. Since there were 73 abstentions, Canada had plenty of company, but gave away a principled position.[11]

On 28 March 2000 the Senate of Canada adopted a motion urging the nuclear weapon states to move to the total elimination of their nuclear weapons, as called for by the Non-Proliferation Treaty (NPT). Douglas Roche, speaking as chairman of the 'Middle Powers Initiative,' urged the government of Canada to work alongside the New Agenda Coalition at the 2000 Non-Proliferation Treaty Review Conference to obtain the nuclear weapon states' reaffirmation of their NPT Article VI commitment "and ensure that governments make new commitments to accelerate the nuclear disarmament process." The motion stated that "the Senate recommends that the Government of Canada urge the Nuclear Weapon States to reaffirm their unequivocal commitment to take action towards the total elimination of their nuclear weapons, as called for by the Non-proliferation Treaty, which will be reviewed April 24-May 19, 2000." As usual, the Canadian government was too fearful of Washington and of developing the 'Kiwi disease,' so nothing was done.

The record clearly shows that Canada refuses to support any resolution that specifies immediate action on a comprehensive approach to ridding the world of nuclear weapons. Canada follows the U.S. and NATO line on the tough nuclear disarmament resolutions. The actions of the Canadian government, as well as its votes in the United Nations, clearly show that neither the Liberal nor the Conservative governments have been ready or willing to take a direct position against nuclear weapons and for ridding the world of such weapons.

The next big issue to follow the cruise missile will be the testing, building, and basing of the new U.S. national missile defense. The Liberals will continue to do little if anything, and hope that this issue does not explode in their faces like cruise missile testing. The Department of National Defence will make greater efforts to encourage both the government and the interested population to support both NORAD and ballistic missile defence. The public relations campaign, already begun at a minimal level, will increase in intensity. Canadians have already witnessed the bizarre spectacle of National Defence Director General Daniel Bon stating in public before the House of Commons that Canada is now directly threatened by missiles and weapons of mass destruction from North Korea. National Defence and the Canadian Forces will continue to place more staff in NORAD and at U.S. Space Command. In addition, space programs in Canada will be enlarged and funding will increase to several hundreds of millions of dollars. The Department of National Defence will support missile defence, and has already succeeded in having its minister make positive statements. DFAIT opposes it, but with Axworthy long gone, it will eventually be brought on side with DND and will support limited Canadian participation in order to ensure Canadian access to NORAD.

In preparation for the necessary change the Chrétien government began the slow move towards public acceptance of a Canadian role in U.S. space warfare and national missile defence plans. Chrétien, who only two months earlier had stated with Russian President Putin that the ABM Treaty was the cornerstone of strategic stability, subsequently stated after a meeting with President George W. Bush that the world was now in a different era regarding the treaty. The minister of national defence had already visited the new U.S. secretary of defense, Donald Rumsfeld, said that he was never adverse to national missile defence, and now wanted "to work together." The road has already been paved for Canada to join national missile defence and thereby to open the doors to the full use of NORAD for U.S. space warfare missions.

The Canadian government frequently suffers from having an insensitive partner, and Washington's actions harm delicate public relations efforts. The reality is that Washington will only give information of a quality and at a time of its own choosing, and there is nothing Ottawa can do to improve this process. By aligning himself with Reagan, Trudeau appeared to be an American puppet in charge of a government run from Washington. At the same time the United States did nothing to assist Trudeau and in fact substantially created the public relations nightmare through clumsy, ill-timed leaks and statements of support that cost Trudeau substantial public credibility. The same pattern has been repeated with Bush on the missile defence issue.

When President Bush announced in mid-May 2001 that the ABM Treaty was dead and that the United States was proceeding with missile defense, the Chrétien government nodded a quiet "ready, aye, ready." Later, after asking the White House to ensure that Bush would not mention the issue in public, Bush twice pumped for his special program during his state visit to Canada in November 2004.

The Canadian government confirmed to Washington that it would seek formal talks on missile defence co-operation in January 2004. On 24 February 2005 Prime Minister Paul Martin struck the ultimate Canadian deal; he officially announced to the public that Canada would not take part in the U.S. anti-ballistic missile programme, but allowed for full co-operation by Canadian NORAD forces in missile defence work. The public was appeased and Washington got another BMD ally. The new prime minister, Stephen Harper, has said that he favours closer military co-operation with Washington, but cannot risk doing much due to the minority status of his government. What both men were able to deliver was the sixteenth largest military budget in the world in 2005-2006, a figure more than twice the world average for military spending per capita.

CONCLUSION

In order to understand the process of U.S. military testing in Canada, it is most important to note that testing is pervasive across the country and within all three military services. The constituency within government extends to both military and civilian sides. The bureaucracy extends across the border and has various components staffed by committed individuals who are doing their best to continue a half-century of cooperation. Although cruise missile testing has ended, testing of U.S. military weapons in Canada will endure.

Since 1952, all Canadian governments have agreed to allow the U.S. Strategic Air Command (SAC), now U.S. Strategic Command, the use of Canadian airspace for flights of nuclear-armed SAC aircraft involved in regular training flights, transit flights, the airborne alert program, and the airborne alert contingency plan. Such flying reached a peak during the Reagan-Mulroney years. With the end of the Cold War, these flights became less frequent but still number in the hundreds, and are scheduled to remain in that number well into the 21st century.

In order to avoid any initial pain from refusing to allow the U.S. Navy to use Canadian facilities, successive governments in Ottawa continue to allow a nuclear-powered and nuclear-armed force to operate in waters and ports, and at Nanoose. The United States Navy has demonstrated that it will go wherever it deems appropriate and will continue to refuse to acknowledge the presence of nuclear weapons on board. International law has increasingly turned against such weapons, and the Canadian government has stated that it is committed to a policy of ridding the world of nuclear weapons. The Canadian government acknowledges in its internal documents that Nanoose is not a military necessity, but rather a political necessity to maintain the U.S. government and military's relationship with the client government in Ottawa. It is clear that the policy is in place not to protect security, but to protect cabinet and Canadian military contractors.

Various testing will continue, and it is worth noting that although the cruise missile is gone from Canadian skies, the agreement is still in place and each year more weapons are tested in the vast and cold spaces of Canada. This will not end, and it is likely that the majority of tests will be kept secret from the public. The Canadian government has adopted a policy of 'don't ask, don't tell' when it comes to U.S. military activity in Canada.

The author with a W-80 nuclear
warhead from an ALCM at Kirtland AFB,
22 December 1999. Photo courtesy of author.

Notes on Sources

We believe that the appropriate security agencies should be
investigating the motives of any individual or organization
coming into possession of such information.
–Memorandum to DND Directorate of Access to Information, 28 July 1998

The documents for this book came from various locales in two countries, from both government and private sources.

FREEDOM OF INFORMATION ACT

The United States *Freedom of Information Act* (FOIA) is perhaps the researcher's best friend when trying to discover what Ottawa is doing without the knowledge of Canadians. Extensive use of FOIA produced a myriad of documents and uncovered various items Ottawa considered better left unseen and unread. Requests under the FOIA were made to the U.S. Air Force, U.S. Navy, U.S. Army, and the U.S. State Department.

DEPARTMENT OF FOREIGN AFFAIRS

The vaults at Foreign Affairs in Ottawa contain a considerable body of political material which may be made available to qualified researchers. Through their academic history program, the staff at Foreign Affairs will grant certain academics the right to inspect original files generated by that Department. In addition, some material has been released by their access to information office either through direct requests, or through consultations with other government departments. However, The access to information process at Foreign Affairs produced almost no actual government documentation in response to direct Access to Information requests. Most of the material released to other researchers was previously public press statements and backgrounders which are not even covered by the *Access to Information Act*. Most substantive information was withheld in contravention of the Act. In addition, material found under the academic access program was heavily censored by the Access to Information

Office before being released. Only an intense battle by the Information Commissioner of Canada brought some of the documentation to light.

The largest problem encountered with the Department of Foreign Affairs is that operational staff have the attitude that the *Access to Information Act* either does not apply to their records, or that they must do everything possible to stop the public from gaining legal access. This makes Foreign Affairs perhaps the worst department with which to deal on *Access to Information Act* matters.

PRIVY COUNCIL OFFICE

The Prime Minister's Office (PMO) and the Privy Council Office (PCO) in Ottawa are the primary source for documents generated by or for the Cabinet and the Cabinet Defence Committee (CDC). The Access to Information Office at PCO was able to provide all the PCO/PMO documents used in this study.

NATIONAL DEFENCE HEADQUARTERS

Most of the material used in this book came indirectly from National Defence Headquarters. This is because National Defence holds most of the files on current Canada-U.S. military co-operation, and specifically the cruise missile files. The Access to Information Directorate at National Defence Headquarters was instrumental in declassifying a vast amount of documentation for a few requesters in recent years. Much of the documentation used in the book had been requested by several people prior to my becoming aware of it. I added to the knowledge base by making additional requests for material to fill in the voids. The Access to Information office at National Defence (known as DAIP), was both helpful and forthcoming at all times.

I would offer a word of caution at this point. There has been a noticeable deterioration in the quality of document releases in the past few years. It seems that National Defence is moving away from openness. In addition, the attitude of official distrust of citizens is not confined to the covert security forces. People who make *Access to Information Act* requests are often viewed with suspicion by civil servants and political leaders. One senior staff member at National Defence, who did not know the name of the applicant, wrote that although the information he was providing was totally unclassified and could be released, "we believe that the appropriate security agencies should be investigating the motives of any individual or organization coming into possession of such information."[1] Such attitudes have a chilling effect on the right of Canadians to know what their government is doing at home and abroad.

DIRECTORATE OF HISTORY AND HERITAGE

Since this was only tangentially a military activity, being more of a political event, there were few strictly military records already archived at National Defence on cruise missile testing. All of the documentation from this book is now part of the collection at the Department of National Defence Directorate of History and Heritage (DHH) in Ottawa. They are filed in the Clearwater Nuclear Weapons Fond (Cruise Missiles), 98/15, and are available without restriction to any and all researchers.

PHOTOGRAPHIC ARCHIVES IN CANADA

The Canadian Forces photographic unit at CFB Cold Lake was the unit responsible for most of the cruise missile photography. However, given the passage of time, most of the negatives were destroyed, but a few were sent to storage at the Central Negative Library in Ottawa. Only photos of record remain, and these few are generally found in annual reports now stored at DHH in Ottawa.

ROYAL CANADIAN MOUNTED POLICE

The RCMP Access to Information Office provided the author with the files on internment of Canadians in case of World War III. This office was most helpful, and made an effort to keep me informed of the continuing status of the documentation at all times.

PROJECT PLOUGHSHARES

The anti-militaristic think tank Project Ploughshares, at Conrad Grebel College in Waterloo, Ontario, provided a large number of early cruise missile documents that had long been lost to the Department of National Defence and the Department of Foreign Affairs and International Trade. In addition, several other items of great use were passed to me for this book. Their contribution helped make the early chapters possible.

BOOKS

Few books have been published in this significant field of Canadian political and military activity. Most works in this field are commonly described by status quo apologists as "critical essays," and date from the early and mid-1980s. However, since these are the only works in the field, and since they did at least try to expose activities, their foundation is important.

The authors of these early works lacked hard proof for their assertions, and it was this weakness that opened them to attack by government supporters. But they did get the story essentially correct. I therefore acknowledge the work done by:

Simon Rosenblum, in *Misguided Missiles: Canada, the Cruise and Star Wars* (Toronto: Lorimer, 1985);

Carole Giangrande, in *The Nuclear North* (Toronto: Anansi, 1983);

Ernie Regehr and Simon Rosenblum, in *Canada and the Nuclear Arms Race* (Toronto: Lorimer, 1983);

Lewis Hertzman, John Warnock and Thomas Hockin, in *Alliances and Illusions* (Edmonton: Hurtig, 1969);

Reg Whitaker and Gary Marcuse, in *Cold War Canada* (Toronto: University of Toronto Press, 1996);

Ernie Regehr, in *Arms Canada* (Toronto: Lorimer, 1987); *The True North Not Strong and Free* (Soules, 1987); and

James Stark, in *Cold War Blues* (Hull, Quebec: Voyageur, 1991).

It was these works in particular which showed that work can be successfully accomplished in this difficult and secretive field, and that secret activities can be exposed.

There had been a proposal for a "Canada & The Nuclear Age" program that was to publish numerous works on these and related subjects, but it failed to get off the ground. The group of academics, scornful of the "critical essay" authors, applied to the federal government for a $1.5 million start-up grant. In the end it was nothing but a failed local attempt to attach a small Canadian component to the international nuclear weapons history project and to the Cold War International History Project.

It produced no known works that would have been of any benefit to the production of this series on nuclear weapons in Canada.

CHRONOLOGY OF ALCM AND ACM TEST FLIGHTS IN CANADA

TEST # 84-1
6 March 1984
captive-carry
319 Bomb Wing B-52G from Grand Forks AFB

TEST # 85-4
15 January 1985
Global Cruise ALCM test
(code means follow-on test and evaluation (FOT&E) of ALCM)
west route, captive-carry
Missile profile: 14 (85-4/14-NS/MO214)
319 Bomb Wing from Grand Forks AFB
B-52G/57-6480

TEST # 85-5
19 February 1985 (Tuesday)
Global Cruise ALCM test
first live launch over Canada
first free-flight over Canada
west route, free-flight
Missile profile: 14 (85-5/14-NS/MO314)
319 Bomb Wing from Grand Forks AFB
46th Bomb Squadron
B-52G/58-0227
Primary missile: 81-0512 (launched)

TEST # 85-5A
25 February 1985
Global Cruise ALCM test
second free-flight over Canada
west route, free-flight
Mission profile: 14 (85-5A/14-NS/MO414)
319 Bomb Wing from Grand Forks AFB
B-52G/58-2594

TEST # 86-x
22 January 1986
Global Cruise ALCM flight test
West route, free-flight
Mission profile: 20 (0120/20-NS)
379 Bomb Wing from Wurtsmith AFB
B-52G/58-0175

TEST # 86-y
25 February 1986
Global Cruise ALCM flight test
west route, free-flight
Profile 21 (0120)
92 Bomb Wing from Fairchild AFB
B-52H/57-6495
ALCM crashed on Beaufort Sea ice

TEST # 87-1
24 February 1987
Global Cruise ALCM flight test
west route, free-flight
Profile 21 (0221)
97 Bomb Wing from Blytheville AFB
B-52G/57-6485

TEST # 87-2
1 March 1987
Global Cruise ALCM flight test
west route, free-flight
Mission profile 21 (0321)
97 Bomb Wing from Blytheville AFB
B-52G/57-6517

TEST # 87-3
27 October 1987
Global Cruise ALCM flight test
Captive-carry, eastern route validation
Mission profile: 32 (0132/32)
92 Bomb Wing from Fairchild AFB
B-52H/61-1031

TEST # 88-1
19 January 1988
Global Cruise ALCM test
east route, free-flight
Mission profile 32 (0232/32NS)
379 Bomb Wing from Wurtsmith AFB
B-52G/58-0168

TEST # 88-2
26 January 1988
Global Cruise ALCM flight test
east route, free-flight
Mission profile: 32 (0532/32NS)
379 Bomb Wing from Wurtsmith AFB
B-52H/58-0168

TEST # 89-4
27 January 1989
Global Cruise ALCM flight test
east route, free-flight, 2nd ANX-Cold
Mission profile 32 (0732/32NS)
416 Bomb Wing from Griffiss AFB
B-52G/57-6498

TEST # 89-(ACM-1)
2 March 1989
Global Shadow ACM captive carry test
(Global Shadow means ACM)
first ACM captive-carry (first ACM in Canada)
east route, captive-carry
410 Bomb Wing from K. I. Sawyer AFB
B-52H

TEST # 90-4
23 January 1990
Global Cruise ALCM free-flight test
east route, free-flight
Mission profile 47 (0147/47NS)
7 Bomb Wing from Dyess AFB
B-52H/60-0062

TEST # 90-4A
29 January 1990
Global Cruise ALCM test
east route, free-flight
Mission profile 47 (0247/47NS)
7 Bomb Wing from Dyess AFB
B-52H/61-0021

TEST # 90-x
24 March 1990
Global Shadow ACM captive-carry test
east route, captive-carry
410 Bomb Wing from K. I. Sawyer AFB
B-52H

TEST # A91-01C
7 November 1990
Global Shadow ACM test flight
east route, captive-carry
410 Bomb Wing from K. I. Sawyer AFB
B-52H/60-0048

TEST # 91-4
31 January 1991
Global Cruise ALCM flight test
east route, free-flight, low launch
Mission profile 54 (0154/54NS)
5 Bomb Wing from Minot AFB
B-52H/61-0024

TEST # 91-5
9 February 1991
Global Cruise ALCM flight test
east route, free-flight, low launch
Mission profile 54 (0454/54NS)
5 Bomb Wing from Minot AFB
B-52H/61-0024

TEST # 92-1
29 October 1991

Global Shadow ACM flight test
east route, captive-carry
mission profile A911 (0191/91NS and A91NSA)
410 Bomb Wing from K. I. Sawyer AFB
B-52H/61-0025

TEST # 92-4
10 February 1992
Global Cruise ALCM test
east route, common strategic rotary launcher
   (CSRL) launch, low launch, free-flight
Mission profile 54 (0654/54NSB)
92 Bomb Wing from Fairchild AFB
B-52H/60-0044

TEST # 93-4
29 January 1993
Global Cruise ALCM flight test
east route, CSRL launch, free-flight
Mission profile 57 (0157/57NSA)
2 Bomb Wing from Barksdale AFB
B-52H/61-013

TEST # A93-04S
29 March 1993
Global Shadow ACM test
first live ACM launch/flight
east route, free-flight
Mission profile: 92
410 Bomb Wing from K. I. Sawyer AFB
B-52H/60-0003

TEST # A94-06 (A193)
6 March 1994
Global Shadow ACM flight test
east route, free-flight
second live ACM launch
Last cruise missile test in Canada
Mission profile A93NSA
410 Bomb Wing from K. I. Sawyer AFB
B-52H/60-0011

AGREEMENTS AND ARRANGEMENTS

THE CANADA/UNITED STATES TEST AND EVALUATION PROGRAM AGREEMENT (CANUS T&E AGREEMENT) 10 FEBRUARY 1983

1. The undertaking pursuant to this Agreement shall be known as "The Canada/United States (CANUS) Test and Evaluation Program." An undertaking under this Program shall be known as a Test and Evaluation (T&E) project.
2. The T&E Program conducted under the provisions of this Agreement shall be governed by the terms of the Agreement between the Parties to the North Atlantic Treaty regarding the Status of their Forces (NATO SOFA) dated 19 June 1951.
3. This agreement is applicable to T&E projects developed under the auspices of the Program and which are mutually agreed upon by the Minister of National Defence on behalf of Canada and the Secretary of Defense on behalf of the United States of America, or their designated representatives. Canada may refuse any T&E projects under this Agreement.
4. A Memorandum of Understanding dealing with general implementation arrangements for this Agreement, including program management and administration, shall be negotiated and concluded by the designated representatives of the Canadian Department of National Defence (DND) and the United States Department of Defense (DOD). A Project Arrangement providing implementation arrangements for each CANUS T&E project shall be negotiated and concluded by DND and DOD.
5. Nothing in this Agreement shall derogate from the applicability of Canadian law in Canada. If, in unusual circumstances, the application of Canadian law may lead to delay or difficulty in the conduct of a T&E project, DOD may request the assistance of Canadian authorities in seeking appropriate alleviation.
6. The Canadian Forces shall exercise command and control over Canadian facilities used by DOD for T&E and Canadian safety regulations and orders shall apply.

7. Specific T&E projects shall be confined to Canadian Forces bases, training areas and agreed airspace. The tests and evaluation will include projects related to weapons, weapons systems, stores and equipment, and electronic warfare systems and may include associated training and tactics development activities.

8. In no case shall nuclear, biological or chemical warfare materials or agents be brought into Canada under this Agreement. Cruise missiles shall be unarmed.

9. Except as provided in paragraph 10, the United States shall bear all the costs and expenditures of the T&E program. Project Arrangements made under the terms and conditions of this Agreement shall not be finalized until such time as it is confirmed that funds have been authorized, appropriated and allocated for this purpose. Subject to Article VIII of NATO SOFA, the United States shall reimburse Canada for all costs incurred by Canada on behalf of the United States as a direct result of the T&E Program.

10. Canada shall have the right to participate in all CANUS T&E projects. The scope, character and financial obligations, if any, of Canadian participation shall be determined for each project through consultation and shall be specified in the associated Project Arrangements.

11. While security for a T&E project will be the responsibility of the Canadian Forces (CF), in special cases such as an unscheduled termination of a test flight or an accident in or adjacent to a CF Base, the U.S. forces may be requested to assume this responsibility on a case by case basis if circumstances so dictate.

12. The use of a specific test area shall be dependent upon the availability of facilities and local resources. Every effort, however, shall be made by DND to accommodate a T&E project in CF plans and to obtain clearances for the use of airspace associated with the test plan.

13. The use of Canadian civil airspace shall be approved and controlled by the Minister of Transport. Flight corridors in Canada to be used for the testing of cruise missiles shall be selected to ensure minimum disruption to civil aircraft operations and minimum disturbance to persons on the ground.

14. DND may review the types of T&E data that are expected to be acquired by DOD during the conduct of a particular project to determine their relevance to DND programs. DND may request that the data acquired during the conduct of the project be provided by DOD. Data provided by DOD shall be at no cost to Canada except as provided in paragraph 10 above. All proprietary information and data exchanged under this program shall be in accordance with the NATO Agreement on the Communication of

Technical Information for Defence Purposes as signed in Brussels on 19 October 1970. All T&E Project Arrangements shall contain the appropriate Intellectual Property provisions.

15. Any classified information and materials exchanged under this Program will be safeguarded in accordance with existing arrangements between Canada and the United States in relation to the protection of classified information.

16. All test and evaluations involving U.S. classified information and/or materials will b carried out under U.S. Government security control unless the specific Project Arrangement specifies otherwise. However, the Canadian Forces shall continue to exercise command and control over Canadian facilities used by DOD for T&E as provided for in paragraph 6 of this Agreement.

17. The release of information to the public concerning any project under this Agreement shall require prior consultation and coordination between appropriate U.S. and Canadian authorities.

18. The DOD shall comply with Canadian laws, regulations and orders applicable to the Canadian Forces in respect of the protection of the environment. DOD shall assume financial responsibility for any environmental studies required under Canadian law, regulations and orders.

19. Claims arising from T&E projects shall be settled in accordance with Article VIII of NATO SOFA. Activities conducted under this Agreement are deemed to be in connection with the operation of the North Atlantic Treaty for the purposes of applying Article VIII, Paragraph 1.

20. DND will provide, on a reimbursable basis, all goods, services and facilities required from Canadian sources during the period of this Agreement.

21. Removal and disposal of United States Government property shall be governed by the Agreement between the United States of America and Canada regarding Disposal of United States Property in Canada effected by the Exchange of Notes signed in Ottawa, 28 August and 1 September 1961. No activities undertaken pursuant to this T&E Agreement shall be deemed "joint exercises for Canadian and United States forces" as that term is used in paragraph 6 of the Note dates 28 August 1961.

22. To the extent that existing laws, regulations and agreements, including NATO SOFA, permit, the import into Canada and purchase in Canada of equipment and goods required for T&E projects shall not be subject to customs duties, federal sales taxes and excise taxes.

23. This Agreement shall remain in force for a period of five years and will be renewed automatically for a further term of five years, subject to the following provisions:

(a.) This Agreement may be terminated in its entirety upon twelve months' notice in writing by either Government, or in whole or in part, by either Government, without advance notice, should either Government consider it necessary by reason of an extreme emergency such as war, invasion, insurrection or riot, real or apprehended;

(b.) In the event of the termination of the Agreement the Governments of Canada and the United States shall negotiate the settlement of outstanding financial issues;

(c.) Either Government shall reserve the right to cancel, suspend, postpone or terminate any specific test and evaluation project, if in its opinion, any unforeseen imperative circumstances should so warrant. In such event the financial obligations of the parties, including reimbursement of costs incurred by a party as a result of cancellation, suspension, postponement or termination by the other party, shall be the subject of separate negotiations;

(d.) This Agreement may be amended by mutual consent of the parties.

For the Government of Canada
(signed by Ambassador Allan Gotlieb)
10 February 1983

for the Government of the United States of America
(signed by Acting Secretary of State Kenneth W. Dam)
10 February 1983

MEMORANDUM OF UNDERSTANDING RELATING TO THE CANUS TEST AND EVALUATION PROGRAM (CANUS T&E MOU) 25 MARCH 1983

1. This Memorandum of Understanding (MOU) is a general implementation agreement between the Canadian Department of National Defence (DND) and the United States Department of Defense (DOD) for the use by the DOD of the Canadian Forces (CF) test sites, training areas and ranges and Canadian airspace for the Test and Evaluation (T&E) of DOD weapons, equipment and tactics, concluded pursuant to paragraph 4 of the Exchange of Notes between Canada and the United States concerning the Test and Evaluation of U.S. Defense Weapon System in Canada, (the Agreement) dated 10 February 1983, and subject to the terms and conditions of the Agreement.

2. A Joint Steering Group, co-chaired by the Under Secretary of Defense, Research and Engineering for the DOD and by the Assistant Deputy

Minister (Material) for the DND, or their designated alternate, and including additional officials, as appropriate, will monitor the T&E Program and provide advice to Departmental authorities and U.S. sponsors. The chairmen will exercise authority over the Program on behalf of their respective Departments.

3. Each Department will appoint a Coordinator who will be responsible for administering the Program, including preparation of Project Arrangements for specific T&E projects, resolution of Program issues and maintaining an awareness of current Program activities and project plans. The DOD Coordinator will be the Director Defense Test and Evaluation or his designated alternate; the DND Coordinator will be the Director, General Military Plans and Operations.

4. The DOD Coordinator will provide to the DND Coordinator, by 1 January of each year, an annual forecast of the probable T&E projects under this program for the next four years, and an estimate of the requirements for the material, airspace and services to be furnished by Canada over the next fifteen months.

5. All matters connected with this implementation of the MOU, other than those which can be resolved by correspondence, will be resolved during a joint meeting of the Steering Group to be held as required, but at least annually, subsequent to the submission of the DOD test forecast, at National Defence Headquarters, Ottawa, or at a location as mutually agreed.

6. The T&E project previously indemnified in the DOD forecast may be proposed directly to the DND Coordinator by a Sponsor who may be one of the authorized DOD Sponsors listed in Appendix 1. Each T&E Project Proposal is to provide sufficient information to enable determination of its applicability under the Program but it must include:

a. a description of the proposed T&E project including details of any extraordinary safety, security or other similar constraints;

b. identification of the desired test site(s) with appropriate details as to those restrictions desired which might affect Canadian plans for current use of the site(s) or adjacent areas;

c. sufficient details of the test site requirements so that the DND Coordinator will be able to suggest suitable alternate sites if the preferred site is not available;

d. duration of the T&E project, in terms of phases if appropriate, with the desired earliest and latest acceptable dates for the commencement of significant activities;

e. description of the desired DND support and the possible options for Canadian participation;

f. any special construction requirements;

g. the total number of U.S. personnel and major items of equipment associated with the project that will be located in Canada at any one time;

h. a list by number, weight and type of explosives or other hazardous materials to be used;

j. a list of potential environmental effects known to, or suspected by DOD; and

k. identification of the DOD Project Manager.

7. The DND Coordinator will advise the DOD Sponsor concerning the acceptability to Canada of the Project Proposal under the Program, but each approval in principle of a Project Proposal will be subject to the negotiation and conclusion of an acceptable Project arrangement. At the same time, the DND Coordinator will indicate any major restrictions that are seen as necessary by Canada as well as the supporting resources Canada may provide, and will identify the Canadian Project Manager. The DND Coordinator will provide the DOD Sponsor an interim reply, if a complete reply is not anticipated to be ready, within 30 working days after the receipt of the Project Proposal.

8. Pursuant to this MOU, a T&E project that is approved in principle will be formalized in a Project arrangement to be approved by the DND Coordinator and the DOD Sponsor and signed by the respective Chairmen of the Steering Group. The Project Arrangement document will contain, as applicable, the following:

a. an outline of the T&E project;

b. a description of the agreed location and the project plan;

c. a full description of access to and use of test sites accorded to DOD including:

(1) details of personnel and equipment to be employed in Canada,

(2) details of troop movements, flight plans, and reconnaissance requirements,

(3) general details of RF emitters (specific details on power and bandwidth will be provided separately to DND for concurrence),

(4) details on access and any plans to provide additional site security that DOD may find necessary, and

(6) any other special requirements;

d. details of the DND control, safety and security precautions for the T&E project;

e. details of the DND support and/or participation;

f. a description of construction requirements;

g. DOD mapping requirements;

h. details of stores and equipment to be expended or left at the test site for DND disposal;

j. a statement of DND rights to data arising from the T&E project;

k. description of management arrangements including the identification of Project Managers for each Department and a statement on reporting requirements;

m. a detailed estimate of the anticipated costs for approved DND support;

n. details of the arrangements for the protection of Intellectual Property;

p. details of arrangements for security;

q. details of arrangements for visits;

r. details of the duration and arrangements for termination of a T&E project before its conclusion; and

s. details of financial arrangements and reimbursement.

9. When a Project arrangement covering a T&E project is concluded, the DOD Sponsor will place in escrow in the U.S. Treasury, prior to the commencement of the T&E Project, an amount equal to the amount of estimated costs of approved DND support to the project. These escrowed funds will be supplied by DOD on request from DND in quarterly allotments in advance or as agreed in the Project Arrangement as appropriate. At the conclusion of the Project, DND will submit an invoice to the DOD Sponsor for the service provided by DND. The amount paid shall be deducted from the invoice with any balance payable within 30 days. If applicable a cheque to refund any unexpended funds on deposit will be issued by DND within 30 days.

10. DND will not be obligated to continue to provide reimbursable support, or otherwise incur costs, in excess of the estimated costs, as set forth in the Project Arrangement, unless the DOD Sponsor has notified the DND Coordinator in writing that additional costs are accepted. However, where resources provided have an actual cost greater than estimated, these actual costs are reimbursable to DND by DOD as and to the extent funds are authorized, appropriated and allocated to a T&E project for this purpose. No notice, communication or representation in any other form, or from any person other than the authorized DOD Sponsor or the DOD Coordinator shall affect the financial obligation of the parties.

11. Additional support requested by the DOD Sponsor, and approved by the DND Coordinator will result in DND providing a revised estimate of costs. If the revised estimate increases the total costs by more than $10,000.00 (CDN) an additional advance of funds from DOD will be required.

12. In accordance with paragraph 20 of the Arrangement, at the request of the DOD Sponsor, DND shall arrange for the provision of material, equipment, installations, transportation, construction and maintenance, supply, services and civil labour from sources in Canada in accordance with the established Canadian Government procedures, terms and conditions which shall be applied as far as is practicable in accordance with U.S. law.

13. At the conclusion of each T&E project a report is to be prepared jointly by the U.S. and Canadian Project Managers that summarizes the project details, particularly as these may affect future T&E Projects under the Program.

14. Within a reasonable amount of time following the completion of a T&E project, the DOD Sponsor will provide to the DND Coordinator the data arising from the project, as agreed under the applicable Project Arrangement.

15. The Memorandum of Understanding and Appendix I may be amended by mutual agreement between the Chairmen of the Steering Group.

16. This Memorandum of Understanding will remain in force during the term of the Agreement.

For the Government of Canada
(signed by Gilles Lamontagne), 21 April 1983

For the Government of the United States of America
(signed by Caspar Weinberger), 25 March 1983

2002 Renewal

The CANUSTEP, CANUS T&E Agreement, was renewed on 10 September 2002 in Las Vegas, by National Defence's Assistant Deputy Minister (Materiel) Alan S. Williams for Canada, and Thomas P. Christie, the Pentagon's Director of Operational Test and Evaluation for the United States. It is to remain binding on Canada for fifteen years, or until 9 September 2017. National Defence at first refused to release the final signed copy of this agreement, but relented after a complaint was made to the Information Commissioner of Canada.

Notes

NOTES TO CHAPTER 1

1   Rosenblum, *Misguided Missiles: Canada, the Cruise and Star Wars* (Toronto: Lorimer, 1985). No documentation has been found amongst the declassified papers to demonstrate this idea. However, since much Strategic Air Command documentation was lost after 1991 when SAC was disbanded, and since little of the early documentation was retained by Canada, it is quite possible that the records no longer exist.

2   29 August 1980, Memo from Col Lorne Broughton, re: proposal to test USAF cruise missile. Obtained by Robert Winters of the *Montreal Gazette* under the *Access to Information Act.*

3   16 June 1982, External Affairs, Clarification to Ross from PMR Johnson, re: cruise missile testing and the connection with the CF-18. Aircraft purchase. 27-16-2-USA.

4   24 January 1983, Memo to DMF (through PFG), from J. R. Francis, Defence Relations, re: Proposed agreement on testing of U.S. defence systems in Canada. DFR-0008. Confidential. 27-8-USA-3.

5   In confirming the first incident, Secretary of State for External Affairs Mark MacGuigan would later state that "Carter requested ... that we allow one of the proposed missile systems, the cruise missile, to be tested in Canada," *Montreal* Gazette, 19 March 1983.

6   Robert Winters, "US plans 3 cruise tests," *Montreal Gazette*, 20 August 1980.

7   14 April 1981, Letter to Dr. J. P. Wade, acting undersecretary of defense for research and development, Pentagon, from L. G. Crutchlow, assistant deputy minister (material), re: Status of discussions on test sites and ALCM testing. 10081-034/338.

8   17–20 February 1981, 158th PJBD Meeting Minutes.

9   6 March 1981, Letter to Prime Minister Trudeau from Chairman G. Hees, Canadian Chairman PJBD, re: 158th Meeting. Secret.

10 14 April 1981, Letter to Dr. J. P. Wade, Acting Under Secretary of Defense for Research and Development, Pentagon, from L. G. Crutchlow, ADM (Materiel), re: Status of discussion on test sites and ALCM testing. 10081-034/338.

11 During the cruise missile period, twelve people held the unwanted post of minister of national defence: four Liberals and eight Conservatives, including the first female defence minister.

Allan McKinnon	1979–1980 (Liberal)
Gilles Lamontagne	1980–1983
Jean-Jacque Blais	1983–1984
Robert Coates	1984–1985 (Conservative)
Joe Clark (Acting)	1985
Eric Nielson	1985–1986
Perrin Beatty	1986–1989
William McKnight	1989–1991
Marcel Masse	1991–1993
Kim Campbell	1993

Tom Siddon   1993

David Collenette   1993–1996 (Liberal)

12   30 April 1981, Letter to Mark MacGuigan, the secretary of state for external affairs, from Minister of National Defence Lamontagne, re: visit by Secretary of Defense Weinberger. Confidential. 27-1-1-3 and 27-16-2-USA. (And) (16) April 1981 DND Note to file, re: "Visit of US Defence Secretary Weinberger, Ottawa, 15 April 1981," Confidential.

13   18 June 1980, Memo to External Affairs from Canadian embassy Washington, re: Release of info relating to Winnipeg 1953 tests. 27-11-CDA-USA. Confidential.

14   DND press release AFN: 26/81, 15 April 1981.

15   16–19 June 1981, 159th PJBD Meeting Minutes. 23 June 1981 Letter to Prime Minister Trudeau from Chairman G. Hees, Canadian Chairman PJBD, re: 159th Meeting. Secret.

16   Benjamin B. Fischer, *A Cold War Conundrum: The 1983 Soviet War Scare.* (Operation RYaN) Centre for the Study of Intelligence, Central Intelligence Agency (CIA), 1997. Unclassified

17   "My fellow Americans, I am pleased to tell you I just signed legislation which outlaws Russia forever. The bombing begins in five minutes." Ronald Reagan said during a radio microphone test, 1984.

18   4 February 1983, Memo to Mr. Riley in the minister's Office, from J. R. Francis, Defence Relations, re: Testing agreement with the United States, DFR-0459. Confidential. 27-16-2-USA.

19   02 February 1982, Memo to DMF from J. R. Francis in DFR, re: "Agreement for testing US defence systems in Canada." Confidential. 27-8-USA-3.

20   16 July 1981, Memorandum to the secretary of state for external affairs from IDR, re: "Cabinet Committee on External Affairs and Defence: Proposed use of Canadian ranges for US military operations and evaluation activities." Secret. DFP-116. (and) 8 July 1981, Memorandum to J. H. Taylor from Cameron, International Security and Arms Control, re: "Draft Memorandum to Cabinet on proposed use of Canadian ranges for US military operational test and evaluation activities." Secret. DFP-104. 27-16-2-USA.

21   30 September 1981, Memorandum to P. Anglin from P. Clement, re: U.S. Cruising Missile Testing Facility in Canada vs. Canadian Security Policy: Initiatives in arms control and disarmament. PMO, Secret.

22   20-23 October 1981, 160th PJBD Meeting Minutes. 30 October 1981 Letter to Prime Minister Trudeau from Chairman G. Hees, Canadian Chairman PJBD, re: 160th Meeting. Secret.

23   27 November 1981, Memorandum for the Prime Minister from Robert Fowler, re: Report of Mr. Hees on the 160th Meeting of the PJBD. Confidential.

24   14 December 1981, Memorandum for the Prime Minister from Robert Fowler, re: Report of Mr. Hees on the 160th Meeting of the PJBD. Confidential.

25   3 November 1983, Memorandum to the EA/MND from ADM (Policy), re: Testing and evaluation of US defence systems in Canada, and attached and talking points.

26   24 March 1982, External Affairs Memorandum re: Current status of US proposal for testing and evaluation of US defence systems in Canada. Confidential. 27-16-2-USA.

27   Walker, "Cabinet gave blessing," *Montreal Gazette*, 18 March 1982. Walker, Southam News, article in *North Bay Nugget*. Walker suggests that the decision was taken by Cabinet in early January 1982 rather than in December 1981. However, this contradicts the secret letter sent to Reagan assuring him that the positive decision had already been made.

28   *Montreal Gazette*, 19 March 1983.

29   2 February 1983, Memo to DMF (through PFG), from J. R. Francis, Defence Relations Division, re: Agreement for testing US defence systems in Canada. DFR-0423. Confidential. 27-8-USA-3.

30   14 December 1981, Memorandum for the Prime Minister from Robert Fowler, re: Report of Mr. Hees on the 160th Meeting of the PJBD. Confidential. (And) 23 December 1981, Memorandum for the Prime Minister from Robert Fowler, re: Testing of United States Weapons Systems. Confidential.

31   30 December 1981, Letter to President Ronald Reagan from Prime Minister Pierre Trudeau, re: Weapons System Testing.

32   17 March 1982, Memorandum for the Prime Minister from R. R. Fowler, re: Testing of United States Weapons Systems in Canada. Confidential; and 24 March 1982 External Affairs Memorandum re: Current status of US proposal for testing and evaluation of US defence systems in Canada. Confidential. 27-16-2-USA.; and c.16 September 1982, External Affairs Current status of U.S. proposal for testing and evaluation of U.S. defence systems in Canada. Confidential. 27-16-2-USA.

33   17 March 1982, Memorandum for the Prime Minister from R. R. Fowler, re: Testing of United States Weapons Systems in Canada. Confidential; and 24 March 1982 External Affairs Memorandum re: Current status of U.S. proposal for testing and evaluation of U.S. defence systems in Canada. Confidential. 27-16-2-USA.

34   16–19 February 1982, 160th PJBD Meeting Minutes. 1 March 1982, Letter to Prime Minister Trudeau from Chairman G. Hees, Canadian Chairman PJBD, re: 161st Meeting. Secret.

35   11 March 1982, Letter to George Hees, Chairman PJBD, from Prime Minister Trudeau, re: 161st Meeting of PJBD.

36   3 February 1983, memo to Mr. Riley in the Minister's Office from J. R. Francis, Defence Relations, External Affairs, re: Testing agreement with the United States. DFR-0451. Confidential. 27-8-USA-3. And attached explanatory note on Articles 8 and 13 of the testing agreement.

37   25 February 1982, Standing Committee on External Affairs and National Defence (SCEAND) meeting #65. P.65:51.

38   11 March 1982, Message from PMR Johnson External Affairs Ottawa to Canadian embassy Washington, D.C., re: U.S. Proposal to test U.S. defence systems in CDA: Press leak. 27-16-2-USA. Confidential.

39   11 March 1982, Memorandum for the minister of national defence from D. P. Wightman PMO, re: Canada/U.S. Weapons Testing Agreement. Confidential.

40   11 March 1982, transcript of minister of national defence and various reporters at the House of Commons, re: cruise missiles. 27-16-2-USA.

41   Canadian Press, "They'd be just dummies, Defence minister looks at Cruise missile issue," *Chronicle Journal*, 12 March 1982.

42   Secretary of State for External Affairs Mark MacGuigan, interview, *Canada AM*, Canadian Television (CTV), 22 March 1982.

43   Carleson, "Canada owes cruise testing to NATO: PET," *Toronto Sun*, 28 March 1983.

44   "NATO delighted," *Sunday Star*, 17 July 1983.

45   Prime Minister Trudeau, interview, CBC Radio Inuvik, NWT, 19 July 1983. Also *Star-Phoenix*, 20 July 1983.

46   McNamara appeared before the joint session of the External Affairs and National Defence Committee on 25 October 1983, and also met with Trudeau. Sears, "Cruise, Pershing needed," *Toronto Star*, 26 October 1983.

47   11 March 1982, Memo from Barlow to Phillips, re: Telephone representation Cruise missile testing in Alberta, 27-16-2-USA Unclassified.

48   11 March 1982, Message from T. C. Hammond External Affairs Ottawa to Canadian embassy Washington, D.C., re: U.S. Proposal to test US defence systems in CDA: Press leak. Attached press guidance. 27-16-2-USA. Confidential.

49   5 January 1983, Telex to Canadian embassy and consulates in USA, from P. E. Heinbecker, External Affairs, re: Canada/US Defence Relations. GNC-0015. Restricted.

50   26 July 1986, Memorandum from DG Information to DAOT and DC Policy, re: ALCM – Proposed 1986 captive carry flight – Public affairs approach. 1350-11410 (DG Info). Secret.

51   General E.L.M. Burns (Ret'd), interview, *CTV National News*, Canadian Television (CTV), 12 March 1982.

52   23 March 1982, letter to Terry Sargeant, MP, from Prime Minister Pierre Trudeau, re: cruise missile tests in Canada.

53   17 March 1982, Memorandum for the Prime Minister from R. R. Fowler, re: Testing of United States Weapons Systems in Canada. Confidential.

54   Ibid. 24 March 1982 External Affairs Memorandum re: Current status of U.S. proposal for testing and evaluation of U.S. defence systems in Canada. Confidential. 27-16-2-USA.

55   19 March 1982, news conference transcript of Prime Minister Pierre Trudeau. The transcript also reveals that Trudeau almost immediately reiterated the falsehood by referring to "these cruise missiles – the SS-20s."

56   House of Commons, Standing Committee on External Affairs and National Defence (SCEAND), *Minutes*, 24 March 1982.

57   Peter Calamai, "Officials lied to hide cost of missiles," *Ottawa Citizen*, 17 March 1989. Sadly, the declassified documents given to Calamai and his wife no longer exist. He had not retained these items, and DND does not normally keep copies of older Access to Information requests and releases past two years. However, the new practice of scanning documents and making them available electronically will save various items for a longer term.

58   8 April 1982, Memorandum to DFR from the minister's office, External Affairs, re: US proposal on testing of US defence systems in Canada. Confidential. 27-16-2-USA.

59   06 May 1982, Telex to External Affairs from Canadian Delegation to NATO, re: "Bilateral: MND-Weinberger." Confidential.

60   25 March 1982, Briefing Note for the Minister of National Defence, re: US Test and Evaluation in Canada – Cruise Missile Testing. Delivered by A. W. Mathewson, CPP, NDHQ.

61   House of Commons, Standing Committee on External Affairs and National Defence, *Minutes*, 27 April 1982.

62   Ibid.

63   *Arms Control Reporter 1984* 611.BA.5.

64   6 October 1982, Memorandum for the Secretary of State for External Affairs, from P.M.R. Johnson, Defence Relations Division, re: Proposed agreement on the use of Canadian test sites for US military. DFR-3242.

65   J. M. Stares of Burlington, Ontario, letter to the editor: "Our politicians should break with their usual line of least resistance and show some intestinal fortitude by firmly prohibiting the trials of those murderous weapons on, or above, our soil," 29 March 1982.

66   Sister Mary Jo Leddy, "Now the hour has come," *The Toronto Star*, 3 April 1982.

67   16 September 1982, Memorandum for the Secretary of State for External Affairs, re: Proposed use of Canadian test sites for US military operational test and evaluation activities (and) current status briefing note. Confidential. DFR-3003. 27-16-2-USA.

68   3 February 1983, memo to Mr. Riley in the minister's office from J. R. Francis, Defence Relations, External Affairs, re: Testing agreement with the United States. DFR-0451. Confidential. 27-8-USA-3. And attached explanatory note on Articles 8 and 13 of the testing agreement. (Paragraph 3).

69   16 September 1982, Memorandum for the Secretary of State for External Affairs from Assistant Deputy Ministers Delworth and Marchand, re: Proposed use of Canadian test sites for US military operational test and evaluation activities. DFR-3003. Confidential. 27-16-2-USA.

70   6 October 1982, Memorandum for the Secretary of State for External Affairs, from Assistant Deputy Ministers Delworth and Marchand, re: Proposed agreement on use of Canadian test sites for US military operational test and evaluation activities. DFR-3242. Confidential.

71   Clearwater, *Canadian Nuclear Weapons* (Toronto: Dundurn, 1998).

72   Rusk, "Technicality delays cruise test pact," *Globe and Mail*, 30 October 1982.

73   6 November 1982, Trudeau speech to the Liberal Party of Canada convention.

74   2 November 1982, Briefing Note for the Minister [of National Defence] from ADM Policy J. F. Anderson, re: Canada/United States Test and Evaluation Agreement.

75   3 November 1982, External Affairs Memo from R. P. Cameron, DFP, re: Proposed agreement on the use of Canadian test sites for US military test and evaluation activities: communication plan. DFP-167. Confidential. 27-16-2-USA.

76   22 December 1982, Memorandum for the Secretary of State for External Affairs, from Delworth and Marchand, re: Proposed agreement on testing of US defence systems in Canada. DFR-4287. Confidential. 27-16-2-USA.

77   10 December 1982 CP article in the *Globe and Mail*, 10 December 1982.

78   2 November 1982, Briefing Note for the Minister from J. F. Anderson, ADM (Policy) and A. W. Mathewson, CPP, re: Canada/United States test and evaluation agreement. A-3613.

79   24 January 1983, Letter to Secretary of State for External Affairs MacEachen from U.S. Secretary of State Shultz, re: U.S.-Canada Weapon Testing Agreement. Confidential.

80   The French text was given to the State Department by the Canadian embassy in Washington, D.C., 9 December 1982.

81   *Toronto Star*, 10 December 1982.

82   Todd, "Eggleton backs request for national cruise vote," *Toronto Star*, 3 August 1983.

83   7 December 1982, Memorandum for the Deputy Prime Minister and Secretary of State for External Affairs, from Delworth and Marchand, re: Proposed use of Canadian test sites for US military operational test and evaluation activities. DFR-4120. Confidential.

84   21 December 1982, Memorandum for the Secretary of State for External Affairs, from the Deputy Minister, re: Proposed agreement on testing of US defence systems in Canada. DFR-4283. Restricted.

85   22 December 1982, Memorandum for the Secretary of State for External Affairs, from Delworth and Marchand, re: Proposed agreement on testing of US defence systems in Canada. DFR-4287. Confidential. 27-16-2-USA.

86   24 December 1982, Memorandum for the Prime Minister from R. R. Fowler and Wightman, re: Report on Cruise Missile Testing from DND, Confidential.

87   6 January 1983, Memo to DMF, from J. R. Francis, Defence Relations, re: Testing agreement with the United States, DFR-0086. Confidential. 27-8-USA-3.

88   10 January 1983, Memo to External Affairs MIP from Defence Relations, re: Testing agreement with USA, DFR-0115. Confidential. 27-16-2-USA.

89   10 January 1983, Memo to External Affairs DMF from J. R. Francis in Defence Relations, re: Testing agreement with USA: Public Affairs, DFR-0102. Confidential. 27-8-USA-3.

90   21 January 1983, Memorandum for the Minister of National Defence from J. F. Anderson, ADM (Policy) re: Test and evaluation: the cruise missile. Confidential.

91   Kaufman, "Canada-US pact on missile tests is delayed," *New York Times*, 22 January 1983.

92   Mollins, "Canada postpones missile pact signing," in *Saskatoon Star-Phoenix*, 26 January 1983.

93   24 January 1983, Letter to SSEA MacEachen from Secretary of State George Shultz, re: test and evaluation agreement importance. Confidential.

94   "Majority in Canada is opposed to cruise," *Toronto Star*, 12 February 1983.

95   Bob Hepburn, "2 out of 3 MPs won't say yes or no to testing the cruise," *Toronto Star*, 16 March 1983.

96   John Ferguson, "Cruise test plans are now favoured," *Montreal Gazette*, 8 October 1983.

97   Mike Sadava, "Majority of Albertans oppose cruise testing – poll," *Edmonton Journal*, 27 October 1983.

98   *Arms Control Reporter 1983* 611.B.70 21.1.83.

99   26 January 1983, Telex to Canadian Delegation NATO (Brussels) from External Affairs Ottawa, re: Cruise missile testing: Canadian demonstration 25 January. DFR03521.

100   1 February 1983, Memo to DMF (through PFG) from J. R. Francis, Defence Relations, re: Testing agreement with the United States, DFR-0421. Confidential. 27-8-USA-3.

101   Wilson in *Washington Post* and *Boston Globe*, 16 February 1983; *Aviation Week & Space Technology* 31 January 1983; Wilson, in *Washington Post*, 27 February 1983.

102   4 February 1983, Telex to Canadian Embassy Washington, D.C., from External Affairs Ottawa, re: Signing of testing agreement with USA. Secret. 27-16-2-USA.

103   8 February 1983, House of Commons Briefing Book for the Secretary of State for External Affairs, re: Possible development of a stealth cruise missile. 27-8-USA-3.

104   20 January 1983, Memo to DMF (through LAP) from R. P. Cameron in DFP, re: Proposed agreement on testing of U.S. defence systems in Canada: Possible court challenge. DFR-0280. Restricted. 27-8-USA-3.

105   Trudeau had quit the Liberal Party in disgust with the pro-nuclear policies of Pearson, only to keep a handful of nuclear weapons throughout his entire time as prime minister. Pearson had both accepted the weapons and put in place the mechanism to have most returned by 1972. Canada would become a staunch supporter of various treaties to control nuclear weapons and proliferation.

106   Southam News, "Signing a secret ritual," *Vancouver Sun*, 11 February 1983.

107   *Hansard*, Volume XX, 1983, 15th session, 32nd Parliament, P.22714.

108   Masser, "Tory MP attacks secrecy," *The Ottawa Citizen*, 11 February 1983.

109   18 January 1983, Memorandum for the Secretary of State for External Affairs, from Delworth and Marchand, re: Proposed agreement on testing of US defence systems in Canada. DFR-248. Confidential. 27-16-2-USA.

110   *Hansard*, 15 February 1983, P.22851.

111   Doug Long, "Soviets 'could exploit' refusal of cruise tests," *Ottawa Citizen*, 18 February 1983.

112   16 February 1983, House of Commons statement by Prime Minister Pierre Trudeau, as reported by the Prime Minister's Office.

113   "Canada hasn't been asked," *Ottawa Citizen*, 16 March 1983.

114   March 1983, Memorandum for the Minister of National Defence, from the Deputy Minister D. B. Dewar, re: Can/US agreement – test and evaluation of US weapons systems Memorandum of Understanding (received 2 March 1983).

115   Benjamin B. Fischer, *A Cold War Conundrum: The 1983 Soviet War Scare* (Operation RYaN). Centre for the Study of Intelligence, Central Intelligence Agency (CIA), 1997. Unclassified.

116   4 February 1983, Facsimile from Canadian Embassy Washington, D.C. to External Affairs, re: Secretary Shultz statement to press. 27-8-USA-3.

117   "Nuclear warning," *Edmonton Sunday Sun*, 13 March 1983.

118   Rosner, "US bombers fire simulated cruises," *Winnipeg Free Press*, 18 May 1983.

119   "Bodyguards grab reporter querying PM," *Ottawa Citizen*, 25 March 1983.

120   "Bush expects Canada to honour agreement on missile testing," *Globe and Mail*, 24 March 1983.

121   "Canada signs arms test memo," *Winnipeg Free Press*, 22 April 1983.

122   Sears, "Canada will test cruise Bush is told," *Toronto Star*, date unknown.

123   23 March 1983, State Dinner for Vice President George Bush hosted by Prime Minister Pierre Trudeau.

124   Anderson, "Just what our leaders have said," *Toronto Star*, 2 April 1983.

125   House of Commons, Standing Committee on External Affairs and National Defence, *Minutes*, no. 99:19, 9 June 1983, 19.

126   "Replies of Yuri Andropov," *Pravda*, 27 March 1983.

127   20 April 1983, Memo to Mr. Riley in the Minister's Office from J. R. Francis, Defence Relations, re: Testing Agreement/MOU. DFR-1345. Confidential. 27-16-2-USA.

128   29 March 1983, Telex to Canadian embassy Washington, D.C. from J. R. Francis, Defence Relations, External Affairs, re: Testing agreement with USA. Confidential.

129   "Cruise missiles here within year," *Ottawa Citizen*, 18 April 1983.

130   "US to request cruise testing," *Brandon Sun*, 12 April 1983.

131   19 April 1983, Letter to Members of Parliament and the Senate, from Secretary of State for External Affairs Allan MacEachen, re: cruise missile testing in House of Commons, Standing Committee on External Affairs and National Defence, *Minutes of Proceedings*, no. 88A:56, 19 April 1983.

132   Cox & Taylor, *A Guide to Canadian Policies on Arms Control, Disarmament, Defence and Conflict Resolution, 1986-87* (Ottawa: CIIPS, 1987), p. 119.

133   27–28 April 1983, Prime Ministerial Visit to Washington, D.C., U.S.A. for meetings with the U.S. President. "PM appears set to approve cruise tests after US visit," *Toronto Star*, 28 April 1983. "PM, Bush avoid issue of cruise tests," *Ottawa Citizen*, 28 April 1983.

134   26 April 1983, Memorandum for the Prime Minister, from R. R. Fowler, re: Visit to Washington April 27–28 – Briefing Book. Confidential.

135   Gwyn, "Trudeau used a debating trick," *Ottawa Citizen*, 12 May 1983.

136   Ibid.

137   "PM gets cruise letters," *Winnipeg Free Press*, 27 May 1983.

138 House of Commons, Standing Committee on External Affairs and National Defence, *Minutes*, no. 33:24, 3-10-1985. Testimony of Director General Military Plans & Operations, BGen C. Bertrand.

139 13 May 1983, Memorandum for Bob Fowler from D. P. Wightman, re: Cruise testing request. Confidential.

140 House of Commons, Standing Committee on External Affairs and National Defence, *Minutes*, 12 May 1983.

141 Cahill, "A fireside chat with Trudeau," *Toronto Star*, 14 May 1983.

142 "Canada will OK cruise test: Kissinger," *Owen Sound Sun Times*, 1 June 1983.

143 6 June 1983, *Hansard* Commons Debates 26075.

144 Walkom, "Lamontagne admits radar can be used for the cruise," *Globe and Mail*, 8 June 1983.

145 circa 12 June 1983, Memorandum to the Minister of National Defence from the Deputy Minister, re: CANUS Test and evaluation agreement air launched cruise missile project.

146 9 June 1983, PMO Note for David Wightman and Maurice Archdeacon to transmit to DND and for use in the memo to the PM, from Robert Fowler, Secret.

147 10 June 1983, Memo from CANUS T&E Coordinator, General A. C. Brown, re: CANUS Test and evaluation review committee cruise missile, 10081-34/0 (DMPC). Confidential.

148 13 June 1983, Memo to DFP from PMR Johnson, re: Cruise missile testing project arrangement proposal: preliminary impressions. DFR-2065. 27-8-USA-3. Confidential.

149 13 June 1983, Memorandum for Mr. Osbaldeston from R. R. Fowler, re: Cruise missile testing request. Secret, no distribution. (And) 14 June 1983 Memorandum for the Prime Minister from Robert Fowler (via Mr. Osbaldeston) re: Cruise missile – request for test facilities. Secret.

150 Undated (circa June 1983) PMO/PCO "Critical path for cruise missile testing agreement." Released by PCO under Access to Information.

151 14 June 1983, Memorandum from Col R. W. Buskard, DC Policy, re: ALCM project proposal, 10081-034-3 (DC Pol 3). Confidential.

152 15 June 1983, Memorandum from LCol J. R. Morency, DSPCA 2, re: ALCM project Proposal, 10081-34-3 (DSPCA 2). Confidential.

153 15 June 1983, Memorandum from Major M. R. Hunt, D Law/I, re: ALCM project proposal, 10081-34-3 (D Law/I).

154 "Colonel urges Moscow Trip," *Victoria Times-Colonist*, 18 July 1983.

155 Rooney, "Cruise protesters convicted," *The Calgary Herald*, 10 May 1984.

156 13 May 1983, Memorandum for R. R. Fowler from General Wightman, re: Cruise missile testing. Confidential.

157 "US officially asks to test cruise," *Saint John Telegraph Journal*, 14 June 1983.

158 House of Commons, Standing Committee on External Affairs and National Defence, *Minutes*, no. 92:24, 12 May 1983.

159 10 June 1983, Memo from CANUS T&E Coordinator, General A. C. Brown, re: CANUS Test and evaluation review committee cruise missile, 10081-34/0 (DMPC). Confidential.

160 14 June 1983, Memorandum from LCol G. M. Ewen, DFSM, re: ALCM project proposal, 2772-14 (DFSM 2). Confidential.

161   15 July 1983, Minutes of Cabinet Priorities & Planning Committee meeting; and Minutes of 15 July 1983 Cabinet meeting, 26-83CBM, Secret, Cabinet Confidence. These documents were closed but leaked to the author. The full records were released to the public in October 2003.

162   15 July 1983, letter to U.S. Secretary of State George Shultz from Secretary of State for External Affairs MacEachen, re: decision to approve ALCM tests.

163   15 July 1983, Government of Canada News Release, "Canada agrees to test cruise missile," 88/83.

164   "Anti-cruise protesters begin vigil," *Toronto Sunday Sun,* 17 July 1983.

165   16 July 1983, TASS (Moscow), in *Portage la Prairie Daily Graphic,* 18 July 1983.

166   "Cruise communist issue: PC aide," *Montreal Gazette,* 6 August 1983.

167   Lowman, "Nobody rallied against Soviets," *Toronto Star,* 3 November 1983.

168   Anderson in *Washington Post,* 28 November 1983.

169   "Shultz praises decision," *Winnipeg Free Press,* 17 October 1983.

170   25 October 1983, Telex to Embassy in Washington from External Affairs, re: "Shultz/ MacEachen bilateral: cruise missile testing." Confidential. 27-8-USA-3.

171   "Communists making use of peace movement: Tory," *Ottawa Citizen,* 5 December 1983.

172   "Communists admit anti-cruise role," *Edmonton Journal,* 23 February 198_. Year unknown.

173   *Arms Control Reporter 1983* 607.B.27 22.11.83.

NOTES TO CHAPTER 2

1   Undated (mid-1984), Briefing note on status of CANUS Test and Evaluation program. (DND)

2   3 March 1984, Memo to the minister of national defence from LCol R. W. Walker, re: Cruise missile testing schedule. Obtained by Robert Winters of the *Montreal Gazette* under the *Access to Information Act.*

3   Rooney, "The cruise from a distance," *Content,* May/June 1984.

4   05 January 1990, Letter to Commodore Bruce Johnson, DND CANUS T&E Coordinator, from Richard Ledesma, DoD CANUS T&E Coordinator, re: 30 month testing forecast. Annex on ALCM testing. Secret.

5   USAF Fact Sheet 96-06, AGM-86B/C Missiles.

6   Definitions courtesy of Rick Green (the Frantics) and Andrew Green (Toronto writer).

7   Full details of the U.S. nuclear weapon deployments to the Canadian military are found in the first volume of this series entitled *Canadian Nuclear Weapons* (Toronto: Dundurn, 1998).

8   The peace petition was given to Mulroney on 22 October 1984. "Cruise tests stay," *Montreal Gazette,* 23 October 1984.

9   *Pravda,* 31 July 1984.

10   TASS 25 August 1984 in USSR UN Mission press release.

11   "Ronald Reagan, The Prime-Time President," *The American President.* http://www. americanpresident.com.

12   9 January 1985, Memorandum for the Prime Minister, re: Cruise missile Testing in Canada. Secret.

13 "Cruise protesters demonstrate," *Portage la Prairie Daily Graphic*, 23 February 1985.

14 25 February 1985, Journal of the PJBD 170th Meeting, Key West, USA, 5–8 February 1985. Secret.

15 11 September 1986, Memorandum to ADM Policy from BGen J. A. Cotter, DC Policy, re: CANUS Nuclear Weapons Arrangements. 3310-1 (DC Pol). Secret.

16 19 February 1985, Message to Embassy in Washington from External Affairs, re: "USA nuclear deployments." Secret

17 14 August 1986, Memo to IDD Mr. D. Peel, from IDD Mr. K. J. Merklinger, re: "Nuclear agreements review meeting with US 0930 August 26 1986." Secret.

18 The following are the agreements and arrangements which were cancelled:

A. 16 August 1963, Agreement on providing nuclear warheads to Canadian forces.

B. 15 October 1973, Host/Tenant agreement between CFB Comox and Det 5, 425 Munitions Maintenance Squadron.

C. 15 October 1974, Amendment 1 to Host/Tenant agreement of 15 October 1973.

D. 01 June 1964, Administrative and logistical support agreement for USAF custodial detachments in Canada.

E. 20 January 1978, Nuclear weapons engineering and test support of CF Aerospace nuclear weapon systems.

F. 19 February 1970, Arrangement for the CF-101/Air 2A.

G. 15 December 1970, USA-Canada CIM-10B/CF-101 weapon inspection plan.

H. 28/30 September 1963, Agreement under which storage of nuclear air-to-air defensive weapons at Goose Bay and Harmon AFB would be permitted.

I. 15 May 1964, Arrangement to supplement and provide for the implementation of the 28/30 September 1963 agreement on nuclear weapons at Goose Bay and Harmon AFB. This referred to the USAF air defence units at Goose Bay and Harmon AFB in Newfoundland that were armed with nuclear-tipped Falcon missiles. All ended by 1968.

J. 27 July 1967, Agreement on the condition under which storage of nuclear anti-submarine weapons in Canada, for use of U.S. forces, would be permitted.

K. 18 December 1967, Arrangement to supplement and provide for the implementation of the 27 July 1967 agreement on U.S. airborne nuclear ASW weapons at a base in Canada.

L. (c.1967) Channel and authorization for exchange of atomic information between the US Navy and DND ZED control officer.

The first document refers to nuclear warheads for the BOMARC, Starfighter, CF-101, and Honest John systems operated by the RCAF and RC Army. The bulk of the documents refer to CF-101/Genie operations in Canada. All such operations ended by mid-1984. The last three obscurely-named documents were for the U.S. navy anti-submarine patrol aircraft carrying nuclear depth bombs deployed to Argentia in Newfoundland. All such activities ended by 1971.

19 23 January 1985, Telex to External Affairs from Embassy in Washington, re: "USA nuclear deployments." Confidential.

20 29 August 1986, Memorandum from DAP 3 to DAR and DAOT, re: Review of Nuclear Agreements – Meeting of 26 August 1986, 1150-110/C2-4 (DAP3). Secret/CEO.

21 4 September 1986, Message to Embassy in Washington from External Affairs, re: "Review of Canada-USA military agreements." Secret.

22 29 August 1986, Memorandum from DAP 3 to DAR and DAOT, re: Review of Nuclear Agreements – Meeting of 26 August 1986. 1150-110/C2-4 (DAP3). Secret/CEO.

23   7 May 1990, *CANUS Index of Agreements.* (Interim). Canada-United States Military Cooperation Committee. Confidential.

24   Items still in force in 1990 included these crucial nuclear-related agreements and arrangements:

A. Agreement for cooperation on civil uses of atomic energy. (With exchange of notes), 15 June 1955.

B. Amendment to agreement for cooperation on civil uses of atomic energy of 15 June 1955. (With exchange of notes), 26 June 1956.

C. Amendment to 15 June 1955 agreement for cooperation regarding atomic information for mutual defence purposes. (With exchange of letters), 22 May 1959.

D. Amendment to agreement for cooperation on civil uses of atomic energy of 15 June 1955. (With exchange of notes), 11 June 1960.

E. Amendment to agreement for cooperation on civil uses of atomic energy of 15 June 1955. (With exchange of notes), 25 May 1962.

F. Agreement between the Government of Canada and the Government of the United States of America for cooperation regarding atomic information for mutual defence purposes. (with exchange of notes), 15 June 1955.

G. Agreement between the Government of the United States of America and the Government of Canada for cooperation on the uses of atomic energy for mutual defence purposes. (with exchange of notes), 22 May 1959.

H. Administrative arrangements to support the agreement between Canada the USA for the cooperation on the uses of atomic energy for mutual defence purposes. 05 January 1961.

I. Administrative arrangements to support the agreement between Canada the USA for the cooperation on the uses of atomic energy for mutual defence purposes. 18 June 1964.

J. Agreement between the parties to the North Atlantic Treaty for cooperation regarding atomic information. 04 May 1965.

K. Technical annex to the Agreement between the parties to the North Atlantic Treaty for cooperation regarding atomic information. 18 June 1964.

L. Security annex to the Agreement between the parties to the North Atlantic Treaty for cooperation regarding atomic information. 18 June 1964.

25   The ten nuclear-related military air items include:

A. Exchange of notes on provision of nuclear weapons for the Canadian Forces. 16 August 1963.

B. Exchange of notes on consultations and procedures related to NORAD alert status and the use of nuclear air defence weapons CINCNORAD. 17 September 1965.

C. Exchange of letters concerning arrangements for intergovernmental consultation in the event of hostilities. 14 June 1973.

D. Canada/USA consultation with respect to situation which might lead to the outbreak of hostilities involving North America. 199x year unknown.

E. Exchange of notes on the establishment of a second low altitude training route in Canada for use by Strategic Air Command. 11 February 1966.

F. Agreement between 24 NORAD Region and CFB Moose Jaw for fighter interceptor support. 5 March 1973.

G. Agreement between 24 NORAD Region and CFB Moose Jaw for IFR Flush procedures at CFB Moose Jaw. 5 March 1973.

H. SAC/NORAD command agreement for Snowtime. 1 January 1976.

I. Agreement between 24 NORAD Region and CFB Winnipeg for fighter interceptor support. 20 February 1974.

J. Agreement between 24 NORAD Region and CFB Winnipeg for Flush procedures at CFB Winnipeg. 20 February 1974.

26 Other nuclear-related items in the 1990 CANUS index are:

A. Agreement concerning air traffic services for USAF-SAC contingency plans operating in Canadian air space. 4 October 1974.

B. Approved methods of clearing flights of SAC bombers and SAC transport aircraft over Canadian territory where the movement of nuclear weapons is involved. 27 June 1979.

C. Exchange of notes on procedures governing the overflight of or emergency landing in Canada by nuclear-armed SAC aircraft experiencing operational or material difficulties. 14 January 1963.

D. Exchange of notes approving in principle overflight of Canadian territory during an airborne alert. 13 January 1984. (This agreement was in force 12 days before Canada signed it.)

E. Exchange of notes concerning arrangements for the emergency deployment and refuelling of aircraft at selected Canadian Forces bases in Canada in times of international crisis. 16 September 1977.

F. Arrangement between SAC 92nd Bomb Wing and CFB Cold Lake governing the emergency deployment and refuelling of United States military aircraft at CFB Cold Lake. 16 September 1977.

G. Memorandum of agreement between CFB Edmonton and SAC 93rd Bomb Wing on conditions governing emergency deployment to CFB Edmonton. 5 April 1979.

H. Exchange of notes on United States nuclear powered warships in foreign ports. 20 February 1967.

27 The six items from the 1997 CANUS index are:

A. Exchange of notes governing the establishment of an integrated system to support the ballistic missile early warning system (BMEWS). 13 July 1959.

B. Exchange of notes for the continued operation and maintenance of the Torpedo Test Range in the Strait of Georgia including the installation and utilization of an Advanced Underwater Acoustic Measurement System at Jervis Inlet. (CFMETR, Nanoose) 14 April 1976.

C. Supplementary and administrative arrangement for the operation of test ranges in the Strait of Georgia and Jervis Inlet, British Columbia. 14 September 1994.

D. CANUSTEP Project Arrangement – Air launched cruise missile (ALCM). 1 December 1985.

E. Exchange of notes between the Government of Canada and the Government of the United States of America constituting an Agreement concerning the reciprocal testing and evaluation of weapons systems. 10 February 1993.

F. Canada-United States Test and Evaluation Program (CANUSTEP). 24 February 1993.

28 Terry Milewski, "Defence Secrets," *The National*, Canadian Broadcasting Corporation, 4 December 1985.

29 11 December 1985, Memorandum for the Prime Minister from Paul Tellier, re: Canada – USA Arrangements in regard to defence, defence production and defence sharing. Secret.

30 Ibid.

31 26 November 1986, Message to JLEB from Karsgaard, Defence Relations (IDR), DFAIT, re: CANUS Index of Agreements. IDR/D 27-1-1-USA. Confidential.

32 4 September 1985, Message to Canadian Embassy Washington D.C., from External Affairs Ottawa, re: review of CDA-USA military agreements. IDR-3120, 27-1-1-USA. Secret.

33 15 January 1984 [maybe a typo for 1985], message to Canadian Embassy Washington D.C., from External Affairs Ottawa, re: nuclear deployments. 27-11-1, 370421. Secret, Canadian Eyes Only.

34 18 January 1985, Ministerial House of Commons Briefing Book, re: deployment of nuclear weapons to CFB Comox and Greenwood aboard U.S. P-3 Orion aircraft. Prepared by IDR for SSEA. 1-11-IDR-2, 27-11-1. Secret.

35 23 January 1985, message to External Affairs Ottawa from Canadian Embassy Washington D.C., re: USA nuclear deployments. 27-1-1-USA, 478674. Confidential.

36 5 February 1985, Memorandum for the Secretary of State for External Affairs, from DM and ADM Int; Security affairs, re: North American defence related issues. IDR-0465, 27-11-1, 373093. Secret.

37 23 January 1985, message to External Affairs Ottawa from Canadian Embassy Washington D.C., re: USA nuclear deployments. 27-1-1-USA, 478674. Confidential.

38 19 February 1985, message to Canadian Embassy Washington D.C., from External Affairs Ottawa, re: USA nuclear deployments. 27-11-1, 378678. Secret.

39 12 February 1985, Memorandum for the Prime Minister re: Cruise missile test program in Canada. Confidential.

40 Ibid.

41 31 March 1985, "History 4201ˢᵗ Test Squadron January-March 1985." DCoS Ops, SAC/USAF, SECRET/NOFORN/RD.

42 31 July 1985, Memorandum for the Prime Minister from Robert Fowler, re: Reply to letter from the Honourable Allan Lawrence. Secret.

43 28 January 1985, Memorandum for the Prime Minister from Paul Tellier, re: Your meeting with Allan Lawrence Wednesday January 29 – 3:15 PM. Secret.

44 31 May 1990, notes to file appended to document 30 May 1990 21:30z message from HQ NORAD to dist list, re: Future NORAD participation in CANUS ALCM tests. Unclassified.

45 13 August 1986, Message to DMC from Karsgaard in IDR, re: "Cruise missile testing programme: planning meeting." Secret. 27-8-USA-3.

46 18 September 1986, Message to Ministerial Delegation from External Affairs, re: "Cruise missile testing in Canada." Secret. 27-8-USA-3.

47 26 July 1986, Memo to Dist List from DG Info, BGen Liston, re: ALCM – Proposed 1986 captive carry flight – public affairs approach. Secret.

48 5 November 1986, Telex to Ministerial Delegation from External affairs, re: "SALT II compliance and ALCM testing." Secret – CEO. 28-6-5-1 and 27-8-USA-3.

49 "Cruise foes play into Soviet hands Clark tells MPs," *Toronto Star*, 2 December 1986.

50 5 January 1987, Letter to U.S. President Reagan from Prime Minister Mulroney regarding SALT II and ALCM testing.

51 6 March 1987, *Hansard*.

52 9 March 1987, *Hansard*.

53 *Times Colonist*, 13 September 1987.

54 1 October 1987, *Hansard*.

55　02 October 1987, Memorandum for the SSEA from Sullivan and Taylor, re: "Cruise missile testing." Secret. 27-8-USA-3.

56　The office of the chief of defence staff admitted that INF deployments "did not arise out of any profound and widely held anxiety among the *peoples* of Western Europe." In the same way, the chief of defence staff was told, Canadians are not supporting cruise missiles, but that the opposition was not communist inspired. 2 December 1982, DAC Pol briefing note for the CDS, re: "Peace movements at home and abroad and their impact on the role of the CF."

57　25 March 1988, *Hansard.*

58　25 March 1988, *Hansard.*

NOTES TO CHAPTER 3

1　The basic facts of the Litton bombing are well known, but the following articles give details from the time and present the facts in a way not yet covered by any historical writings. Romain, "Litton is negotiating pact to build system for US cruise missiles," *Globe and Mail*, 3 April 1979; Lowman, "Cruise missile 'brain' spurs business for Toronto firm," *Toronto Star*, 8 April 1982; Lowman, "Litton delivers first navigational 'brain' for deadly cruise missile," *Toronto Star*, 11 April 1982;Erdle, "16 Charged in anti-missile rally at Litton," *Toronto Star*, 7 August 1982;, Kaufman, "7 Hurt in blast at Toronto plant," *New York Times*, 16 October 1982; "Five injured in blast at missile parts plant," *Winnipeg Free Press*,15 October 1982; Ferguson and Slotnick, "Litton bombing called work of experts as police question anti-missile groups," *Globe and Mail*, 16 October 1982; Clifford, "Litton assembly areas undisturbed by blast," *Globe and Mail*, 16 October 1982; Slotnick, "Group lays claim to Litton bombing," *Globe and Mail*, 21 October 1982; Slotnick, "Litton bombing: Group claims responsibility," *Toronto Star*, 21 October 1982; "100 Anti-nuclear demonstrators arrested at Litton's factory," *Ottawa Citizen*, 12 November 1982; Kashmeri, "Police conduct raid in search for leads to Litton bombing," *Globe and Mail*, 15 December 1982; Stancu, "Metro cops charge 5 in Litton blast," *Toronto Sun*, 13 April 1983; "Teacher guilty in Litton protest," *Toronto Star*, 28 April 1983;, Scotton, "Snaring the Squamish Five," *Toronto Star*, 8 June 1985; "Litton cruise protesters charged," *Saskatoon Star-Phoenix*, 10 August 1983; "16 Charged with trespass in anti-cruise protest at Litton offices," *Montreal Gazette*, 10 August 1983; "Reports seen as biased against alleged bombers," *Ottawa Citizen*, 14 September 1983; Bohuslawsky, "They're victims of peace," *Toronto Sunday Sun*, 28 November 1983; McAteer, "72 arrested in Litton plant missile protest," *Toronto Star*, 13 November 1982; "29 women charged at Litton march," *Toronto Star*, 15 November 1983; Cox, "70 arrested at Litton protest kept in jail for night by police," *Globe and Mail*, 19 November 1983; Ferri, "81 arrested during protest at Litton plant," and "Protester may lose teaching job," *Toronto Star*, 19 November 1983; "Queen's University professor convicted of resisting arrest at Litton protest," Canadian Press, 14 December 1983; O'Neill, "Man, 24, convicted in protest at Litton," *Toronto Star*, 20 December 1983; Mulgrew, "20-Year jail term for Litton bomber," *Globe and Mail*, 19 May 1984; "$19,000 awarded to trio injured in Litton bombing," *Ottawa Citizen*, 31 May 1984; "Admits Litton bombing, woman called frustrated activist," *Kitchener-Waterloo Record*, 5 June 1984. "Bomber gets life term, hurls tomato at judge," *Globe and Mail*, 3 June 1984; Mulgrew, "The defiant Squamish five: down to earth with a thud," *Globe and Mail*, 19 June 1984; Moore, "12 Cruise protesters charged after skirmish at Litton plant," *Toronto Star*, 15 November 1984; Chapman, "Plea deal for Litton bombers is disgusting," *Toronto Sun*, 20 March 1984; "3 Litton protesters choose jail over curtailed activities," *Toronto Sunday Star*, 12 August 1984; Tripp, "Litton bomber earns BA in jail," *Toronto Star*, 5 June 1989; Matas, "Protesters admit defeat as defence firm booms," *Globe and Mail*, 25 September

1987; "3 Litton protesters under court order," *Toronto Star,* 6 February 1991; Gargiulo, "31 Nabbed at Litton demo," *Toronto Saturday Sun,* 9 March 1991.

2   Late October 1982, RCMP Initial Subject Evaluation Report (SER) on the Cruise Missile Conversion Project (CMCP), pursuant to DDG(OPS)-088 of 19 October 1982. Secret.

3   The level 4 OPRC operation began on 18 October 1982, as per SWOAC message SS(D)1933/235 of 18 October 82.

4   Late October 1982, message from RCMP Chief Superintendent R. L. Duff, Area Commander, SWOAC, re: Bomb incident – bombing of Litton Systems Etobicoke, 14 October 1982. Secret.

5   4 November 1982, Memo to SWOAC from Chairman, OPRC, F. J. Bosse, re: OPRC General meeting 4 November 1982. Secret.

6   15 November 1982, Memo to OIC D Ops, from OIC D-1 Supt J. A. Venner, re: Cruise missile conversion project. Secret.

7   24 November 1982, Memo to the chairman, OPRC, from OIC D Operations, SWOAC, I. W. Taylor, re: Cruise Missile Conversion Project. Secret.

8   30 November 1982, Memo to OIC D Ops from OPRC chairman F. J. Bosse, re: Cruise Missile Conversion Project (CMCP). Secret.

9   16 December 1982, Memo to the OPRC chairman from OIC D Ops, re: CMCP. Secret; 20 January 1983, Transit Slip from Venner re: OPRC meeting 19 January 1983; 19/20 January 1983, Message to SWOAC from OPRC 19 January 1983 meeting, re: CMCP. Secret.

10   16 June 1983, Memorandum from Col R. T. Hall, DSecur, re: Security Considerations (C) ALCM project proposal, 2115-0 (DSecur) Confidential.

11   *Winnipeg Free Press,* 15 June 1983.

12   10 August 2000, *Access to Information Act* release from National Archives, #AH-1999-00008/dg, re: RG146, Volume 3246, "CMCP Canada" Part 1. The files were released only after an extensive battle involving the Information Commissioner of Canada, CSIS, and the National Archives.

NOTES TO CHAPTER 4

1   5 February 1985, Memorandum for the Secretary of State for External Affairs, from DM and ADM Int; Security affairs, re: North American defence related issues. IDR-0465, 27-11-1, 373093. Secret. Section I. Canada-US Test and Evaluation Agreement (Cruise Missile Testing). Refers to initial proposals for "Stealth" ALCM being withdrawn by U.S. by 1985.

2   "Will Canada be asked," *Montreal Gazette,* 8 October 1983.

3   12 June 1986, Memorandum for the SSEA from the DM and ADM (PISA), re: Advanced cruise missile testing proposal, IDR-1976, 27-8-USA-3. Secret – Canadian Eyes Only.

4   14 July 1986, letter to Prime Minister Brian Mulroney from Honourable Allan Lawrence, Chairman, Canadian Section, PJBD, re: 174th Meeting of PJBD, 10-13/6/86. Secret.

5   31 July 1986, letter to Allan Lawrence, Chairman, Canadian Section, PJBD, from Prime Minister Brian Mulroney, re: 174th PJBD Meeting.

6   15 July 1986, Memorandum to the VCDS, DCDS, DM and CDS, from ADM (Pol), re: Cruise Missile Testing. Secret.

7   14 July 1986, Letter to Prime Minister Brian Mulroney, from Honourable Allan Lawrence, Chairman Canadian Section, PJBD, re: 174th Meeting of PJBD, 10-13/6/86. Secret.

8   16 July 1986, Memorandum for Paul Meyer, External Affairs, from Gordon Reay, Foreign and Defence Policy office, PMO, re: Report of the Canadian chairman of the PJBD. Confidential.

9   18 July 1986, letter to DND Assistant Deputy Minister for Policy, Robert Fowler, from Reid Morden, Assistant Secretary to the Cabinet Foreign and Defence Policy, re: PCO comments on U.S. proposal to test ACM in Canada. Secret (CEO).

10 18 July 1986, Memorandum for the Prime Minister, from Paul M. Tellier, Clerk of the Privy Council, re: Reply to letter from Mr. Lawrence. Secret.

11 31 July 1986, Letter to Allan Lawrence from Prime Minister Mulroney, re: 174th PJBD meeting and invitation to meeting with prime minister, secretary of state for external affairs, and minister of national defence.

12 6 April 1988, External Affairs, MINT/Crosbie's briefing book, "Air launched cruise missile (ALCM) testing in Canada," Secret, Canadian Eyes Only. 27-8-USA-3. (And) 5 August 1986, External Affairs Memo to under-secretary of state from IDD (Karsgaard), re: Signature by the minister of the Memorandum on cruise missile testing. Secret. 27-8-USA-3.

13 9 September 1986, Message to Embassy in Washington from External Affairs, re: "Cruise missile testing in Canada." Secret. (And) 10 September 1986, Message to External Affairs from the Embassy in Washington, re: Cruise missile testing. Secret, Canadian Eyes Only. 27-8-USA-3.

14 25 August 1986, telex from Canadian embassy, Washington, to External Affairs, re: Cruise missile testing in Canada. Secret. 27-8-USA-3.

15 25 August 1986, Note for the secretary of state for external affairs for Derek H. Burney, re: Cruise missile testing in Canada. Secret. 27-8-USA-3.

16 5 September 1986, Message to Embassy in Washington from External Affairs, re: "Cruise missile testing in Canada." Secret. 27-8-USA-3.

17 1 September 1986, External Affairs, "The Withdraw Pitch," Secret. 27-8-USA-3, Volume 3.

18 Ibid.

19 10 September 1986, Message to the Ministerial Delegation at the Embassy in Washington, from External Affairs, re: "Cruise missile testing in Canada." Secret, Canadian Eyes Only, No Distribution. 27-8-USA-3.

20 16 September 1986, Message to secretary of state for external affairs only, from External Affairs deputy minister, re: "Weinberger/Beatty meeting September 12." Secret, Canadian Eyes Only. 27-8-USA-3.

21 10 September 1986, Message to External Affairs from the Embassy in Washington, re: Cruise missile testing. Secret, Canadian Eyes Only. 27-8-USA-3.

22 16 September 1986, Memorandum for DM/CDS, from ADM (Pol), re Post Washington Actions. Secret.

23 11 September 1986, Memorandum for Paul Tellier from Reid Morden, re: Issues for next week. Secret. 19 September 1986, Memorandum for Bob Blackburn from Reid Morden, re: Issues for next week. Secret.

24 11 September 1986, telex to the Ministerial Delegation at the Embassy in Washington, from External Affairs, re: "Cruise missile testing." Secret, Canadian Eyes Only, No Distribution. 27-8-USA-3.

25 7 October 1986, Telex from External Affairs to Embassy in Washington, re: "Canadian/ USA relations: meeting between SSEA and Amb Niles," Confidential. 27-8-USA-3.

26 18 November 1986, Letter to Prime Minister Mulroney, from Honourable Allan Lawrence, Chairman, Canadian Section, PJBD, re: 175th Meeting of PJBD, 14-17/10/86. Secret.

27 1 December 1986, telex to the Embassy in Washington from External Affairs, re: "ACM testing in Canada," Secret, Canadian Eyes Only, No Distribution. 27-8-USA-3.

28 24 November 1986, Message to Embassy in Washington from External Affairs, re: "SSEA/Shultz bilateral: cruise missile testing." Confidential. Late November 1986, Telex to Embassy in Washington from External Affairs, re: "SSEA/Shultz bilateral: cruise testing."

29 10 November 1986, Memo to USS from IDR, re: Proposed meeting between SSEA and MND. Secret. 27-8-USA-3.

30 24 September 1986, House of Commons Briefing Book for External Affairs, re: cruise missile testing. Secret.

31 5 January 1987, Message to file from IDR, External Affairs, re: Visit of Dep. Asst Sec Def J. Maresca. IDR-0003, 27-1-1-USA, 477482. Secret.

32 Circa November 1986, Jan–Oct 1986, Ministerial Briefing Note List, Office of the Minister of National Defence. Secret. Item number 50 refers to a briefing note from the ADM (Mat) on 21 April 1986 on the Project Proposal for Captive-Carry test on the AGM-129 Advanced Cruise Missile (ACM).

33 2 February 1987, Hansard. p. 2974.

34 3 February 1987, Message to Embassy in Washington from External Affairs, re: "Advanced cruise missile testing," Secret.

35 3 February 1987, Hansard. p. 3032

36 9 September 1987, Letter to Project Ploughshares from the Information Commissioner of Canada, re: case 3100-1085 on the ACM briefing note at DND of 21 April 1986.

37 27 August 1985, Revision 1, IAW Para 15 of MOU, re: Restatement of the Memorandum of Understanding relating to the CANUS Test and Evaluation Program Incorporating Agreed Upon Amendments.

38 30 June 1987, Memorandum for the SSEA from the DM, re: "ACM testing: letter from Mr. Weinberger to Mr. Beatty of May 12," Confidential. 27-8-USA-3

39 14 August 1987, Letter to Robert Fowler, ADM (Policy), DND, from Reid Morden, Assistant Secretary to the Cabinet, Foreign and Defence Policy, re: ACM testing. Secret (CEO).

40 14 August 1987, Letter to ADM (Policy), DND, from Asst Sec to the Cabinet, Foreign and Defence Policy, re: ACM testing. Annex of Statement to US Government. Secret (CEO).

41 2 September 1987, Memorandum to DM/CDS from Robert Fowler, ADM (Pol), re: Correspondence Mr. Beatty – Mr. Weinberger. Secret.

42 1 September 1987, Letter to General D. Huddleston, A/ADM (Policy), from Reid Morden, Assistant Secretary to the Cabinet, Foreign and Defence Policy, re: Beatty/Weinberger letter. Secret. (Asking that the now-agreed version be presented to the MND)

43 27 August 1987, Letter to J. H. Taylor, under-secretary of state for external affairs, from Reid Morden, assistant secretary to the cabinet, foreign and defence policy, re: Beatty/ Weinberger letter. Secret

44 Jeff Sallot, "Ottawa to allow new cruise missile testing," Globe and Mail, 1 October 1987. P.A1.

45 29 September 1987, Memorandum to MND Press Secretary, from Col D. A. Fraser, DC Pol, re: Cruise Missile Testing/Possible INF Agreement.

46 21 December 1987, Memorandum to the Prime Minister, from Glen Shortliffe, re: Advanced cruise missile testing. Secret.

47 21 December 1987 Memorandum to the Prime Minister from the Secretary of State for External affairs, Joe Clark, re: ACM testing. Secret. 6 January 1988, Memorandum to the Deputy Minister DND, re: SSEA Memo to PM ACM Testing. Secret.

48 Secretary of State for External Affairs Joe Clark's response to Question 242, tabled by Dan Heap in the House of Commons, 29 January 1988.

49 6 January 1988, Telex to External Affairs from Ministerial Delegation in Paris, re: "Anticipated ACM test request: SSEA/Shultz discussion Paris Jan 6," Corrected copy, Secret, Canadian Eyes Only. 27-8-USA-3.

50 7 January 1988, Telex to External Affairs from Burney in Embassy in Washington, re: "SSEA/Shultz meeting 11 Jan – ACM testing," Secret, Canadian Eyes Only.

51 3 February 1988, Letter from Thomas Niles, U.S. Ambassador, to Taylor, under-secretary of state for External Affairs, transmitting the letter to the secretary of state for external affairs from George Shultz. Confidential. 3 February 1988, Message to USS from IDR, re: "ACM testing in Canada," Secret. 27-8-USA-3.

52 25 January 1988, Letter to Minister of National Defence Perrin Beatty, from U.S. Ambassador Thomas M. T. Niles, re: ACM Testing Proposal. Secret.

53 9 February 1988, Memorandum for the SSEA from Taylor and Bild, re: "Advanced cruise missile (ACM) testing in Canada." Secret (CEO).

54 11 February 1988, Letter to U.S. Secretary of State George Shultz from Secretary of State for External Affairs Joe Clark, re: rejection of ACM tests. Confidential. 27-8-USA-3. (And) 06 April 1988, MINT/Crosbie's briefing book, re: "Air launched cruise missile (ALCM) testing in Canada." Secret – Canadian Eyes Only.

55 12 February 1988, Letter to Prime Minister Brian Mulroney from U.S. President Ronald Reagan. The message was delivered electronically, by fax and by hand to the Prime Minister's Office.

56 19 January 1989, Telex to External Affairs from Burney at Embassy in Washington, re: "Call on Deputy Secretary Whitehead." Confidential.

57 16 February 1988, Letter to U.S. President Reagan from Prime Minister Mulroney, re: ACM testing, secret. Found in MGen Charles Gauthier study for DND entitled "Formulation of Defence Policy from 1970 to 1990." Secret (CC).

58 30 March 1988, Letter to Prime Minister Brian Mulroney, from Honourable Allan Lawrence, Chairman Canadian Section PJBD, re: PJBD Meeting, 1-4/03/88. Secret.

59 2 February 1988, Memo to PCO from Jim Wright, PMO, re: Update on ACM testing.

60 Circa 1 June 1988, briefing note for the SSEA on the Clark/Shultz meeting in Madrid on 9 June, re: "Advanced cruise missile – request to test in Canada." Secret. 27-8-USA-3.

61 27 January 1989, Telex to External Affairs from Burney in Embassy in Washington, re: "ACM testing," Confidential, Canadian Eyes Only. 27-8-USA-3.

62 3 May 1988, Memo for Derek Burney from Ernest Hebert, re: ACM testing public disclosure policy. Secret.

63 11 April 1988, Memorandum for the SSEA from Taylor and Bild, re: "Advanced cruise missile (ACM) testing – press line." Secret – CEO. The comments from Taylor appear as marginalia after his signature on the last page, and are dated 22 April.

64 10 August 1988, Memorandum to the DM/CDS, from ADM (Pol), re ACM Testing. Secret. 16 August 1988, Briefing Note to the Minister of National Defence from the DM/CDS, re: Advanced Cruise missile Testing. Secret.

65 31 May 1988, Memorandum for ADM (Pol) from BGen Doupe, A/DGC Pol, re: ACM Testing Public Disclosure Policy. Secret.

66   12 August 1988, Memorandum for the Prime Minister, from Paul Tellier, re: Advanced cruise missile testing. Secret (CEO).

67   25 November 1988, Memorandum for the SSEA, re: "US request to test the advanced cruise missile (ACM)." Secret. IDD-0138.

68   7 December 1988, Memo pad note to IDD from MINA (SSEA), re: "Your memorandum IDD-0138 of November 25, 1988."

69   25 November 1988, Telex to Embassy in Washington from External Affairs, re: "ACM – anticipated request for testing." Secret, Canadian Eyes Only. IDR2822.

70   "Canada to US: Ready, aye ready," *Toronto Star*, 3 February 1989.

71   19 January 1989, Telex to External Affairs from Burney at Embassy in Washington, re: "Call on dpty secy Whitehead." Confidential.

72   31 January 1989, Message to Embassy in Washington from External Affairs, re: "ACM testing." Confidential – CEO. The message detailed the content and recommendation of submission to cabinet by MND and SSEA for ACM testing at P&P cabinet meeting that day.

73   23 January 1989, Memorandum (Rush) for the EA/DM, from LCol P. Cantin, office of the Minister of National Defence, re: Advanced cruise missile testing. 269-3 TD 3589. Secret.

74   27 January 1989, Memorandum for the Prime Minister, from Paul Tellier, re: Timing of the advanced cruise missile testing announcement. Secret.

75   23 January 1089, Memorandum for ADM (Pol), from Col D. K. Lett, DC Pol, re: Advanced Cruise Missile. Secret.

76   circa 29 October 1992, Briefing to DM/CDS on Renewal of T&E Agreement and free-flight testing of the advanced cruise missile. Secret (CC). p. 7.

77   24 January 1989, press release on Liberal convention issued by Deputy Opposition Leader Herb Gray. Courtesy of John Harvard, MP for Winnipeg St. James. 1 February 1989.

78   31 January 1989, Letter to U.S. Secretary of Defense, from Minister of National Defence, William McKnight, re: Approval of ACM testing in Canada.

79   31 January 1989, 23:55z, Message to Cdn Embassy Washington, from John Noble, IDD, External Affairs, re: ACM testing. Confidential.

80   3 February 1989, Letter to US Ambassador Thomas Niles, from USS External Affairs, J. Taylor, re: ACM testing approval letter to SoD from MND. Secret.

81   1 December 1985, CANUS Test and Evaluation of the Air Launched Cruise Missile (ALCM) Project Arrangement. Signed by USA 18 December 1985, and by Canada 12 November 1985.

82   25 August 1983, CANUS Test and Evaluation of AGM-86B Air Launched Cruise Missile (ALCM) Project Arrangement. Signed by USA 04 January 1984, and by Canada 14 February 1984.

83   27/28 February 1989, Change 3 to ALCM Project Arrangement (to allow captive-carry testing of ACM).

84   31 January 1989, 17:01z, Message to Canadian Embassy Washington, from John Noble, IDD, External Affairs, re: ACM testing. Confidential (CEO).

85   1 February 1989, National Defence News Release, AFN: 06/89, re: Government Announces Approval for Unarmed Advanced Cruise Missile Testing.

86   10 February 1989, Letter to Members of Parliament (Progressive Conservative Party members only), from the minister of national defence, the Honourable William McKnight, re: Announcement of decision to allow the USAF to test the AGM-129 ACM in Canada.

87 1 February 1989, Memorandum for Correspondents, from the Office of the Assistant Secretary of Defense for Public Affairs, re: Advanced cruise missile testing.

88 6 February 1989, Memo to IFB from John Noble, IDD Director, External Affairs, re: ACM test decision – CCACD comments. IDD-0018. Unclassified.

89 "Cruise tests opposed by 57%, Gallup says," *The Toronto Star*, 26 February 1990.

90 "51% oppose tests of cruise, poll says," *The Toronto Star*, 6 April 1989.

91 22 January 1990, Privy Council Office question and answer briefing note, re: Advanced cruise missile testing.

92 3 December 1989, Cruise Missile Brief, Consultative Group Meeting, IDR, External Affairs, Unclassified.

93 24 April 1991, Memorandum to DC Policy, from LCol Bacon, DC Pol 3, re: ALCM 1991 lessons learned conference – 16–18 Apr 91. 10081-34-3 (DC Pol 3). Secret.

94 7 March 1991, Briefing note to the Minister [of National Defence] from ADM Material, re: Canada-United States test and evaluation program – review of 1991 annual forecast of projects. Secret. (And) 11 March 1991 Memo to Distribution List from R. D. Gillespie, Chairman CANUS T&E Steering Group, re: CANUS test and evaluation programme 1991 annual forecast of projects. 10081-34-0 (ADM(Mat)). Unclassified.

95 11 March 1991, Memo to Dist List from R. D. Gillespie, Chairman CANUS T&E Steering Group, re: CANUS test and evaluation programme 1991 annual forecast of projects. 10081-34-0 (ADM(Mat)). Unclassified.

96 18 November 1991, Information Memorandum for the Secretary of State for External Affairs from J.K.B. Kinsman, ADM Political and Intl Security Affairs, re: Bush initiative for nuclear weapons reductions: Effect on cruise missile tests in Canada. IDR-3114. Confidential.

97 28 September 1991, Memorandum for the Secretaries of the Military Departments, the Chairman of the Joint Chiefs of Staff, the Under-Secretaries of Defense, and the Assistant Secretary of Defense for Command Control Communications and Intelligence, from Secretary of Defense Dick Cheney, re: Reducing the united States Nuclear Arsenal.

98 24 January 1992, Memorandum for the Prime Minister, from Paul Tellier, Clerk of the Privy Council, re: Cruise missile testing. Confidential. (It is noted that the Prime Minister made no comments.)

99 circa 6 April 1992, Memorandum to Dist List, from LCol Clark, DAOT 6, re: Trip report – Global Cruise missile lessons learned meeting. 10081-34 (DAOT 6). Confidential.

100 26 May 1992, 2230z, message from Charles Johnson of 49 TESTS, Barksdale AFB, re: FY93 Canadian/US (CANUS) cruise missile Global Cruise/Global Shadow mission schedule. Confidential.

101 13 August 1992, Memorandum for the ADM (Pol & Comm), from Col. Keith Coulter, DC Pol, re: Briefing Notes on Test and Evaluation and cruise missile testing. Secret.

102 6 April 1992, Memorandum to DG Pol Ops through DC Pol, from LCol Bacon, DC Pol 3, re: Note on an air launched cruise missile (ALCM) annual lessons learned meeting 31 March to 2 April 92. 10081-34 (DC Pol 3). Confidential.

103 circa 6 April 1992, Memorandum to Dist List, from LCol Clark, DAOT 6, re: Trip report – CANUS Global Cruise missile lessons learned meeting. 10081-34 (DAOT 6). Confidential. para. 9.a-d.

104 15 September 1992, Memorandum to ADM (Mat) and Dist List, from Ken Calder, ADM (Pol & Com), re: US request for renewal of CANUS T&E Agreement and amendment to ALCM project arrangement. 10081-34-0 (DC Pol 3). Secret.

105 13 August 1992, Briefing Note for the DM/CDS on proposed US amendments to the air launched cruise missile project arrangement. Prepared by LCol Hincke, DC Pol 3. Secret. para.7.

106 2 October 1992, ACM Environmental Assessment Update, by K.C. Kavanagh, Director Environmental Protection, Chief of Defence Staff, National Defence, 10081-34-3 (Denvp 2-2).

107 November 1992, Briefing note to MND from DM/CDS, re: Amendment to Cruise Missile Project Arrangement. Secret (CC). para.15.

108 6 November 1992, Memorandum to the DM/CDS from Ken Calder, ADM (Pol & Comm), re: Free-flight testing of the ACM. Secret (CC).

109 November 1992, Briefing note to MND from DM/CDS, re: Amendment to Cruise Missile Project Arrangement. Secret (CC). para.14.

110 Ibid., para.12.

111 18 December 1992, Handwritten note to file by Mark Mayhew, D Cabinet Liaison, re: ACM free-flight testing. Secret (CC).

112 16 December 1992, Handwritten memo to ADM (Pol & Comm) from Colonel Coulter, DC Pol, re: latest twist in the ACM story.

113 11 December 1992, Memorandum for the Prime Minister from Glen Shortliffe, Clerk of the Privy Council, re: Cruise missile testing. Secret.

114 7 December 1992, Note to Glen Shortliffe from Jim Judd, PCO, re: Cruise missile testing. Secret.

115 20 November 1992, Letter to the Minister of National Defence Marcel Masse, from Deputy Minister Fowler and Chief of Defence Staff General de Chastelain, re: Amendment to Cruise Missile Project Arrangement. Secret (CC).

116 20 November 1992, Handwritten note to Deputy Secretary of State for External Affairs Reid Morden, from Deputy Minister of National Defence Bob Fowler, re: Cruise missile testing. Secret. (cc. To Jim Judd, PCO)

117 Undated (circa August-October 1992) [National Defence] Public Affairs Assessment Test and Evaluation and Cruise Missile Agreements. Secret.

118 29 December 1992, "Change 4 to ALCM Project Arrangement" (to allow free-flight testing of AGM-129), originally dated 1 December 1985.

119 2 March 1993, 14:55, handwritten minutes of meeting of DM on ACM free-flight testing.

120 6 April 1992, Memorandum to DG Policy Operations through DC Pol, from LCol Bacon, DC Pol 3, re: Note on an air launched cruise missile (ALCM) annual lessons learned meeting 31 March to 2 April 92. 10081-34 (DC Pol 3). Confidential.

121 7 January 1993, Briefing note for the DM/CDS, re: Update of current plans for cruise missile testing. By LCol J. Hincke, DC Pol 3. Secret.

122 19 February 1993, Briefing note for the MND, re: Timing of the next cruise missile test. By LCol J. Hincke, DC Pol 3. Confidential.

123 (no date) circa mid-March 1993, Question Period notes for minister of national defence, re: cruise missile testing. Prepared by Col. Coulter and LCol. Hincke, DC Pol.

124 Originally DND had few details, as shown in the 16 December 1992 minute sheet "Cruise missile test program status update," written by LCol Hincke, DC Pol 3. Confidential.

125 17 December 1992, Note to file by LCol Joe Hincke, DC Pol 3, National Defence, re Telecon LCol Hincke/Maj Lytor 17 Dec 92.

126 12 February 1993, message from Eglin AFB to NDHQ, re: Missile mishap investigation, Global Shadow A93-03 Almag final report. Unclassified.

127 __ February 1993, Minute Sheet from DC Pol Colonel Coulter, to ADM Pol & Comm Dr. Calder, re: ACM Test Status. Secret.

128 15 February 1993, Transcript of Question Period, question by L. Axworthy for Minister of National Defence Campbell.

129 16 March 1993, Memorandum for the Minister from DM/CDS, re: Update – cruise missile testing in Canada. Secret.

130 15 January 1993, Briefing note for the minister from DM/CDS, re: Cruise missile testing in Canada. Secret. The popularity of testing had dropped from a high of 45% in 1985 to the current Gallup Poll low of 36%.

131 Charles Gordon, "Cruise control: testing the logic of bureaucrats and military men," *Ottawa Citizen*, 26 January 199?, year unknown.

NOTES TO CHAPTER 5

1 "Cruise pact to be renewed; no hitches in Tuesday's test," *Calgary Herald*, 25 February 1987; "Canada to Renew pact for more cruise tests," *Ottawa Citizen*, 25 February 1987; "Cruise pact extended 5 years," *Kitchener-Waterloo Record*, 25 February 1987; "Cruise test is a success; Canada extends treaty," *Moncton Times Transcript*, 25 February 1987.

2 17 March 1987, Memorandum to the Minister of National Defence, from D. B. Dewar, Deputy Minister, and General Paul Manson, CDS, re: CANUS T&E Agreement. Confidential.

3 6 March 1987, *Hansard*.

4 Hunter, "Soviets may see tests of cruise," *Ottawa Citizen*, 10 January 1990.

5 28 January 1992, message to various embassies and offices, from M. Brock, IDR, External Affairs Ottawa, re: USA State of Union Nuclear. Unclassified.

6 13 May 1992, letter to LCol Hugh Bacon, D Continental Policy, NDHQ, from J. T. Devlin, A/D International Security and Defence Relations Division, External Affairs, re: CANUS T&E Agreement. IDR-1815. No classification.

7 1 June 1992, 19:45z, Message to Associate assistant deputy minister (material), NDHQ, from CDLS (Canadian Defence Liaison Staff) (Wash), re: Legalization of MOUs. Unclassified.

8 19 June 1992, Memorandum to J3 Plans, DDIR, D Fin S(#), D Law/I, from Col. H.R. Leduc, DC Pol, re: CANUS T&E Agreement renewal. 10081-34-0(DC Pol 3).

9 12 June 1992, Memorandum to ADM (Mat) from MGen P. E. Woods, Assoc ADM (Mat), re: CANUS Test and evaluation (T&E) programme proposed amendments to agreement. 10081-34 (DAS Eng 4-5).

10 12 June 1992, Memo to ADM (Mat) from Assoc ADM (Mat), re: CANUS Test and evaluation (T&E) programme proposed amendments to agreement.

11 13 August 1992, Briefing Note for the DM/CDS on the impending expiry of the CANUS Test and Evaluation (T&E) Agreement. By LCol J.D.A. Hinke, DC Pol 3. Confidential.

12 7 August 1992, Memo to JIX (Access to Information Division), from the Acting Director General, Bureau of International Security, re: Consultation from DND Cruise missile testing. ADS-2242. Secret.

13 13 August 1992, Briefing Note for the DM/CDS on the impending expiry of the CANUS Test and Evaluation (T&E) Agreement. By LCol J.D.A. Hinke, DC Pol 3. Confidential.

14 Ibid.

15 15 September 1992, Memorandum to various offices at NDHQ, from Ken Calder, ADM (Pol & Comm), re: US request for renewal of CANUS T&E Agreement and amendment to ALCM project arrangement. 10081-34-0(DC Pol 3). Secret.

16 Ibid.

17 Circa 29 October 1992, Briefing to DM/CDS on Renewal of T&E Agreement and free-flight testing of the advanced cruise missile. Secret (CC)., p. 8.

18 24 September 1994, Memorandum to DDIR 6, from LCdr J. J. Priddle, D Law/—2, re: CANUS Test and Evaluation Programme.

19 21 October 1992, Memorandum to CS, from C.A. Kerr, DGIIP, re: CANUSTEP Renegotiation. Secret (CC).

20 24 September 1992, Proposed changes and comments to Note #64. Appendix A to 3440-1-26 (D Law/—2), JAG/NDHQ.

21 24 September 1992, Appendix B, to Proposed changes and comments to Note #64. Appendix A to 3440-1-26 (D Law/—2), JAG/NDHQ.

22 25 September 1992, Memo and draft for Mr. Craig Farr, Office of the deputy Director, Strategic Weapons System Assessment/STEP, Pentagon, from Col. J. Hincke, DC Pol 3, re: Proposed text of exchange of notes to renew CANUS T&E agreement. (Sent that day through USDAO).

23 29 September 1992, Memorandum for Col. J. Hincke, DC Pol 3, from Mr. Craig Farr, Office of the deputy Director, Strategic Weapons System Assessment/STEP, Pentagon, re: Proposed text of exchange of notes to renew Canadian/United States (CANUS) Test and Evaluation (T&E) agreement.

24 6 October 1994, Memorandum to DDIR 6, from LCdr J. J. Priddle, D Law/—2, re: CANUS Test and Evaluation Programme. 3440-1-26 (D Law/—2).

25 9 October 1992, Fax and draft note for Mr. Craig Farr, Office of the deputy Director, Strategic Weapons System Assessment/STEP, Pentagon, from Col. J. Hincke, DC Pol 3, re: Proposed text of exchange of notes to renew CANUS T&E agreement.

26 16 October 1992, Note to file, by LCol Joe Hinke, DC Pol 3, re: Telecon Craig Farr/Joe Hinke 16/10/92 T&E Dip Note.

27 20 October 1992, Memorandum to DDIR 6, from LCdr J. J. Priddle, D Law/—2, re: Exchange of notes Canada/US. 3440-1-26 (D Law/—2).

28 19 October 1992, Cover memo for DC Pol, from B. A. Goetze, DG Pol Ops, re: consequences on non-renewal. Secret. Attached document entitled: CANUSTEP, Implications of non-renewal. By M. J. Slack and H. J. Skynner, DDIR-6. Secret (CC).

29 19 October 1992, Memo to Assoc ADM (Pol & Comm) thru DG Pol Ops, from DC Pol, re: T&E/ACM. Secret.

30 Circa 21 October 1992, Aide-Memoire on consequences of delays in Cabinet consideration of CANUS T&E renewal and ACM free-flight testing, by LCol J. Hincke. Secret/Confidential.

31 15 October 1992, Fax and attached draft agreement to LCol Joe Hincke, DC Pol 3, from Craig Farr, OSD/DDDRE (T&E), Pentagon, re: CANUS T&E Agreement.

32 16 October 1992, Note to File, by Mark Mayhew, D Cabinet Ln. re: Renewal of T&E Agreement w/US, ref: Discussion DM/D Cabinet Ln 16 Oct 92. Secret (CC).

33 Circa 18 October 1992, Memo to Assoc ADM (Pol & Comm) through DG Pol Ops, from Col. K. A. Coulter, DC Pol, re: T&E/ACM. Secret.

34 21 October 1992, Memorandum to CS, from C. A. Kerr, DGIIP, re: CANUSTEP Renegotiation. Secret (CC).

35 27 October 1992, Memo to DGIIP/CS, from B. L. Thomas, DDIR, re: draft CANUSTEP.

36   27 October 1992, Memo to DGIIP/CS, from B. L. Thomas, DDIR, re: draft CANUSTEP. Note #1 by John Skynner, DDIR 4, re: MC (Memo to Cabinet) route changed by direction of DM. (10/12/92).

37   Circa 29 October 1992, Briefing to DM/CDS on Renewal of T&E Agreement and free-flight testing of the advanced cruise missile. Secret (CC). p. 7–8.

38   Ibid., p. 10.

39   Ibid., p. 15.

40   Circa 26 October 1992, Memo to D Cabinet Ln, from Col Keith Coulter, DC Pol, re: first draft of the essential argument.

41   Circa 25 October 1992, Public affairs assessment: Test and evaluation and cruise missile agreements; Strategic communications plan: advanced cruise missile testing. National Defence. Secret.

42   Circa 25 October 1992, Public affairs assessment: Test.and evaluation and cruise missile agreements. National Defence. Secret.

43   Ibid.

44   29 October 1992, Note to Glen Shortliffe, Clerk of the Privy Council, from Jim Judd, PCO, re: Canada-US testing and evaluation agreement. Secret.

45   30 October 1992, Fax and attached draft agreement to LCol Joe Hincke, DC Pol 3, from Craig Farr, OSD/DDDRE (T&E), Pentagon, re: CANUS T&E Agreement.

46   30 October 1992, Memorandum to DDIR from D Law/—2, re: draft CANUS MOU. 3440-1-26 (D Law/—2), JAG/NDHQ.

47   9 November 1992, Note to file by William George, D Cabinet Ln 5, re: Meeting between the deputy minister, under-secretary of state for external affairs, and assistant secretary to cabinet on ACM free-flight testing and renewal of Test and Evaluation Agreement (5 November 1992). Secret (CC) (Cabinet Confidence).

48   Circa 4 November 1992, Deputy minister's meeting with the under-secretary of state for external affairs, Speaking points for the Deputy minister on Why Canada should renew the Canada-US Test and Evaluation Agreement. Assistant deputy minister (policy and communications), NDHQ. Secret (CC).

49   Circa 4 November 1992, Deputy minister's meeting with the under-secretary of state for external affairs on ACM free-flight testing and the renewal of Canada-U.S. Test and Evaluation Agreement. Speaking points for the deputy minister on why continue to test cruise missiles and why Canada should agree to test the advanced cruise missile in free-flight. Assistant deputy minister (policy and communications), NDHQ. Secret (CC).

50   9 November 1992, Memorandum to A/ADM (Mat), Ray Sturgeon, from Ken Calder, ADM (Pol & Comm), re: Renewal of T&E Agreement preparation of draft MOU. 10081-34-0 (DC Pol 3). Secret.

51   18 November 1992, Memorandum to DDIR 6, from J. Cabana-Marshall, NDMOUC, re: draft renewal/amendment of DND/US DoD T&E MOU. NDMOUC review comments on the T&E MOU (17/11/92). Secret.

52   13 November 1992, Fax and attached draft agreement to LCol Joe Hincke, DC Pol 3, from Craig Farr, OSD/DDDRE (T&E), Pentagon, re: (nil entered) CANUS T&E Agreement.

53   11 November 1992, Memorandum to Dist List, from Ray Sturgeon, A/ADM (Mat) and CANUS T&E Steering Group Chairman, re: Renewal of T&E Agreement preparation of draft MOU. 10081-34-0 (A/ADM (Mat)). Secret.

54   18 November 1992, Memorandum to A/ADM (Mat), from Ray Sturgeon, CS/ADM (Mat), re: CANUSTEP Renegotiation. 10055-15 (DGIIP). Secret.

55   Ibid., para.3.

56   27 November 1992, Memorandum to DDIR 6-3 from Lcdr J. J. Priddle, D Law/—2, re: Draft CANUS Note. 3440-1-26 (D Law/—2). 30 November 1992, Memorandum to DDIR 6-3 from Lcdr J. J. Priddle, D Law/—2, re: Draft Canada-US MOU. 3440-1-26 (D Law/—2).

57   2 December 1992, Memo to JLAB URR TAG, from Carol Markham, IDS, North American Defence Relations, re: DND revised texts. IDS-3036. Secret.

58   7 January 1993, Briefing Note for DM/CDS from ADM Policy Calder, re: Update of current plans for cruise missile testing during the Jan – Mar 93 testing period. Secret.

59   23 November 1992, Memorandum for the Prime Minister, from Glen Shortliffe, Clerk of the Privy Council, re: Meeting with US Ambassador Teeley, November 24, 1992, Cruise missile testing - (Responsive only). Confidential.

60   Circa January 1993, Briefing Note for DM/CDS, re: Update of current plans for cruise missile testing in the Jan–Mar 93 testing period. Secret. para.2.

61   23 December 1992, Draft MOU relating to the CANUS Test and Evaluation Program.

62   30 December 1992, Memorandum to ADM (Mat), from C. A. Kerr, DGIIP, re: CANUSTEP. 10055-15 TD2350 DGIIP). Secret.

63   22 December 1992, Memo to ADM (Pol & Comm), from Col. Coulter, DC Pol, re: draft agreement and MOU and package for DM.

64   31 December 1992, Memo to ADM (Mat), from Ken Calder, ADM (Pol & Comm), re: Aide-Memoire for Ministers on the renewal of the Canada-US Test and Evaluation Agreement. Secret (CC).

65   22 December 1992, 15:30, draft Aide-Memoire for Ministers on the renewal of the Canada-U.S. Test and Evaluation Agreement. Secret.

66   4 January 1993, Memo for Mike Slack, A/DDIR 6, from Craig Farr, OSD/DDDR, Pentagon, re: Text of EoN and the MOU to renew the Canadian/United States (CANUS) Test and Evaluation (T&E) Agreement.

67   6 January 1993, External Affairs IDS Division draft and comments on the CANUS T&E Agreement.

68   7 January 1993, Memorandum for the DM, CDS, VCDS, and ADM(Mat), from Ken Calder, ADM (Pol & Comm), re: Renewal of the Canada-US Test and Evaluation Agreement. Secret (CC). para.5.

69   8 January 1993, draft timetable for T&E renewal. DND.

70   7 January 1993, Memorandum for the DM, CDS, VCDS, and ADM(Mat), from Ken Calder, ADM (Pol & Comm), re: Renewal of the Canada-U.S. Test and Evaluation Agreement. Secret (CC); Outline for oral briefing to MND, re: renewal of CANUS T&E Agreement. Secret.

71   8 January 1993, draft timetable for T&E renewal. DND.

72   11 January 1993, Checklist for ADM (Pol & Comm) meeting with DM on T&E renewal, 11 January 1993, 10:00 hours. Secret (CC).

73   6 January 1993, draft Aide-Memoire for Ministers on the renewal of the Canada-US Test and Evaluation Agreement. Secret; 7 January 1993, Memorandum for the DM, CDS, VCDS, and ADM(Mat), from Ken Calder, ADM (Pol & Comm), re: Renewal of the Canada-US Test and Evaluation Agreement. Secret (CC).

74   8 January 1993, Memo to CoS J3, D Law M, D Law S, NDMOUC, and DC Pol, from C.A. Kerr, DGIIP, re: CANUSTEP. 1055-15 TD2350 (DDIR 6-4).

75   11 January 1993, Letter to Pierre Gravelle, DM Revenue Canada, from Robert Fowler, DM DND, re: CANUS T&E Agreement. Confidential.

76   11 January 1993, Memo to A/ADM (Supply), from T. M. Williams, DG Supply, re: CANUS Test and Evaluation program customs duties and taxation.

77   11 January 1993 fax and attachment to Craig Farr, OSD/DDDR, from LCol Hincke, DC Pol, re: new draft text.

78   9 January 1993, Informal Message to Michael Dawson and Paul Meyer, Cdn Embassy Washington DC, from Carol Markham, IDS, External Affairs, re: New agreement on reciprocal T&E. Secret.

79   11 January 1993, Checklist for ADM (Pol & Comm) meeting with DM on T&E renewal, 11 January 1993, 10:00 hours. Secret (CC)

80   18 January 1993, Message to Canadian Embassy Washington, from IDS, External Affairs, re: Aide Memoire Qs and As, draft press release, and final texts for T and E agreement. Secret.

81   8 January 1993, Draft timetable for T&E renewal. Secret (CC).

82   13 January 1993, Memo to Nancy Wildgoose, NDHQ, from Carol Markham, IDS, re: Explanatory memorandum and External Affairs renewal schedule. Secret.

83   January 1993, Minute Sheet to EA ADM (Mat, from LCol Joe Hincke, DC Pol 3, re: ADM (Mat) signature-CANUS T&E MOU and ALCM P.A..

84   14 January 1993, Memorandum to Sr ADM (Mat from Pierre Lagueux, A/ADM (Sup), re: CANUSTEP. Secret (CC).

85   9 February 1993, Memorandum to Sr ADM (Mat), from Pierre Lagueux, A/ADM (Sup), re: CANUSTEP. 10055-15 TD2350 (Sr ADM (Sup)).

86   11 January 1993, Memorandum for DDIR 6, from Lcol Joe Hincke, DC Pol 3, re: Renewal of CANUSTEP – Draft MOU – Continuation of ALCM project arrangement. 10081-34-0(DC Pol 3).

87   15 January 1993, Fax to Capt. Eric Burnet, from Craig Farr, OSD/DDDRE (T&E), Pentagon, re: Proposed Project Arrangement under the Canadian/United States (CANUS) Test and Evaluation (T&E) Agreement for the ALCM test program.

88   20 January 1993, Memorandum to the Minister of National Defence, from DM Robert Fowler and CDS General de Chastelain, re: Renewal of the Canada/United States Test and Evaluation Agreement. Secret (CC). paras.6,8.

89   19 January 1993, Action Memorandum for the Secretary of State for External Affairs, from the Deputy Minister, J. R. Morden, re: Canada-U.S.A.. reciprocal test and evaluation agreement. IDS-1100. Secret

90   22 January 1993, Memorandum to the Prime Minister from the Clerk of the Privy Council, re: Cruise missile testing. Confidential.

91   22 January 1992, Memorandum to Senator Murray from Marie-P. Poulin, Deputy Secretary to the Cabinet Communications and Consultation, re: Cruise missile test - Test and evaluation agreement. Secret.

92   28 January 1993, Memo to URR (via IDD and IFB), from D. Dhavernas, Director International Security, re: Prime Minister Mulroney/President Clinton, call for briefs. IDS-1167. Secret; Canada-USA reciprocal test and evaluation agreement briefing note. Secret.

93   18 January 1993, Memorandum to Ken Calder from John Dixon, re: Minister's briefing book on T&E Agreement.

94   28 January 1983, transcript of media scrum with MND Kim Campbell.

95   4 February 1993, Memorandum to Senator Murray from Marie-P. Poulin, Deputy Secretary to the Cabinet, re: Canada-US Test and Evaluation Agreement.

96 15 February 1993, Question Period, rough transcript. Question by Lloyd Axworthy and answers by Minister of National Defence Kim Campbell.

97 29 January 1993, Letter to Cmdre D. Cogdon, DND CANUS T&E Coordinator, from Richard Ledesma, DoD CANUS T&E Coordinator, re: Change 5.

98 1 February 1993, Handwritten note to Ken Calder, assistant deputy minister (policy and communications), from Colonel Keith Coulter, re: T&E update.

99 c.8 January 1993, Actions to be completed by Department of External Affairs and Department of National Defence, External Affairs.

100 10 February 1993, Situation report, Test and Evaluation Agreement. NDHQ. point #4.

101 3 February 1993, Message to IDS External Affairs, from Cdn Embassy Washington, re: T and E Agreement USA comments on texts. Secret.

102 3 February 1993, Message to Canadian Embassy Washington, from IDS External Affairs, re: T and E Agreement USA comments. Secret.

103 10 February 1993, Diplomatic Note to the US Secretary of State, The Honourable Warren M. Christopher, Department of State, Washington, from Marc-Andre Brault, Charge d'Affaires ad interim, Embassy of Canada, re: Note No. 24 of 10 February 1993.

104 10 February 1993, Diplomatic Reply Note to The Honourable Marc-Andre Brault, Charge d'Affaires ad interim, Embassy of Canada, from the U.S. Secretary of State, Department of State, Washington (signed by Thomas Niles), re: Canadian Note #24 of 10 February 1993.

105 10 February 1993, Situation report, Test and Evaluation Agreement. NDHQ. point #5.

106 11 February 1993, Questions and answers regarding "Why should the government renew the test and evaluation agreement," by Miller and Judd, Foreign and Defence Policy, PCO.

107 11 January 1993, News Release, "Canada Renews Military Testing Agreement," Government of Canada, AFN: 03/93.

108 2 March 1993, 14:55, handwritten notes on meeting of Deputy Minister on ACM free-flight testing with ADM (pol), Assoc ADM (Pol), and DC Pol.

109 Global Cruise/Global Shadow Lessons Learned Conference, Barksdale AFB, 18–20 May 1993.

NOTES TO CHAPTER 6

1 22 November 1993, Memorandum for the DM and CDS, from ADM (Pol & Comm), re: Cruise missile testing in Canada. Secret. Rubber stamp marks on the memo indicate that the memo was received by the deputy minister that same day.

2 Circa late December 1993, National Defence briefing note on Cruise Missile Testing. Secret (CC).

3 25 January 1994, Minute to Deputy Minister from ADM Ken Calder (Pol & Comm), re: "US Embassy call to DFA." Confidential.

4 7 January 1994, Aide-Memoire for the MND, re: Value of the Canada-U.S. Test and Evaluation Program (CANUSTEP). DDIR Beth Thomas.

5 22 November 1993, Memorandum to the Minister of National Defence, David Collenette, from Deputy Minister Robert Fowler, and Chief of Defence Staff Admiral J. R. Anderson, re: Cruise Missile Testing in Canada. Secret.

6   22 November 1993, Memorandum to the MND, David Collenette, from DM Fowler, and CDS Anderson, re: Cruise Missile Testing in Canada. Secret. Signed copy (30 November) provided by the office of the Deputy Minister.

7   Circa 20 November 1993, Memo to ADM (Pol & Comm) from AADM (Pol), re: draft memo to MFA on Can-US defence issues.

8   26 November 1993, Note to A/ADM (Policy) General John Boyle from Mark Moher, DG IDD, External Affairs, re: final text.

9   20 November 1993, Action Memorandum for André Ouellet, Minister of Foreign Affairs, from Gaetan Lavertu, ADM Political and International Security Affairs, re: Several issues in Canada-U.S. defence cooperation are at a stage requiring Ministerial decisions. IDD-0230. Secret.

10 Ibid.

11 26 November 1993, Cosics-Informal message to James Junke, URR, from Jean Riople, URR, External Affairs, re: Bilateral defence relations.

12 10 December 1993, Letter to Pierre Lagueux, DND Assistant Deputy Minister (Supply), from Richard R. Ledesma, DoD CANUS T&E Coordinator, re: CANUS T&E MOU 30 Month Forecast of Tests. Secret.

13 (undated) circa 7 January 1994, Memorandum to the DM and CDS, from ADM (Pol & Comm), re: Cruise missile testing in Canada – Government decision. 10081-34-3 (ADM (Pol & Comm)). Secret (CC).

14 Ibid. Annex entitled CANUSTEP: Future Cruise missile testing issue summary & points to register. 2/4. Secret.

15 Ibid. 7 January 1994, Annex entitled Aide-Memoire for the Minister of National Defence, Value of the Canada-US Test and Evaluation program (CANUSTEP).

16 "Cruise test resumption not decided, Chretien says," *Ottawa Citizen*, 8 January 1994.

17 7 January 1994, Fax from Christopher Davis, Privy Council Office, Communications and Consultation, to Valerie Keyes and Don Marsh, re: Talking points on cruise missile testing.

18 21 January 1994, DND (draft) Fact Sheet, re: Canada-United States test and evaluation program and cruise missile testing. para. 6.

19 "Chretien denies story: US not yet permitted to test cruise missiles," *Victoria Times-Colonist*, 8 January 1994.

20 (no date) circa 7 January 7 1994, Memorandum for Jim Judd from Valerie Keyes, PCO, re: Cruise missile testing. Secret.

21 7 January 1994, Memo to the Prime Minister from Jim Judd, re: Cruise missiles.

22 10 January 1994, Memo to DC Pol-3, from Colonel R. W. Guidinger, Director Continental Policy, re: CDS request for briefing note on ALCM testing.

23 10 January 1994, Memo to DC Pol (thru DC Pol Ops), from A/ADM (Pol), General John Boyle, re: Decision by DM/CDS to delay tests.

24 10 January 1994, Memo to DC Pol from A/ADM (Pol), re: Decision by DM/CDS. Notes at bottom added by DC Pol-3, 10/1/94.

25 10 January 1994, 20:00z, message to Air Command HQ from 939 RQW, re: cruise missile testing.

26 7 January 1994, 23:01z, message to Air Command HQ from 79 RQW, re: cruise missile testing.

27 11 January 1994, Memorandum for Jim Judd from Dusty E. Miller, PCO, re: NATO summit. Secret.

28 12 January 1994, 18:06z, message to ADM (Pol), NDHQ, from Canadian Embassy Washington, re: Cruise missile testing. Confidential; 20 January 1994, Memorandum for Sr ADM Mat, from ADM (S), Pierre Lagueux, re: CANUSTEP Cruise Missile Testing. 10055-15-7 (DGIIP). Secret.

29 20 January 1994, 12:40z, Message from Canadian Embassy Washington, to NDHQ, re: U.S. response to points raised by PM on cruise missile tests. Confidential.

30 26 November 1993, Action Memorandum for the Minister of Foreign Affairs, from Gaetan Lavertu, ADM Pol & IDS DFAIT, re: Several issues in Canada-U.S.A. defence cooperation are at stages requiring Ministerial decisions. IDD-0230. Secret.

31 18 January 1994, Talking points for meeting with Mr. Stephen Oxman, State Dept., Jan. 18, 1994, contained in facsimile from M. Kergin, Canadian Embassy Washington, to FAITC – IDD. Protected.

32 18 January 1994, DFAIT talking points for meeting with Stephen Oxman, State Department, on cruise missiles and Bosnia. Protected.

33 20 January 1994, 12:40z, message to ADM (Pol) NDHQ from Canadian Embassy Washington, re: Charge met with State. Confidential. Para. 1.

34 Ibid., Para. 2-3. 20 January 1994, 12:40z, message to ADM (Pol) NDHQ from Canadian Embassy Washington, re: Charge met with State. Confidential. Para. 1.

35 20 January 1994, 12:40z, message to ADM (Pol) NDHQ from Canadian Embassy Washington, re: Charge met with State. Confidential. Para. 4.

36 Ibid., Para. 5.

37 19 January 1994, Fax to FAITC-IDD from M. Kergin, Cdn Embassy Washington, re: Meeting with Stephen Oxman. Talking points for meeting with Mr. Stephen Oxman, State Dept., 18 January 1994. Protected.

38 20 January 1994, 12:40z, message to ADM (Pol) NDHQ from Canadian Embassy Washington, re: Charge met with State. Confidential. Para. 5.

39 20 January 1994, Memorandum to Sr ADM (Mat from Pierre Lagueux, ADM (S), re: CANUSTEP, Cruise missile testing. 10055-15-7 (DGIIP). Secret.

40 19 January 1994, 16:00z, message to various USAF units from AIRCOM Winnipeg, re: Foreign flight request and visit notification for FY 94 CANUS cruise missile tests. Confidential.

41 21 January 1994, 23:02z, message from USAFAWC/CV to various USAF/CF units, re: Global Shadow A94-04 reschedule/cancellation.

42 20 or 21 January 1994, transcript of scrum between MND Collenette and press, House of Commons lobby, provided by PCO Communications Monitoring: Foreign & Defence.

43 21 January 1994, Memorandum for Chaviva Hosek, from Valerie Keyes, PCO, re: Cruise missile testing.

44 20 January 1994, *Hansard.*

45 24 January 1994, Fax to Mark Mayhew, Director Cabinet Liaison, DND, from Dusty Miller, PCO, re: Need comments on which wording Defence would prefer.

46 21 January 1994, Draft Motion, Cruise missile testing – Sponsored by the Minister of National Defence. Foreign and Defence Policy office, PCO. Text in brackets represent wording used in the actual House of Commons debate.

47 (no date) circa 25 January 1994, Talking points for a speaker in favour of cruise missile testing in Canada, House of Commons, January 26, 1994. PMO.

48 26 January 1994, Question/Suggested Answer notes for Masse, Cruise missile testing. Keyes/Judd, Foreign and Defence Policy, PCO.

49   25 January 1994, Memo to DG Pol Coordinator, from DG Pol Ops, ADM (Pol & Comm), re: Pre-DEM on contact in US Administration on decision.

50   28 January 1994, message from 79 TEG, Eglin AFB, to NDHQ, re: reschedule of ACM flight test. Confidential.

51   25 January 1994, Minute Sheet to DM and CDS, from Ken Calder, ADM (Pol & Comm), re: U.S. Embassy call to DFA. Confidential.

52   26 January 1994, Speaking notes for David Collenette, PC, MP, Minister of National Defence, for the House of Commons debate on cruise missile testing, Ottawa, Ontario.

53   (no date) circa 21-25 January 1994, Proposed statement by the Minister of National Defence in the House of Commons, Cruise missile testing.

54   27 January 1994, Memorandum to the Prime Minister from the Clerk of the Privy Council, re: Cruise missile debate – Summary. Confidential. Attached was the National Defence "Summary of the debate in the House of Commons on cruise missile testing in Canada, Wednesday January 26th, 1994" by Katherine Baird, Director Cabinet Liaison 5-2. (00:45, 27/1/94).

55   Jeff Sallot, "Keep testing cruise, Bloc, Reform urge," *Globe and Mail*, 27 January 1994, p. A1.

56   Allan Thompson, "MPs support cruise missile tests in North," *Toronto Star*, 27 January 1994, p. A8.

57   "Former critics silent as MPs from all parties endorse more cruise tests," *Victoria Times-Colonist*, 27 January 1994, p. A20.

58   28 January 1994, 18:44z, message from 79 TEG at Eglin AFB, to various USAF and CF units, re: Global Shadow A94-04 reschedule. Confidential.

59   Ibid.

60   7 February 1994, Briefing Note for the Minister of National Defence, re: Cruise missile testing – 1994 test window extension. By Colonel Guidinger, DC Pol. Confidential.

61   28 January 1994, 18:44z, message from 79 TEG at Eglin AFB, to various USAF and CF units, re: Global Shadow A94-04 reschedule. Confidential. para. 3.A.

62   Jeff Sallot, "Liberals split over testing of cruise missiles," *Globe and Mail*, 3 February 1994, p. A3.

63   3 February 1994, Question Period Digest, Question Period transcript. Gilles Duceppe and David Collenette.

64   3 February 1994, National Defence News Release, Canada to Review Cruise Missile Testing. AFN: NR-94.001.

65   John Ward, Canadian Press article on Liberal approval of cruise missile testing. Various newspapers.

66   Jeff Sallot, "Approval of missile tests divides cabinet," *Globe and Mail*, 4 February 1994, p. A3.

67   Telecon AIRCOM G3 Coord and NDHQ DC Pol with USAF, 04/2/94, referenced in 4 February 1994, 12:08z, message from 79 TEG to various USAF and CF units, re: Global Shadow A94-04 reschedule. Confidential.

68   7 February 1994, Briefing Note for the Minister of National Defence, re: Cruise missile testing – 1994 test window extension. By Colonel Guidinger, DC Pol. Confidential.

69   4 February 1994, 12:08z, message from 79 TEG to various USAF and CF units, re: Global Shadow A94-04 reschedule. Confidential.

70 10 February 1994, 16:30z, Formal Message to External Affairs Ottawa, from Michael Dawson, Canadian Embassy Washington, re: Canada-U.S.A. defence cooperation Umbrella agreement. Protected.

71 11 February 1994 (arrival date), Letter from U.S. CANUS T&E Coordinator, Richard Ledesma, to ADM (Supply) Pierre Lagueux, re: 30 month forecast for CANUS T&E testing in Canada. Secret.

72 28 February 1994, Memorandum to the Prime Minister from the Clerk of the Privy Council, re: Cruise missile test – March 1, 1994. Confidential.

73 (Undated) circa early 1995, DND "Chronology – CANUS T&E and Cruise Testing." Secret Cabinet Confidence. Released by DND under AIA.

74 31 March 1994, Memorandum to CICS from ADM (Pol & Comm), re: Briefing note for DM and CDS - Cruise missile testing in Canada. 29 March 1994, Briefing Note for the DM and CDS, re: Cruise missile test spring 1994. By LCol J.D.A. Hincke, DC Pol-3.

75 7 March 1994, 23:35z, message from 28 TESTS, Eglin AFB, to various USAF and CF units, re: Canadian Global Shadow mission update. Unclassified, Priority.

76 8 April 1994, 16:00z, message from 49 TESTS at Barksdale AFB, to various USAF and CF units, re: Canadian-U.S. (CANUS) Global Cruise/Shadow lessons learned conference and FY95 panning meeting. Unclassified.

77 29 March 1994, Briefing Note for the DM and CDS, re: Cruise missile test spring 1994. By LCol J.D.A. Hincke, DC Pol-3.

78 Handwritten note to DC Pol-3 from DC Pol, Col. Guidinger, in bottom margin of 8 April 1994, 16:00z, message from 49 TESTS, re: Canadian-US (CANUS) Global Cruise/Shadow lessons learned conference and FY95 panning meeting. Unclassified.

79 Edward Greenspon, "Ouellet rules out more cruise testing," *Globe and Mail*, 14 May 1994, p. A4.

80 Rosemary Speirs, "Liberal delegates denounce tests of US cruise missiles," *Toronto Star*, 14 May 1994, p. A16.

81 Ibid.

82 13 May 1994, TVA (Montreal), Le Canada n'autorise plus les essays des missiles cruise au-dessus de son territoire. French newscast on Liberal party convention and cruise missile vote by delegates, with interview of Ouellet and Chrétien.

83 (no date) circa 15 May 1994, briefing note from ADM (Pol & Comm) on Cruise missile testing - Canada-U.S.-Test and evaluation agreement. No classification. 2 pages.

84 16 May 1994, Briefing Note for MND, from ADM (Pol & Comm) and DC Pol-3, re: Recent DFA statements in press regarding Cancellation of cruise missile testing in Canada. No classification.

85 Department of Defense transcript of Secretary Perry's comments on cruise missile testing, made in Ottawa on 16 May 1994, courtesy of the Office of the Secretary of Defense, Directorate of Testing and Evaluation.

86 David Visnneau, "Cruise tests may be over, US hints," *Toronto Star*, 17 May 1994, p. A24.

87 1 June 1994, 21:41z, message to NDHQ and ADM (Pol & Com), from M. Kergin, Canadian Embassy Washington, re: Cruise missile testing. Confidential. Document references the 19 January 1994 message on previous State Department representation on the importance of continuing the tests.

88 13 June 1994, letter to Richard Ledesma, Deputy Director Test and Evaluation, Pentagon, from ADM (Supply) Pierre Lagueux, re: Follow-up to discussion between Secretary Perry and MND and MFA.

89 4 August 1994, Memorandum for the Record, re: Minutes of CANUS cruise missile archive meeting, Air Command HQ, CFB Winnipeg, 3–4 August 1994. 10081-3 (G3 Coord), Captain N. W. Coull.

90 1994 National Defence *White Paper*, Canada-United States Defence Cooperation, Canada-United States Test and Evaluation Program. Chapter 5.

91 (Undated) circa early 1995, DND "Chronology - CANUS T&E and Cruise Testing." Secret Cabinet Confidence. Released by DND under AIA.

92 25 September 1994, Briefing letter for the Minister of National Defence from Deputy Minister Robert Fowler and Chief of Defence Staff General John de Chastelain, re: Canada-US test and evaluation program, Response to the U.S. fiscal year 1994 forecast. Secret.

NOTES TO CONCLUSION

1 "Upgraded cruise missile shows greater accuracy in flight test," *Defense News*, 28 May 2001.

2 Kenneth Werrell, *The Evolution of the Cruise Missile* (Maxwell AFB, AL: Air University Press, 1985), 227.

3 12 June 1997, Briefing Note for the Minister of National Defence, "Canadian Forces Maritime Experimental and Test Ranges (CFMETR)," Commander JED Byrtus (DC Pol), for Dr. Kenneth J. Calder (ADM Policy, National Defence), Secret (CC).

4 Ibid.

5 New Zealand Nuclear Free Zone, Disarmament, and Arms Control Act, June 1987.

6 Rosemary Speirs, "Liberal delegates denounce tests of US cruise missiles," *Toronto Star*, 14 May 1994, p. A16.

7 C. Gordon, "Cruise control; Testing the logic of bureaucrats and military men," *Ottawa Citizen*, 26 January 199x year unknown. p. A11.

8 26 November 1993, Action Memorandum for the Minister of Foreign Affairs, from Gaetan Lavertu, ADM Pol & IDS DFAIT, re: Several issues in Canada-USA defence cooperation are at stages requiring Ministerial decisions. IDD-0230. Secret.

9 18 November 1992, Memorandum to A/ADM (Mat), from Ray Sturgeon, CS/ADM (Mat), re: CANUSTEP Renegotiation. 10055-15 (DGIIP). Secret.

10 Douglas Roche, "Canada's voting record at the U.N. First Committee," *Project Ploughshares Monitor*, 18 November 1999.

11 Ibid.

NOTE TO NOTES ON SOURCES

1 28 July 1998, Memorandum to DAIP from DSTCIM, re 98/1000. 1463-(A)978/0857. Unclassified.

Index

6 March 1984 (first test), 64

6 March 1994 (last test), 176, 193–194

9 September 2017 (new termination date), 230

10 February 1983 (signing), 36–38

10 February 1993 (renewal), 169–76

10 September 2002 (renewal), 230

11 March 1982 ("dummies" cabinet meeting), 1

13 June 1983 (first request), 50–51

15 April 1981 (Weinberger meeting), 6

15 July 1983 (cabinet decision), 53–54

18 December (Reagan letter), 11

19 February 1985 (first flight test), 82–84

22 January 1986 (first air attacks on ALCM), 87–88

25 March 1983 (MOU signed), 43

28 TEST Squadron, 195, 197

30 November 1993 (test approval), 179, 185

31 January 1989 (cabinet agrees to ACM), 127

49 TEST Squadron, 134, 197

79 TEG, 183, 190, 192

80 treaty-level agreements, 200–201

250 MOUs, 200–201

319 Bomb Wing, 64, 83

417 Squadron (Helicopter), 146, 173

436 Bomb Wing, 64

441 Squadron (Fighter), 154–55

600 bilateral arrangements, 186

600 letters, 24

1000 letters, 24

1991 withdrawal of tactical nuclear weapons, 133

1994 White Paper on Defence, 197

2,500 high-priority targets, 59

3,500 letters, 46

6,570 personal letters, 45

420,000 Canadians, 72

A

A-1331-83, 58

ABM, 32, 207–8

ABM Treaty, 94, 205–8

Access to Information Act (AIA), xiii, 7,
        94–95, 108, 118, 159, 211–13

acid rain, 127

acoustic submarine tracking facility, 179,
        192

advanced cruise missile (ACM) (see also
        AGM-129), 68, 111–40, 117–18,
        131, 149

    B-52 flight, 149

    begin free-flight, 168

    Cabinet agrees to test, 127

    CF-18 escort, 150

    CF-18 intercepts, 137–38

    first free-flight, 139–40

    first test, 129

    first captive-carry, 129

    H of C answer, 122

    "pleased to approve", 129

    no parachute, 135

    no request to test, 118–19

    test request, 111

    withdraw request, 91, 113–14

Advanced range instrumentation aircraft
        (ARIA), 59, 68, 83, 190–91

AETE, 150, 191, 197

Afghanistan, 199

Agent Orange, 7

AGM-86A (ALCM-A), 67

AGM-86B (ALCM-B), 11, 35, 66–68, 141
        specifications, 66–68

AGM-86C (ALCM-C), 68, 199

AGM-129 (ACM), 68, 111–40, 117–18,
        131, 149, 190, 193

agreements
    air defence, 78

nuclear weapons, 78–79, 240–42

number, 200–201

review of, 77–79

secret, 79–80

storage, 80

termination of, 77–80

Air Combat Command (ACC), xiii, 187

Air Command, 76, 182, 185, 197

    anti-cruise flights (CMDI), 76, 86–88,
        93, 148, 153–54, 157, 172, 191,
        204

air defence, 78

Air Defence Initiative (ADI), 112

airborne alert program, 208

Alberta, 51

ALCM Project Arrangement, 128

Allmand, MP Warren, 52, 89

alternative way of life, 51

Amarillo, Texas, 72

American puppet, 207

Anderson, Admiral J.R., 177–78

Andre, MP Harvie, 60

Andropov, Yuri, 8–9, 40, 42, 63

Anglin, Perry, 10

annual forecast (thirty-month forecast), 44,
        63, 111, 119, 131, 179, 180, 193,
        227, 239, 250, 258, 261, 262

April 26 Coalition, 106

"approved 30/11/93", 179, 185

Arctic sovereignty and defence, 86, 112

Argentia naval station, 77, 80, 192

Arkin, William, 79, 81

armed warheads, 13

arms control
    Canadian policy, 17, 45
    INF, 12, 21, 24, 25, 72, 95–96, 116,
        121–22
    SALT II, 18, 24, 30, 60–61, 70, 91, 94,
        112–14, 116

START, 24, 126, 129, 133

START I, 132–33, 181

START IA, 134–35

START II, 135, 168–69

United States' policy, 113

Arms Control Reporter, 61

arrest without charge, 205

AS-15 (ALCM), 73

AS-19 (ALCM), 130

Ashton, Mark, 83

Aspin, Les, 187

Assistant Deputy Minister Material (ADM
Mat), 119, 159, 185, 227

atomic energy for mutual defence
purposes, 241

Atwood, Margaret, 39

Aurora (CP-140), 93, 157

author, 210

authorization (nuclear), 25, 79

automatic renewal, 92

Aviation Week & Space Technology, 36

"avoid jeopardizing our testing", 180

AWACS, 68, 83, 93, 97, 139, 140

Axworthy, MP Lloyd, 91, 139, 180, 182,
186, 190

B

B-1A (experimental bomber), 3, 67

B-1B (bomber), 7

B-2 (stealth bomber), 7, 118, 180, 198

B-52 (heavy bomber), 18, 30, 41, 52, 64,
68–70, 118, 141, 144, 156

"bad news announcement", 137, 165

bad weather, 50, 75, 93, 139, 140, 154–55,
157–58, 173, 193–94

Bader, George, 123

Bagotville, CFB, 6, 16, 27, 72

Baily, Leo, 102

Baker, MP George, 52

balloon, 82–83, 89

Barksdale AFB, 68, 134, 176, 195

Basic Security Plan, 5

Bay of Fundy, 25

BBC, 33

Beatty, MP Perrin, 111, 112, 116, 118–19,
120

letter to Weinberger, 121

Weinberger meeting, 114

Beaufort Sea, 89–90, 93, 151, 173, 193

crash (*see also* ALCM crash), 89–90, 93

beginning of a request, 5

Belmas, Juliet Caroline, 101, 105, 244

Berg, Jim, 74

Berlin Wall, 130–32

BGM-109G (GLCM), 12, 21, 30, 40, 42, 47,
58–61, 96, 111, 121, 122

Bilderberg Group, 48

Binnie, Ian, 58, 62

BL-10 (ALCM), 73

Blais, MP Jean-Jacques, 57, 62, 100

bloated military hierarchy, 203

Blondin-Andrew, MP Ethel, 190

Blundon, Barry, 102

Blytheville AFB, 92–93

Boeing, 11, 66, 69

BoMARC, 72, 77, 240

bombing

"is madness", 99, 102

Litton, 99–109

Russia, 232

Southeast Asia, 69

Bon, Daniel, 208

Bosse, F.J., 107

Bouchard, MP Lucien, 188

Boyer, Corporal Bruno, 108

Boyle, General John, 179, 182–83

Brault, Marc, 175

Brezhnev, Leonid, 8, 21, 28

Brink's truck, 105

British Columbia, 23, 51

Broadbent, MP Edward, 38, 52

Broughton, Colonel Lorne, 3

Brown, Angela, 56

Brown, General A.C., 49

budget, military, 12, 32, 203, 208

BUIC, 78

Bumpers, Senator Dale, 61

Burch, Brian, 55

Burger, Nancy, 17

Burney, Ambassador Derek, 113, 123,
    126–27

Bush, President George H.W. (1988–1992),
    42, 126, 132–33, 156, 169

Bush, President George W. (2000–2008),
    207–8

Burns, General E.L.M., 18

Byrtus, Commander J.E.D., 262n3

C

Cabana-Marshall, J., 166

Cabinet
    agreed to testing, 54
    approval, 163
    battle, 31–32
    committees
        Foreign & Defence Policy, 9,
            29, 116
        Priorities & Planning, 53–54,
            127, 160, 170, 172
    confidence, 159, 201
    decision challenged in court, 57–58,
    decisions reviewable by court, 61, 86
        limits to tests, 191
    meetings, 40, 48–49, 53–54, 91, 113,
        115, 124–25, 127, 171
    timetable to approve tests, 48–49

Caccia, MP Charles, 189

CADIN, 78

CALCM (*see also* AGM-86C), 68, 199

Calder, Dr. Ken, 135, 160–61, 179–80, 195,
    200

Cameron, R.P., 28, 35

Campbell, Prime Minister Kim, 139, 151,
    169, 172, 178

Canada and the nuclear age, 214

Canada-US defence co-operation, 166

Canadian arms control policy, 17, 45

Canadian Aviation Safety Board, 89

Canadian Defence Liaison Staff Washington
    (CDLS-W), 158, 182

Canadian Disarmament Information
    Network (CANDIS), 60

Canadian Forces Maritime Experimental
    Test Range (CFMETR), 200–202

Canadian Institute for Strategic Studies
    (CISS), 157

Canadian military industries, 169

Canadian Nuclear Weapons, 1

Canadian Press, 192

Canadian Security Intelligence Service
    (CSIS), 99, 108, 205

Canadian Test & Evaluation Steering Group,
    44, 112, 160

Canadian United Nations Association, 24

cancel agreements, 77, 80

cancellation consequences, 184

cancelled acquisition, 35

cancelled agreements, 240

CANUS Index of Agreement, 78–79, 241–42

CANUS T&E, 29, 36–38, 119, 151
    agreement text, 223–26
    automatic renewal, 152
    changes, 128, 136–37, 172, 174–75
    flush away, 180
    MOU text, 226–30
    renew, 151–76

renewal in 2002, 230

termination, 96

captive-carry test, 59, 64, 87, 120,129, 133

carbon fibres, 155

Carlson, Stan, 10

Carrie Jane Grey Park, 75

Carter, President Jimmy, 3

Carter, Susan, 10

Cashore, John, 62

Cattanach, Justice Alex, 57

censored documents, xiii, 118–19, 159,
 211–12, 230

CF-18, 8, 14, 19

 acquisition, 9

 CMDI, 86–88, 148,150, 153–54, 157,
  173–74, 204

 crash, 154–55

 escorts, 76, 82, 93, 97, 148, 150

 far north, 154–55

 intercept ACM, 137–38, 150

 production, 9

CF-101 VooDoo, 27, 72, 77, 240

CF-104 Starfighter, 72, 77, 240

CFMETR, 200–202, 242

chain link fence, 65

Chambers, William, 152

de Champlain, Captain Heather, 197

changes to ALCM project arrangement,
 128, 136–37, 172, 174, 175

Chapeau agreement, 192

Charlottetown Accord, 160

Charter of Rights and Freedoms, 32,
 57–58, 61, 86

de Chastelain, General John, 136

Cheekeye-Dunsmuir powerlines, 100, 105

chemical weapon testing, 7

Chernyenko, Constantin, 63

Chikowski, Terry, 102

Chmara, Major, 192

Chouinard, Justice Julien, 62, 75

Chrétien, Prime Minister Jean, 96, 127,
 182, 195, 205

Christie, Thomas P., 230

Christopher, Warren, 175, 183

chronology of tests, 217–21

Churchill, Fort, 79

civil disobedience, 106

civil use of atomic energy, 241

Clark, Prime Minister Joe, 86, 112, 122–23,
 124, 152

Clark, Matthew, 56

Clearwater Nuclear Weapons Fond 98/15,
 2, 213

Clement, Philippe, 10

Clements, Bill, 67

Clinton, President William, 169, 173

Coe, Stephanie, 43–44, 53

Cold Lake, CFB, 17, 41, 51, 62, 64–65, 76,
 90, 107, 134, 142, 144, 213

 fence, 65

 public affairs, 64–65

cold war ended, 157

Collenette, MP David, 177, 179, 185, 188,
 197

"commie shit", 55

commitment of the previous government,
 177, 184, 185, 191, 195, 202

common strategic rotary launcher (CSRL),
 69, 157, 172

communication strategy, 136–37

communist financing, 60

Communist Party of Canada (CPC), 60

Comox, CFB, 16, 72, 81

Conference on Disarmament, 33–34, 54

consequence of refusal, 199–202

Constitution, 55–56

consultation on release, 79

Consultative Group Meeting on cruise

missiles, 130

coordinating group, 44

Copps, MP Sheila, 174, 190

Corver, Captain Richard, 154–55

cost effectiveness, 197

cost of tests, 66

costs and consequences, 184

costs to Canada, 159

Cotler, Irwin, 58

Coull, Captain Norman, 197

Coulter, Keith, 136

Courvoisier, Guy, 101

crashes
    ACM, 138, 167
    ALCM, 18, 31, 50, 87, 88, 89, 91, 93,
        114, 167
    B-52, 52
    CF-18, 154–55
    GLCM, 30

critical essays, 214

crucial test from White House, 178

cruise catcher, 82

Cruise Missile Archive Meeting, 197

Cruise Missile Conversion Project
    (CMCP), 32, 55, 100, 103,
    103–9, 204–5

Cruise Missile Defence Initiative (CMDI),
    76, 86–88, 93, 148, 153–54, 157,
    172, 191, 204

cruise missiles shall be unarmed, 13

Cruise Missile Technical Group, 48

cruise testing if necessary, 121, 202

Crutchlow, L.D., 4

Cubana Airlines, 41

CUPE, 55

CUPW, 55

customs duties, 170

D

daily executive meeting (DEM), 163

le Dain, Justice Gerald, 58

DAIP, xiii, 119, 211–13

Dam, Kenneth W., 36–38

"damage our defence relationship", 123

Davis, Pauline, 62

Dawson, Michael, 192

death of cruise missile testing, 196–97

decreased fiscal resources, 197

Defence Industrial Production Programme
    (DIPP), 9

Defence Industrial Relations (DDIR), 161,
    170, 172

defence policy review, 191, 197

defence production, 20

Defence Production Sharing Agreement,
    19, 198

defensive anti-cruise missile capability, 174

DDR dissolves, 130–32

debates, 30, 38, 185–86

"defrocked priest of peace", 203

delay ACM tests, 123, 126

delays in renewal, 158–68

delays in signing, 33

delays in testing, 182

Delworth, W.T., 26

demarche, 114, 178, 187

Department of Industry, 9

Devlin, J.T., 158

DEW Line, 5, 78–79

Dewar, D.B. (Bev), 40, 47–49, 125

Dick, MP Paul, 152

Dickson, Justice Brian, 75, 86

Diefenbaker, Prime Minister John, 13, 38,
    203

diplomatic complaint, 53

Direct Action, 102–6, 244–45

Directorate of Access to Information

(DAIP), xiii, 119, 211–13

Directorate of History (DHH), 2, 213

Dixon, John, 174

"don't ask, don't tell", 209

Douglas, MP Tommy, 203

Dr. Strangelove (film), 69

dual-track decision (NATO), 15–16, 19, 22–23, 46–47, 61

Duceppe, MP Gilles, 191

Duff, R.L., 107

dummy protestors, 104

Duncan, Robert, 128

Dundas, Peter, 55

Dungery, Harry, 101

Dyer, Gwynne, 111

Dyess AFB, 153, 154

E

Eagle, Reverend Glen, 17

east corridor, 87, 95

Easter protest, 72

economic benefits, 20

Edwards, Commodore, 4

Eggleton, Mayor Art, 29, 32, 103

Eglin AFB, xiii, 183, 190, 192, 197

Ehrnman, Bruce, 184

elimination of MIRVed ICBMs, 134–35

Ellis, Deb, 29

Elmendorf AFB, 139, 140, 152, 155, 190, 193, 194

emergency locator transmitter (ELT), 135, 138

"enemy is everywhere", 189

end of cruise missile testing, 196–97

engine intake cover, 89

environment, 12, 23, 87, 94, 130, 135–36, 225, 228, 251

    Initial Environmental Evaluation (IEE), 94

laws, 12

Ernest Harmon AFB, 77, 80, 240

escorts, 76, 82, 93, 97, 148, 150

Estey, Justice Willard, 75

Evolution of the Cruise Missile, 199

exchange of notes, 37, 170

External Affairs (Foreign Affairs)

    AIA withholds, xiii, 159, 211–12

external observable differences, 30, 70

F

facility barter system, 159

Fairchild AFB, 95, 157

Farr, Craig, 161–62, 165, 169

Farrell, Mike, 89

"fast for peace", 41, 53

Federal Bureau of Investigation (FBI), 53

federal court, 32, 57–58, 61, 62,

financial responsibility, 12, 26, 29

first ACM test, 129

first ACM free-flight, 139–40

first captive-carry test, 64–65

First Committee (Disarmament), 205–6

first free-flight test, 82–84

first official request, 4

first operational test, 68

first request, 50–52

first test, 64–65

Firth, MP Doug, 52

Fitzpatrick, William, 82–83

Five plus five (5+5), 151

flight safety, 23, 59, 94, 154–55

Flush procedures, 80, 241

forecast of tests (*see also* annual forecast), 44, 63, 111, 119, 131, 179, 180, 193, 227, 239, 250, 258, 261, 262

Foreign Affairs (*see* External Affairs)

foreign policy review, 191

Forman, Gideon, 157

Forward Operating Location (FOL),
  154–55
Fort Churchill, 79
Foster, K.F., 56
Fowler, Robert R., 11, 20, 30, 49, 50, 112,
      118, 123, 136–37, 163, 166,
      177–78
Francis, J.R., 31
Frantics, The, 239
Fraser, MP John, 52
Frazer, Colonel J., 121
Frazer, MP Jack, 188
Fredricton, NB, 25
free-flight test, 64
free trade, 126, 167
Freedom of Information Act (FOIA), xiii,
      7, 211
freedom of speech, 51–52, 57
freedom run wild, 7
French translation, 25–26, 29, 167, 170,
      175
friendly persuasion, 189
FTA (NAFTA), 126, 167
funding, 12, 125,
fuze, 85

G

Gagetown, CFB, 25, 47,
Gallaway, MP Roger, 190
Gallup poll, 130
Gauley-Gage Cartage, 101
General Motors, 157
Geneva talks, 33–34, 54
Genie rocket, 16, 27, 72, 77
Glenn, Brig. General, 123
Global Cruise, 68, 74, 82, 83, 84, 88, 89, 92,
      93, 95, 96, 97, 152, 153, 154, 155,
      157, 172
global positioning system (GPS), 66

Global Shadow, 118, 129, 131, 133, 134,
      139, 193
Globe and Mail, 190–91
Gomberg, Richard, 56–57
Goose Bay, 23, 77, 80
Gorbachev, General Secretary Mikhail, 47,
      95, 115, 121, 132
Gordon, Charles, 140
Gotlieb, Ambassador Alan, 26, 33, 36–38,
      81
Grand Forks AFB, 34, 41, 64, 82–84,
grand gesture by Trudeau, 204
Gray, MP Herb, 127, 186, 188
Grayson, Peter, 55–56
Grenada, 58
      Cuban construction workers, 58
      U.K. support for workers, 58
      U.S. invasion of, 58
Greenham Common, 29, 31, 61
Greenpeace, 40, 51, 82, 88, 142, 144
Greenspon, Lawrence, 32, 57, 58, 62
Greenwood, CFB, 81
Grey, MP Deborah, 189
Griffiss AFB, 30, 34, 41, 55, 68, 152
ground launched cruise missile (GLCM),
      12, 21, 30, 40, 42, 47, 58–61, 96,
      111, 121, 122
GST, 170
Guidinger, Colonel R.W., 192, 195
Gustafson, Roger, 83
Gwyn, Richard, 46

H

Haig, Alexander, 6, 19
Halifax submarine tracking facility, 179,
      192
Hancock, Ken, 103, 108
Hannah, Gerald (Useless), 101, 104–5, 244
Hansen, Ann Britt, 103, 105, 244

Harcourt, Mayor Michael, 44

Harmon AFB, 77, 80, 240

Harney, Private Doug, 122

Harper, Prime Minister Stephen, 208

Harris, Dave, 51

Harrison, Karen, 41–42

Heap, MP Dan, 63, 122,

heavy bombers, 132–33

Hees, MP George, 5, 13

Helms, Jesse, 60

Hendrie family, 58

high-altitude route (*see also* low-altitude),
52–53

Hill AFB (*see also* Utah), 88, 173, 199

Hinke, Colonel Joe, 161–62

Holy Trinity Church, 60

Honest John rocket, 72, 77, 240

Hound Dog (ALCM), 70

Huddleston, General, 126

Hugessen, Justice James, 58

Hughes Missile System, 117

Hunt, Major, 51

Hussein, Saddam (*see also* Iraq), 174

I

ICBM (*see also* START), 133, 168–69, 181

ICBM tests, 50

IDD, 170

IDR, 171

Ikle, Fred, 7, 81

inconsistency, 22

incremental costs, 159, 162, 165

Inertial Navigation System (INS), 100, 109

INF, 12, 21, 24, 25, 72, 116

INF Treaty, 95–96, 121–22

infiltration of peace groups, 108, 205

Information Commissioner, 94, 119–20,
212

initial environmental evaluation (*see also*

environment), 94–95

Intermediate Nuclear Forces (INF), 12, 21,
24, 25, 72, 116

International Industry Programme, 167,
193

international law, 209

International Telecommunications Union
(ITU), 53

Inuit, 190

Inuvik, 154

"investigating the motives", 211, 213

Iraq, 68, 131, 140, 203
ACM initial strikes, 131

Irwin, MP Ron, 52

Ittinaur, MP Peter, 52

J

Jaworsky, Sonny, 104

Jewett, MP Pauline, 1, 9, 13, 22, 38, 54, 94,
96, 118–19

joint Canada-US steering committee, 166

Joyce, Tom, 101

Judd, Jim, 165, 182

Judge Advocate General (JAG), 161,
165–66

"just dummies", 1, 15

K

Kaplan, Robert, 108

Karsgaard, David, 123

Kashton, William, 60

Kaufman, Michael, 33

Kavanagh, 136

Kergin, M., 183–85, 197

Kerr, C.A., 167

K.I. Sawyer AFB, 129, 134, 139, 149, 190,
193–94

Kirtland AFB, 210

Kissinger, Henry, 48

Kiwi disease, 200–202, 206

Korea, North, 208

Korean Airlines (KAL), 58

Kravchuk, President Leonid, 181

Kuse, Corporal Robert, 103

Kvitsinsky, Yuli, 25

L

Lagueux, Pierre, 172, 178, 180, 185, 197

Lajoie, Sue, xiii

Lamontagne, MP Gilles, 1, 6, 15, 17, 23, 28,
    40, 44, 48, 52

    meeting with Weinberger, 7–8,
        28–29, 43

Landry, George, 94

LANTIRN, 47, 63

Laskin, Chief Justice Bora, 62

last ACM test, 176, 193–94

Lavertu, Gaetan, 179

Lavigne, MP L., 189

Lawrence, Allan, 112

Lawrence Livermore National Lab, 24, 71

Lawson, Colonel Thomas, 51

Layton, Jack, 44

leak of information, 14, 53, 116

LeCouvie, Ivan, 104

Leddy, Sister Mary Jo, 24

Ledesma, Richard, 135, 169, 170, 179

Leduc, Colonel, 156

Leigh, Lt Colonel, 107

lessons learned, 176, 195

"lessons learned" conference, 195

letters of protest, 19, 24, 45, 46, 120, 125,
    237

Liberal
    convention, 28, 127, 195
    flush away CANUS T&E, 180
    office, 56
    split, 28, 179, 182, 260

"typical sleazy tactic", 55

life cycle of weapon, 51

Light, Robert, 53

ling, 29

litmus test, 123, 187

Litton, 24, 29, 62, 99–109, 244–45
    bombing of, 27, 99–109
    "Bombing is madness", 99, 102
    credits, 15, 99
    guidance system, 99–100, 109
    interest-free loans, 99
    Litton Systems Canada, 9, 99
    unionize, 100

list of tests, 194, 217–21

live warheads, 12, 15, 25

locator beacon (see also ELT), 135, 138

Locke, W.M., 100

Loring AFB, 47

Los Alamos National Laboratory (LANL),
    xiii, 70–72, 142–43

low-angle measurement, 48

low-level training routes (see also high-
    altitude), 18, 52–53, 91, 198, 241

LRNA, 132–33

Lysyshyn, Ralph, 153

Lyter, Major, 138

M

MacAdam, Murray, 104

MacEachen, MP Allan, 6, 10, 24, 26–27,
    29–30, 33, 35–36, 38–40, 43,
    50, 54, 59

MacDonald, Clarke, 27

MacDonald, Jim, 24

Macdonnell Douglas, 14, 100,

MacGuigan, MP Mark, 10, 13, 19, 57
    meeting with Shultz, 27

Mackenzie King, 5, 121, 202

MacKinnon, MP Allan, 38, 52

Manitoba legislature, 94

Manson, General, 125

Maple Flag, 41

Marceau, Louis, 58, 61

Marchand, de Montigny, 26, 30

Maresca, J., 118

Martin, Prime Minister Paul, 207–8

Martinsen, Major Jan, 132

M.A.S.H., 89

Masse, MP Marcel, 137

    approves ACM, 137

Matusiak, Norm, 62, 104

Mayhew, Mark, 163, 172

McCreary, Lt Colonel, 123

McFarlane, Roy, 54

McIntyre, Justice William, 62, 75

McKay, Steve, 83

McKnight, MP Bill, 119, 128–29

McLean, MP Walter, 52

McMurtry, Roy, 108

McNamara, Robert, 16

McRae, MP Paul, 38, 49, 52

media coverage, 64–65

Meech Lake

    accord, 94, 160

    cabinet retreat, 171

Meinheit, 156

memorandum of understanding (MOU),
    25, 40, 43–44, 165, 226–30

Memorandum to Cabinet (MC), 9, 77, 160,
    163, 164

Mid-Canada Line, 5

Middle Powers Initiative, 206

Military Co-operation Committee (MCC),
    5, 77

Miller, Commodore Dusty, 170

ministers of national defence (MND), 231

Minot AFB, 155, 156

MIRV, 61, 135, 169

Misguided Missiles, 214, 231

missile defence, 207–8

MIT, 48

Mk-57 bomb, 81

Mobilization for Survival, 56

Moher, Mark, 170, 179

Mom, v

Moose Jaw, CFB, 80, 241

Moran, High Commissioner John, 16

Morden, R., 112, 165, 172

Morrison, Colonel Alex, 157

Morrison, Dave, 53

Mother's Day rally, 46–47

motion in House of Commons, 52, 94, 96,
    186

Moxley, Andrew, 108

Mulroney, PM Brian, 39, 74, 80, 109, 204

    letter on ACM, 120–21

    letter to Reagan, 91–92, 124

    meeting with Clinton, 173–75

    meeting with Reagan, 73, 86

    meeting with Teeley, 167

    Reagan and NORAD, 90

    Reagan years, 208

    unconvinced on ACM, 112

Murray, Admiral Larry, 136

Murta, MP Jack, 52

MX missile (Peacekeeper), 7, 12, 26, 32,
    50, 133

N

NAFTA, 124, 167

Nanoose, 200–201, 209

National Archives, 55–56

National Defence Act, 122

National Missile Defense (NMD), 207–8

NATO, 16, 32, 42, 181

    commitments, 41

    dual-track decision, 15–16, 19, 22,
        46–47, 61

fig leaf, 16

Flying Training Centre, 200–201

foreign ministers, 91

Nuclear Planning group, 43

North Atlantic Council, 121

posture, 15

requirements, 17

solidarity, 43

target list, 59

NDMOUC, 166

neutron bomb, 25, 40

New Agenda Coalition (NAC), 205–6

New Democratic Party (NDP), 38, 54, 94

New York Times, 33

New Zealand, 200–201

Nicholson, MP Aideen, 41

Nielson, MP Erik, 86

Niles, Ambassador Thomas, 114–15, 127–28, 152, 175

Nitze, Paul, 25

Nixon, Richard, 67

"no ALCM testing can be assured", 195

"no decision made", 182

no request to test ACM, 118–19

Noble, John, 128

Non-Proliferation Treaty (NPT), 206

non-renewal, 151

NORAD, 5–6, 19, 38, 73, 78, 80, 179, 207, 208

    Alert Agreement, 241

    anti-cruise operations, 76

    CINCNORAD, 79, 241

    CMDI, 76, 86–88, 93, 148, 153–54, 157, 172, 191, 204

    consultation, 79

    flush procedures, 80, 241–42

    intercept ACM, 191

    renewal, 90, 156

    signing, 38

North Korea, 208

North Pole, 63

Northwest Territories (NWT), 50–51

NOTAM, 49

Note #24, 175

Note #64, 36–38

Note #352, 79

Note #397, 30

nuclear agreements, 77–79, 241

nuclear allergy, 77, 81, 200–202

nuclear anti-submarine weapons, 80–81

nuclear depth bomb, 81

nuclear-free city, 32

nuclear posture review (NPR), 181

nuclear-powered warships, 78, 80

nuclear warheads

    W-25, 16, 72, 77–78

    W-80, 66, 70–72,117, 142–43

nuclear weapons agreements, 77–79, 241

nuclear weapons consultation, 75, 79, 241

0

official list, 194

offsetting costs, 159

Ogdensburg Declaration, 5

open letter from Trudeau, 45–46

open letter to Trudeau, 39

Open Skies Treaty, 153

Operation Dismantle, 32, 40, 54, 57, 75

Operation *RYaN*, 8–9, 40, 59

"operational necessity", 179

Operational Research Division Study, 30

Order-in-Council, 20, 26, 163, 170

Ouellet, MP Andre, 96, 179, 188, 195

overflights, 179, 241, 242

Oxman, Stephen, 183–85

P

Padgham, Paddy, 17

Pangborn, William, 83

Pantex Plant, 71

"pants down", 66

parachute, 83, 135, 145, 152

Parliament Hill, 27, 40, 43–44, 46, 51, 53,
     99, 109–10

parliamentary supremacy, 57–58

Pauling, Dr. Linus, 26

Peace Camp, 43–44, 53

Peace Mom, 62

Peace Tower, 51

Peacekeeper (MX) missile, 7, 12, 32, 50
     railroad project, 133

Pearson, PM Lester B., 72, 202–3
     "defrocked priest of peace", 203

People in Sport for Peace, 89

Permanent Joint Board on Defence (PJBD)
     4, 8, 10, 13, 27, 76, 77, 85, 86,
     112, 115,116,124, 183

Pentagon decrees end to tests, 204

Perry, Dr. William, 4, 26, 187, 196–97, 202

Pershing II MRBM, 21, 40, 47, 59–60, 72,
     96, 111

Pervomaysk, 181

Peters, Mary Ann, 184

petitions, 72, 89

Petzinger, Bonnie (DAIP), xiii

Pierce, Karen, 40

pilot training, 188

Pinetree Line, 5, 78

Pitcairn, 11

"planning may proceed", 198

political action to please Washington, 84

polls, public opinion, 33–34, 85, 96, 123,
     130, 164, 176

poll question, 130

postponed tests, 88, 140, 152–53, 155–56,

     157–58, 172–73, 184, 193–94

Powell, Deb, 29

Power, Sue, 53

Pratte, Justice Louis, 58

Pravda, 73

pre-clearance for nuclear use, 25, 79

precision guided munitions, 25

Prime Minister's Office (PMO), 10–11, 15,
     17, 21, 22–23, 30–31, 45, 50,
     125, 189, 212

Primrose Lake, 65, 82, 140, 145–46, 150,
     153, 176, 194

Privy Council Office (PCO), xiii, 47, 112,
     125, 136, 165, 212

Progressive Conservative, 38
     convention, 33, 39
     Red Tory, 52, 205–6
     Reform, 188, 208

Project Arrangements
     Change #3, 128
     Change #4, 136–37,
     Change #5, 172, 174, 175

Project Ploughshares, xiii, 39, 46, 118, 157,
     213

project proposal, 118

Prongos, Peter, 26

proprietary data, 12

protest in Canadian municipalities
     Bagotville, 27
     Calgary, 56, 60
     Charlottetown, 60
     Cold Lake, 17, 45, 88
     Edmonton, 17, 60
     Grand Centre, 17
     Halifax, 60
     Hamilton, 60
     Kingston, 60
     Lakeland, 17
     London, 60

Montreal, 26

Ottawa, 60

Parliament Hill, 26

Peace River, 89

Prince Albert, 60

Prince George, 75

Queen's Park, 44, 56

Regina, 56, 60

Saint John, 60

St. John's, 60

Saskatoon, 45, 56, 60

Thunder Bay, 60

Toronto, 32, 44, 51, 56

Vancouver, 24, 44, 56, 60

Vernon, 60

Victoria, 60

Wandering River, 82

Windsor, 60

Winnipeg, 27, 60, 75, 122

Yellowknife, 54–55

protest in Europe

Comiso, 17

Easter, 72

Greenham Common, 29, 31, 61

Munich, 17

Rome, 17

protest events in Canada

banner, 51

chained, 40

Constitution, 55–56

Easter, 72

"fast for peace", 41

forecast for poor attendance, 84–85

Hiroshima Day, 101

hunger strike/fast, 41, 53

Litton, 100–109

Mother's Day, 46–47

Parliament Hill, 99

peace camp, 43–44, 53, 108

Peace Mom, 62

Peace Tower, 51

Public Gallery, 33

Remembrance Day, 100, 103

"very polite", 19

Recruiting Centre, 51

protest groups

in Alberta, 120

Canadian Disarmament Information
Service (CANDIS), 60

Cruise Missile Conversion Project
(CMCP), 32, 55, 100, 103, 103–
9, 204–5, 245

Edmontonians for a Non-Nuclear
Future, 17

Greenpeace, 40, 51, 82, 88, 93, 142,
144

Lakeland Area Non-Nuclear
Coalition, 17

Mobilization for Survival, 56

Operation Dismantle, 32, 40, 54, 57,
75, 204–5

People in Sport for Peace, 89

Physicians for Social Responsibility,
55

Project Ploughshares, 39, 46, 118,
157, 213

Refuse the Cruise, 27, 29

Toronto Disarmament Network, 56

Toronto Peace Alliance, 157

Winnipeg Coordinating Committee
for Disarmament (WCCD), 75

World Emergency Project, 104

press release, 50, 191

Priddle, Lt Commander J.J., 161–62

process of Canadian government, 1

public affairs, 18, 90, 125, 136, 165, 175

public opinion polls, 33–34, 85, 96, 123,
130, 164, 176

Putin, President Vladimir, 207

PVO-Strany, 58

Q

Quebec, federal powers to, 94, 160

Quebec Bloc, 188

question period (QP), 119, 175, 251

R

Raby, Wilfrid, 53

race to test, 6

radar cross-section, 26, 66, 117

radioactive half life, 70

RCMP, 46–47, 99, 103, 106–9, 205, 213

"ready, aye, ready", 208

Reagan, President Ronald, 4, 42, 45, 63, 74,
        95, 115, 204

    letter to Mulroney, 124, 126

    letter to Trudeau, 11

    "not rational", 127

reciprocity, 159, 161–62, 177–78

red herring, 22

Red Hot Video, 103

red ink, 55–56

reduced costs, 180

Reform Party, 188

Refuse the Cruise, 27, 29

Reis, Dr. Victor H., 171

Rennie, Justice Gordon, 51

request to renew, 158

Resistance magazine, 103

re-targeting missiles, 181

Revenue Canada, 170

review of cabinet decisions, 61, 86

Reykyavik, 115

ribbon bridge transporter, 180

Robinson, Dr. Bill, 118, 157

Robinson, Ambassador Paul, 40–41

Robinson, MP Svend, 139, 186, 189

Roche, Senator/MP Douglas, 52, 205–6

Rodionov, Ambassador, 129

Romanow, Roy, 21

Rosenblum, Simon, 214

Rosetto, Captain Luigi, 74

Royal Canadian Mounted Police (RCMP),
        46–47, 99, 103, 106–9, 205, 213

Royal Canadian Regiment (RCR), 25, 51

RSD-10 (SS-20), 12, 21, 96

Rubin, Ken, 118

Rumsfeld, Donald, 207

Ryan, Justice William, 58

RYaN, Operation, 8–9, 40, 59

Rynd, Aaron, 51

S

safety issues, 59, 94

safety review, 23, 198

Saint John, NB, 25–26

Sallot, Jeff, 121, 190–91, 192

SALT II, 18, 24, 30, 91

    compliance, 60–61

    external differences, 30, 70

    Senate, 60–61

    violation, 70, 91, 94, 112–14, 116

Salt Shaker, 70

sanctions, 200

Sargeant, MP Terry, 18, 48

Saskatchewan, 20

Saskatoon, 20

Savage, Dave, 43

SCEAND, 22, 42, 47, 79

Scientology, 7

Scott, Jamie, 57

scrum, 42

SDI, 32, 42

sea-launched ballistic missile (SLBM), 7,
        135, 168–69

sea-launched cruise missile (SLCM), 26, 67,

73, 114, 131

second test, 74–75

secret agreements, 79–80

secret police, 99, 103, 106–9

Secret Squirrel, 68

Section 69 Cabinet Confidences, 159

security agreement, 79

Sellar, Don, 14, 53

Senecal, Nicole, 45

"serve Canada's ... interests", 164

Sewell, John, 44

sharp end of the stick, 203

Sharpsword, xiv

"shock to the system", 192

Shortliffe, Glen, 136, 165, 190, 193

"show stopper", 138

Shultz, George, 27, 29, 33, 40–41, 43, 54,
        59, 116, 124

    letter to Clark, 123

Siberia, 65, 140

SIOP, 134, 168

Skynner, John, 197

Slack, Mike, 169

sleazy tactic, 55

Slocum,Walter, 184

Sloscan, Operation, 140, 154–55

Smith, French, 53

Smith, Gordon, 111

SNDV, 132–33

Snore Control, 173

snow on ground, 65

Snowtime, 241

solicited request, 9, 11

Southam News, 14, 34

Southern Alberta and Iraq, 68, 140, 203

Soviet funding of protest, 60

Soviet observers, 153

Space Command, 207

Spock, Dr. Benjamin, 47

Squamish, 101

Squamish Five, 100–106, 244–45

SR-71 (Blackbird), 93

SRAM, 69–70, 133

SS-20 (see also RSD-10), 16, 21, 47–48, 96

St. John's harbour, 114

Stalinism, 62, 104, 132

stand-down of nuclear weapons in 1991, 133

Standing Committee on External Affairs &
        National Defence (SCEAND), 22,
        42, 47, 79

Standing Consultative Commission (SCC), 61

Star Wars (SDI), 32

Starfighter (CF-104), 72, 77, 240

Stark, T. James, 32, 57, 75, 214

Starodubov, General Victor, 26

START, 24, 126, 129, 133

START I, 132–33, 181

START IA, 134–35

START II, 135, 168–69

State Department meeting, 183–85

stealth bomber (B-2), 7, 118, 198

stealth cruise missile (ACM, AGM-129) 26,
        35–36, 68, 111–40, 117–18, 131,
        149, 190, 193

stealth fighter (F-117), 7, 117, 180

steering group, 44, 112

Stevenson, Susan, 75

Stewart, Douglas, 105, 244

Strait of Juan de Fuca, 80

Strangelove, Dr. (film), 69

Strategic Air Command, 3, 52, 208, 242

Strategic Command, xiii

Strategic Defense Initiative (SDI), 32, 42

strategic integrated operational plan (SIOP),
        134, 168

Strategic Weapons System Assessment, 161

Sturgeon, Ray, 172, 175

Subject Evaluation Report (SER), 106

submarine tracking facility, 179, 192

submarine transit of Canadian waters, 80

submission to council, 26

suffocation strategy, 3, 16, 20

Summer, Cole, 75

Supreme Court, 62, 75, 86

    decisions of cabinet are reviewable, 86

Suzuki, David, 39

swept for bugs, 123

T

T-1679-83, 32

tabled agreement, 37–38

tactical nuclear weapons stand-down, 133

Taft, William, 128

talking points, 186

target sets, 180

Target Vancouver, 27

Tayles, James, 102

Taylor, Brent, 101–5, 244

Taylor, I.W., 107

Taylor, J.H., 128

technological determinism, 199

Teeley, Ambassador Peter, 167

ten principles, 63–64

ten-year agreement, 151

TERCOM, 66–67, 102, 131, 134, 140, 155

termination, 196–97

testing in USA, 159, 161–62, 177–78

testing lists, 194, 217–21

testing outside allowed season, 95

tests, 217–21

    # 84-1, 6 March 1984, 64

    # 85-x, 15 January 1985, 74–75

    # 85-y, 19 February 1985, 83

    # 85-z, 25 February 1985, 84

    # 86-1, 22 January 1986, 88

    # 86-2, 25 February 1986, 89–90

    # 87-1, 24 February1987, 92–93

    # 87-2, 1 March 1987, 93

    # 87-3, 27 October 1987, 95

    # 88-1, 19 January 1988, 96-97

    # 88-2, 26 January 1988, 97

    # 89-4, 27 January 1989, 152–53

    # 89-(ACM-1), 2 March 1989, 129–30

    # A91-01C, 7 November 1990, 131–32

    # 90-4, 23 January 1990, 153–54

    # 90-4A, 29 January 1990, 154

    # 91-4, 31 January 1991, 155

    # 91-5, 9 February 1991, 155–56

    # 92-1, 29 October 1991, 133–34

    # 92-4, 10 February 1992, 157–58

    # 93-4, 29 January 1993, 172–73

    # A93-04S, 29 March 1993, 139–40

    # A94-06 (A193), 6 March 1994, 193–94

Theatre Nuclear Forces (see also INF), 111

Thatcher, Prime Minister Margaret, 16

Theriault, General, 52–53

thirty-month forecast (see also annual
        forecast), 44, 63, 111, 119, 131,
        179, 180, 193, 227, 239, 250, 258,
        261, 262

Thomas, Beth, 170

Thompson, Allan, 190

Tiananmen Square, 54

Tomahawk (SLCM), 26, 67, 73, 114

Toronto Disarmament Network, 56

Toronto Peace Alliance, 157

torpedo test range, 200–202, 242

Toy, Justice S.M., 105

trading partner, 176

training flights, 18, 52–53, 91, 208

Transport Canada, 197

Trent University, 104

Trilateral Agreement, 181

Trident

    SLBM, 7

    SSBN, 32, 61

Trudeau, Prime Minister Pierre, 3
  Arctic trip, 54–55
  ALCM issue a problem, 39
  American puppet, 207
  cabinet meetings, 40, 48–49, 53–54
  convention, 28
  English interview, 47
  grand gesture, 204
  hagiography, 28
  judgement, 38
  letters, 19, 24, 45, 46
  meeting with Bush, 42
  meeting with Reagan, 45, 62
  open letter, 45–46
  Peace Mission, 62
  philosopher prince, 46
  pique, 10
  rambling defence, 19
  retires, 64
  scrum, 42
  Trudeamania, 20
  "tired, stale and peevish", 46
  "We all know the cruise is at the end
    of the road", 3, 39
  "We must reduce our cruise missiles",
    22
Tu-95 (bomber), 73
  first ALCM-carrying mock attack,
    73–74
Tu-160 (bomber), 87
Turner, Prime Minister John, 94
Typhoon (SSBN), 63
typical flight, 85–86
typical sleazy liberal tactic, 55

U

Ukraine, 168–69
unarmed, 13, 25
United Auto Workers (UAW), 55

United Church, 27, 57
United Nations
  Disarmament Week, 27
  Special Session on Disarmament, 20,
    22–23
unpredictable response, 179
UNSSOD, 20, 22–23
U.S. Air Force xiii, 3, 4, 11, 12, 14, 18, 21, 24,
    26, 30, 34, 35, 42, 47, 48, 54, 64, 65, 68,
    74, 75, 77, 86, 89, 91, 113114, 120, 123,
    134, 135, 138, 139, 157, 161, 162, 164,
    177, 183, 185, 193–94, 199, 211
U.S. Air Force Museum, 84
U.S. arms control policy, 113
U.S. military testing in Canada, 199–202
U.S. Navy, 73, 200, 209
U.S. Nuclear Weapons in Canada, 1
U.S.S.R. disintegrates, 130
Utah test range (see also Hill AFB), 74, 88,
    138
unionize, 100

V

V-22 aircraft, 180
veiled threats, 184–85
Venner, J.A., 107
veto, 15, 82
VooDoo, 27, 72, 240
votes
  Charlottetown Accord referendum, 160
  House of Commons, 30, 38, 52, 94, 96
  Manitoba on Meech, 94
  Meech Lake Accord, 94
  Toronto nuclear-free, 29
  US Senate on SALT II, 61
voyeurs of USAF cloud shovelling, 203

W

W-25 warhead, 16, 72, 77–78

W-80 warhead, 66, 68, 70–72, 117, 138, 142–43

walk in the woods, 25

Walker, John, 14

Walker, Michael, 83

Ward, John, 192

Warsaw Treaty Organization (WTO), 8, 73, 129–30, 153

Weatherhead, MP David, 52

Weinberger, Caspar, 4, 6–7, 11, 23, 36, 40, 43, 114

letter to Beatty, 120

Weizfeld, Abraham, 42–43

Werrell, Ken, 199

western alienation, 20

western test corridor, 75–76

White House pressure, 11, 124, 126, 169, 173

White Paper on Defence, 197

Whitehead, 127

Wightman, 11, 15, 30, 49

Williams, Alan S., 230

Willis, John, 40, 51

Williston, John, 182

Wilson, Justice Bertha, 75

Winnipeg, 7, 27, 34, 51, 60, 64, 75, 76, 107, 115, 122, 183, 185, 197

Winnipeg Coordinating Committee for Disarmament (WCCD), 75

Withers, General Ramsey M., 42

Woods, General P.E., 159,

World Emergency Project, 104

Wright-Patterson AFB, 69

Wurtsmith AFB, 34, 96–97

Y

Yellowknife, 54–55

Yeltsin, President Boris, 134, 169

Z

Zeilig, Martin, 40